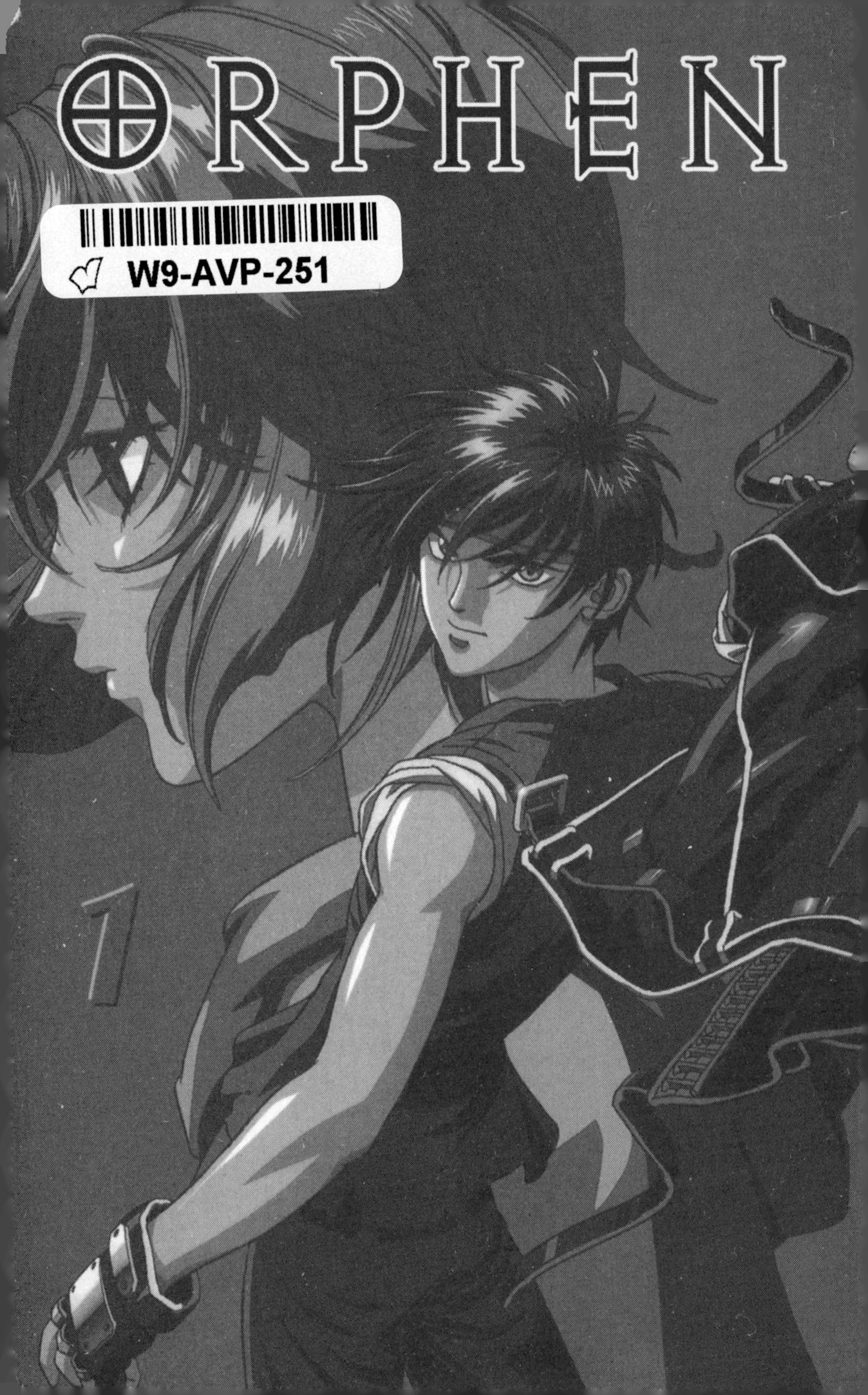
ORPHEN
1

ORPHEN

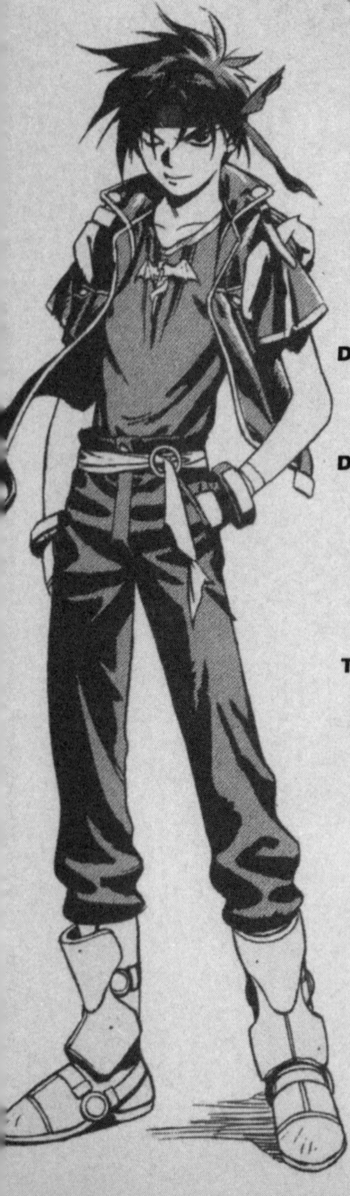

CONTENTS

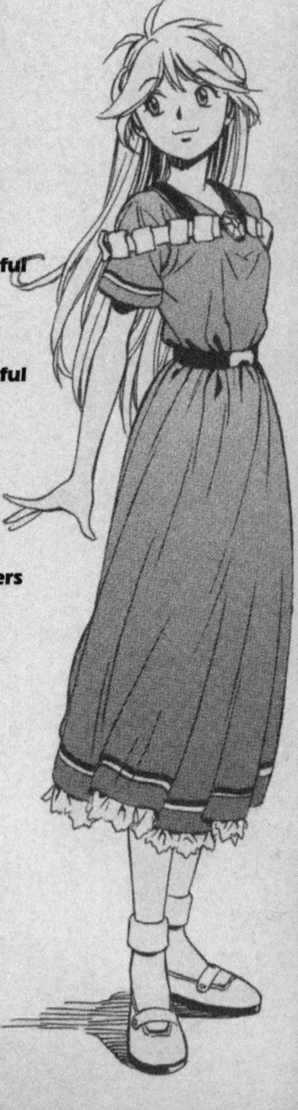

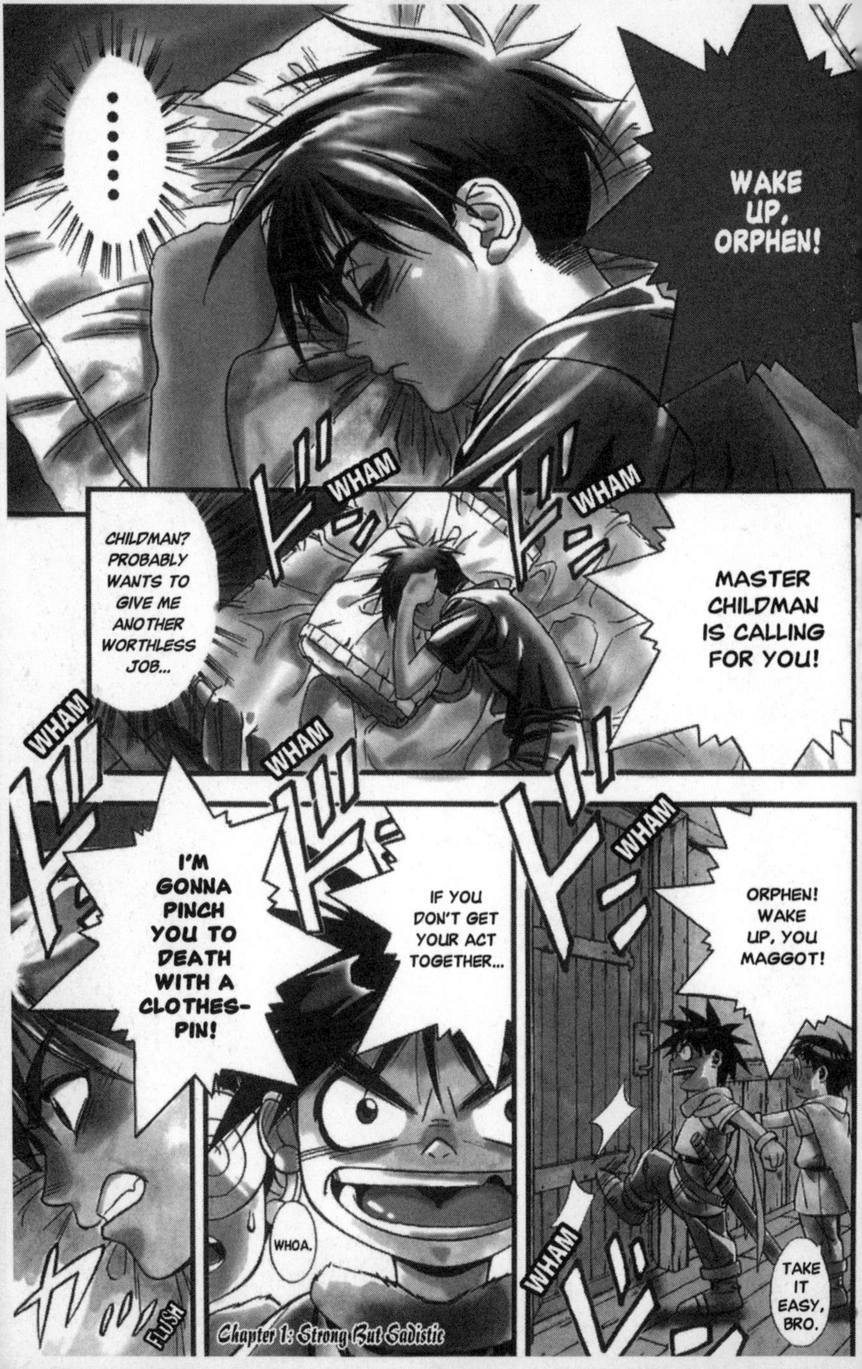
WAKE UP, ORPHEN!
WHAM
WHAM
MASTER CHILDMAN IS CALLING FOR YOU!
CHILDMAN? PROBABLY WANTS TO GIVE ME ANOTHER WORTHLESS JOB...
WHAM
WHAM
WHAM
ORPHEN! WAKE UP, YOU MAGGOT!
WHAM
TAKE IT EASY, BRO.
IF YOU DON'T GET YOUR ACT TOGETHER...
WHOA.
I'M GONNA PINCH YOU TO DEATH WITH A CLOTHES-PIN!
FLUSH
Chapter 1: Strong But Sadistic

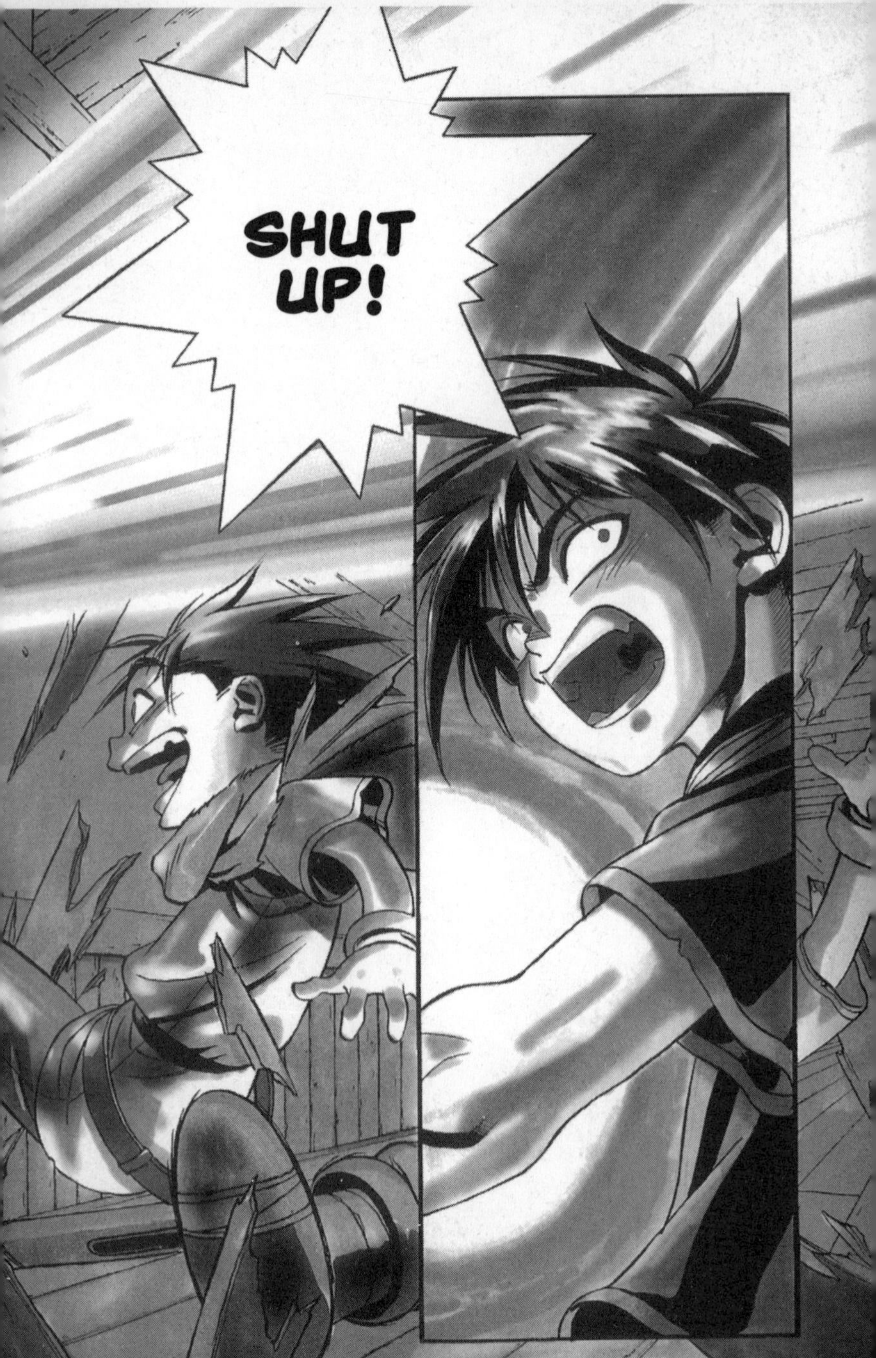
SHUT UP!

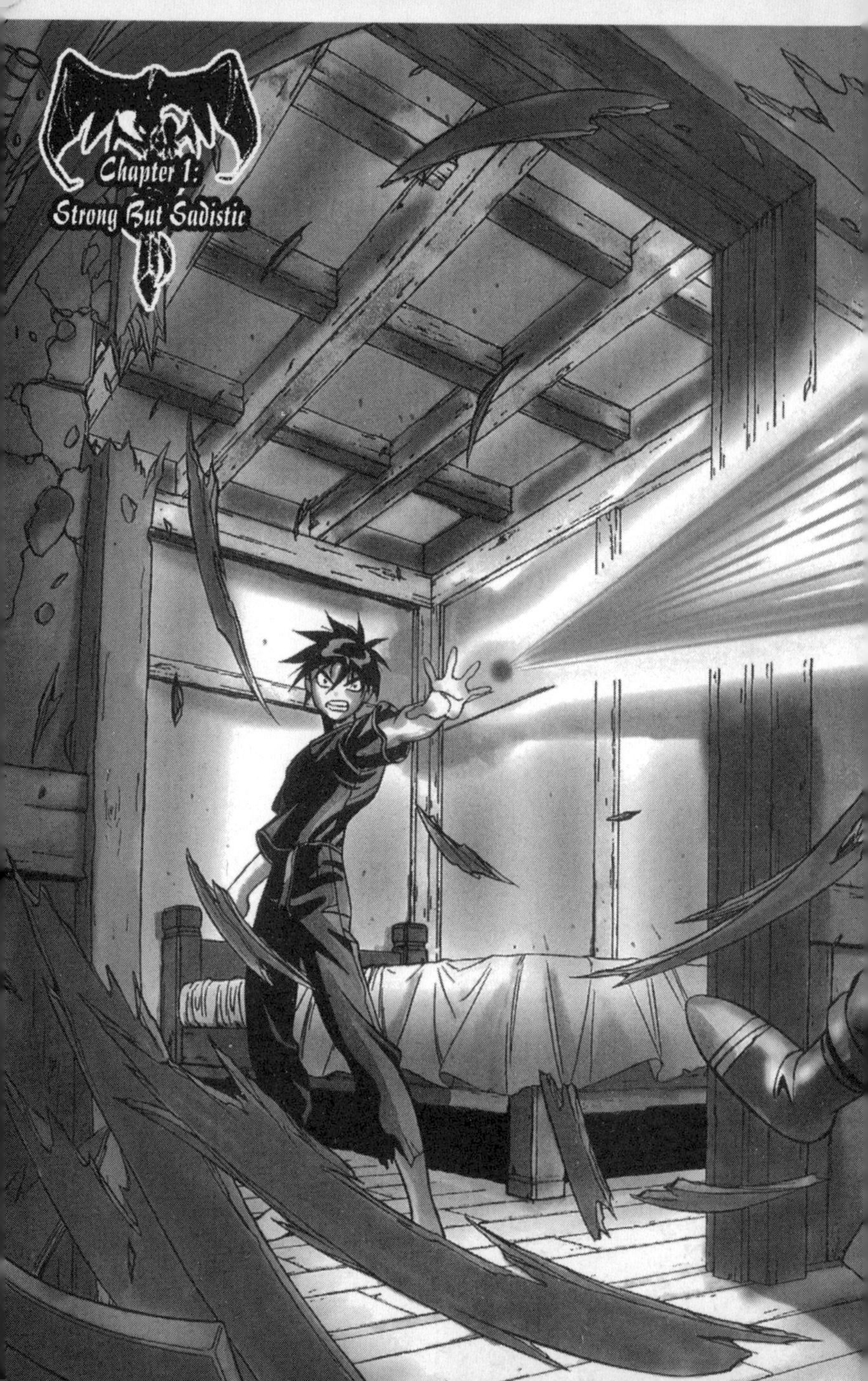
Chapter 1:
Strong But Sadistic

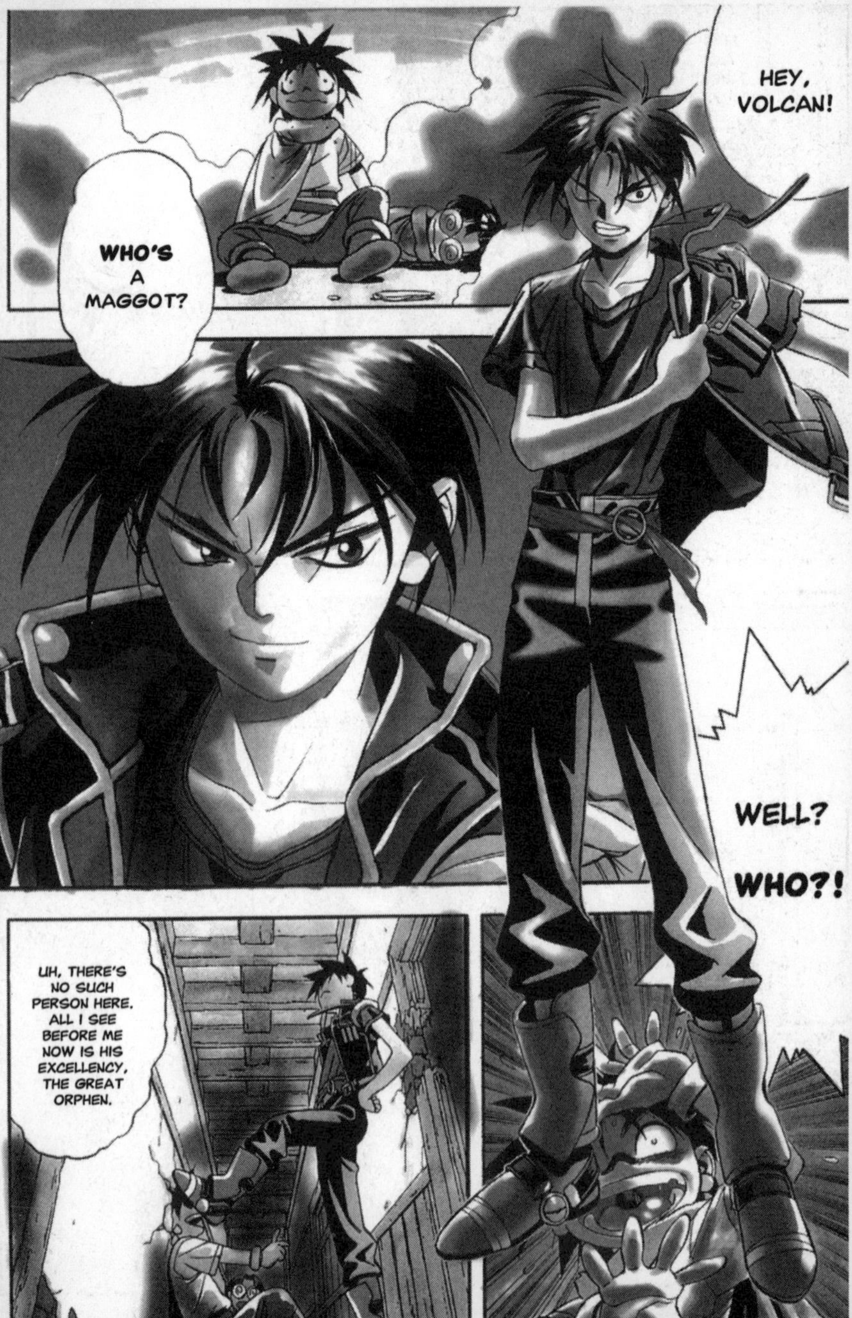
HEY, VOLCAN!
WHO'S A MAGGOT?
WELL?
WHO?!
UH, THERE'S NO SUCH PERSON HERE. ALL I SEE BEFORE ME NOW IS HIS EXCELLENCY, THE GREAT ORPHEN.

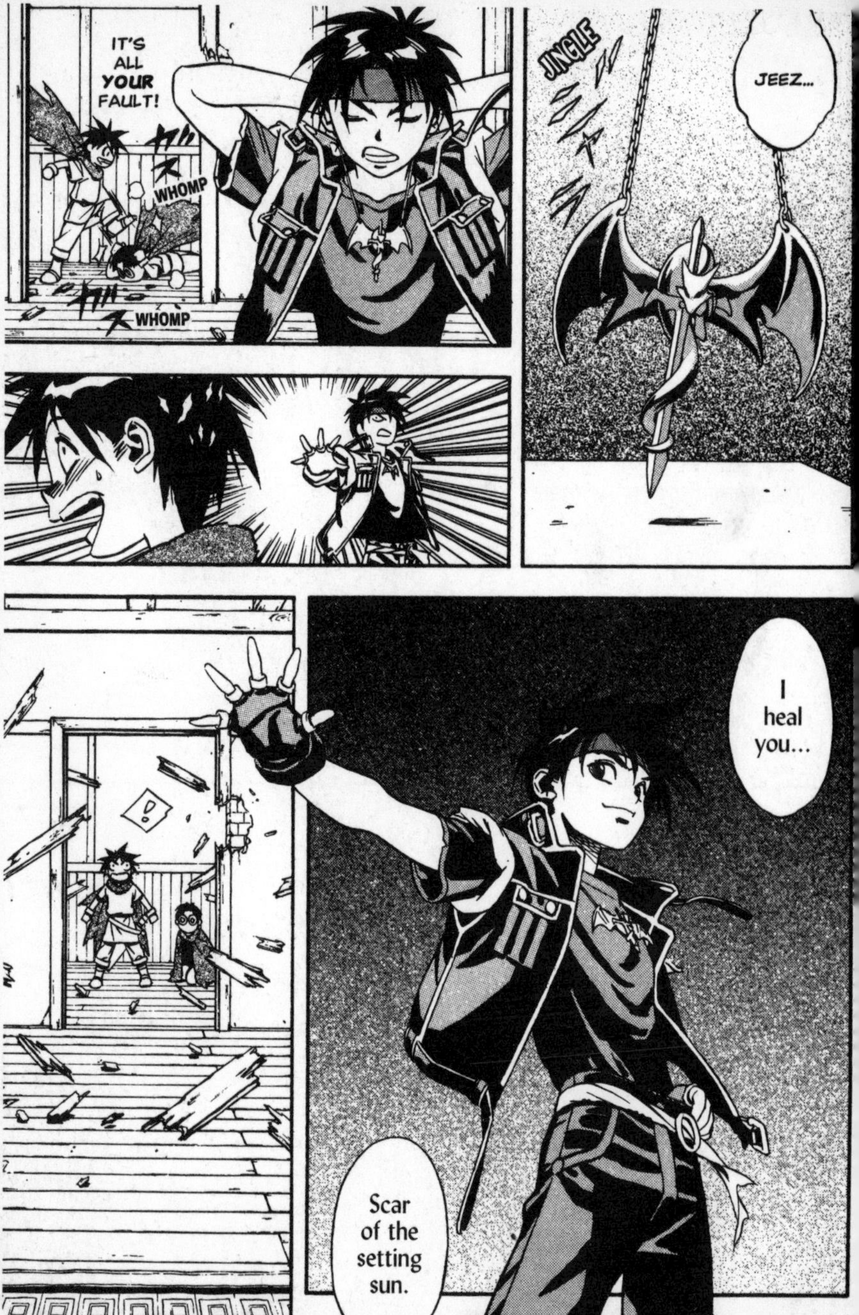
JINGLE
JEEZ...
IT'S ALL YOUR FAULT!
WHOMP
WHOMP
!
I heal you...
Scar of the setting sun.

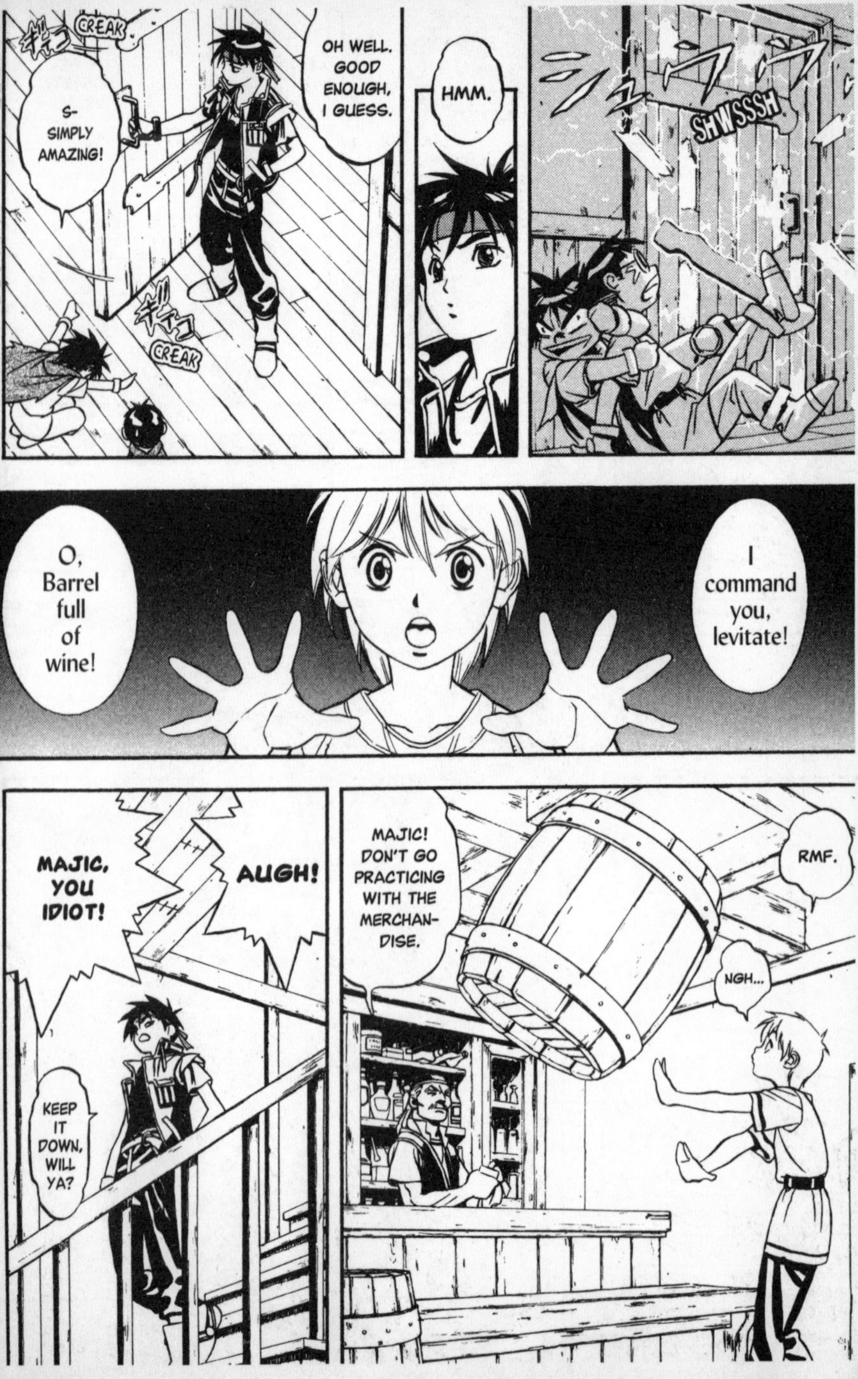
SHWSSSH
HMM.
OH WELL. GOOD ENOUGH, I GUESS.
S-SIMPLY AMAZING!
CREAK
CREAK
O, Barrel full of wine!
I command you, levitate!
RMF.
NGH...
MAJIC! DON'T GO PRACTICING WITH THE MERCHANDISE.
AUGH!
MAJIC, YOU IDIOT!
KEEP IT DOWN, WILL YA?

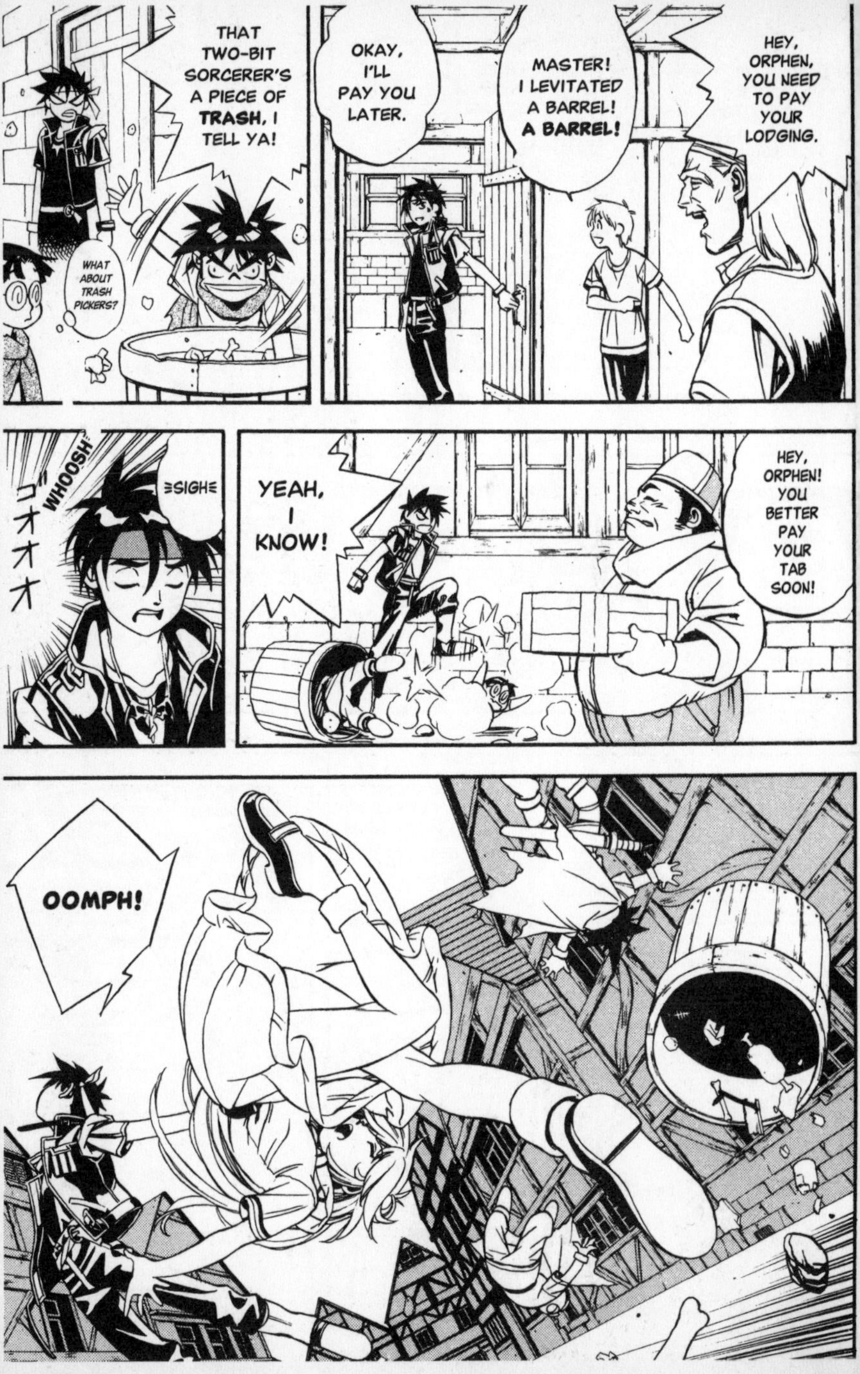
HEY, ORPHEN, YOU NEED TO PAY YOUR LODGING.
MASTER! I LEVITATED A BARREL! A BARREL!
OKAY, I'LL PAY YOU LATER.
THAT TWO-BIT SORCERER'S A PIECE OF TRASH, I TELL YA!
WHAT ABOUT TRASH PICKERS?
HEY, ORPHEN! YOU BETTER PAY YOUR TAB SOON!
YEAH, I KNOW!
≡SIGH≡
WHOOSH
ゴオオオ
OOMPH!

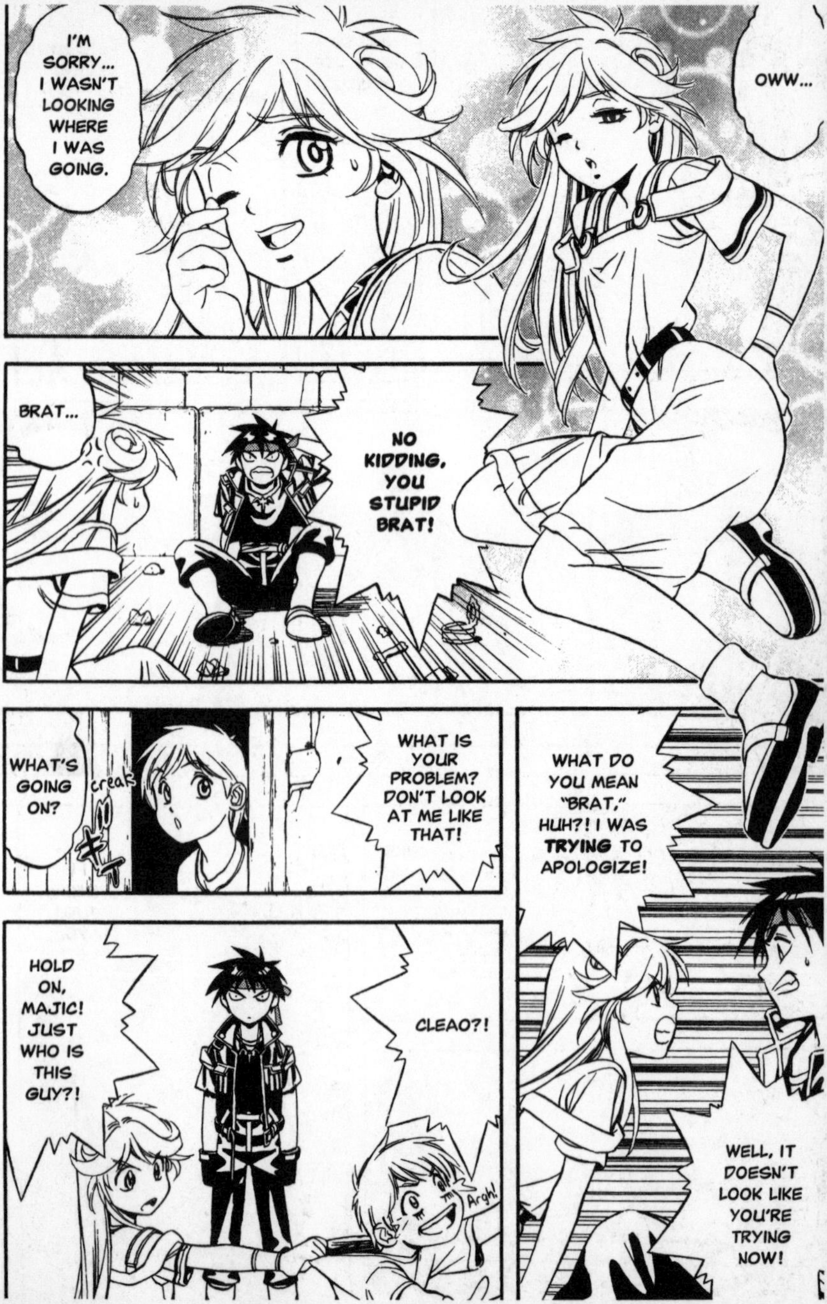
OWW...
I'M SORRY... I WASN'T LOOKING WHERE I WAS GOING.
NO KIDDING, YOU STUPID BRAT!
BRAT...
WHAT DO YOU MEAN "BRAT," HUH?! I WAS TRYING TO APOLOGIZE!
WHAT IS YOUR PROBLEM? DON'T LOOK AT ME LIKE THAT!
creak
WHAT'S GOING ON?
WELL, IT DOESN'T LOOK LIKE YOU'RE TRYING NOW!
CLEAO?!
HOLD ON, MAJIC! JUST WHO IS THIS GUY?!
Argh!

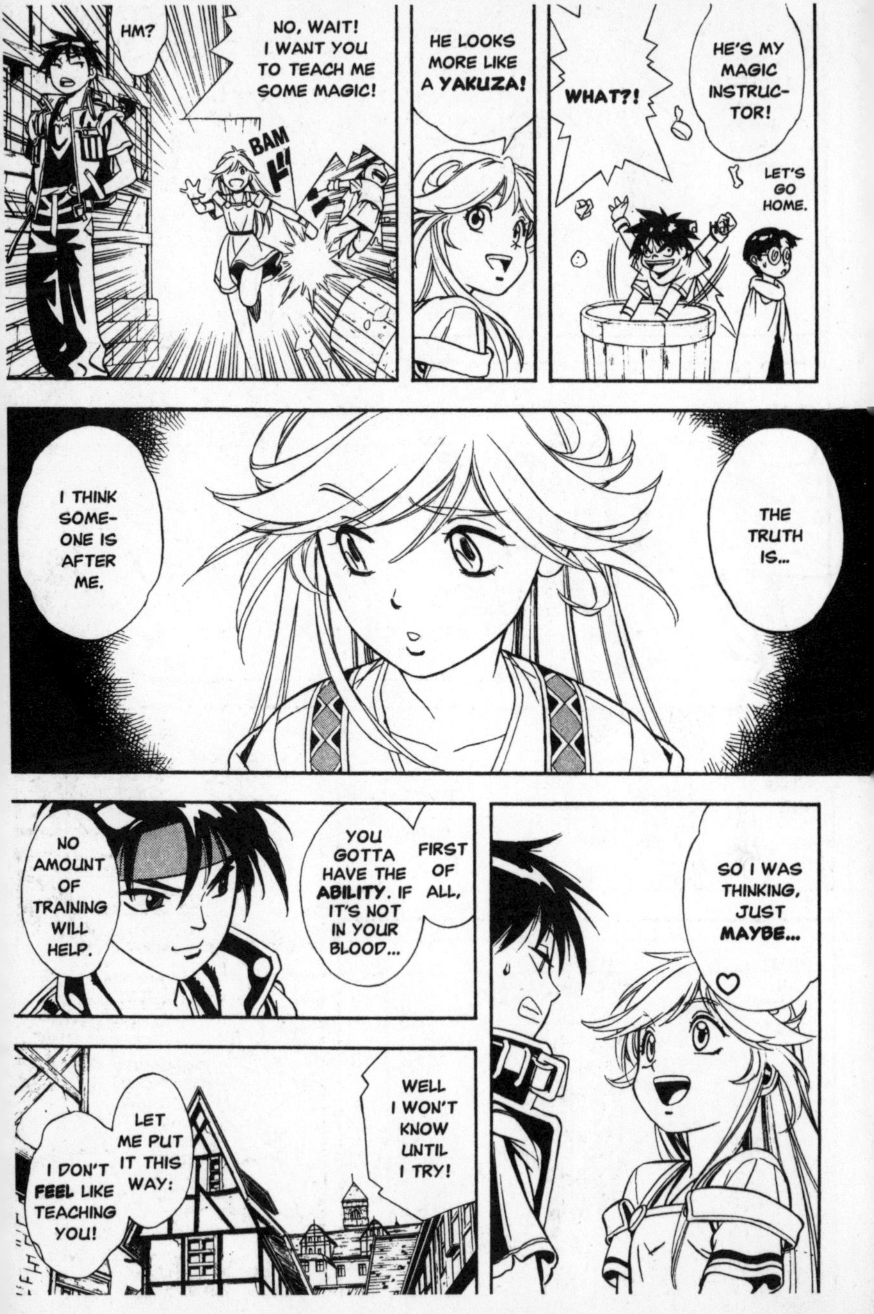
HE'S MY MAGIC INSTRUCTOR!
WHAT?!
LET'S GO HOME.
HE LOOKS MORE LIKE A YAKUZA!
NO, WAIT! I WANT YOU TO TEACH ME SOME MAGIC!
BAM
HM?
THE TRUTH IS...
I THINK SOMEONE IS AFTER ME.
SO I WAS THINKING, JUST MAYBE...
FIRST OF ALL,
YOU GOTTA HAVE THE ABILITY. IF IT'S NOT IN YOUR BLOOD...
NO AMOUNT OF TRAINING WILL HELP.
WELL I WON'T KNOW UNTIL I TRY!
LET ME PUT IT THIS WAY:
I DON'T FEEL LIKE TEACHING YOU!

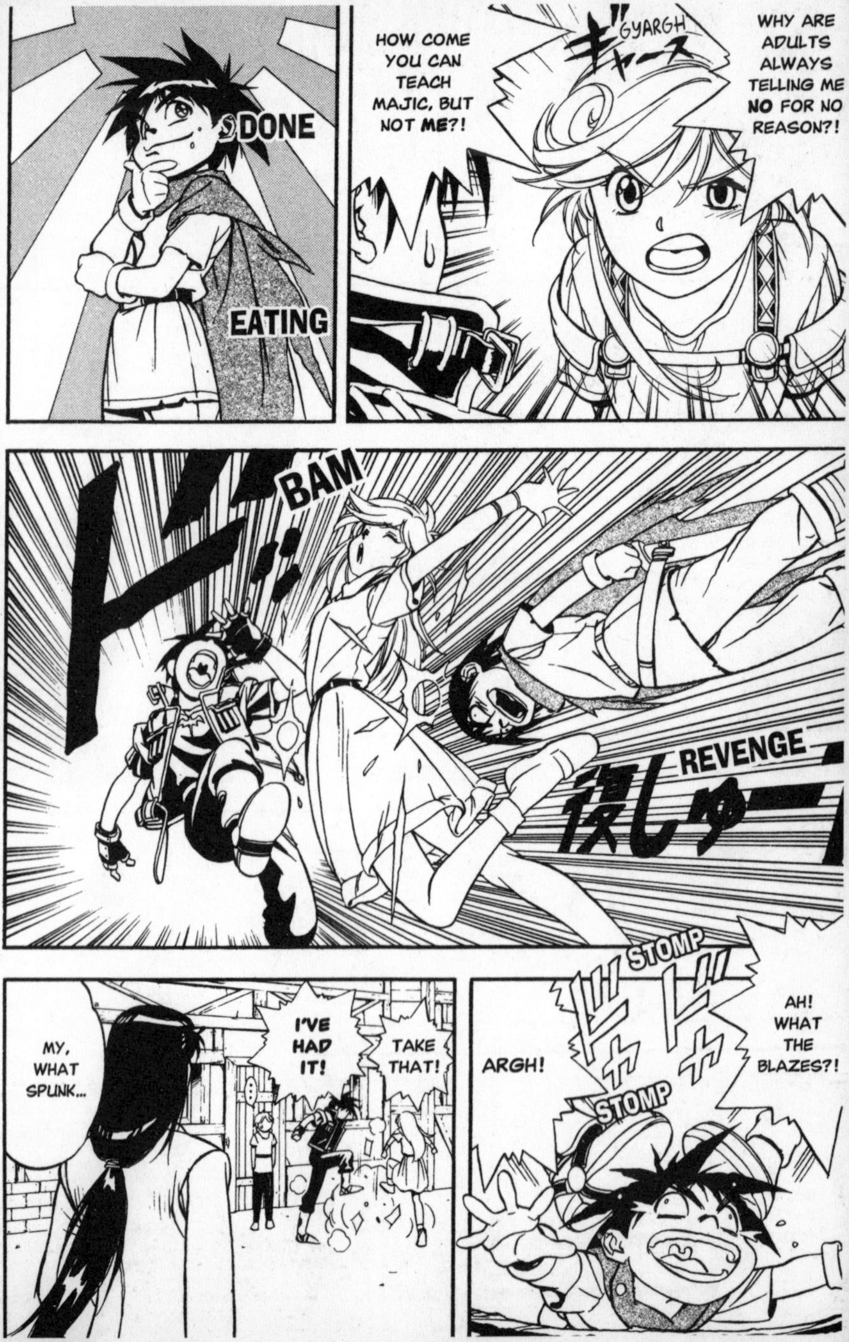
GYARGH
WHY ARE ADULTS ALWAYS TELLING ME NO FOR NO REASON?!
HOW COME YOU CAN TEACH MAJIC, BUT NOT ME?!
DONE EATING
BAM
REVENGE
STOMP
STOMP
AH! WHAT THE BLAZES?!
ARGH!
TAKE THAT!
I'VE HAD IT!
MY, WHAT SPUNK...

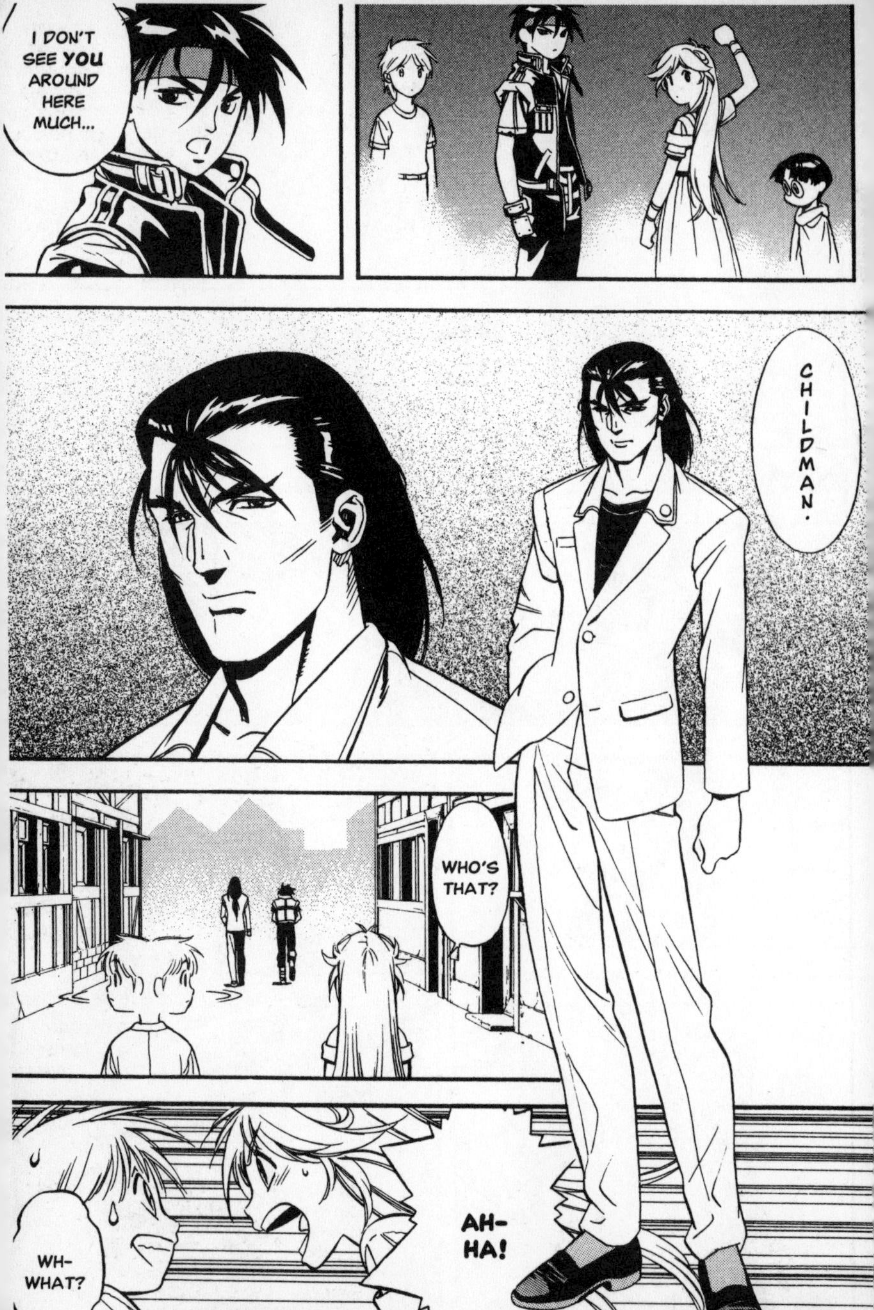
I DON'T SEE YOU AROUND HERE MUCH...
CHILDMAN.
WHO'S THAT?
WH- WHAT?
AH- HA!

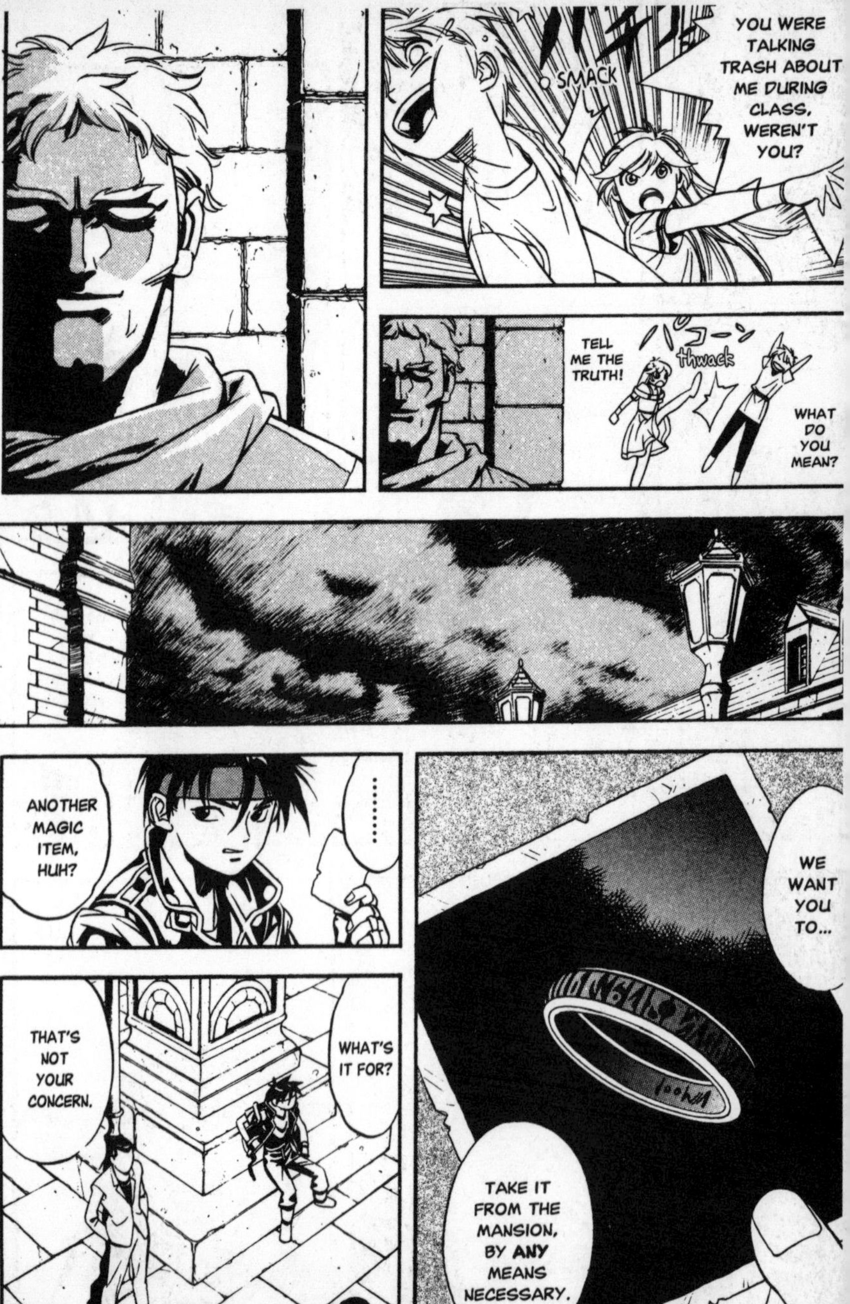
SMACK
YOU WERE TALKING TRASH ABOUT ME DURING CLASS, WEREN'T YOU?
TELL ME THE TRUTH!
thwack
WHAT DO YOU MEAN?
WE WANT YOU TO...
TAKE IT FROM THE MANSION, BY ANY MEANS NECESSARY.
ANOTHER MAGIC ITEM, HUH?
....
WHAT'S IT FOR?
THAT'S NOT YOUR CONCERN.

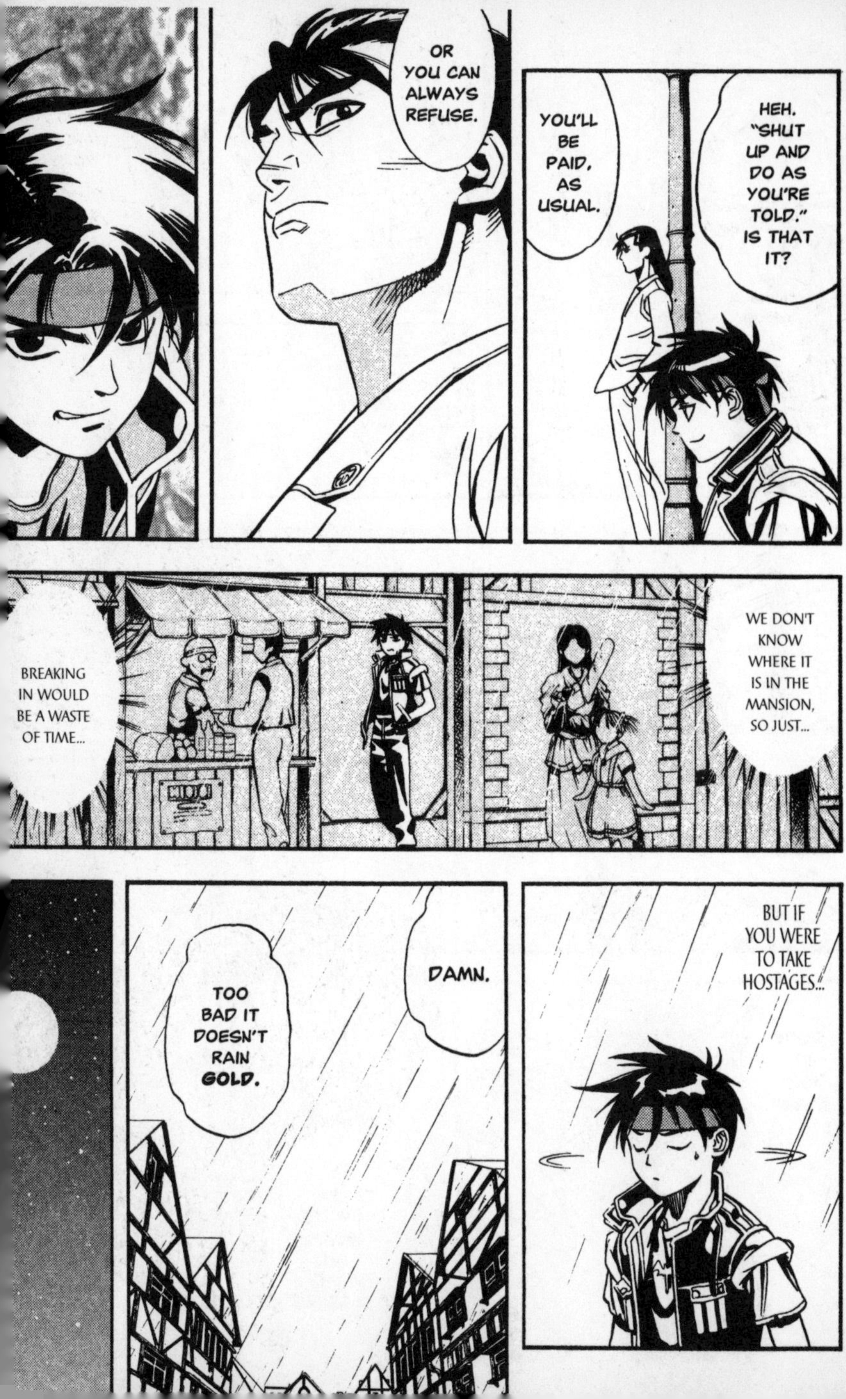
HEH. "SHUT UP AND DO AS YOU'RE TOLD." IS THAT IT?
YOU'LL BE PAID, AS USUAL.
OR YOU CAN ALWAYS REFUSE.
WE DON'T KNOW WHERE IT IS IN THE MANSION, SO JUST...
BREAKING IN WOULD BE A WASTE OF TIME...
BUT IF YOU WERE TO TAKE HOSTAGES...
DAMN.
TOO BAD IT DOESN'T RAIN GOLD.

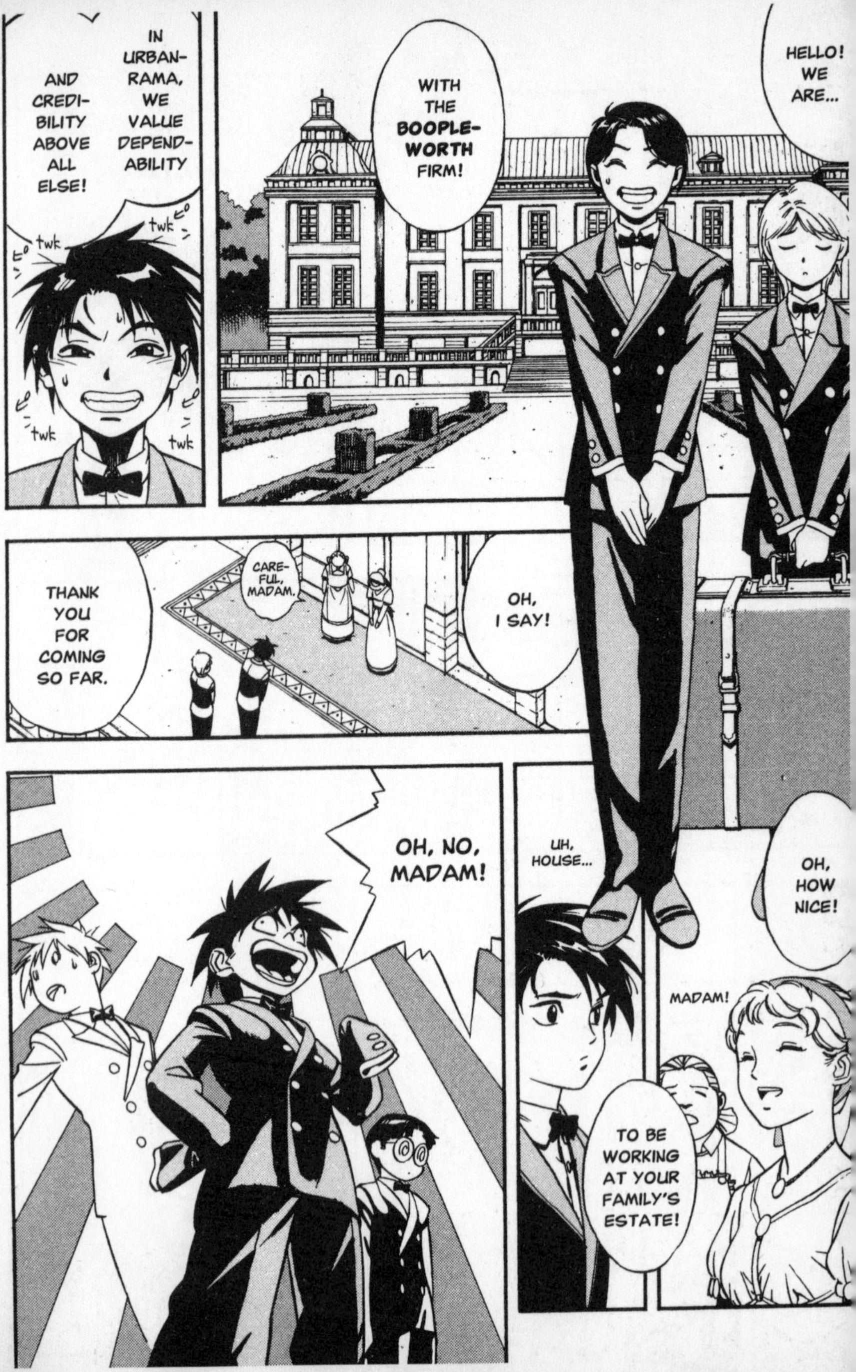
HELLO! WE ARE...
WITH THE BOOPLE-WORTH FIRM!
IN URBAN-RAMA, WE VALUE DEPEND-ABILITY
AND CREDI-BILITY ABOVE ALL ELSE!
twk
twk
twk
twk
OH, I SAY!
CARE-FUL, MADAM.
THANK YOU FOR COMING SO FAR.
OH, HOW NICE!
MADAM!
TO BE WORKING AT YOUR FAMILY'S ESTATE!
UH, HOUSE...
OH, NO, MADAM!

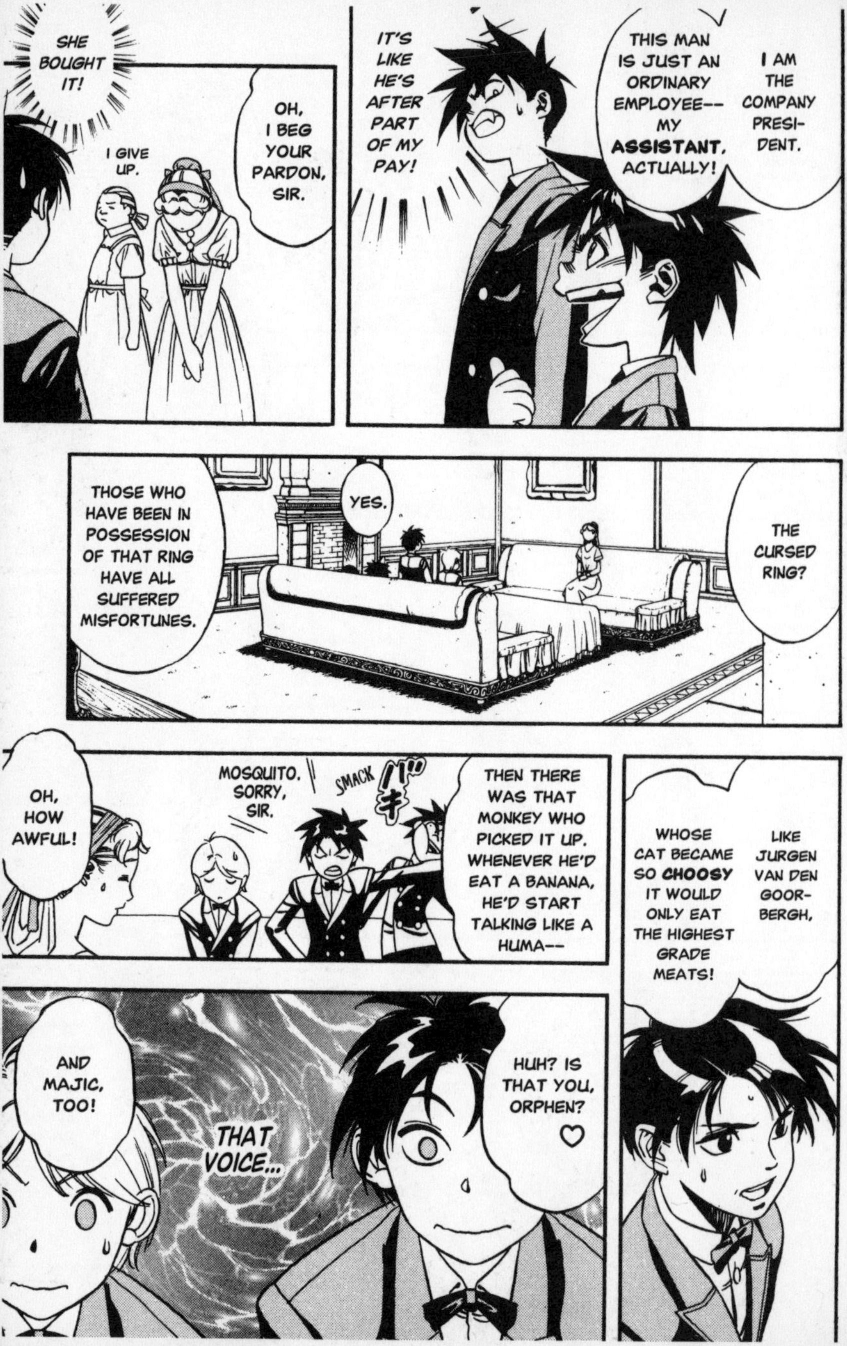
I AM THE COMPANY PRESIDENT.
THIS MAN IS JUST AN ORDINARY EMPLOYEE-- MY ASSISTANT, ACTUALLY!
IT'S LIKE HE'S AFTER PART OF MY PAY!
OH, I BEG YOUR PARDON, SIR.
I GIVE UP.
SHE BOUGHT IT!
THE CURSED RING?
YES.
THOSE WHO HAVE BEEN IN POSSESSION OF THAT RING HAVE ALL SUFFERED MISFORTUNES.
LIKE JURGEN VAN DEN GOORBERGH,
WHOSE CAT BECAME SO CHOOSY IT WOULD ONLY EAT THE HIGHEST GRADE MEATS!
THEN THERE WAS THAT MONKEY WHO PICKED IT UP. WHENEVER HE'D EAT A BANANA, HE'D START TALKING LIKE A HUMA--
SMACK
MOSQUITO. SORRY, SIR.
OH, HOW AWFUL!
HUH? IS THAT YOU, ORPHEN? ♥
THAT VOICE...
AND MAJIC, TOO!

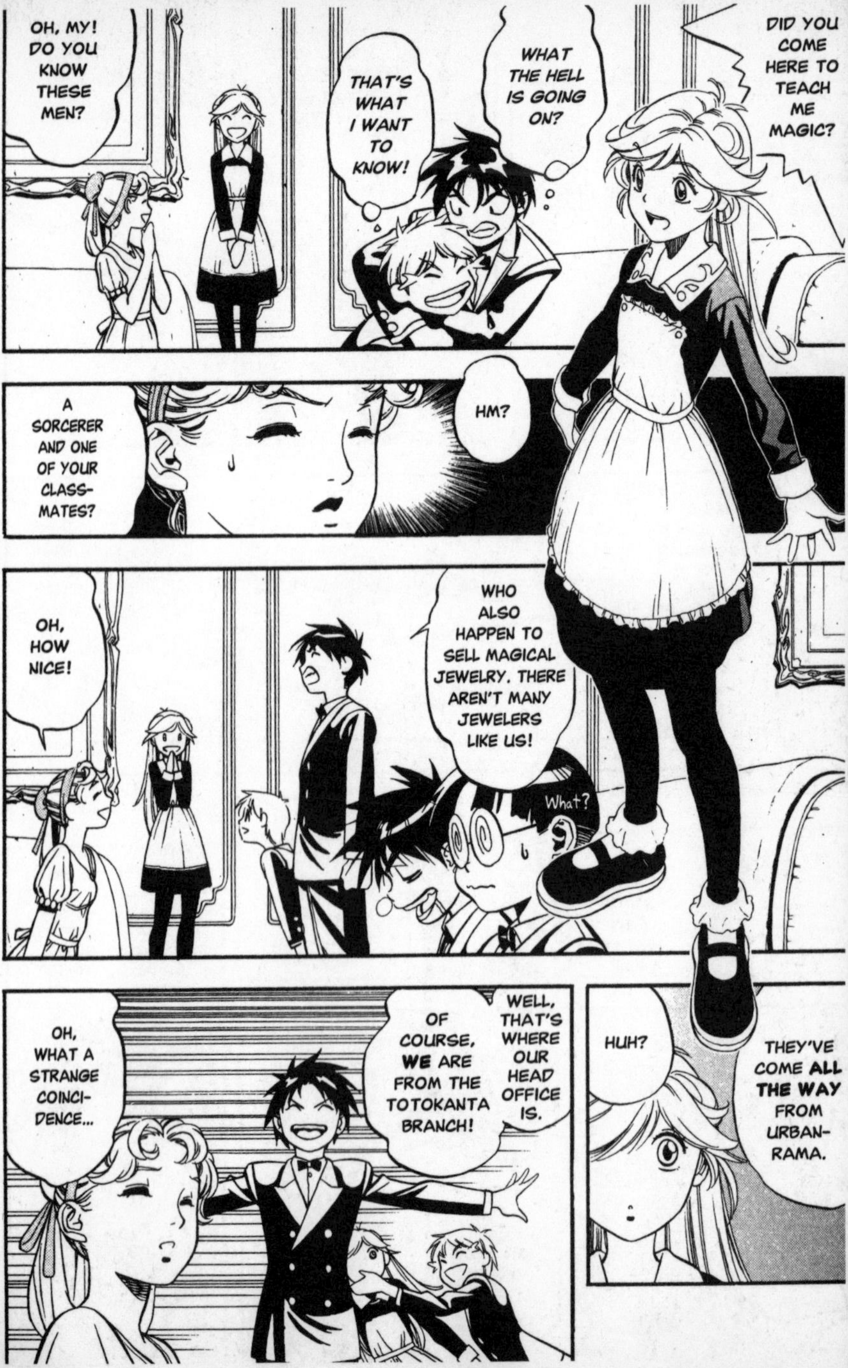
OH, MY! DO YOU KNOW THESE MEN?
THAT'S WHAT I WANT TO KNOW!
WHAT THE HELL IS GOING ON?
DID YOU COME HERE TO TEACH ME MAGIC?
A SORCERER AND ONE OF YOUR CLASS-MATES?
HM?
OH, HOW NICE!
WHO ALSO HAPPEN TO SELL MAGICAL JEWELRY. THERE AREN'T MANY JEWELERS LIKE US!
What?
OH, WHAT A STRANGE COINCI-DENCE...
OF COURSE, WE ARE FROM THE TOTOKANTA BRANCH!
WELL, THAT'S WHERE OUR HEAD OFFICE IS.
HUH?
THEY'VE COME ALL THE WAY FROM URBAN-RAMA.

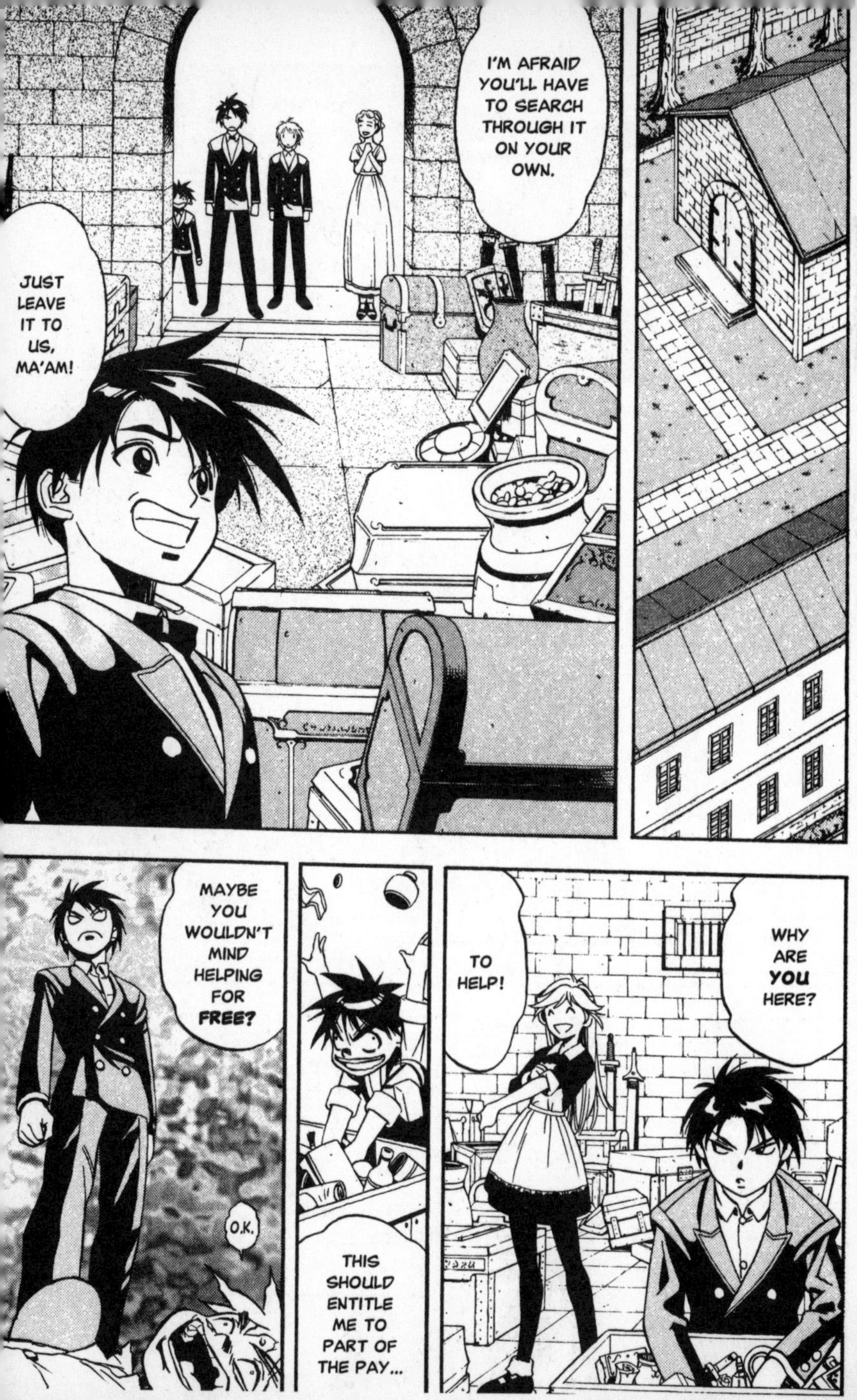
I'M AFRAID YOU'LL HAVE TO SEARCH THROUGH IT ON YOUR OWN.
JUST LEAVE IT TO US, MA'AM!
WHY ARE YOU HERE?
TO HELP!
THIS SHOULD ENTITLE ME TO PART OF THE PAY...
MAYBE YOU WOULDN'T MIND HELPING FOR FREE?
O.K.

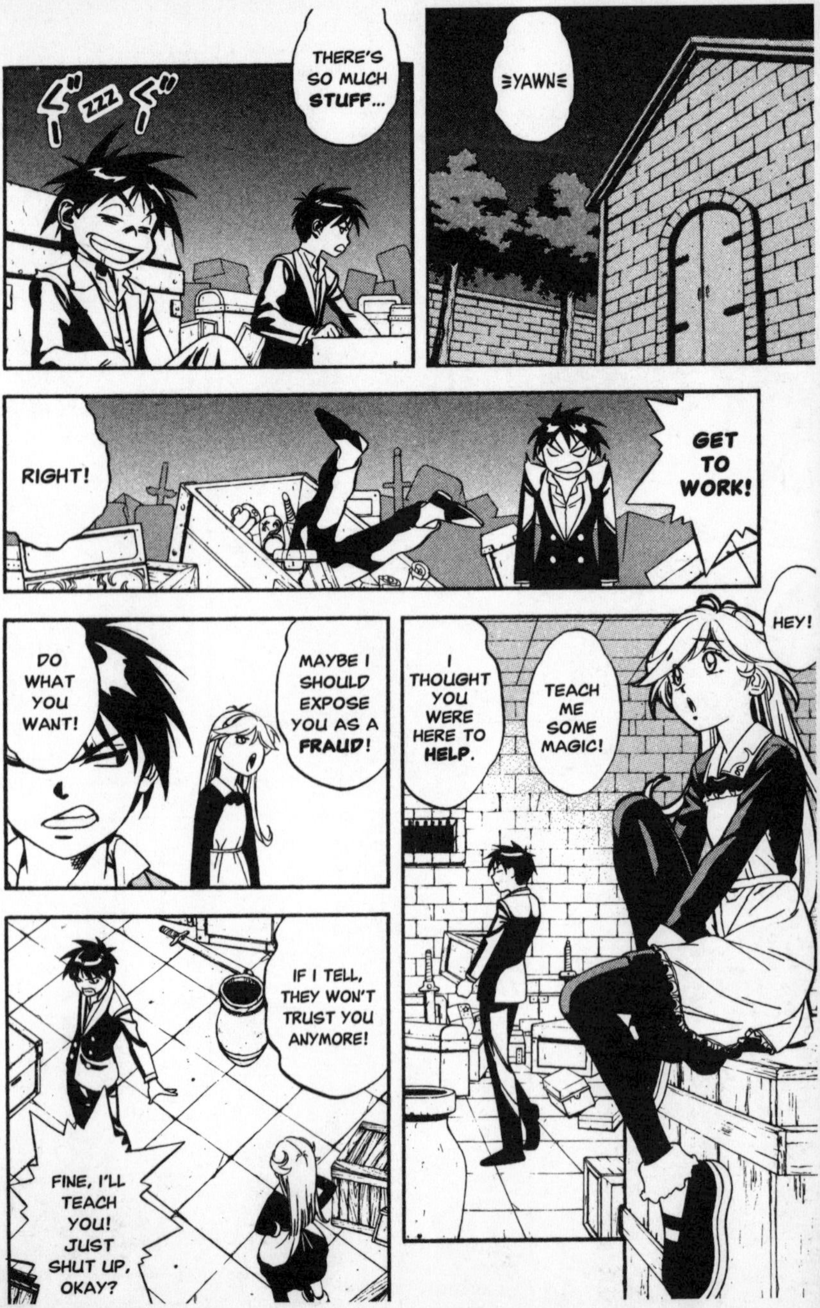

≡YAWN≡
THERE'S SO MUCH STUFF...
ZZZ
GET TO WORK!
RIGHT!
HEY!
TEACH ME SOME MAGIC!
I THOUGHT YOU WERE HERE TO HELP.
MAYBE I SHOULD EXPOSE YOU AS A FRAUD!
DO WHAT YOU WANT!
IF I TELL, THEY WON'T TRUST YOU ANYMORE!
FINE, I'LL TEACH YOU! JUST SHUT UP, OKAY?

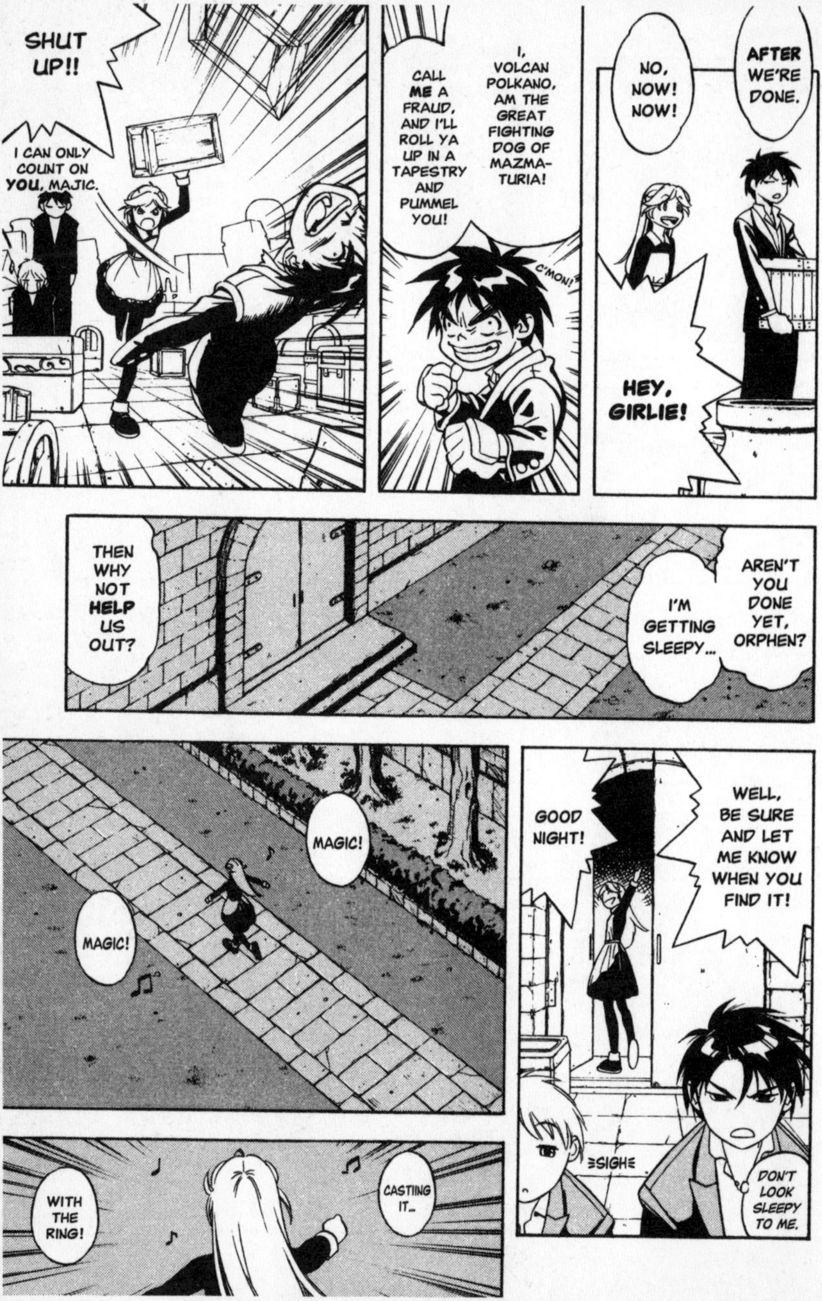
AFTER WE'RE DONE.
NO, NOW! NOW!
HEY, GIRLIE!
I, VOLCAN POLKANO, AM THE GREAT FIGHTING DOG OF MAZMA-TURIA!
CALL ME A FRAUD, AND I'LL ROLL YA UP IN A TAPESTRY AND PUMMEL YOU!
C'MON!
SHUT UP!!
I CAN ONLY COUNT ON YOU, MAJIC.
AREN'T YOU DONE YET, ORPHEN?
I'M GETTING SLEEPY...
THEN WHY NOT HELP US OUT?
WELL, BE SURE AND LET ME KNOW WHEN YOU FIND IT!
GOOD NIGHT!
SIGH
DON'T LOOK SLEEPY TO ME.
MAGIC!
MAGIC!
CASTING IT...
WITH THE RING!

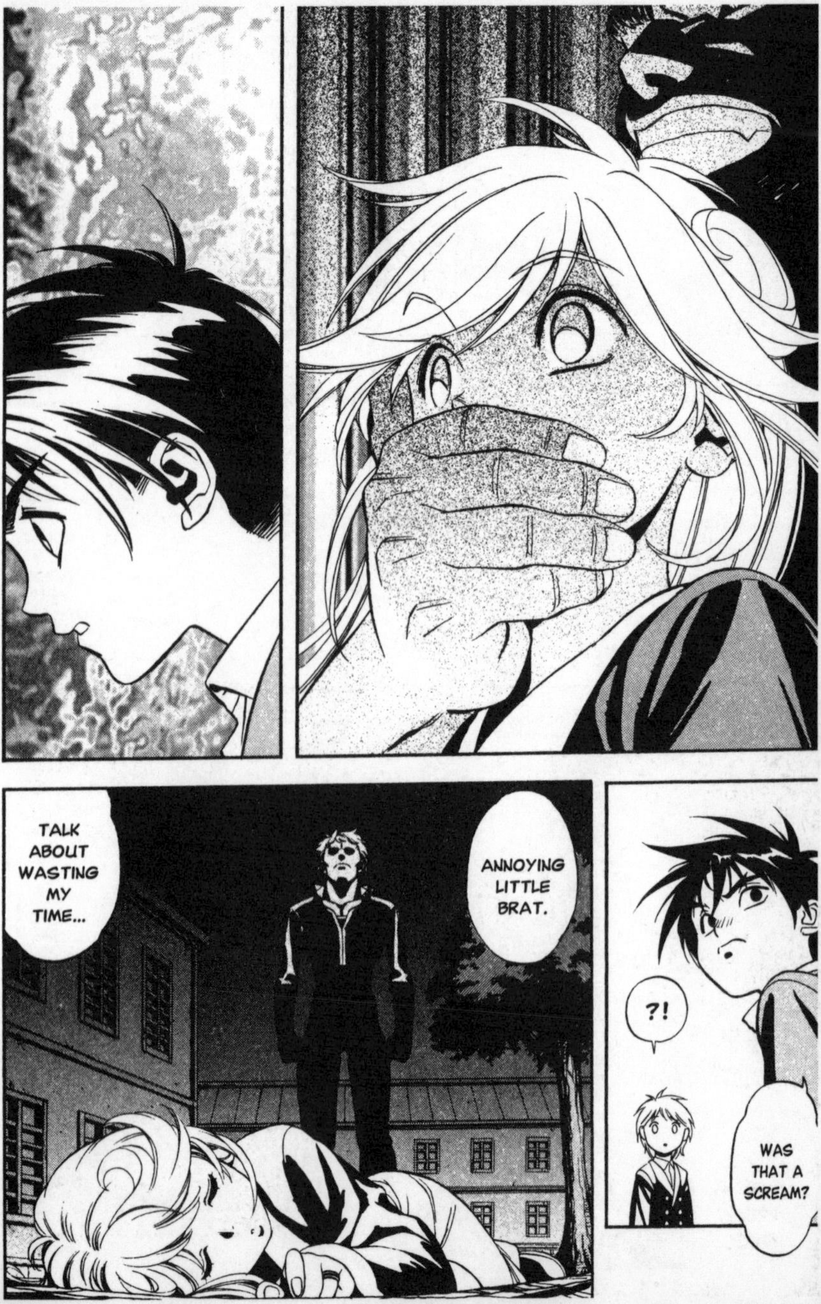
?!
WAS THAT A SCREAM?
ANNOYING LITTLE BRAT.
TALK ABOUT WASTING MY TIME...

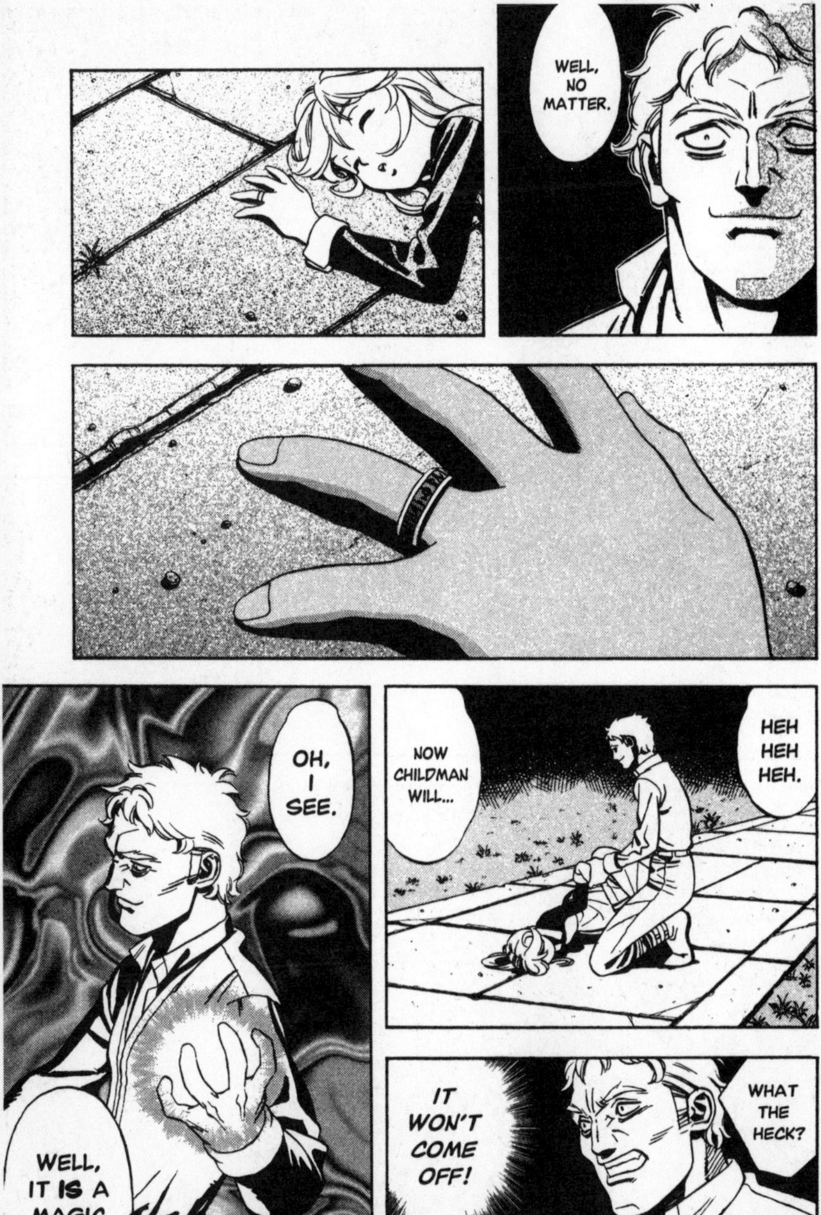
WELL, NO MATTER.
NOW CHILDMAN WILL...
HEH HEH HEH.
WHAT THE HECK?
IT WON'T COME OFF!
OH, I SEE.
WELL, IT IS A MAGIC RING.

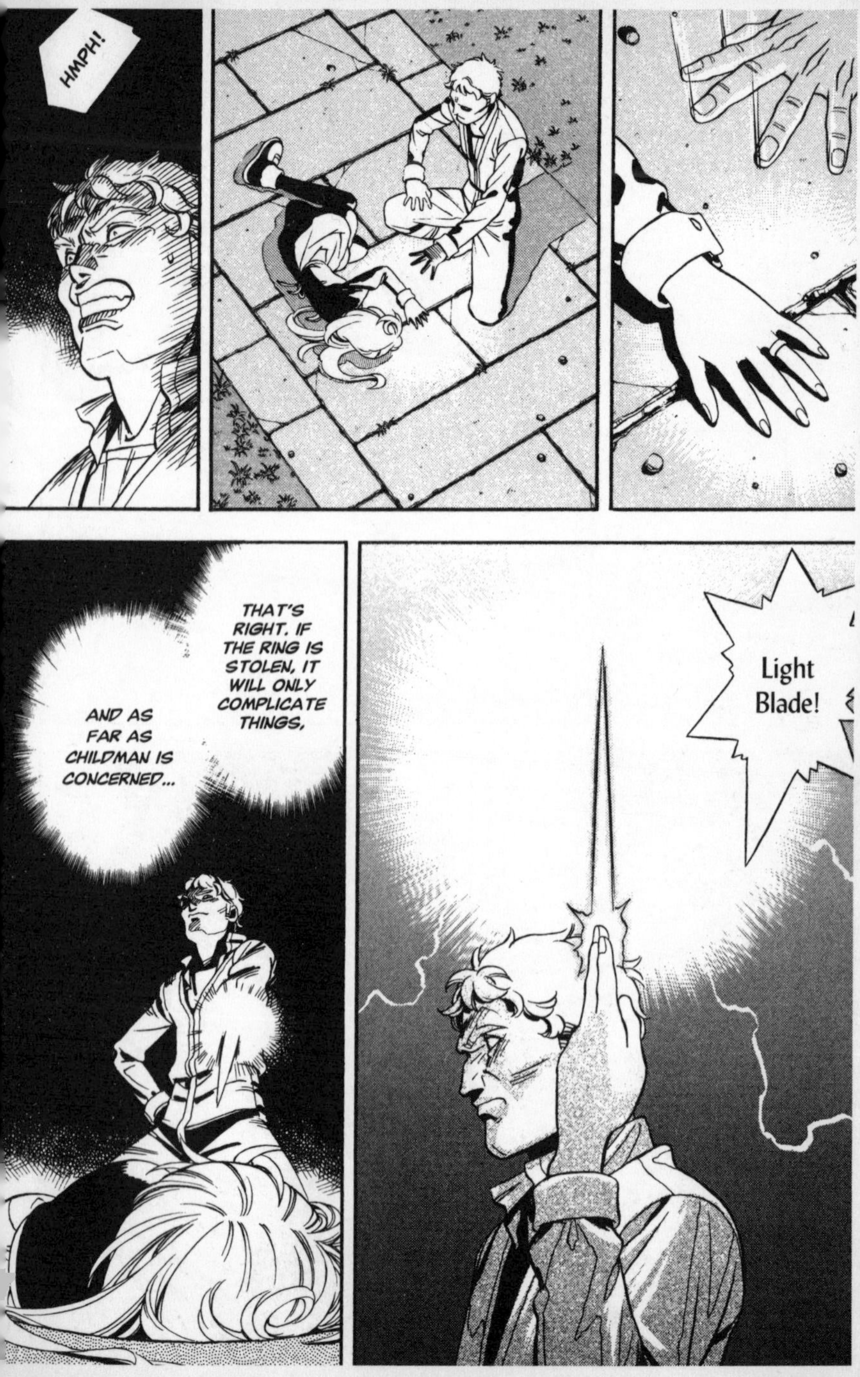
HMPH!
THAT'S RIGHT. IF THE RING IS STOLEN, IT WILL ONLY COMPLICATE THINGS,
AND AS FAR AS CHILDMAN IS CONCERNED...
Light Blade!

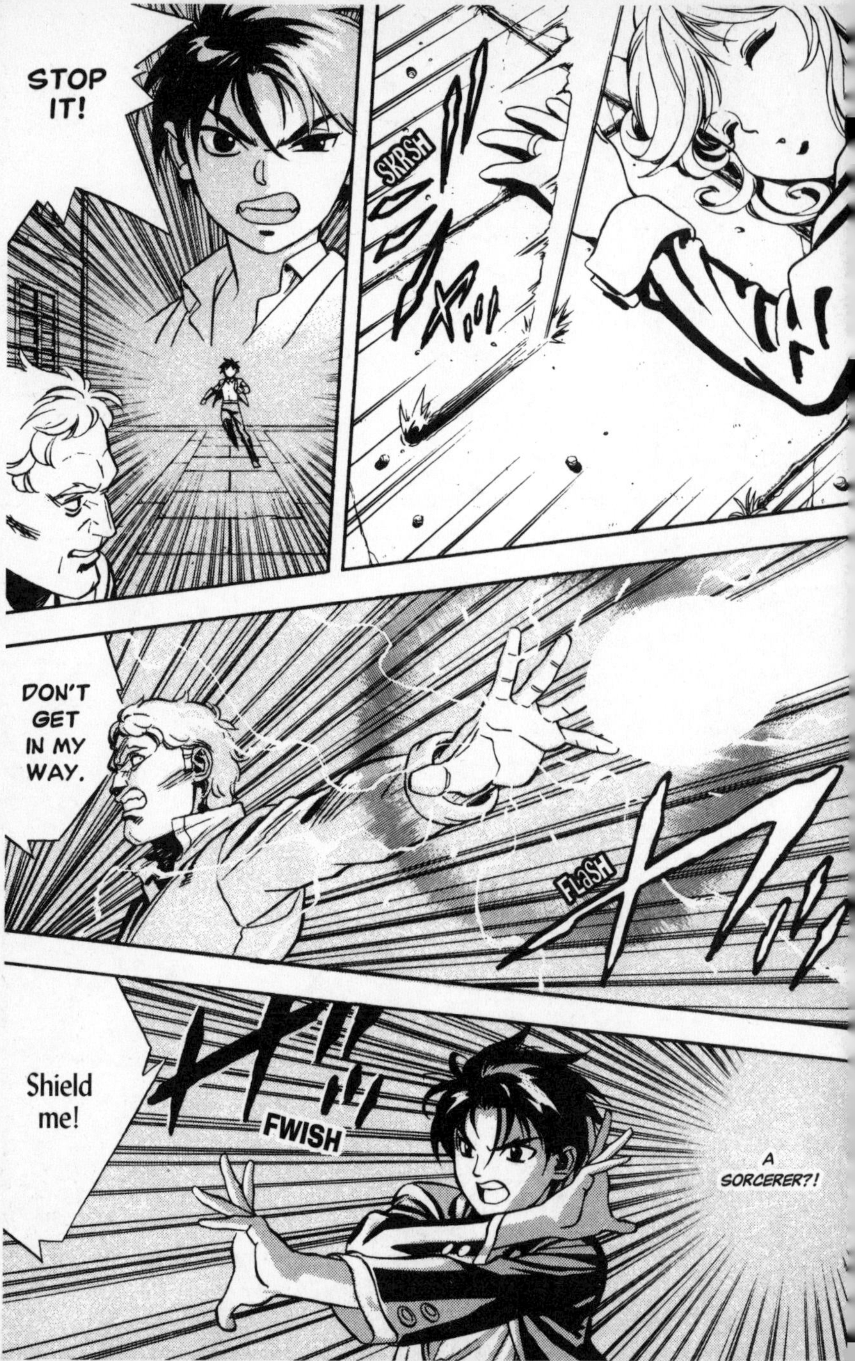
STOP IT!
SKRSH
DON'T GET IN MY WAY.
FLASH
Shield me!
FWISH
A SORCERER?!

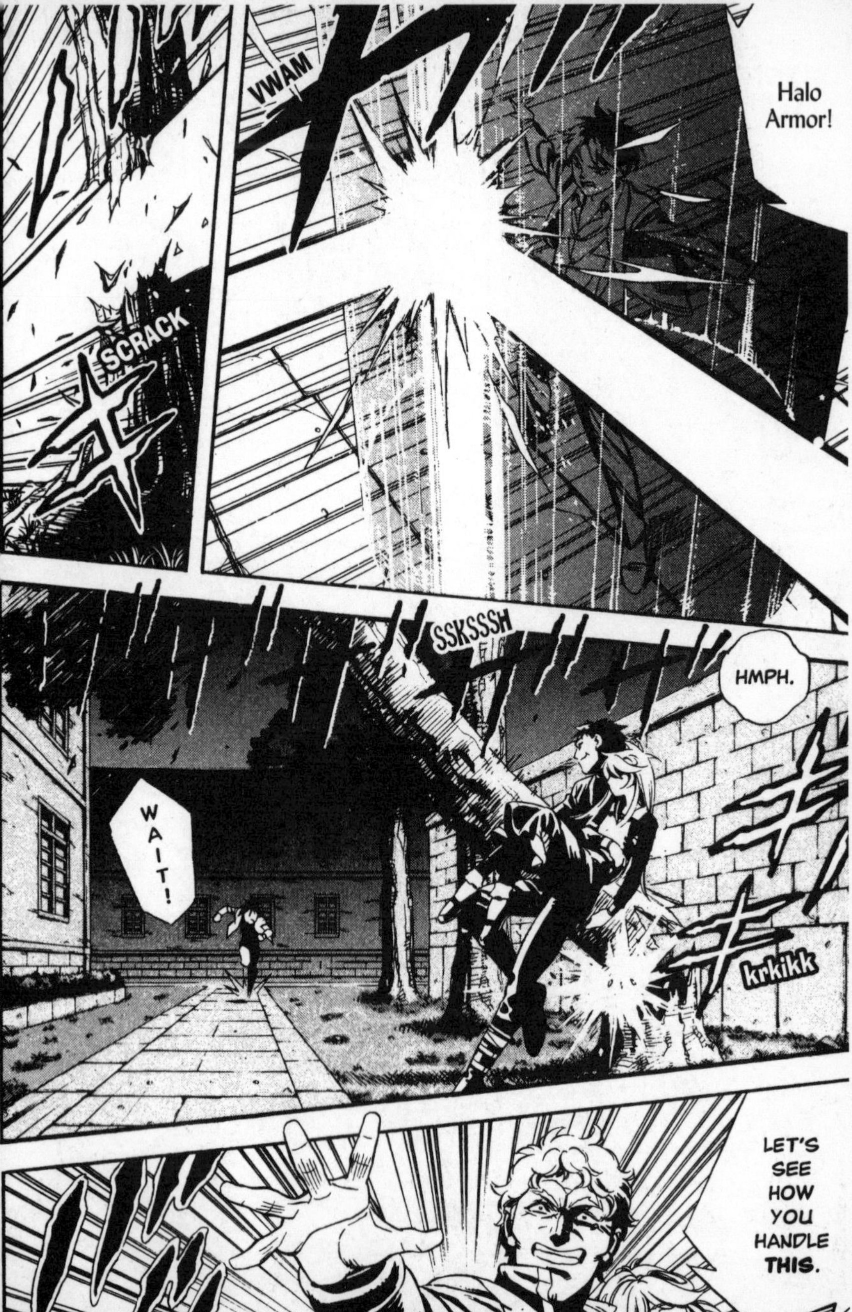
VWAM
Halo Armor!
SCRACK
SSKSSSH
HMPH.
WAIT!
krkikk
LET'S SEE HOW YOU HANDLE **THIS.**
FWIP

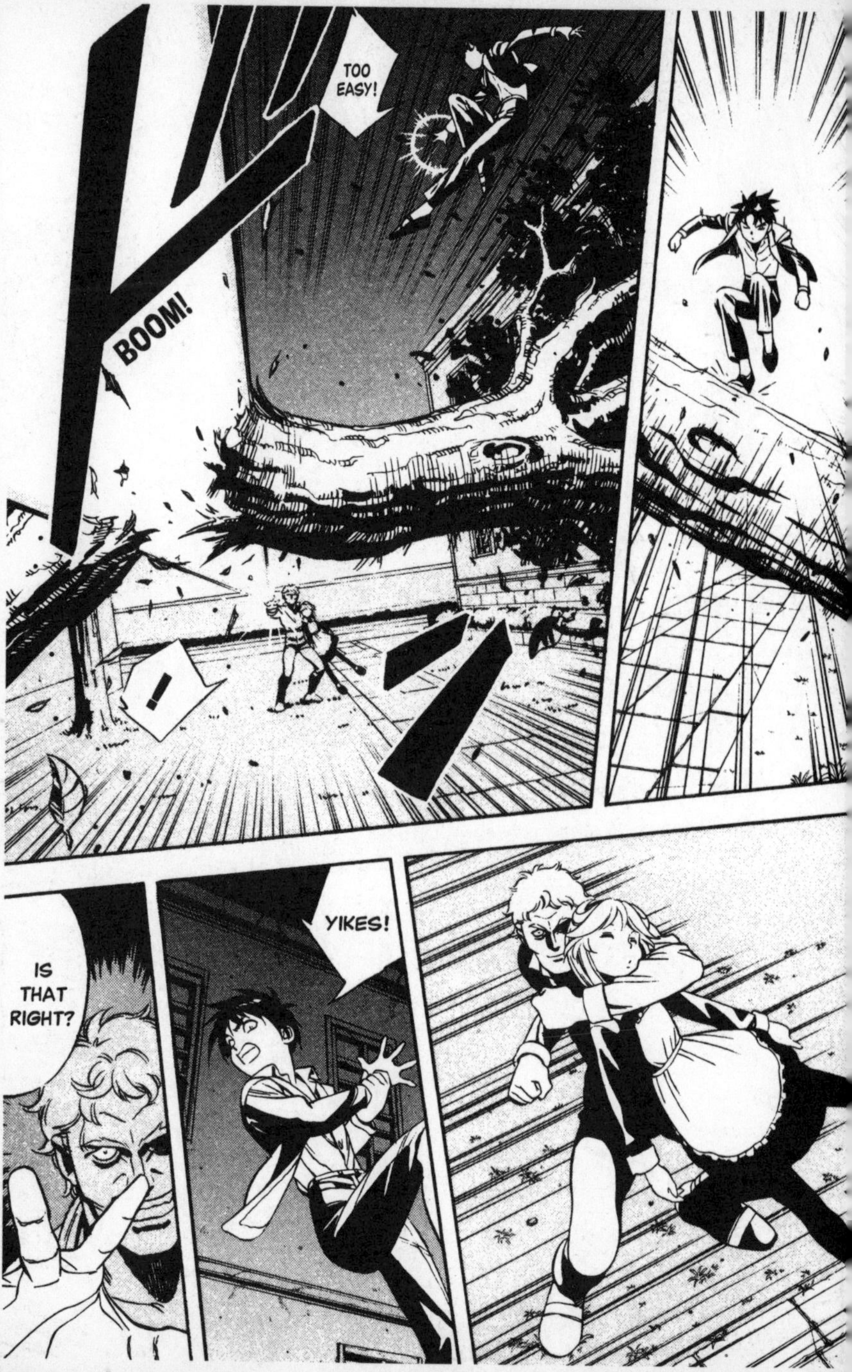
TOO EASY!
BOOM!
!
YIKES!
IS THAT RIGHT?

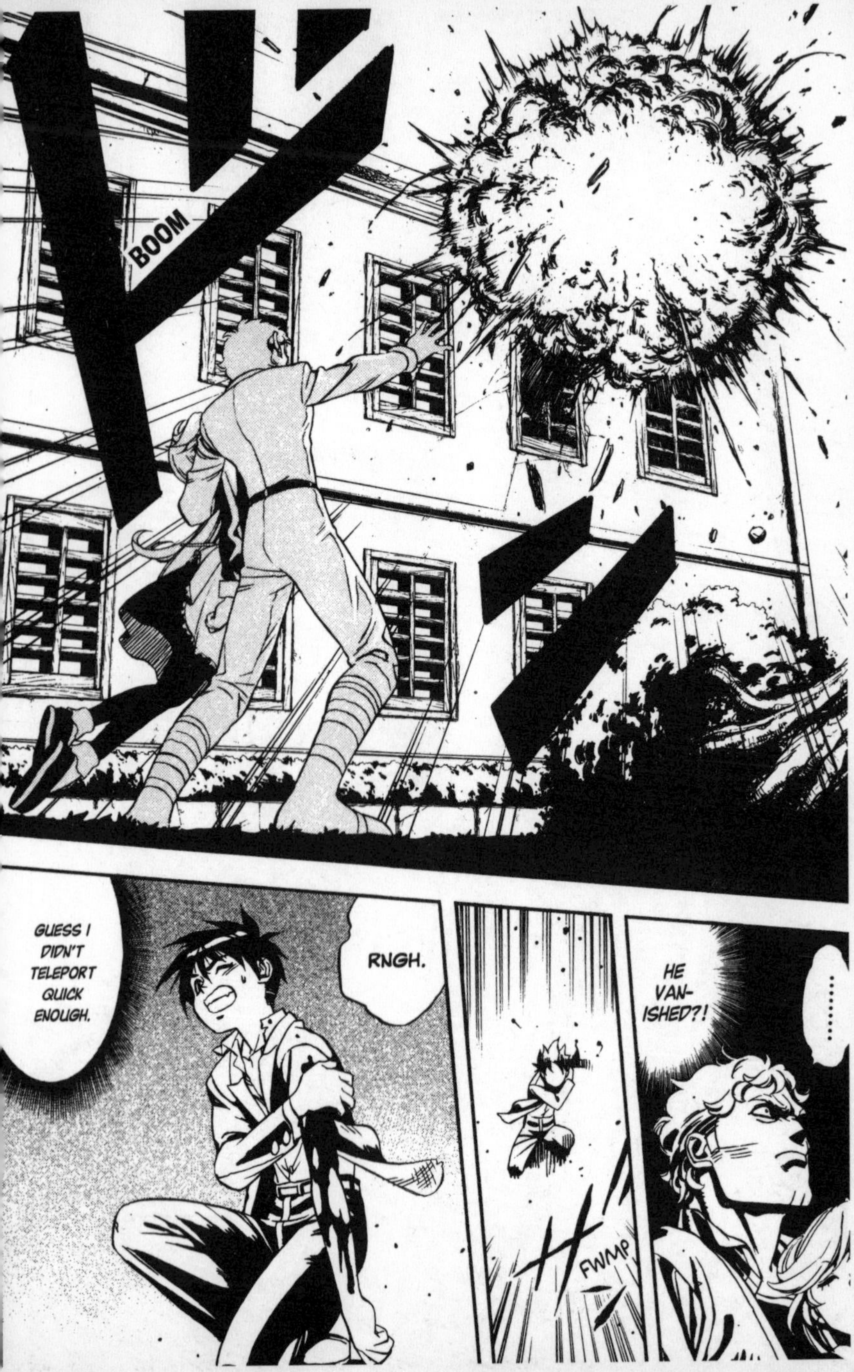
BOOM
......
HE VANISHED?!
FWMP
RNGH.
GUESS I DIDN'T TELEPORT QUICK ENOUGH.

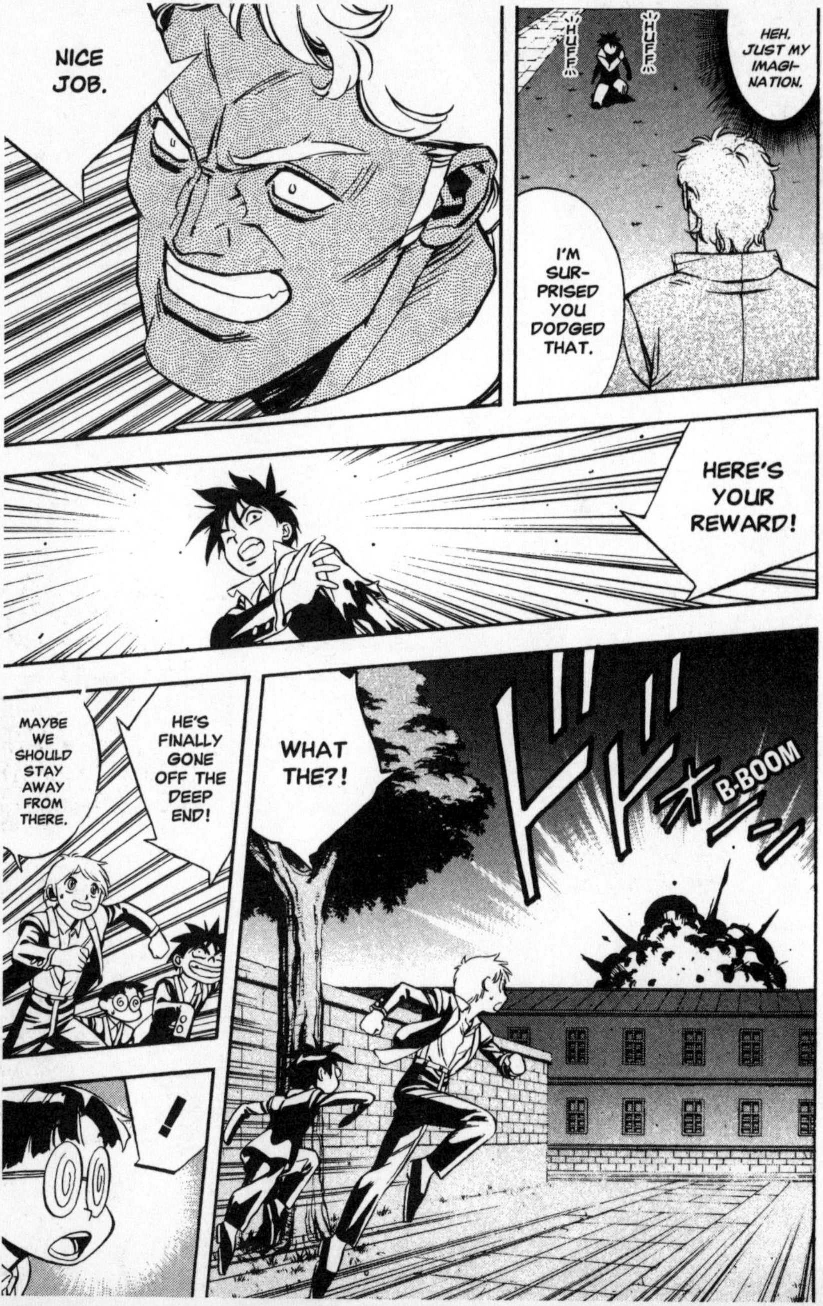
HUFF
HUFF
HEH. JUST MY IMAGI-NATION.
I'M SUR-PRISED YOU DODGED THAT.
NICE JOB.
HERE'S YOUR REWARD!
B-BOOM
WHAT THE?!
HE'S FINALLY GONE OFF THE DEEP END!
MAYBE WE SHOULD STAY AWAY FROM THERE.
!

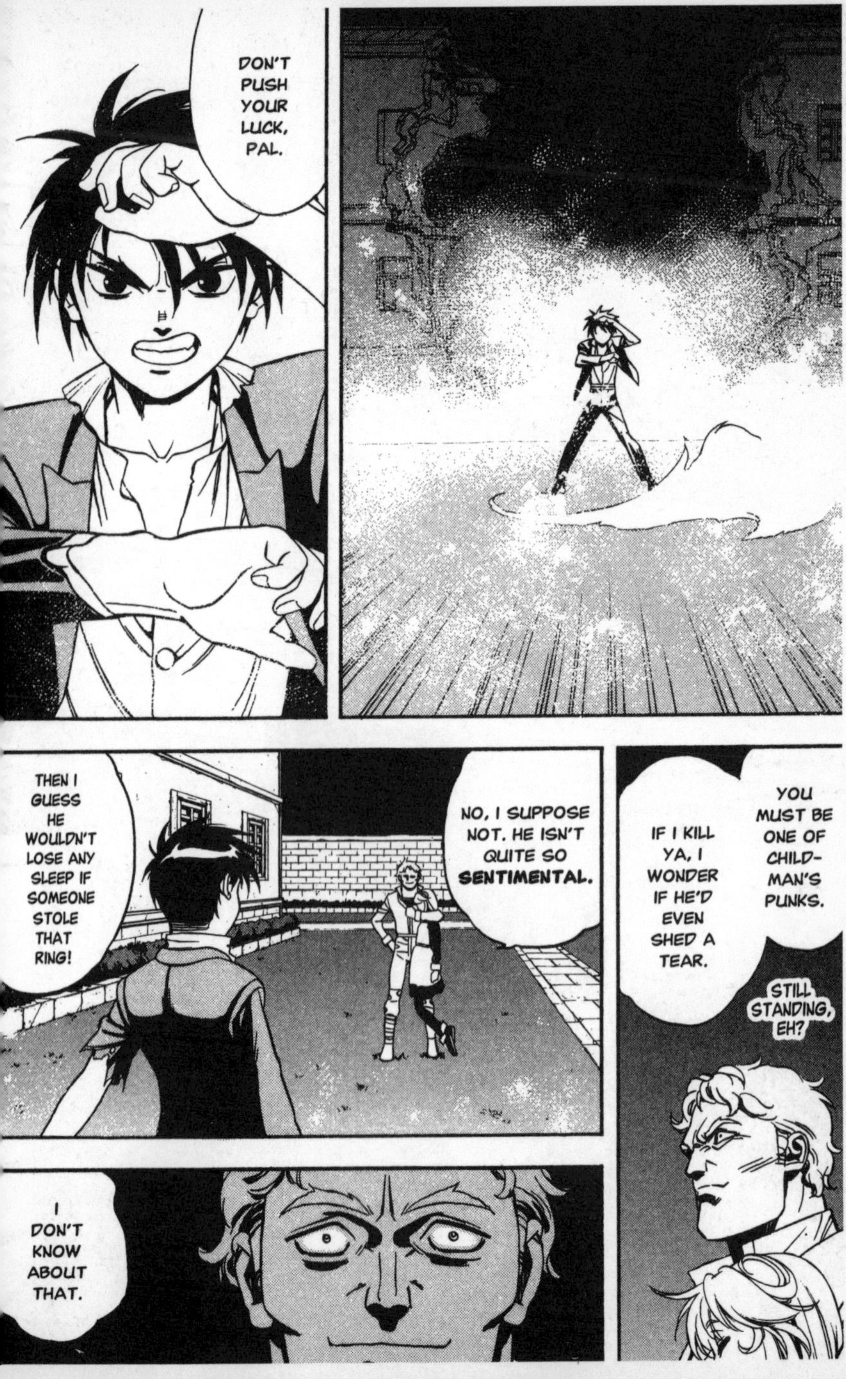
DON'T PUSH YOUR LUCK, PAL.
STILL STANDING, EH?
YOU MUST BE ONE OF CHILD-MAN'S PUNKS.
IF I KILL YA, I WONDER IF HE'D EVEN SHED A TEAR.
NO, I SUPPOSE NOT. HE ISN'T QUITE SO **SENTIMENTAL.**
THEN I GUESS HE WOULDN'T LOSE ANY SLEEP IF SOMEONE STOLE THAT RING!
I DON'T KNOW ABOUT THAT.

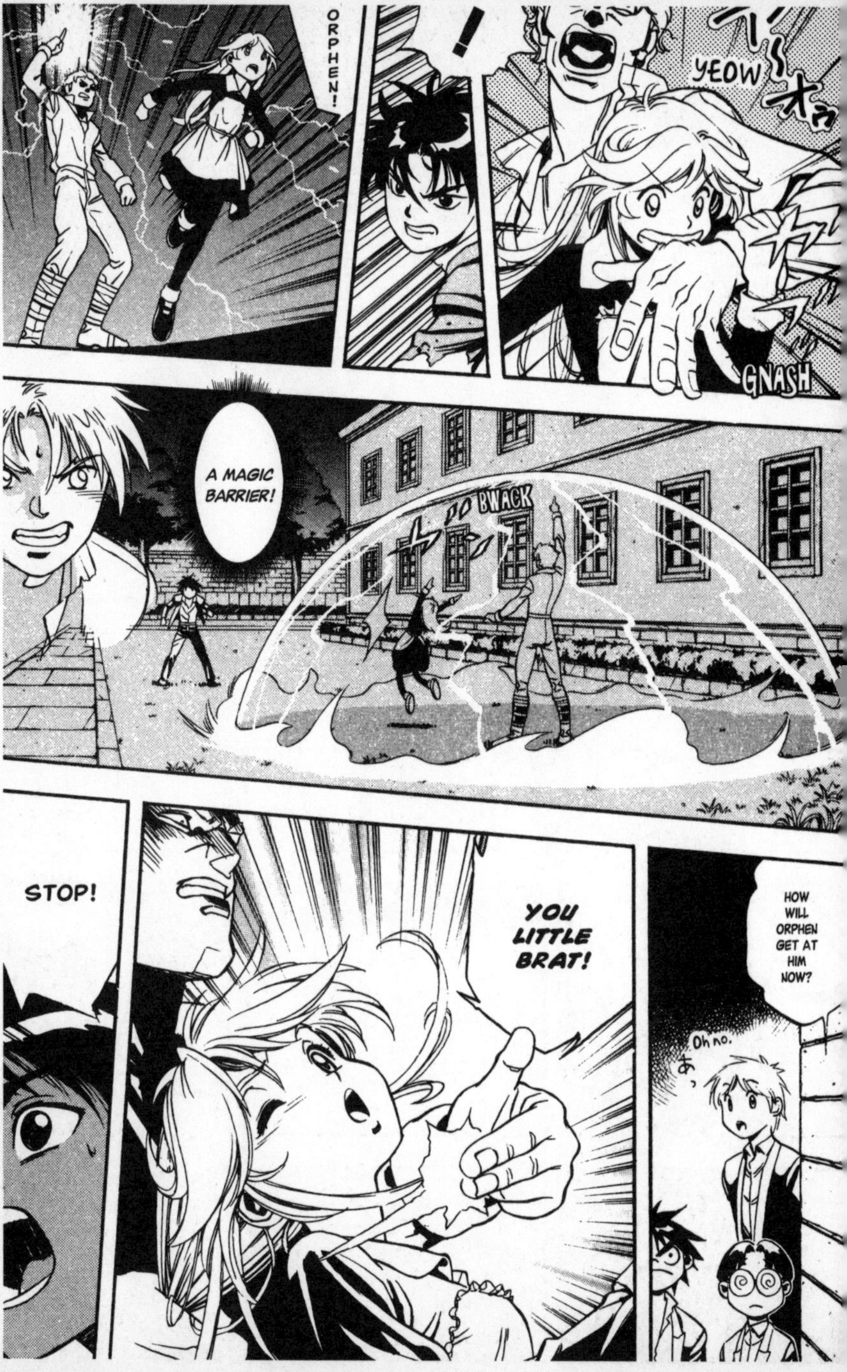
YEOW
GNASH
!
ORPHEN!
BWACK
A MAGIC BARRIER!
HOW WILL ORPHEN GET AT HIM NOW?
Oh no.
あ,
YOU LITTLE BRAT!
STOP!

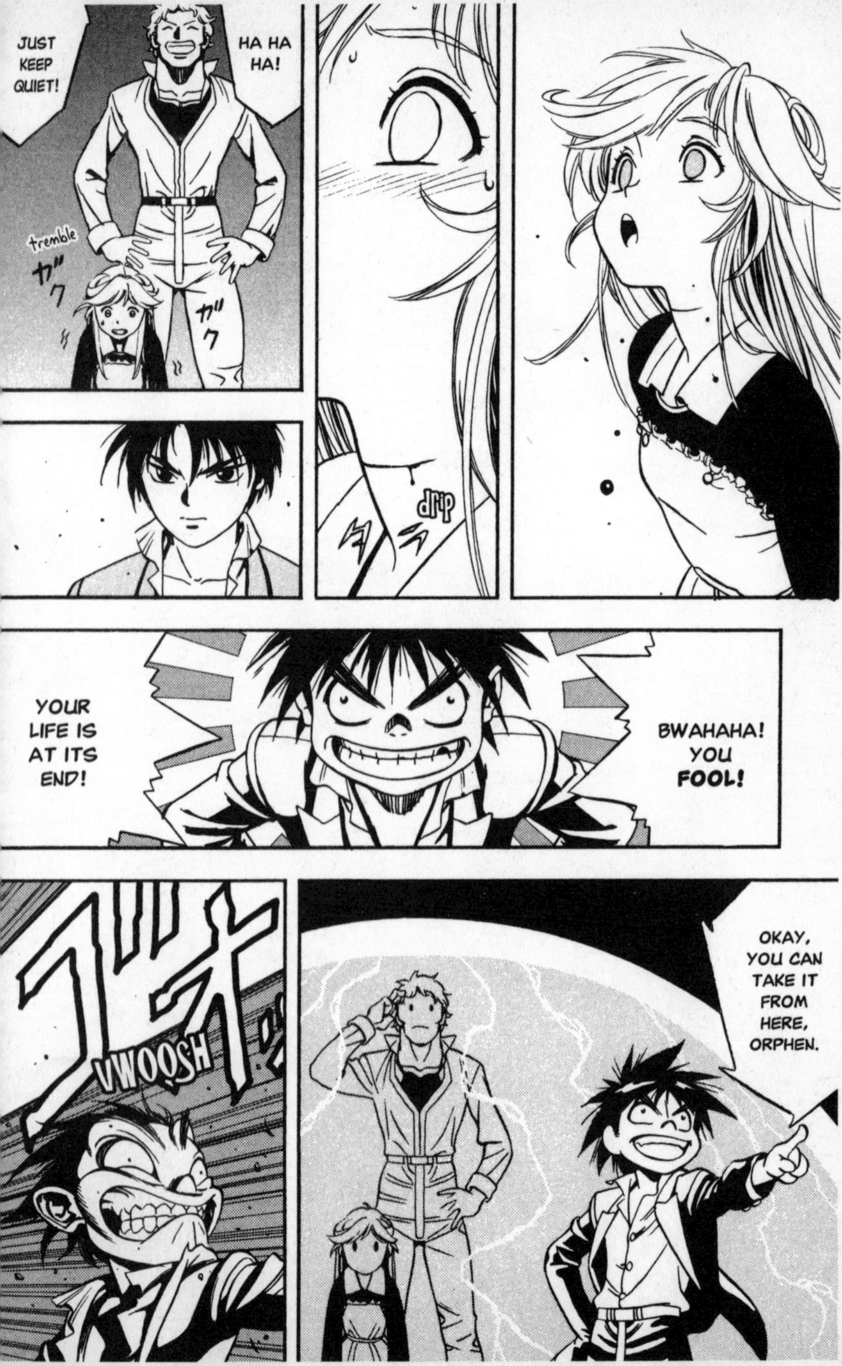
JUST KEEP QUIET!
HA HA HA!
tremble
ガク
ガク
drip
YOUR LIFE IS AT ITS END!
BWAHAHA! YOU FOOL!
VWOOSH
OKAY, YOU CAN TAKE IT FROM HERE, ORPHEN.

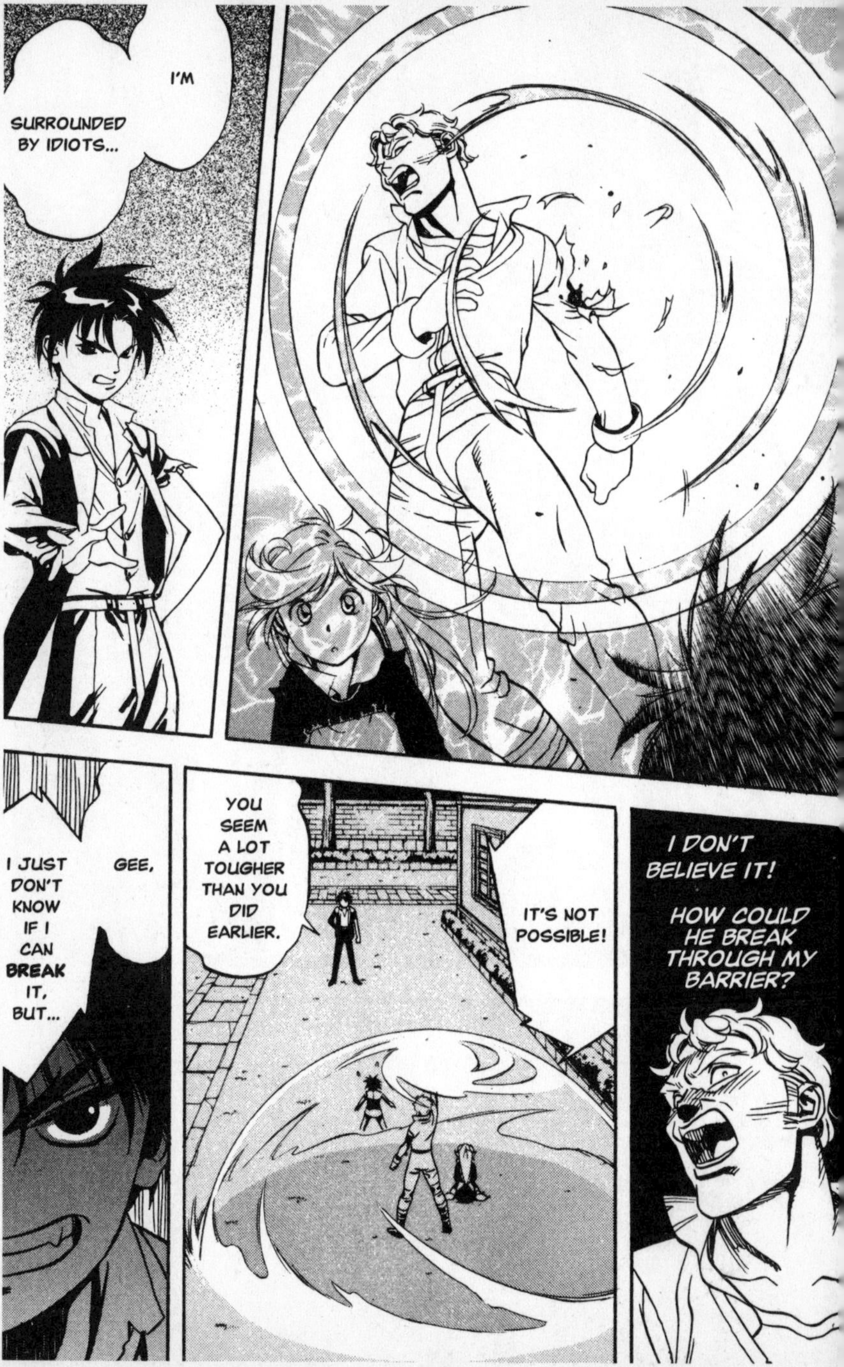
I'M SURROUNDED BY IDIOTS...
I DON'T BELIEVE IT!
HOW COULD HE BREAK THROUGH MY BARRIER?
IT'S NOT POSSIBLE!
YOU SEEM A LOT TOUGHER THAN YOU DID EARLIER.
GEE,
I JUST DON'T KNOW IF I CAN BREAK IT, BUT...

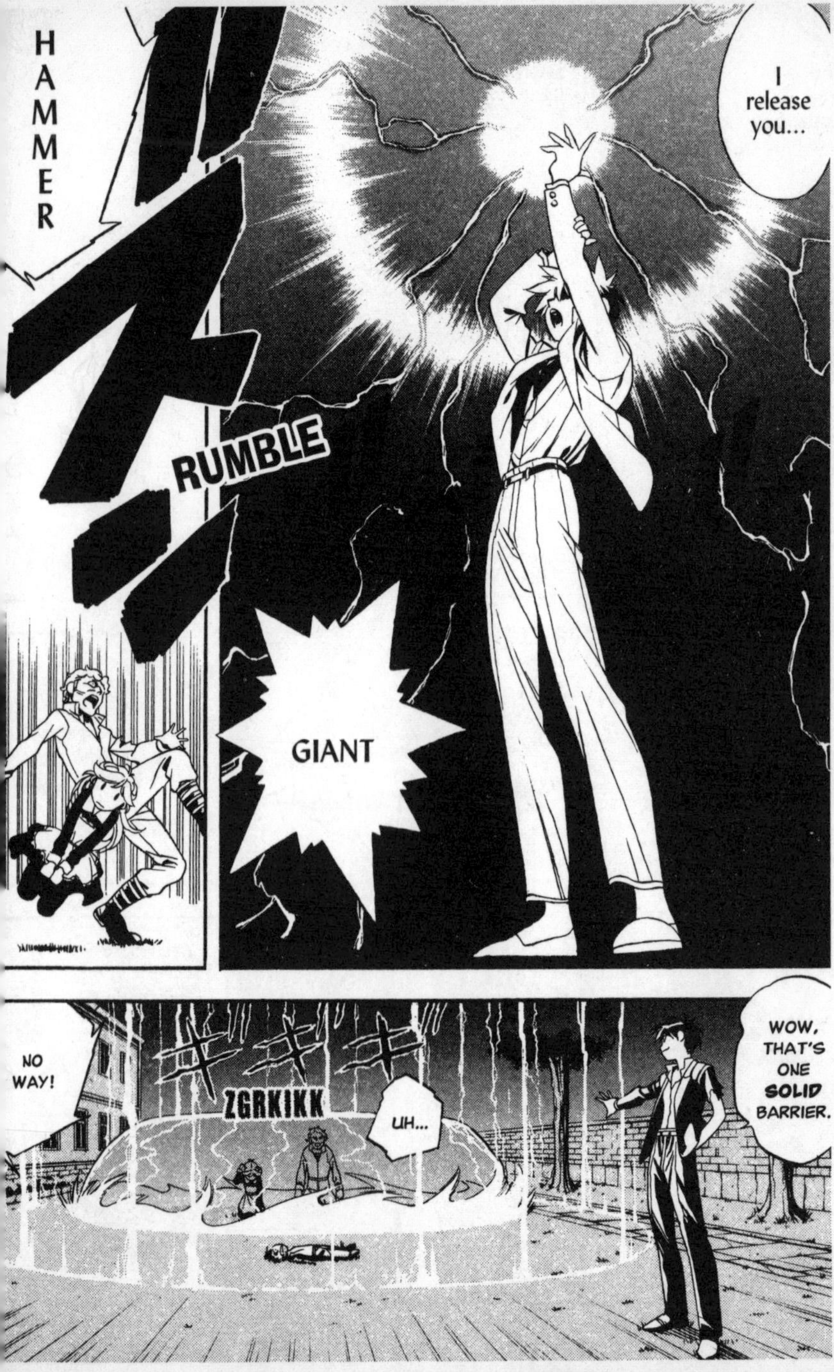
I release you...
HAMMER
RUMBLE
GIANT
WOW, THAT'S ONE SOLID BARRIER.
UH...
ZGRKIKK
NO WAY!

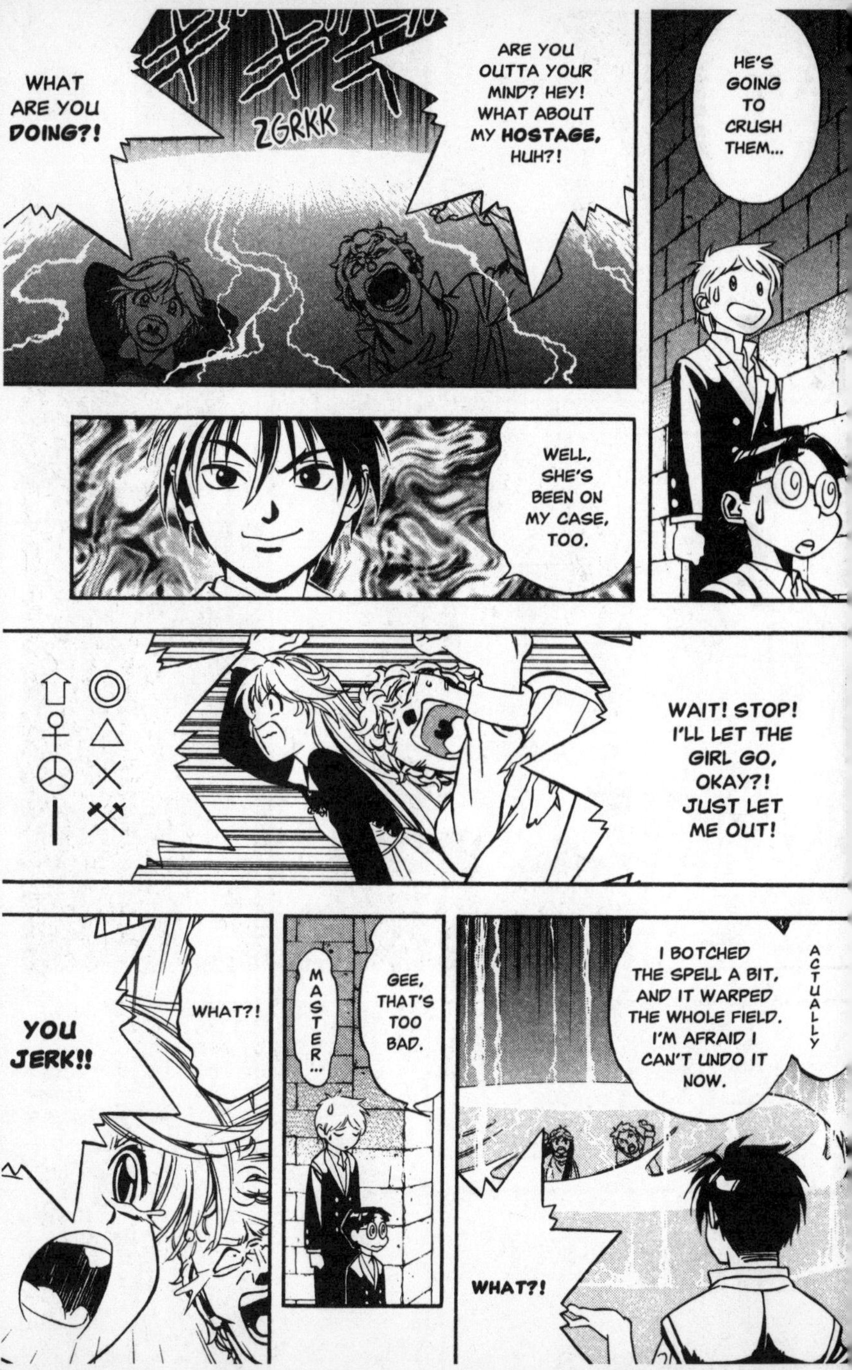
HE'S GOING TO CRUSH THEM...
ARE YOU OUTTA YOUR MIND? HEY! WHAT ABOUT MY **HOSTAGE,** HUH?!
ZGRKK
WHAT ARE YOU **DOING?!**
WELL, SHE'S BEEN ON MY CASE, TOO.
WAIT! STOP! I'LL LET THE GIRL GO, OKAY?! JUST LET ME OUT!
ACTUALLY
I BOTCHED THE SPELL A BIT, AND IT WARPED THE WHOLE FIELD. I'M AFRAID I CAN'T UNDO IT NOW.
WHAT?!
GEE, THAT'S TOO BAD.
MASTER...
WHAT?!
YOU JERK!!

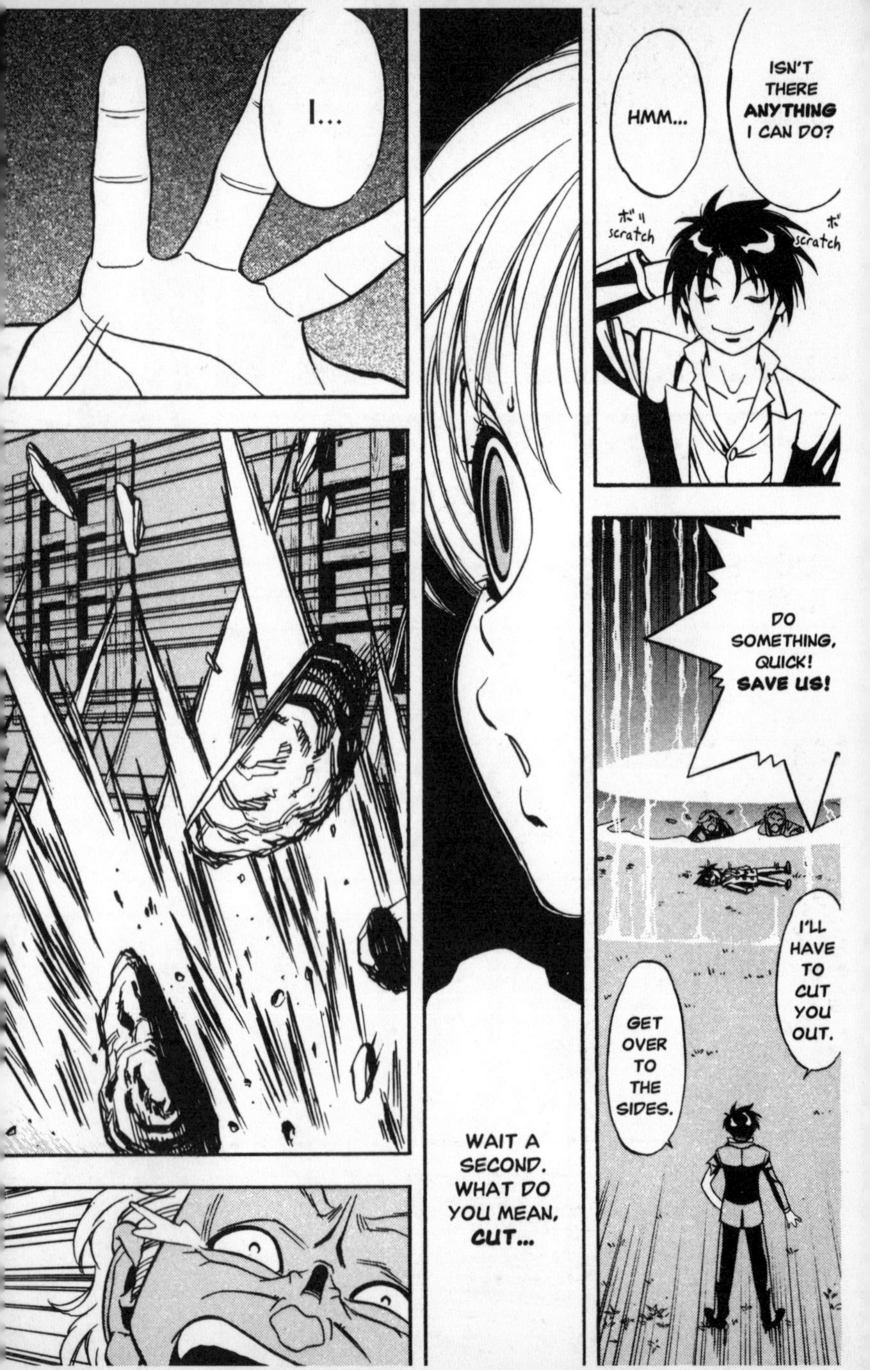

ISN'T THERE ANYTHING I CAN DO?
HMM...
ボ scratch
ボリ scratch
I...
DO SOMETHING, QUICK! SAVE US!
I'LL HAVE TO CUT YOU OUT.
GET OVER TO THE SIDES.
WAIT A SECOND. WHAT DO YOU MEAN, CUT...

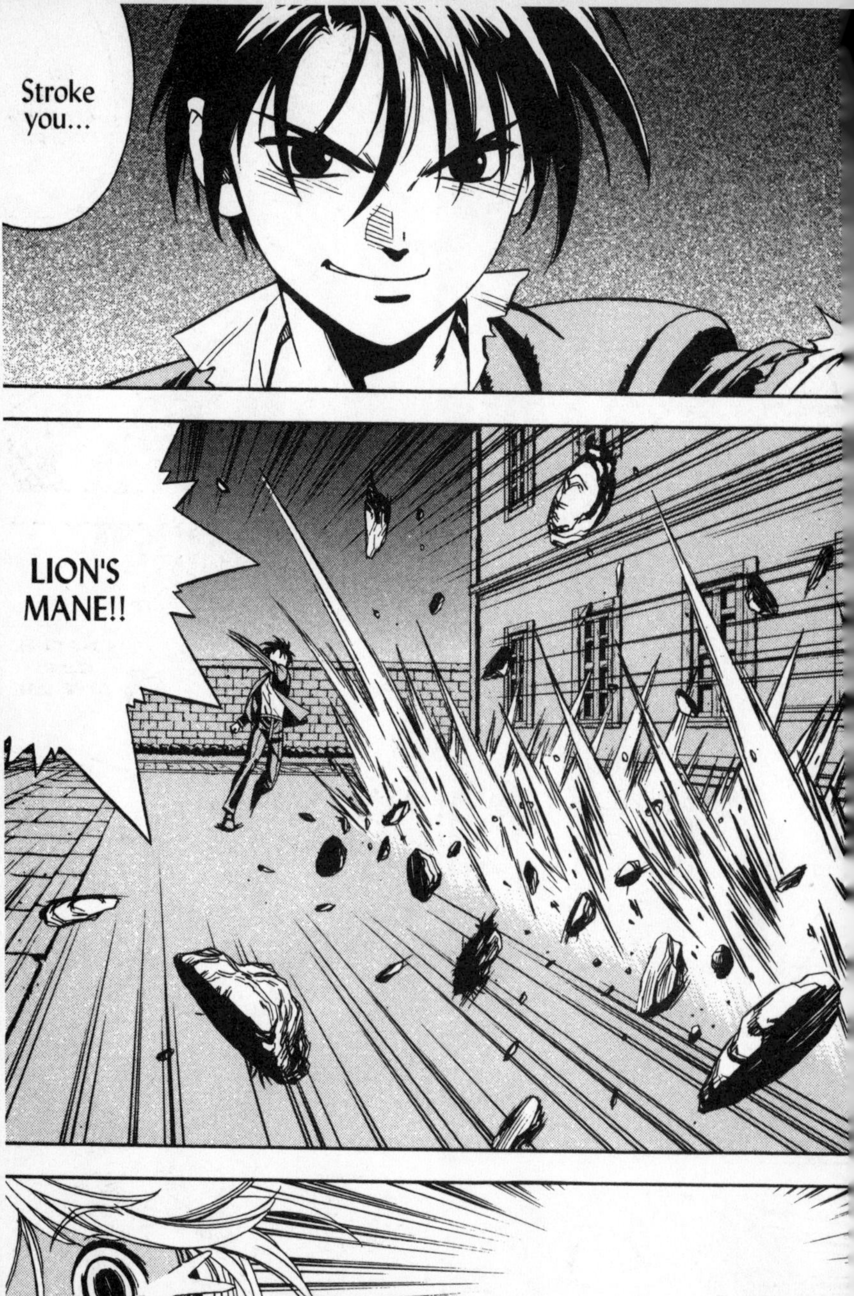

Stroke you...
LION'S MANE!!

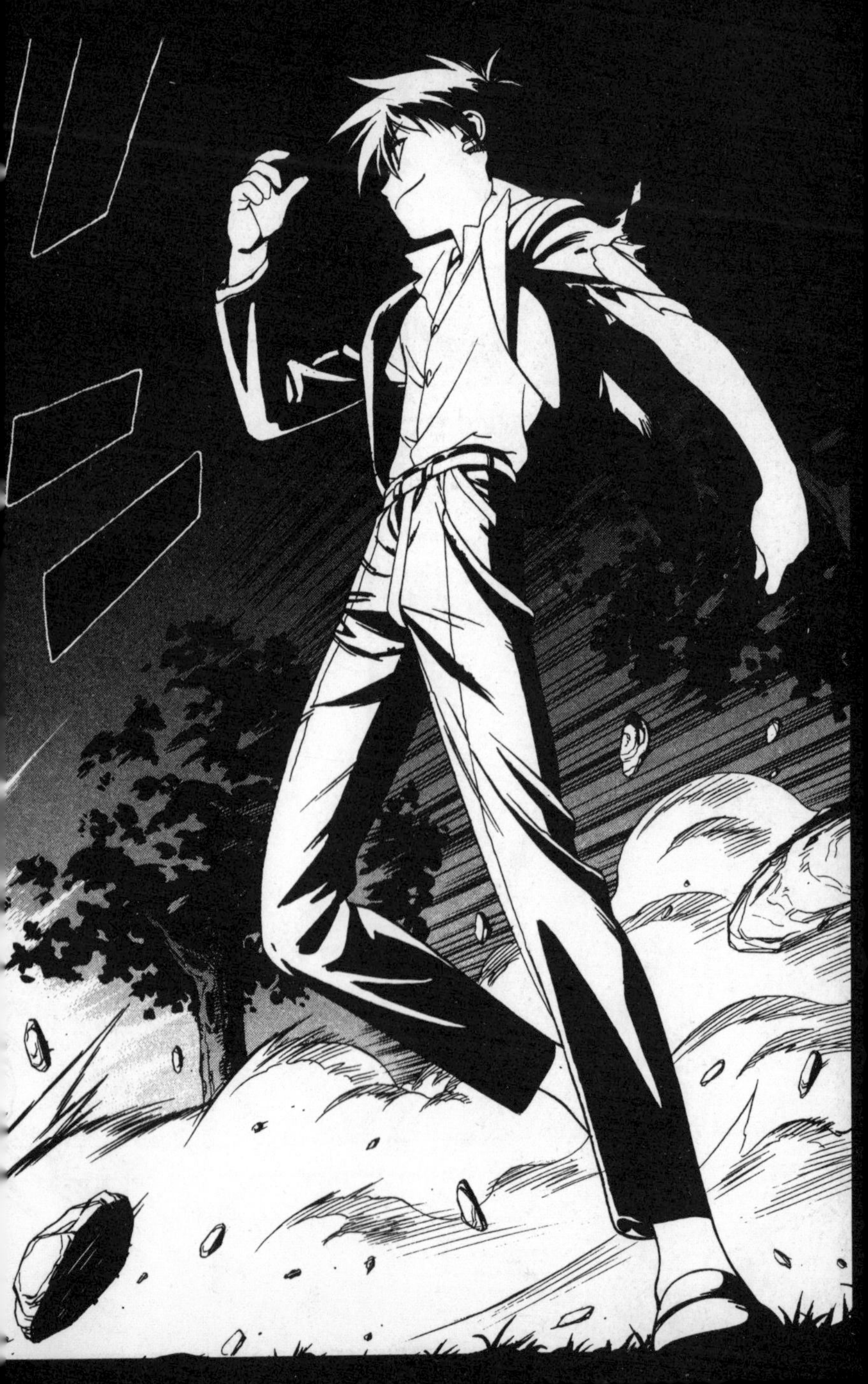

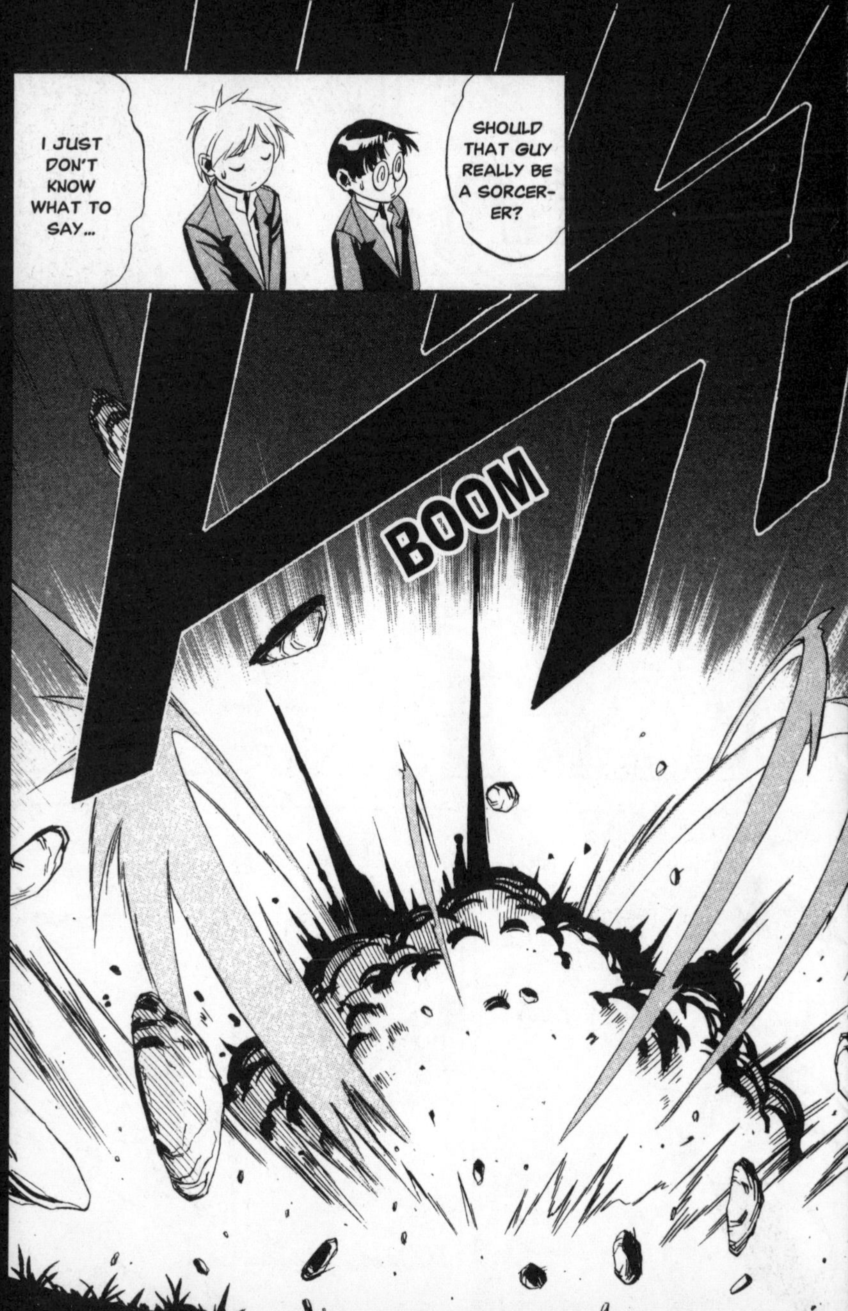
SHOULD THAT GUY REALLY BE A SORCER-ER?
I JUST DON'T KNOW WHAT TO SAY...
BOOM

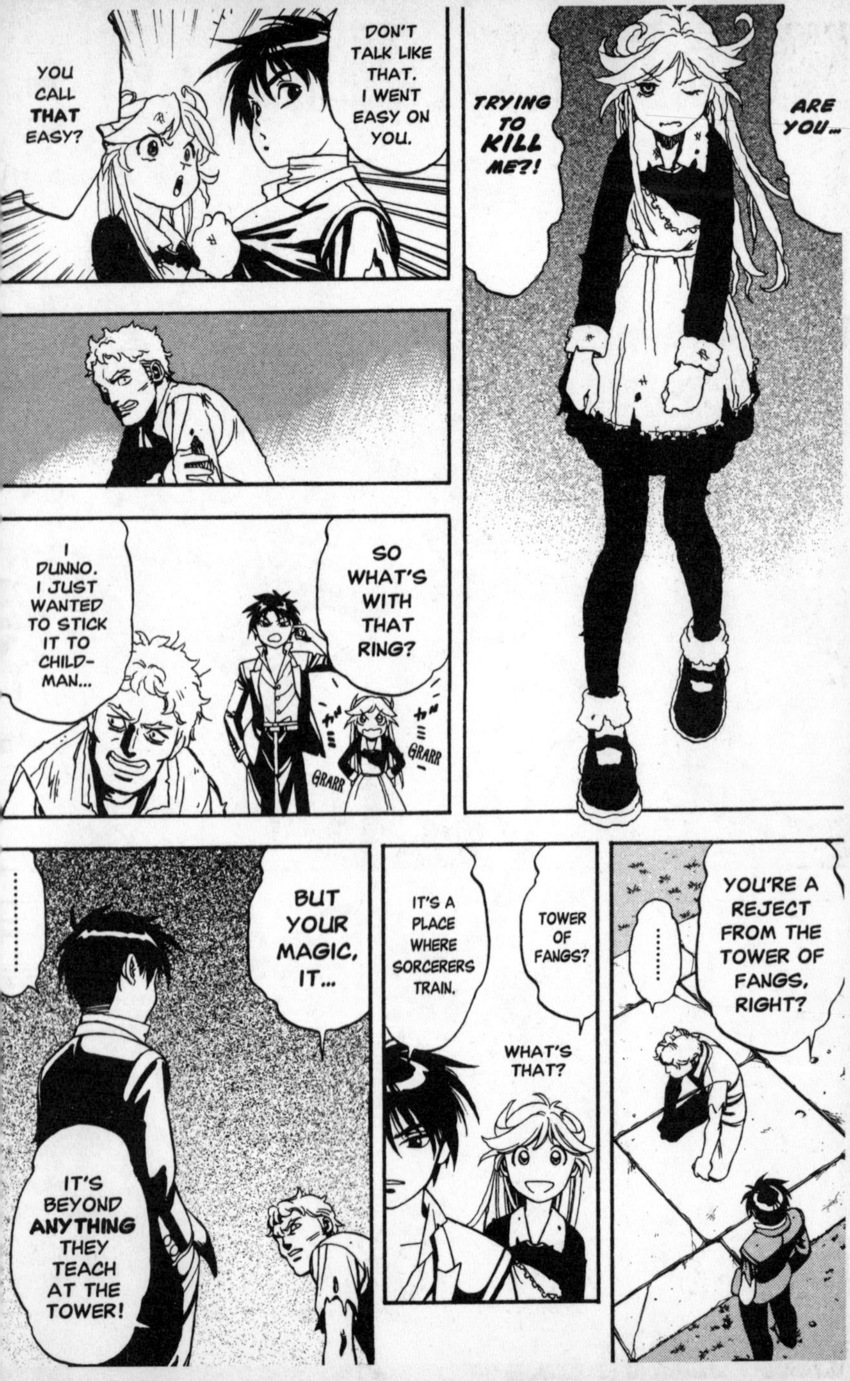
ARE YOU...
TRYING TO KILL ME?!
DON'T TALK LIKE THAT. I WENT EASY ON YOU.
YOU CALL THAT EASY?
SO WHAT'S WITH THAT RING?
GRARR
GRARR
I DUNNO. I JUST WANTED TO STICK IT TO CHILD-MAN...
YOU'RE A REJECT FROM THE TOWER OF FANGS, RIGHT?
......
TOWER OF FANGS?
WHAT'S THAT?
IT'S A PLACE WHERE SORCERERS TRAIN.
BUT YOUR MAGIC, IT...
......
IT'S BEYOND ANYTHING THEY TEACH AT THE TOWER!

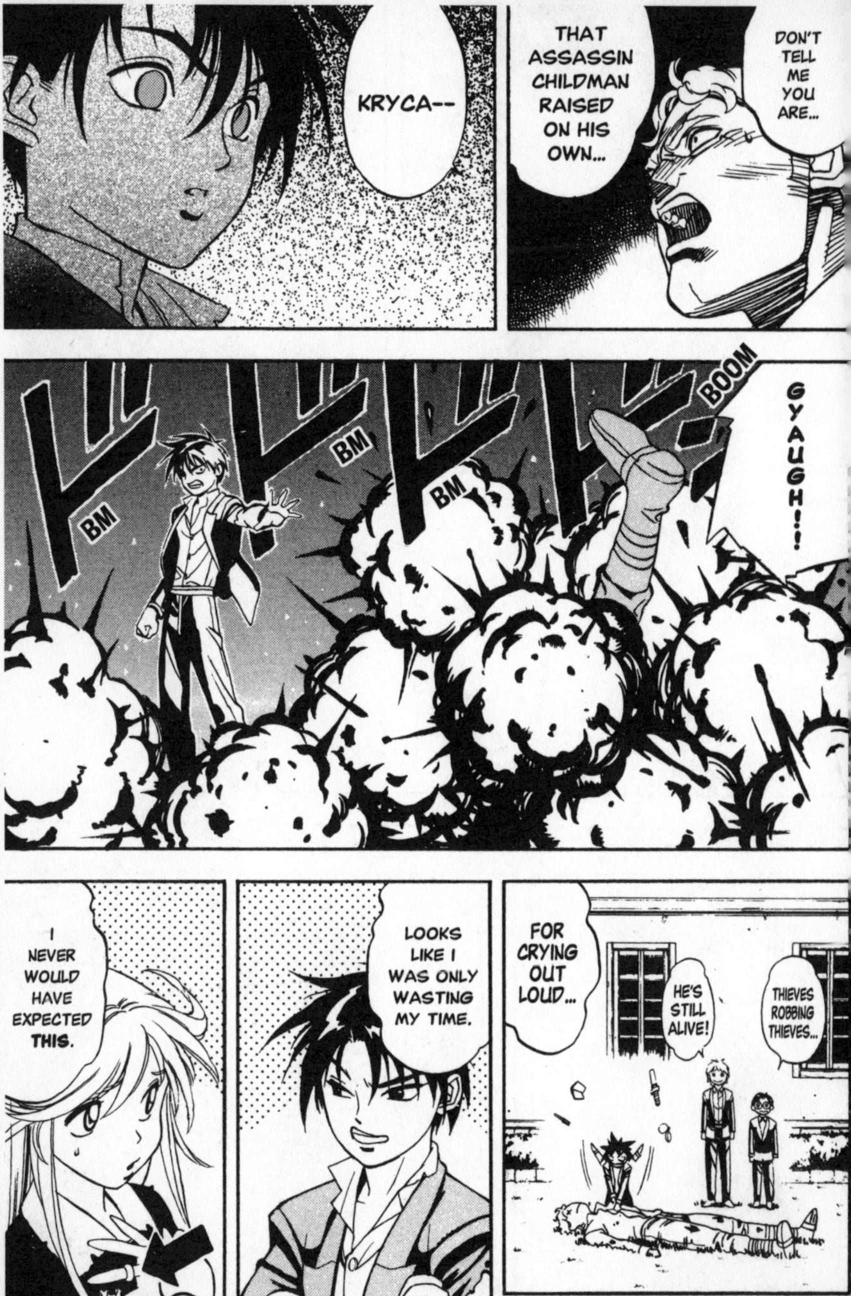
KRYCA--
THAT ASSASSIN CHILDMAN RAISED ON HIS OWN...
DON'T TELL ME YOU ARE...
BM
BM
BM
BOOM
GYAUGH!!
I NEVER WOULD HAVE EXPECTED THIS.
LOOKS LIKE I WAS ONLY WASTING MY TIME.
FOR CRYING OUT LOUD...
HE'S STILL ALIVE!
THIEVES ROBBING THIEVES...

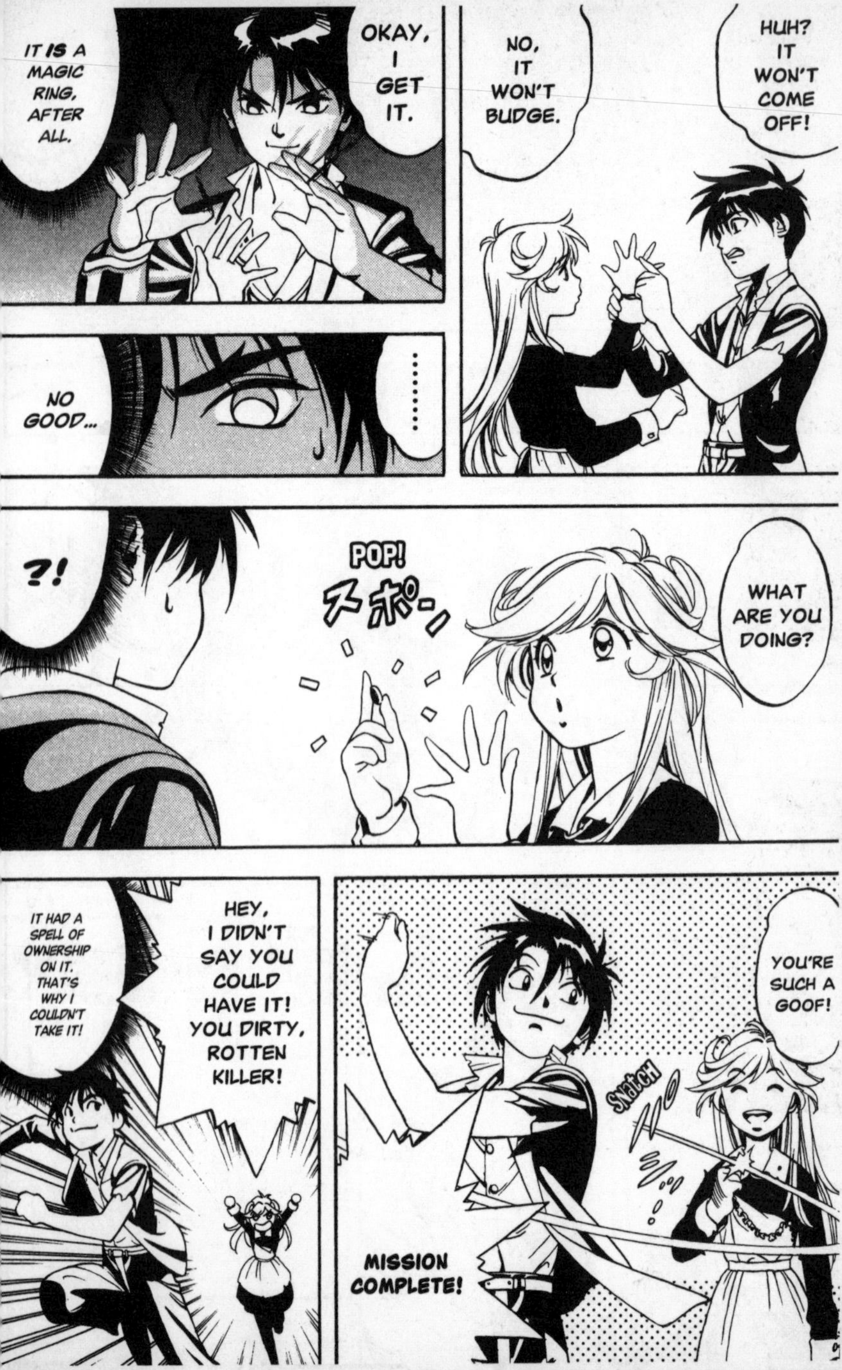
HUH? IT WON'T COME OFF!
NO, IT WON'T BUDGE.
OKAY, I GET IT.
IT IS A MAGIC RING, AFTER ALL.
......
NO GOOD...
WHAT ARE YOU DOING?
POP!
スポーン
?!
YOU'RE SUCH A GOOF!
SNATCH
MISSION COMPLETE!
HEY, I DIDN'T SAY YOU COULD HAVE IT! YOU DIRTY, ROTTEN KILLER!
IT HAD A SPELL OF OWNERSHIP ON IT. THAT'S WHY I COULDN'T TAKE IT!

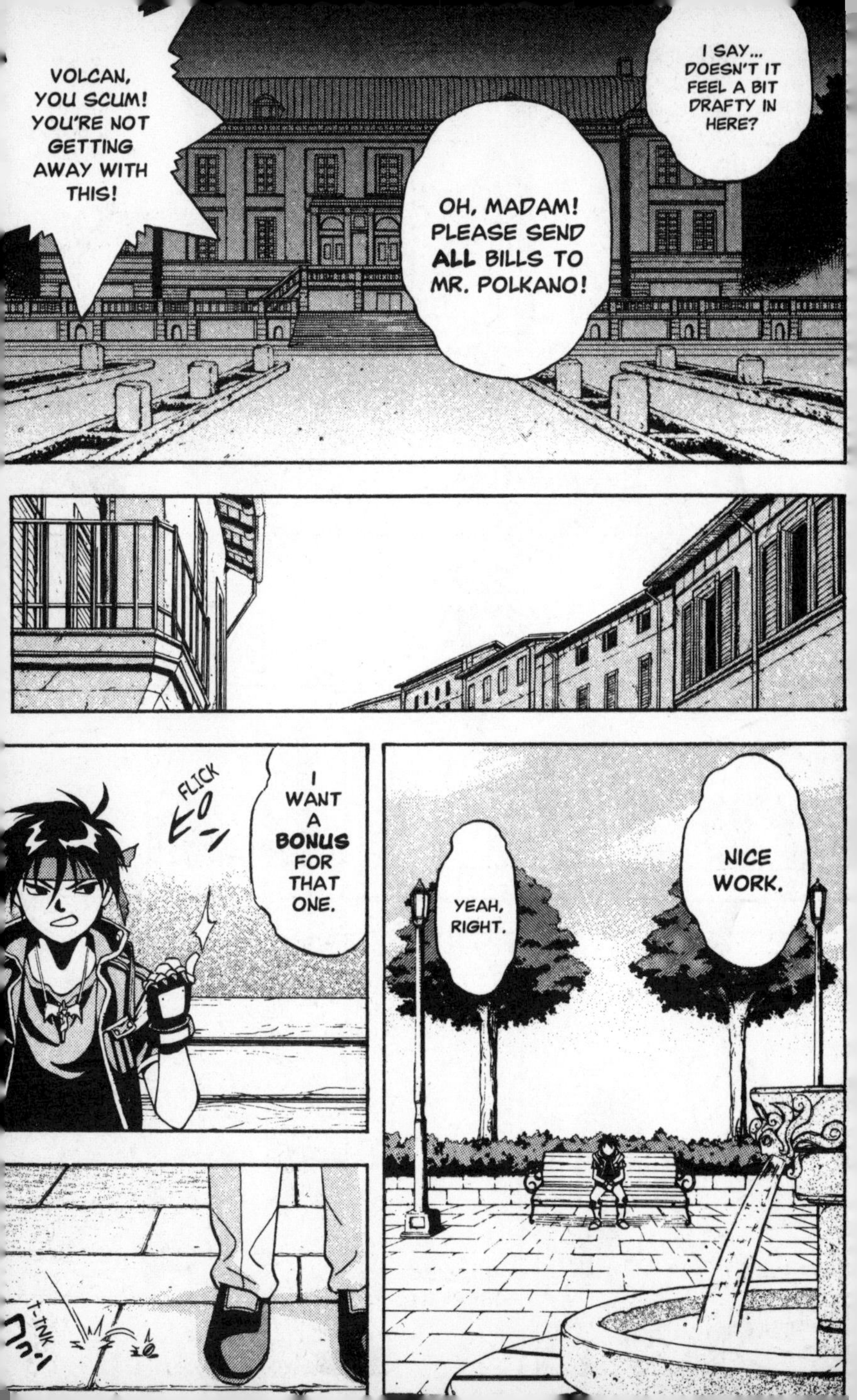
I SAY... DOESN'T IT FEEL A BIT DRAFTY IN HERE?
OH, MADAM! PLEASE SEND **ALL** BILLS TO MR. POLKANO!
VOLCAN, YOU SCUM! YOU'RE NOT GETTING AWAY WITH THIS!
NICE WORK.
YEAH, RIGHT.
I WANT A **BONUS** FOR THAT ONE.
FLICK
T-TINK

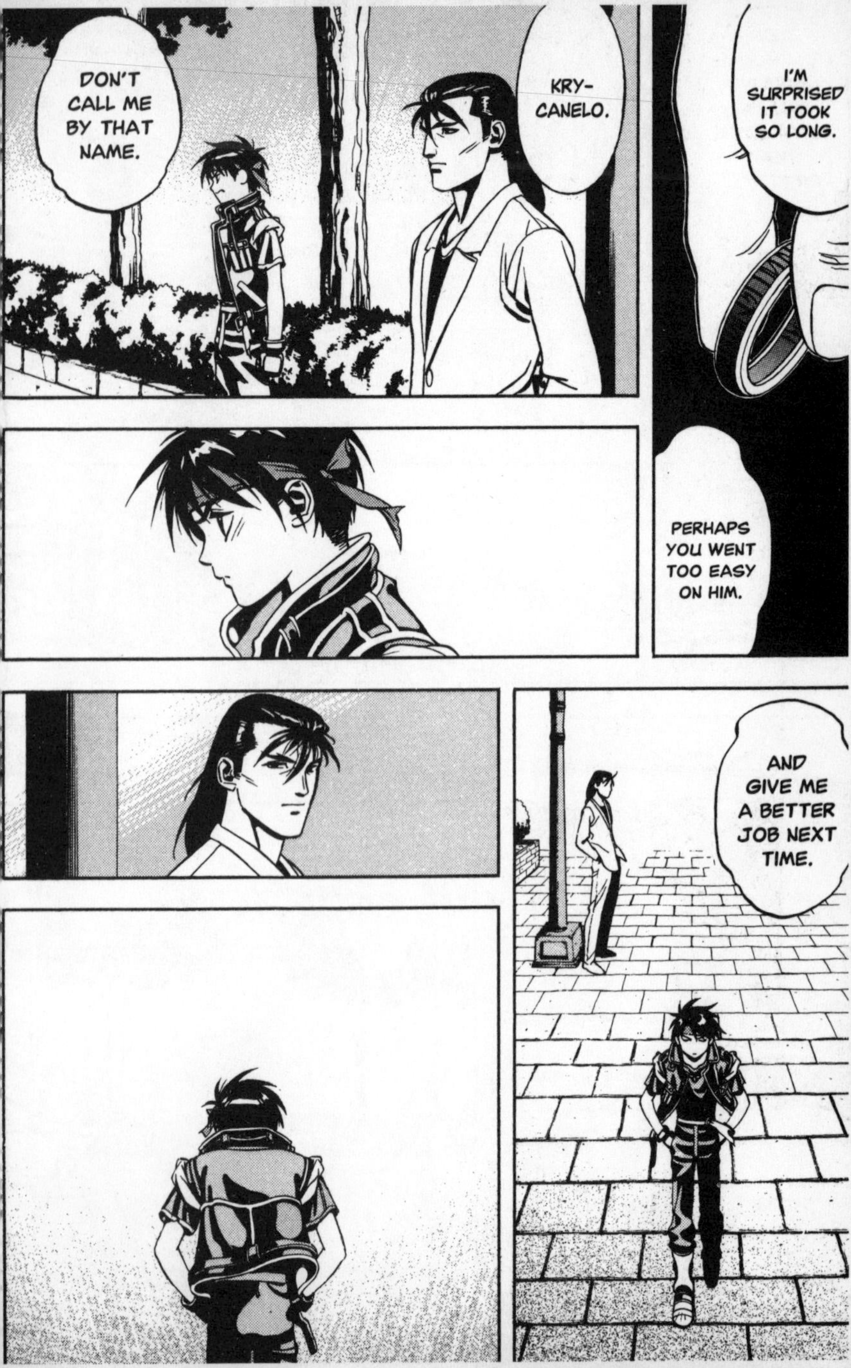
I'M SURPRISED IT TOOK SO LONG.
PERHAPS YOU WENT TOO EASY ON HIM.
KRY-CANELO.
DON'T CALL ME BY THAT NAME.
AND GIVE ME A BETTER JOB NEXT TIME.

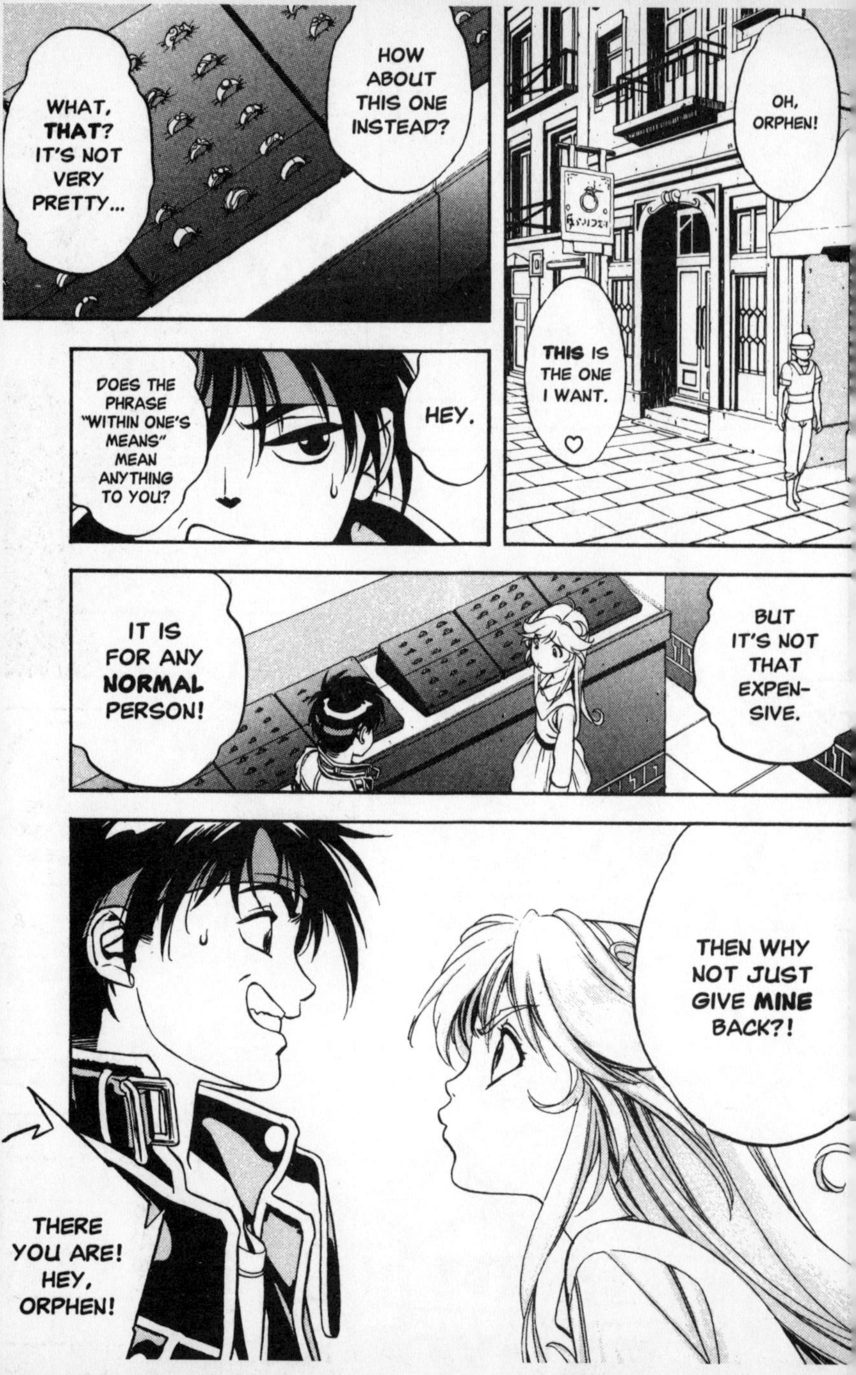
OH, ORPHEN!
HOW ABOUT THIS ONE INSTEAD?
WHAT, THAT? IT'S NOT VERY PRETTY...
THIS IS THE ONE I WANT. ♡
HEY.
DOES THE PHRASE "WITHIN ONE'S MEANS" MEAN ANYTHING TO YOU?
BUT IT'S NOT THAT EXPEN-SIVE.
IT IS FOR ANY NORMAL PERSON!
THEN WHY NOT JUST GIVE MINE BACK?!
THERE YOU ARE! HEY, ORPHEN!

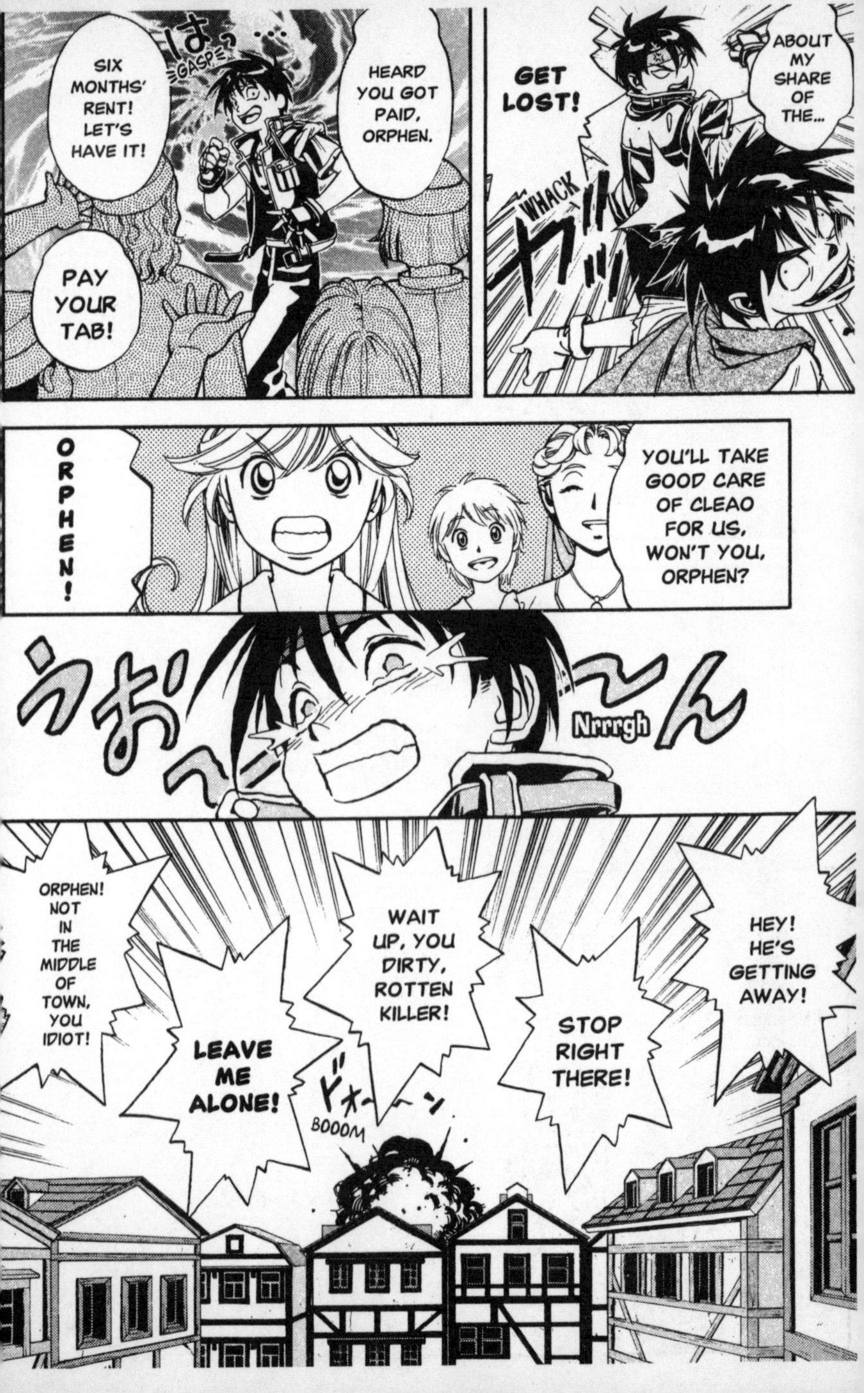

ABOUT MY SHARE OF THE...
GET LOST!
WHACK
HEARD YOU GOT PAID, ORPHEN.
GASP
SIX MONTHS' RENT! LET'S HAVE IT!
PAY YOUR TAB!
YOU'LL TAKE GOOD CARE OF CLEAO FOR US, WON'T YOU, ORPHEN?
ORPHEN!
Nrrrgh
HEY! HE'S GETTING AWAY!
STOP RIGHT THERE!
WAIT UP, YOU DIRTY, ROTTEN KILLER!
LEAVE ME ALONE!
BOOOM
ORPHEN! NOT IN THE MIDDLE OF TOWN, YOU IDIOT!

ORPHEN
Wandering Journey

CLEAO?!
ARGH!
HOLD ON, MAJIC! JUST WHO IS THIS GUY?!

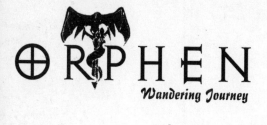

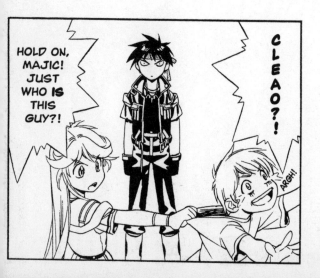

ORPHEN

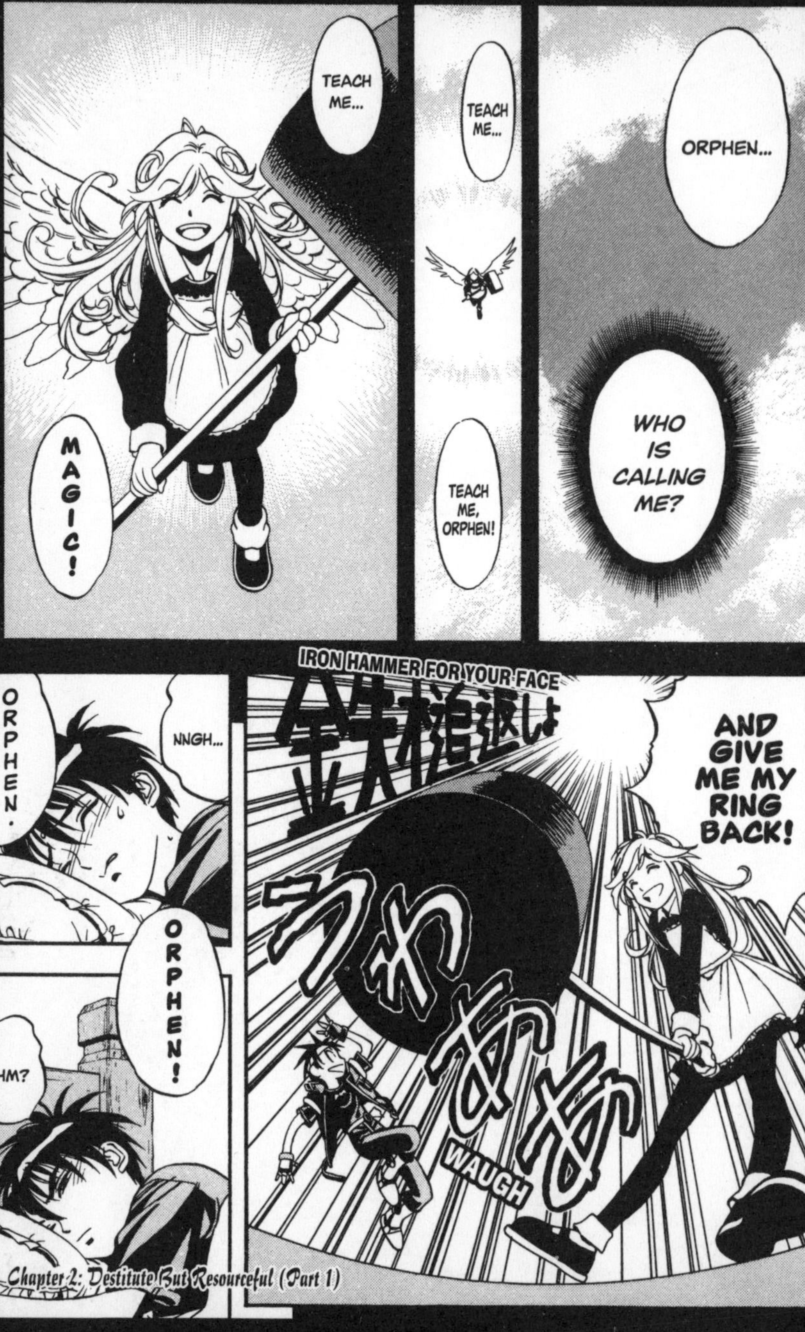
ORPHEN...
WHO IS CALLING ME?
TEACH ME...
TEACH ME, ORPHEN!
TEACH ME...
MAGIC!
IRON HAMMER FOR YOUR FACE
AND GIVE ME MY RING BACK!
WAUGH
ORPHEN.
NNGH...
ORPHEN!
HM?

Chapter 2: Destitute But Resourceful (Part 1)

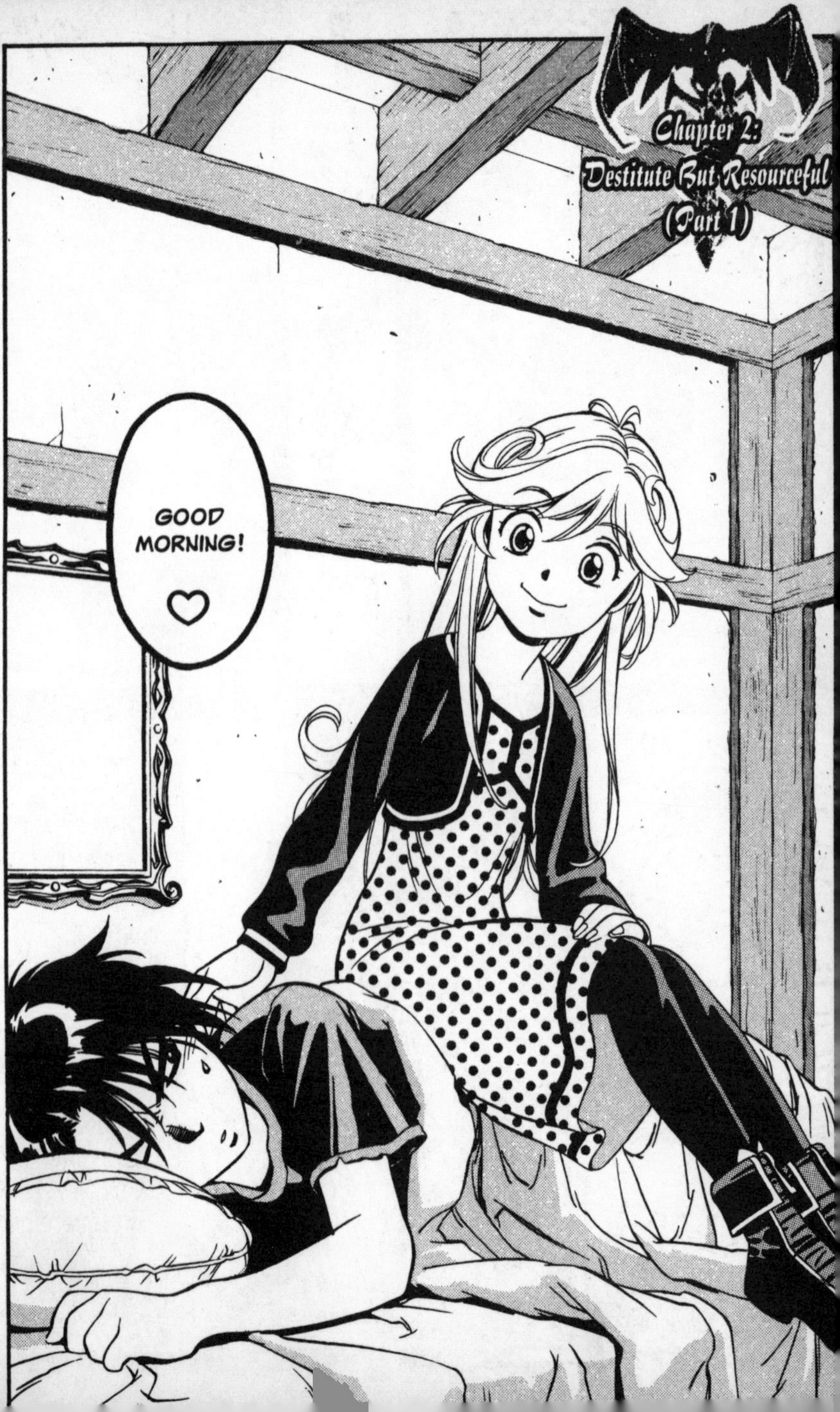
Chapter 2:
Destitute But Resourceful
(Part 1)
GOOD MORNING! ♡

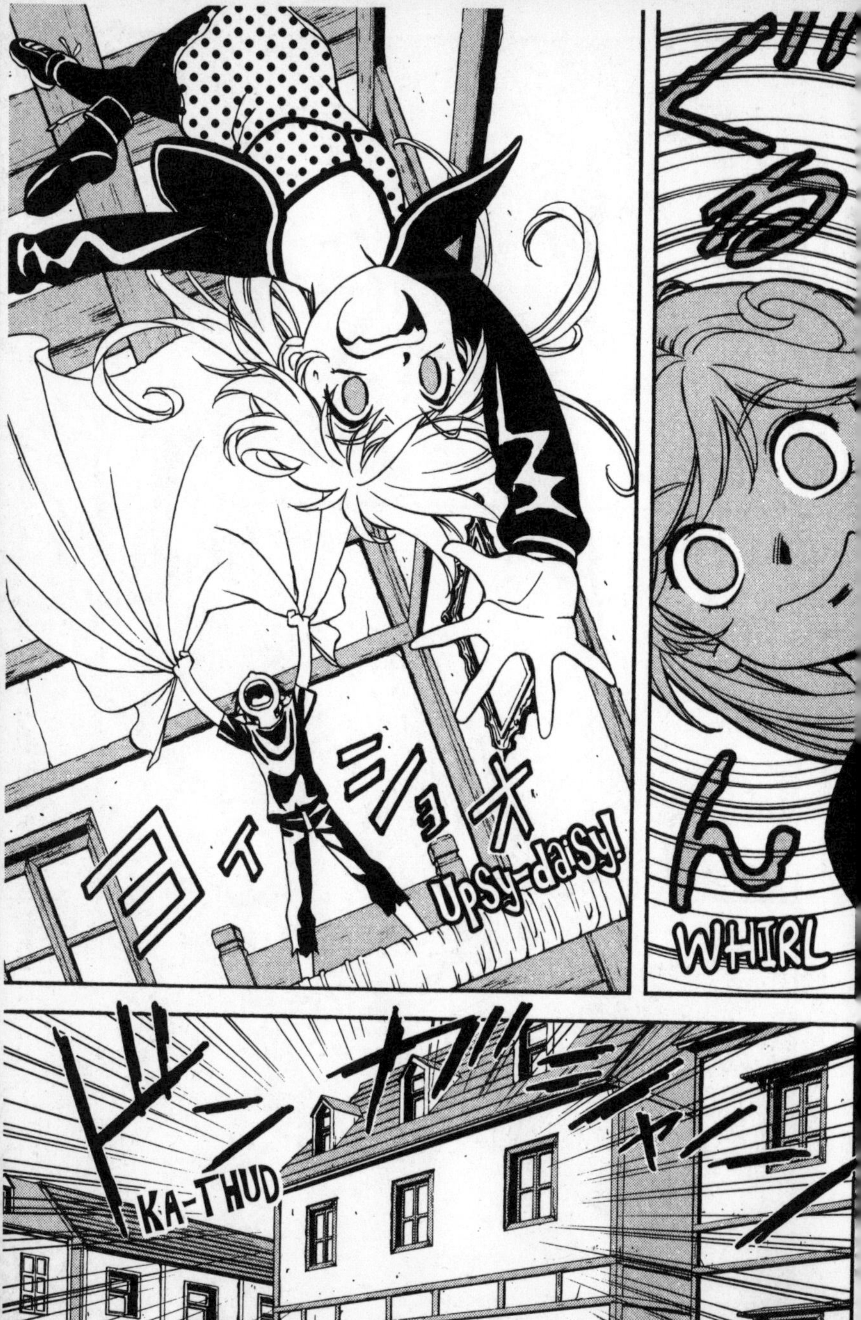

WHIRL
Upsy-daisy!
KA-THUD

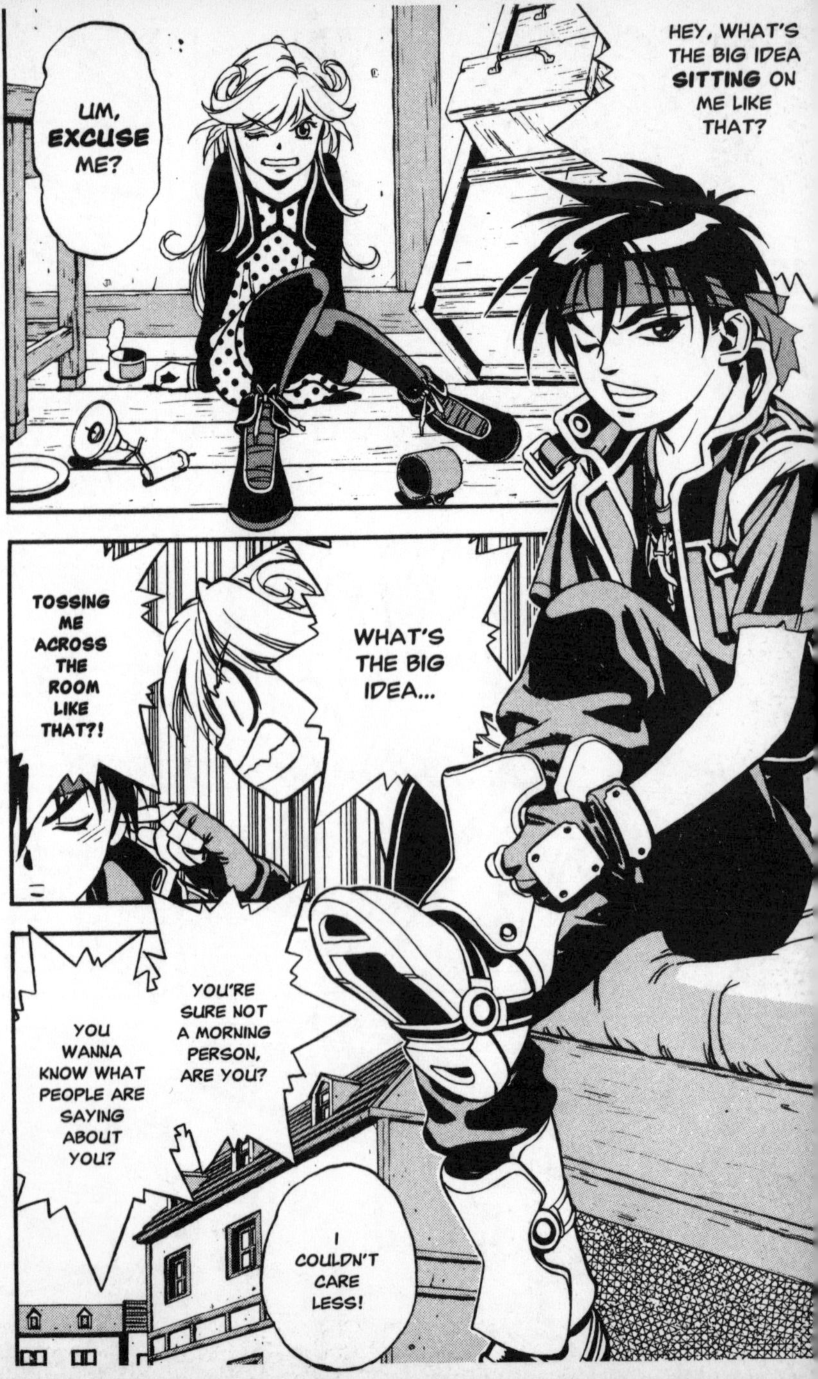
HEY, WHAT'S THE BIG IDEA SITTING ON ME LIKE THAT?
UM, EXCUSE ME?
WHAT'S THE BIG IDEA...
TOSSING ME ACROSS THE ROOM LIKE THAT?!
YOU'RE SURE NOT A MORNING PERSON, ARE YOU?
YOU WANNA KNOW WHAT PEOPLE ARE SAYING ABOUT YOU?
I COULDN'T CARE LESS!

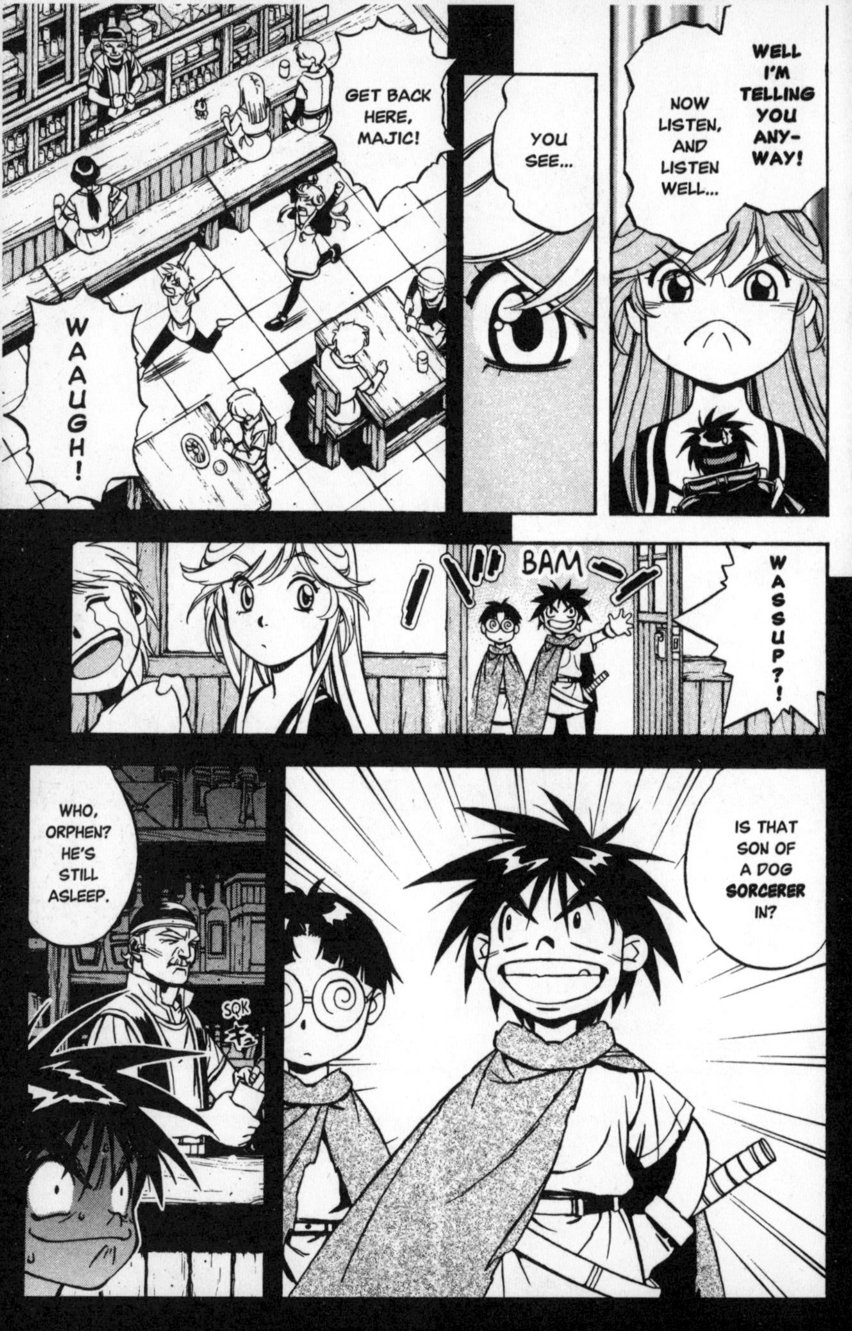
WELL I'M TELLING YOU ANYWAY!
NOW LISTEN, AND LISTEN WELL...
YOU SEE...
GET BACK HERE, MAJIC!
WAAAUGH!
WASSUP?!
BAM
IS THAT SON OF A DOG SORCERER IN?
WHO, ORPHEN? HE'S STILL ASLEEP.
SQK

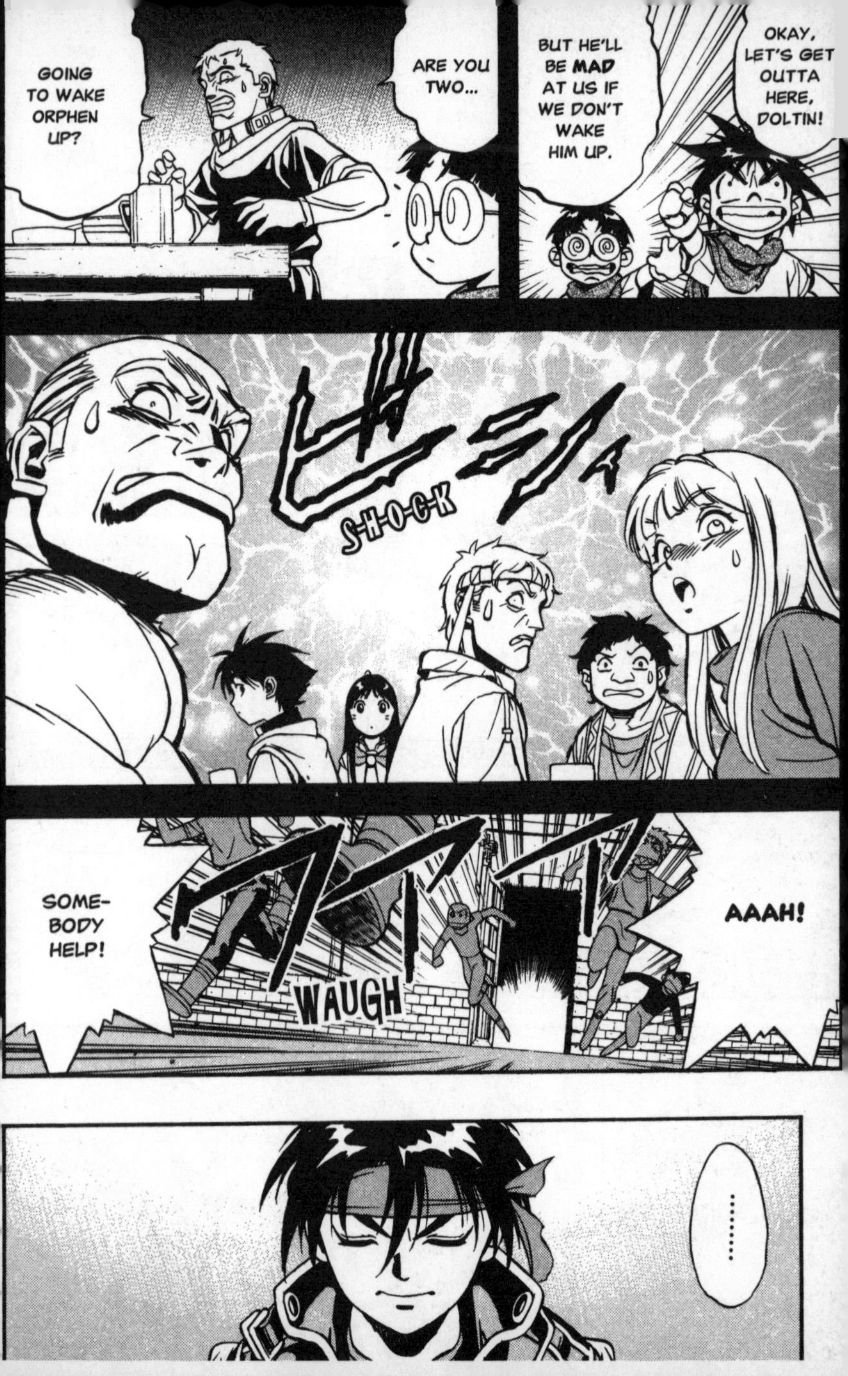
OKAY, LET'S GET OUTTA HERE, DOLTIN!
BUT HE'LL BE **MAD** AT US IF WE DON'T WAKE HIM UP.
ARE YOU TWO...
GOING TO WAKE ORPHEN UP?
SHOCK
AAAH!
WAUGH
SOME-BODY HELP!
......

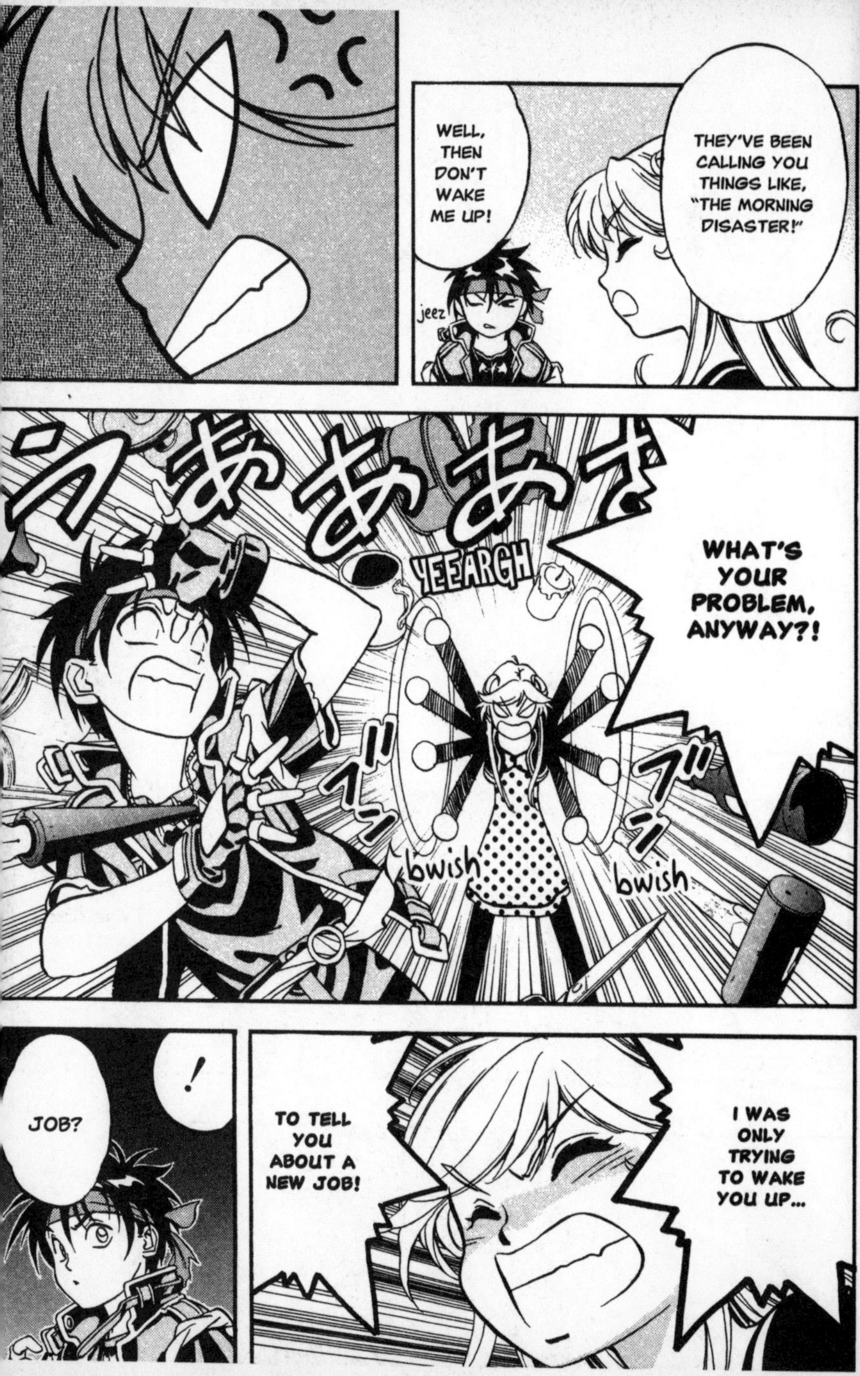
THEY'VE BEEN CALLING YOU THINGS LIKE, "THE MORNING DISASTER!"
WELL, THEN DON'T WAKE ME UP!
jeez
YEEARGH
WHAT'S YOUR PROBLEM, ANYWAY?!
bwish
bwish
I WAS ONLY TRYING TO WAKE YOU UP...
TO TELL YOU ABOUT A NEW JOB!
!
JOB?

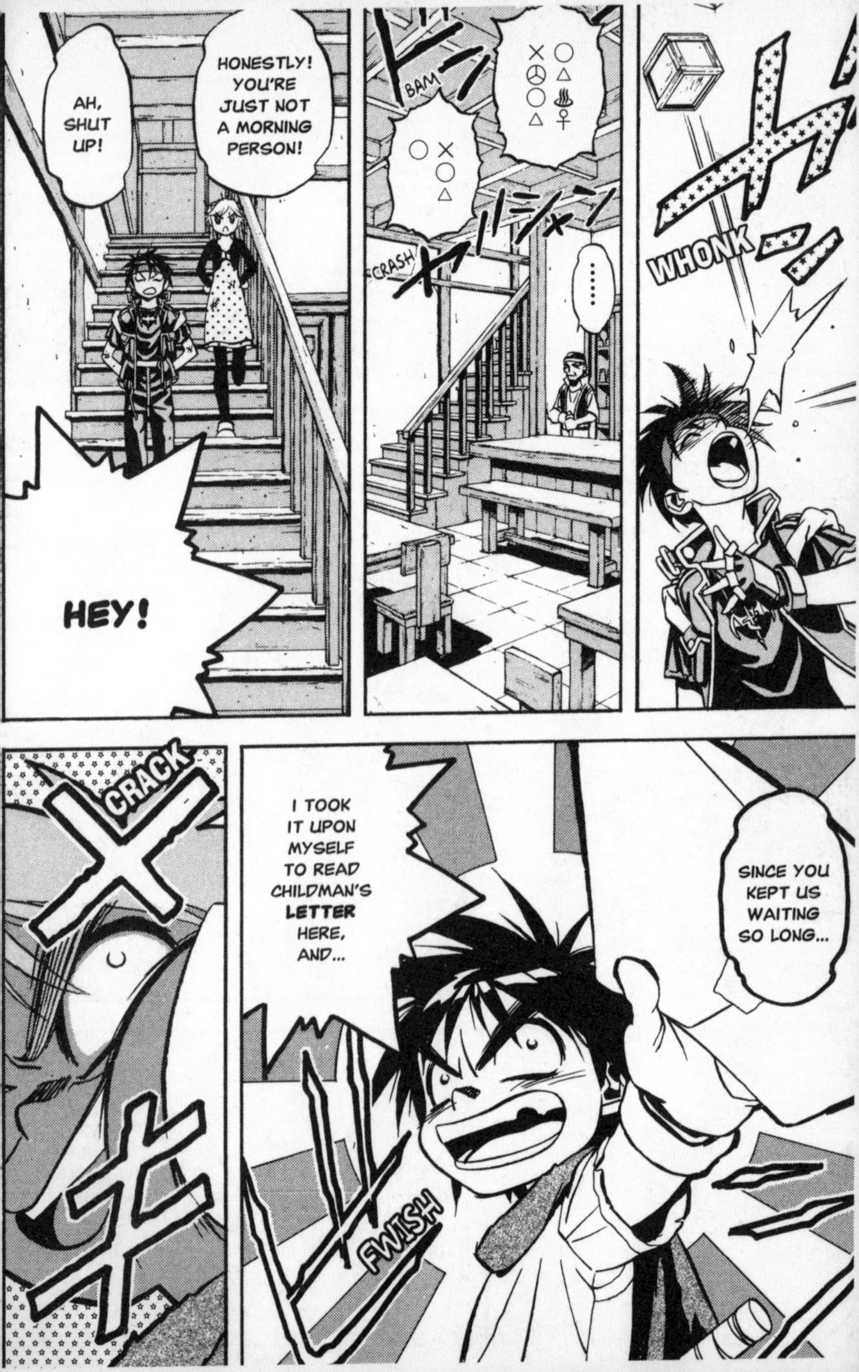
WHONK
BAM
CRASH
......
HONESTLY! YOU'RE JUST NOT A MORNING PERSON!
AH, SHUT UP!
HEY!
SINCE YOU KEPT US WAITING SO LONG...
I TOOK IT UPON MYSELF TO READ CHILDMAN'S **LETTER** HERE, AND...
FWISH
CRACK

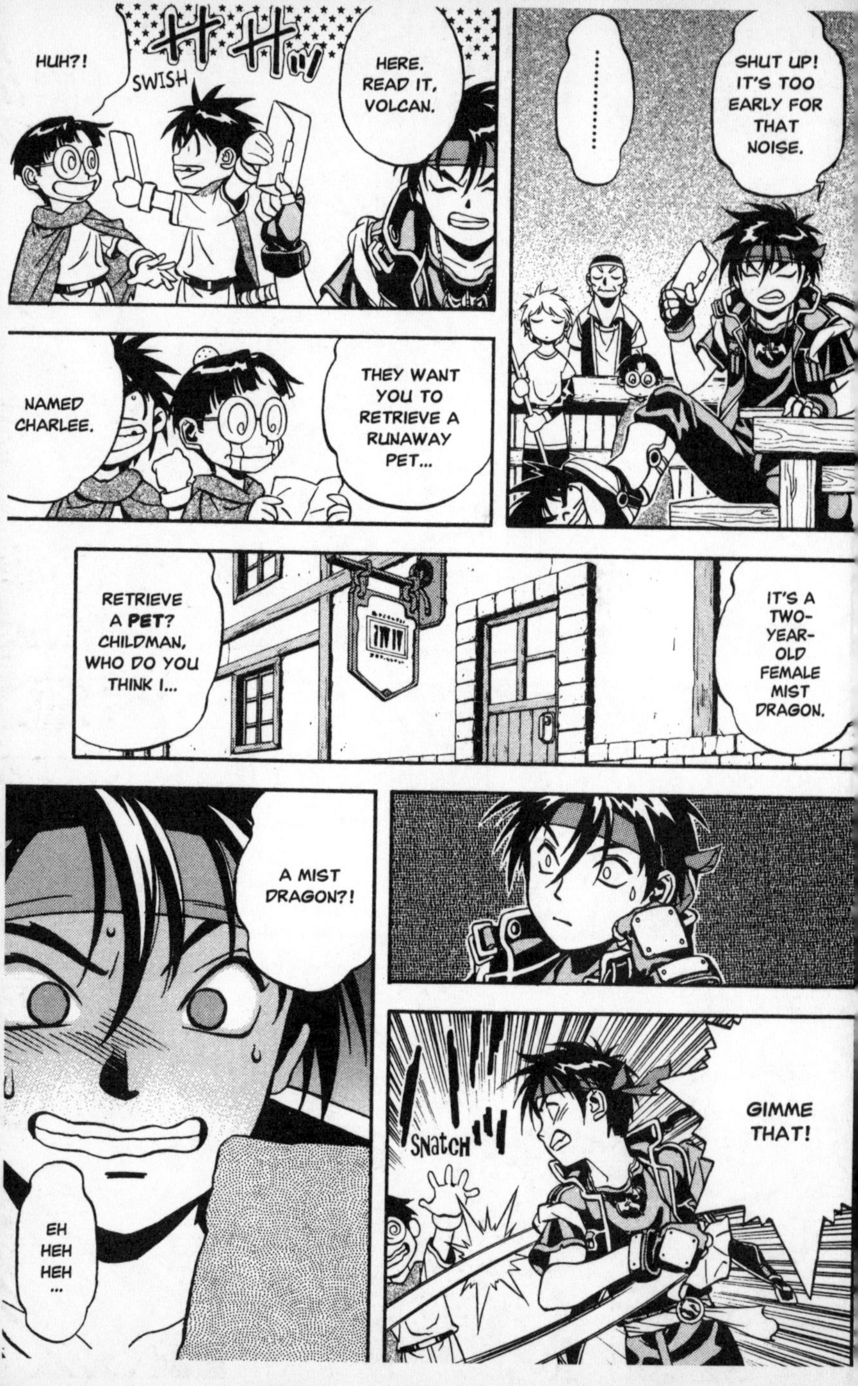
SHUT UP! IT'S TOO EARLY FOR THAT NOISE.
......
HERE. READ IT, VOLCAN.
SWISH
HUH?!
THEY WANT YOU TO RETRIEVE A RUNAWAY PET...
NAMED CHARLEE.
RETRIEVE A **PET**? CHILDMAN, WHO DO YOU THINK I...
IT'S A TWO-YEAR-OLD FEMALE MIST DRAGON.
A MIST DRAGON?!
EH HEH HEH ...
SNATCH
GIMME THAT!

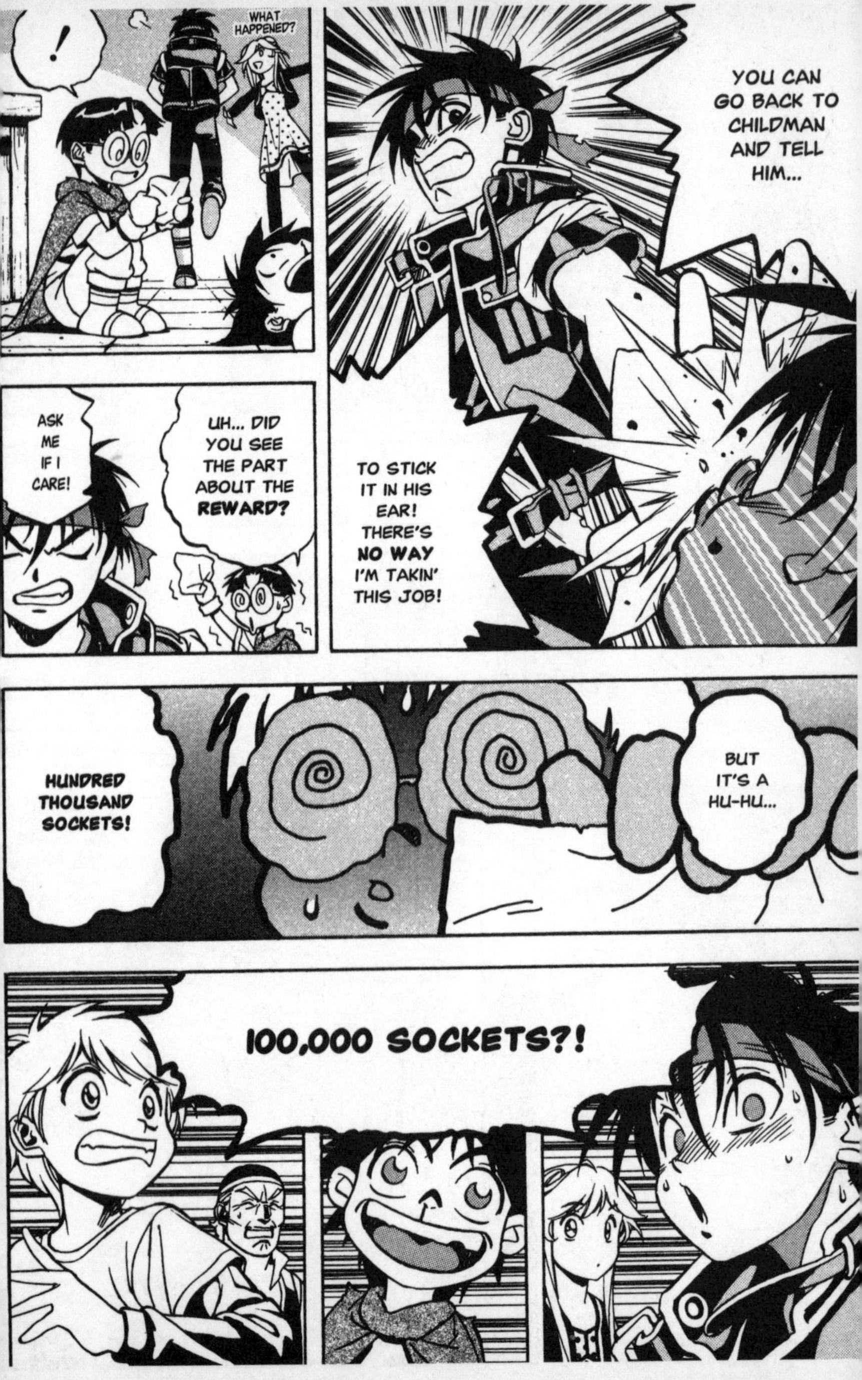
!
WHAT HAPPENED?
YOU CAN GO BACK TO CHILDMAN AND TELL HIM...
TO STICK IT IN HIS EAR! THERE'S NO WAY I'M TAKIN' THIS JOB!
UH... DID YOU SEE THE PART ABOUT THE REWARD?
ASK ME IF I CARE!
BUT IT'S A HU-HU...
HUNDRED THOUSAND SOCKETS!
100,000 SOCKETS?!

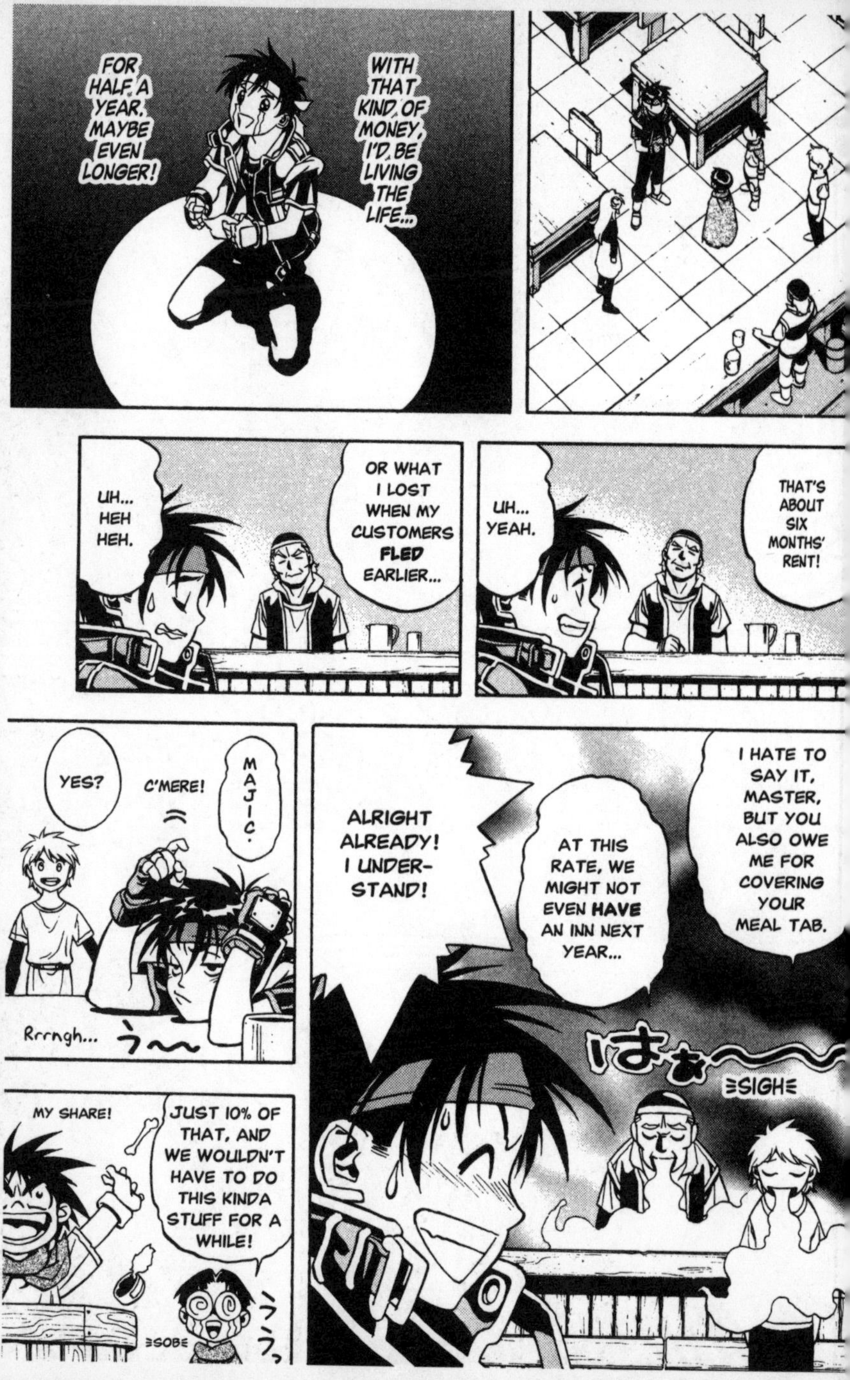

WITH THAT KIND OF MONEY, I'D BE LIVING THE LIFE...
FOR HALF A YEAR. MAYBE EVEN LONGER!
THAT'S ABOUT SIX MONTHS' RENT!
UH... YEAH.
OR WHAT I LOST WHEN MY CUSTOMERS **FLED** EARLIER...
UH... HEH HEH.
I HATE TO SAY IT, MASTER, BUT YOU ALSO OWE ME FOR COVERING YOUR MEAL TAB.
AT THIS RATE, WE MIGHT NOT EVEN **HAVE** AN INN NEXT YEAR...
ALRIGHT ALREADY! I UNDER-STAND!
はぁ〜〜
SIGH
MAJIC.
C'MERE!
YES?
Rrrngh... う〜
JUST 10% OF THAT, AND WE WOULDN'T HAVE TO DO THIS KINDA STUFF FOR A WHILE!
MY SHARE!
うぅっ
SOB

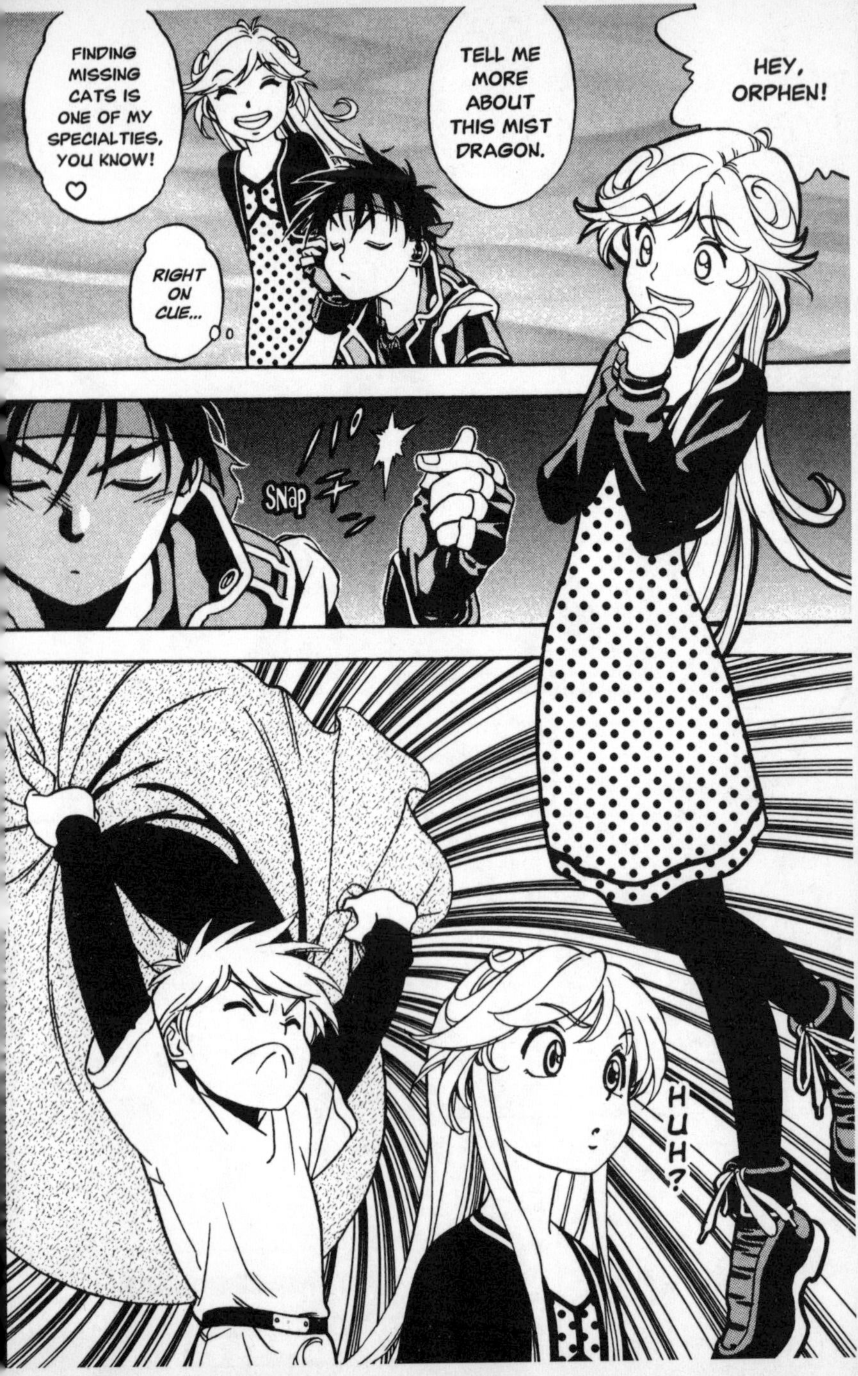
HEY, ORPHEN!
TELL ME MORE ABOUT THIS MIST DRAGON.
FINDING MISSING CATS IS ONE OF MY SPECIALTIES, YOU KNOW! ♡
RIGHT ON CUE...
SNAP
HUH?

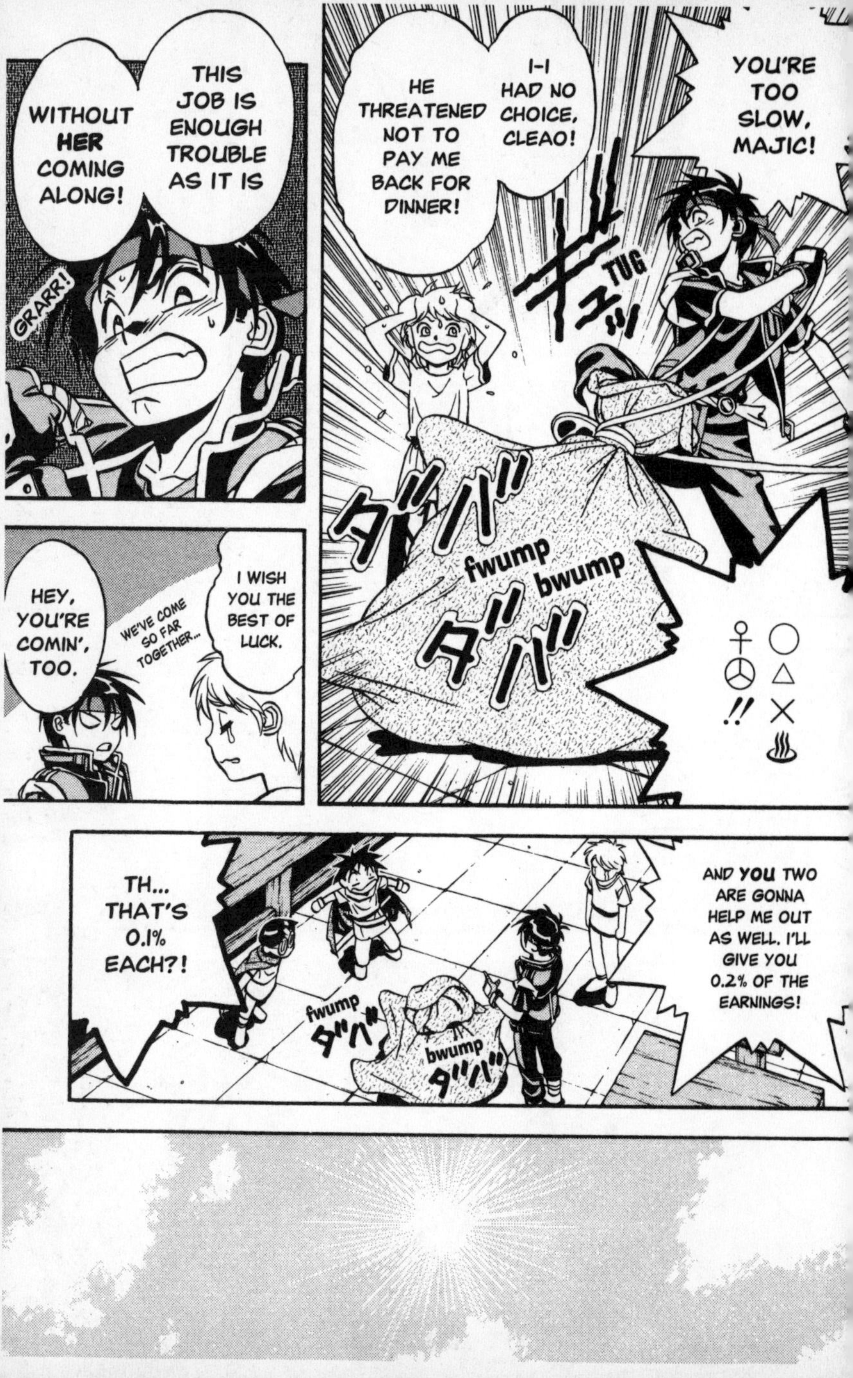

YOU'RE TOO SLOW, MAJIC!
I-I HAD NO CHOICE, CLEAO!
HE THREATENED NOT TO PAY ME BACK FOR DINNER!
TUG
fwump
bwump
THIS JOB IS ENOUGH TROUBLE AS IT IS
WITHOUT HER COMING ALONG!
GRARR!
I WISH YOU THE BEST OF LUCK.
WE'VE COME SO FAR TOGETHER...
HEY, YOU'RE COMIN', TOO.
AND YOU TWO ARE GONNA HELP ME OUT AS WELL. I'LL GIVE YOU 0.2% OF THE EARNINGS!
TH... THAT'S 0.1% EACH?!
fwump
bwump

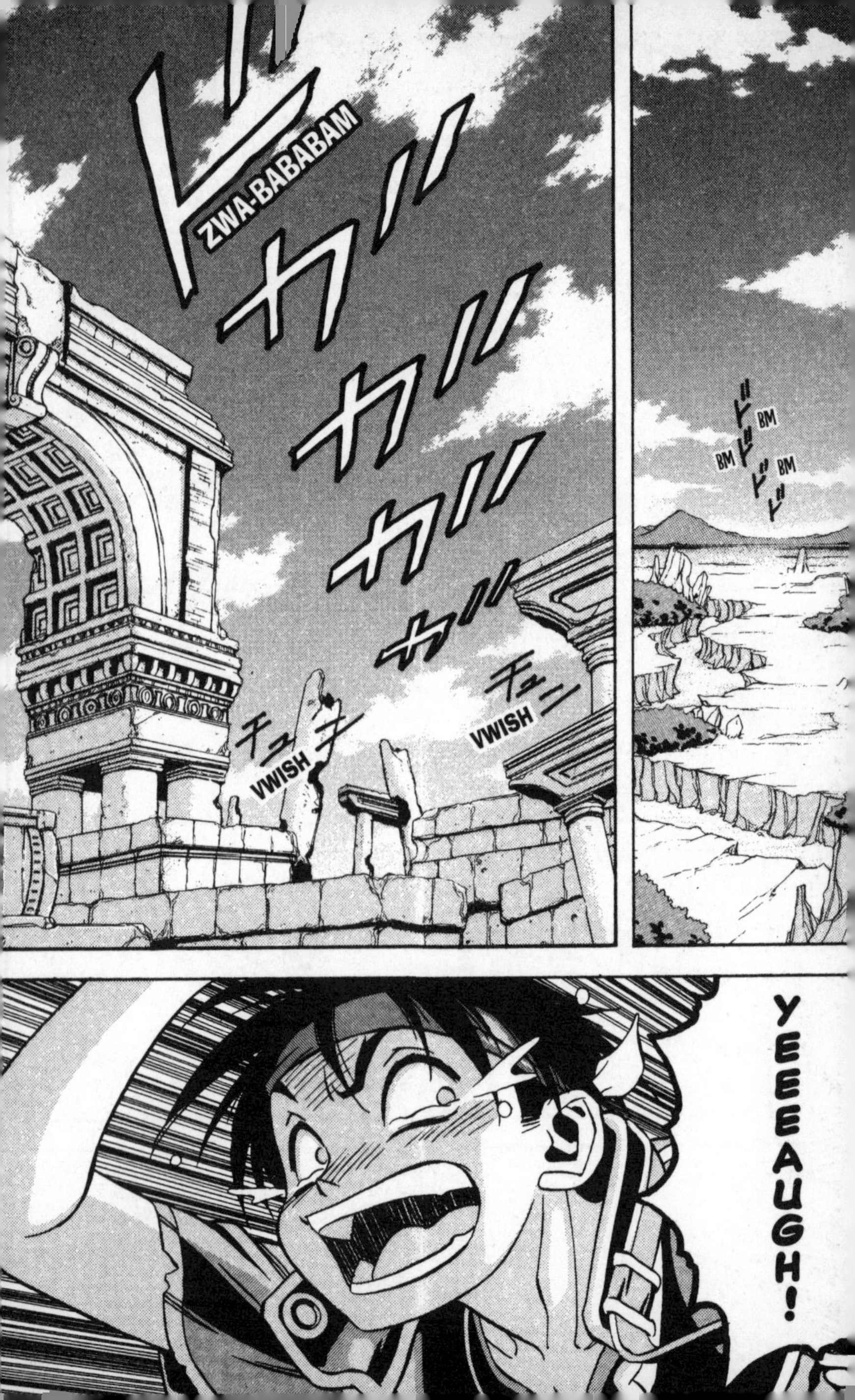
BM
BM
BM
ZWA-BABABAM
VWISH
VWISH
YEEEAUGH!

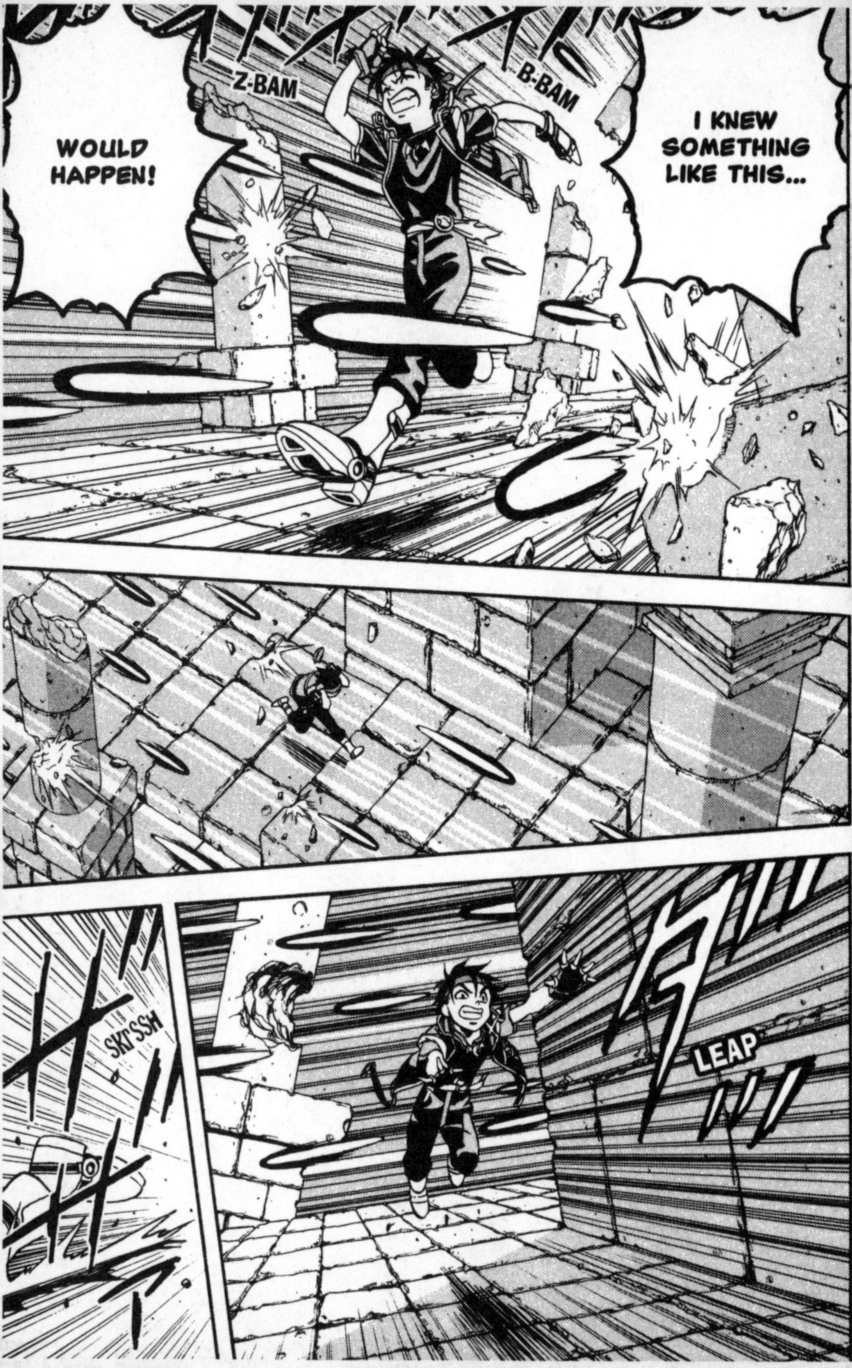
Z-BAM
B-BAM
I KNEW SOMETHING LIKE THIS...
WOULD HAPPEN!
SKT'SSH
LEAP

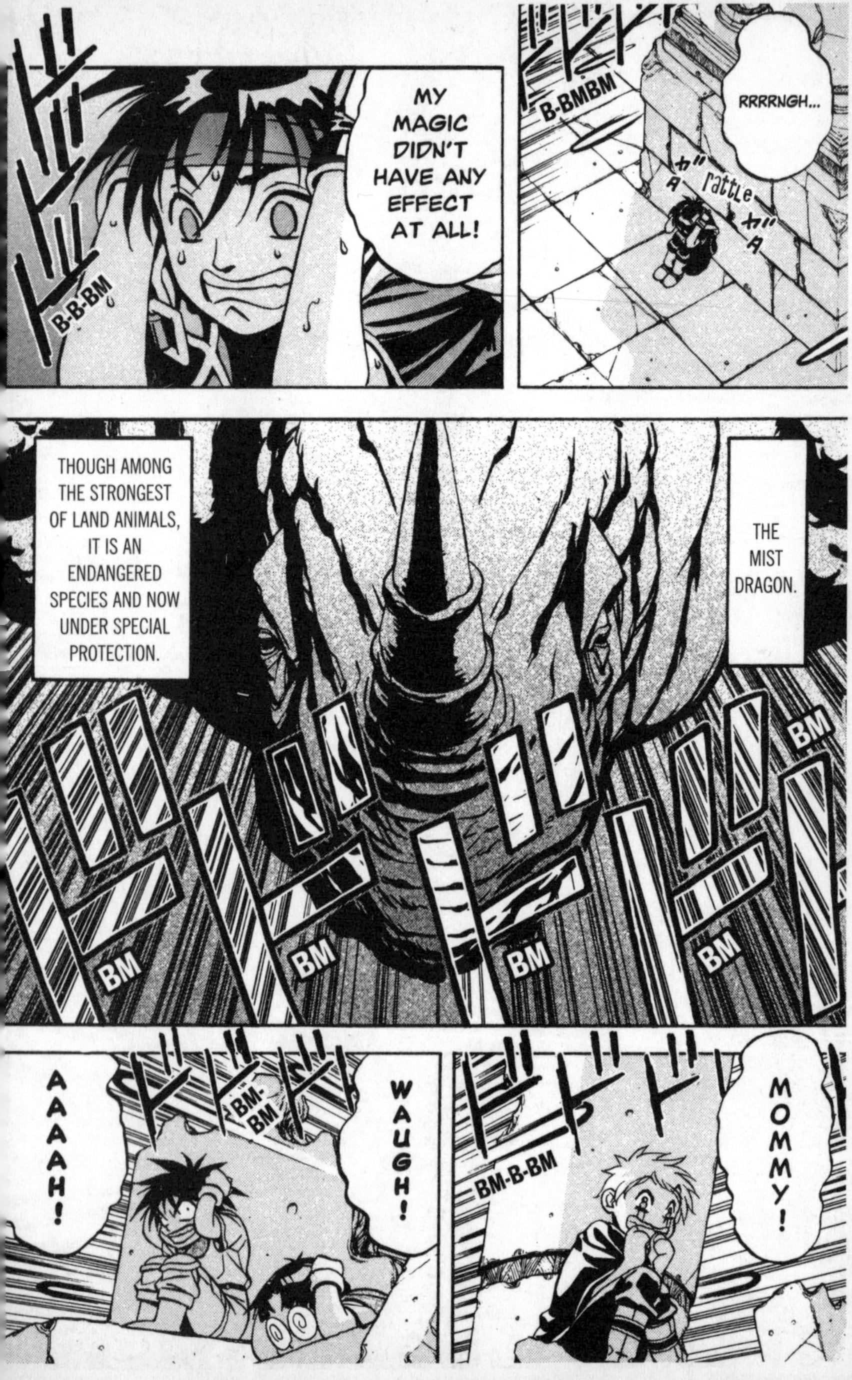
B-BMBM
RRRRNGH...
rattle
MY MAGIC DIDN'T HAVE ANY EFFECT AT ALL!
B-B-BM
THE MIST DRAGON.
THOUGH AMONG THE STRONGEST OF LAND ANIMALS, IT IS AN ENDANGERED SPECIES AND NOW UNDER SPECIAL PROTECTION.
BM
BM
BM
BM
BM
MOMMY!
BM-B-BM
WAUGH!
BM-BM
AAAAH!

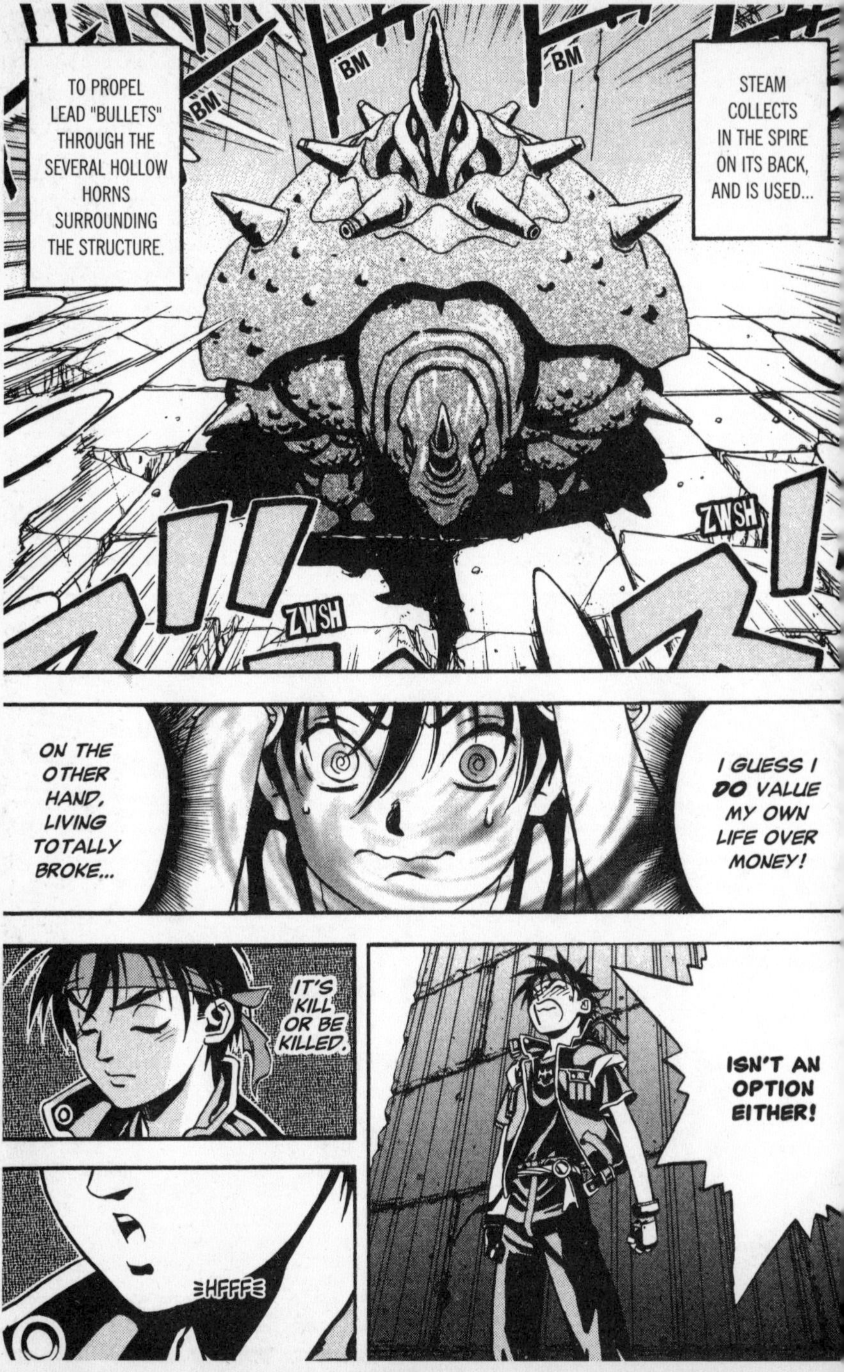
STEAM COLLECTS IN THE SPIRE ON ITS BACK, AND IS USED...
BM
BM
BM
TO PROPEL LEAD "BULLETS" THROUGH THE SEVERAL HOLLOW HORNS SURROUNDING THE STRUCTURE.
ZWSH
ZWSH
I GUESS I DO VALUE MY OWN LIFE OVER MONEY!
ON THE OTHER HAND, LIVING TOTALLY BROKE...
ISN'T AN OPTION EITHER!
IT'S KILL OR BE KILLED.
HFFF

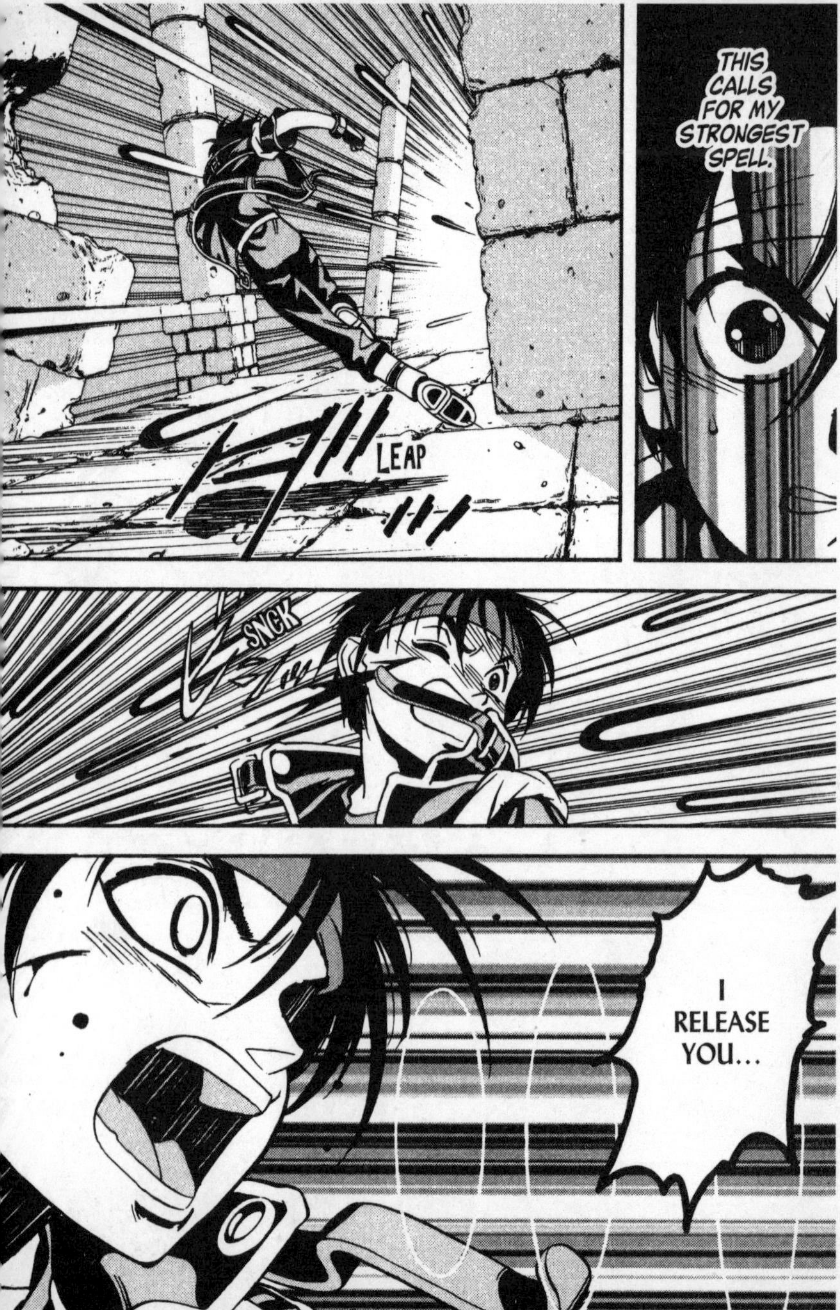
THIS CALLS FOR MY STRONGEST SPELL.
LEAP
SNCK
I RELEASE YOU...

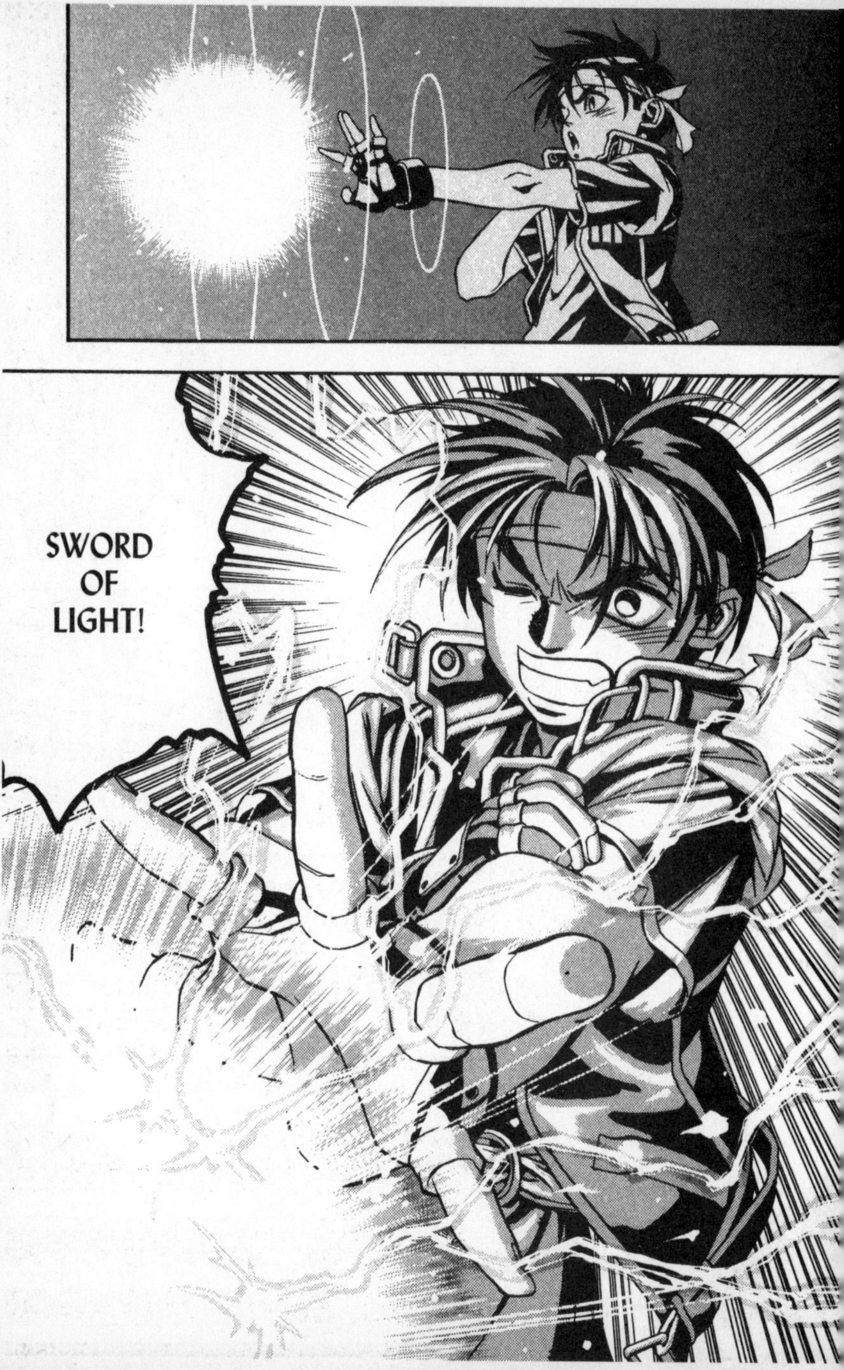
SWORD OF LIGHT!

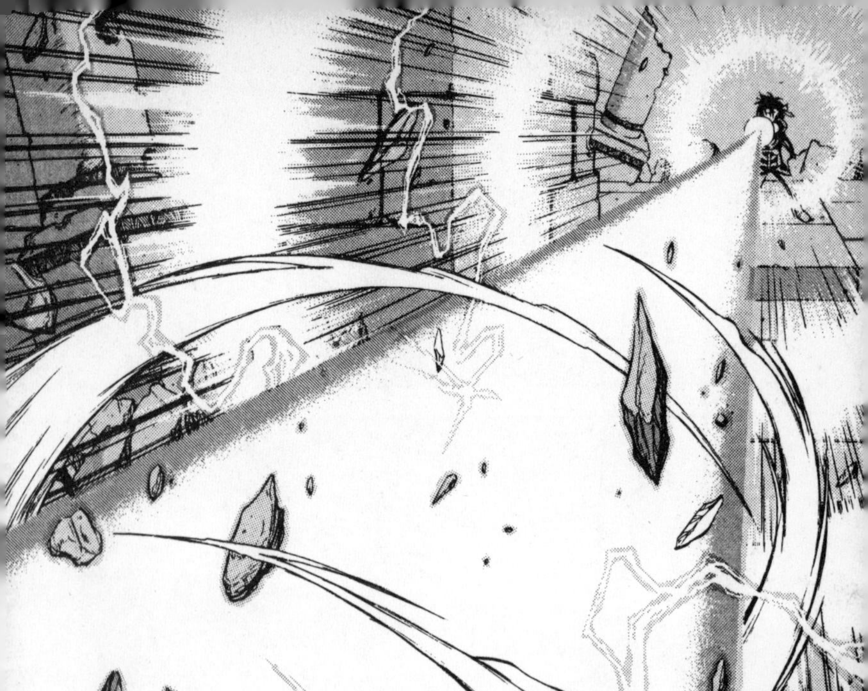

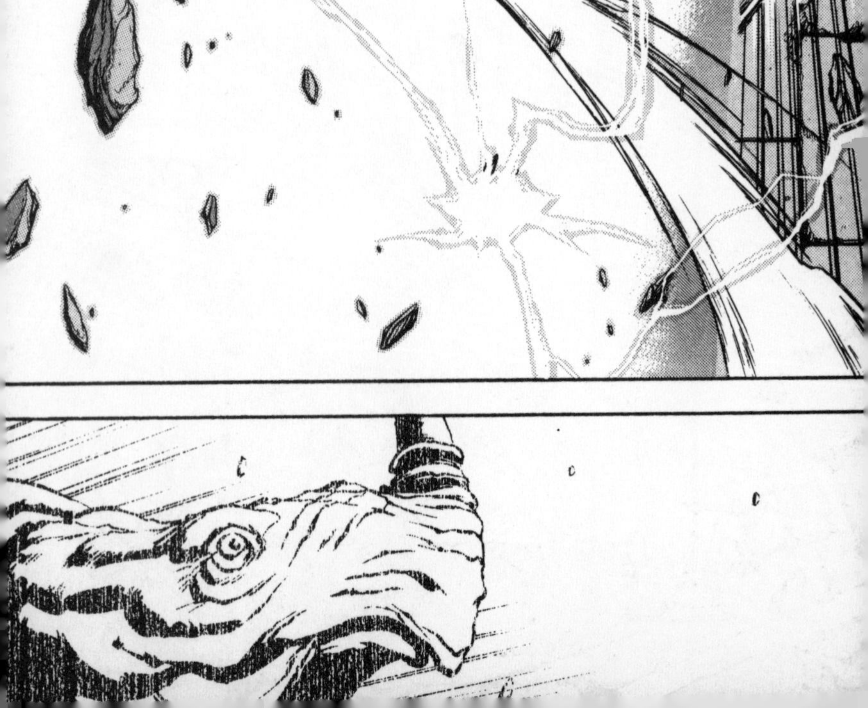

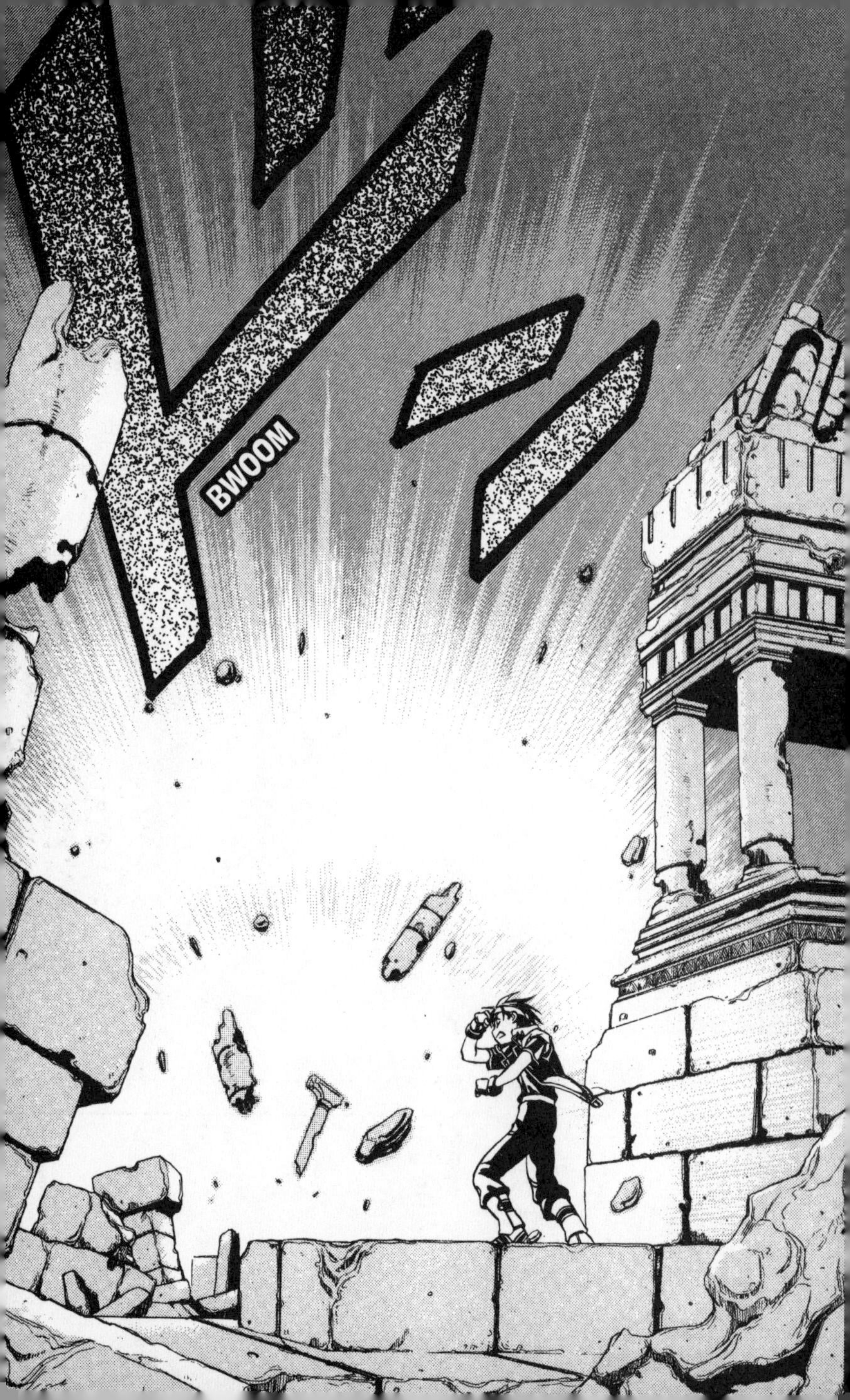
BWOOM

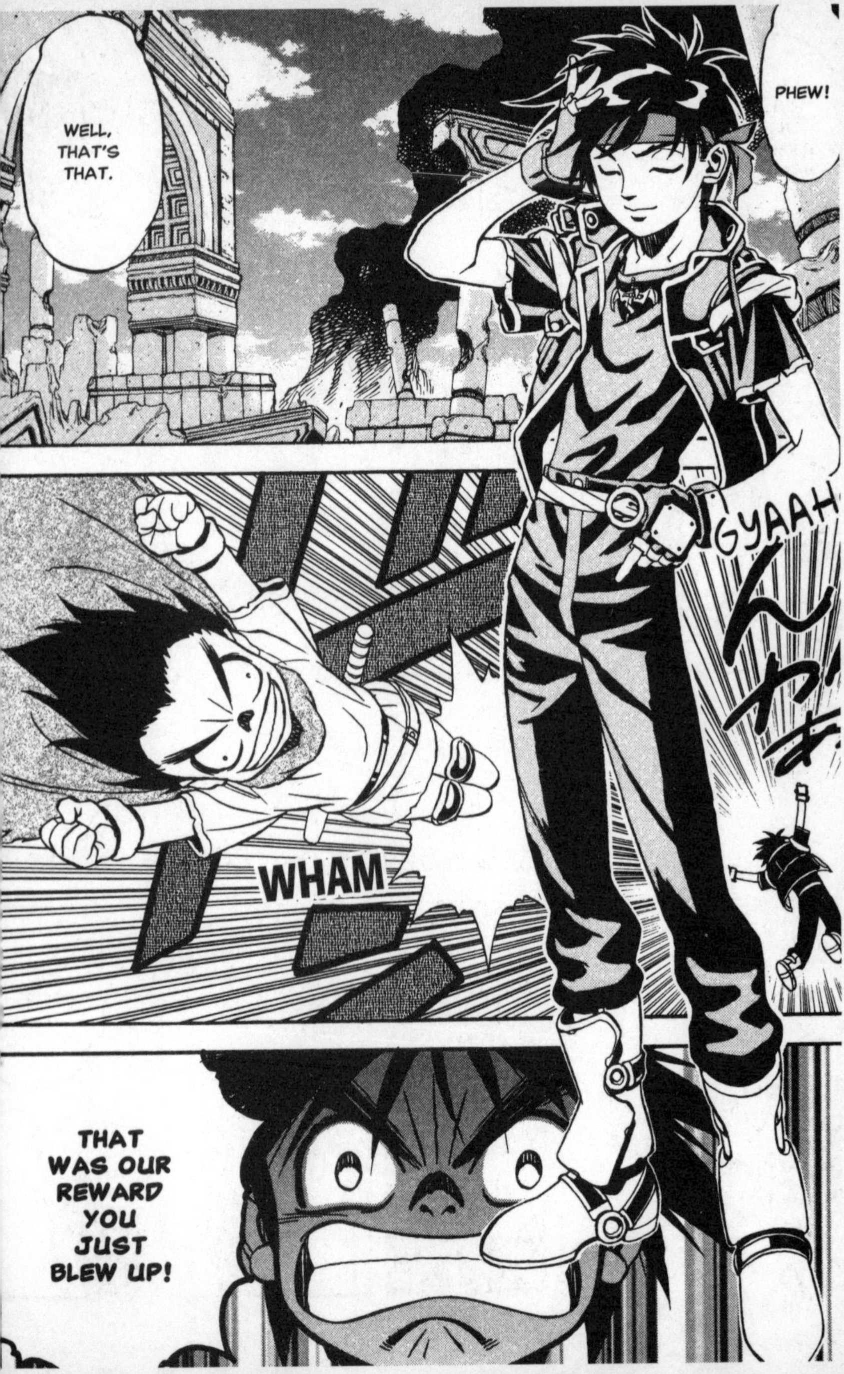
PHEW!
WELL, THAT'S THAT.
WHAM
THAT WAS OUR REWARD YOU JUST BLEW UP!

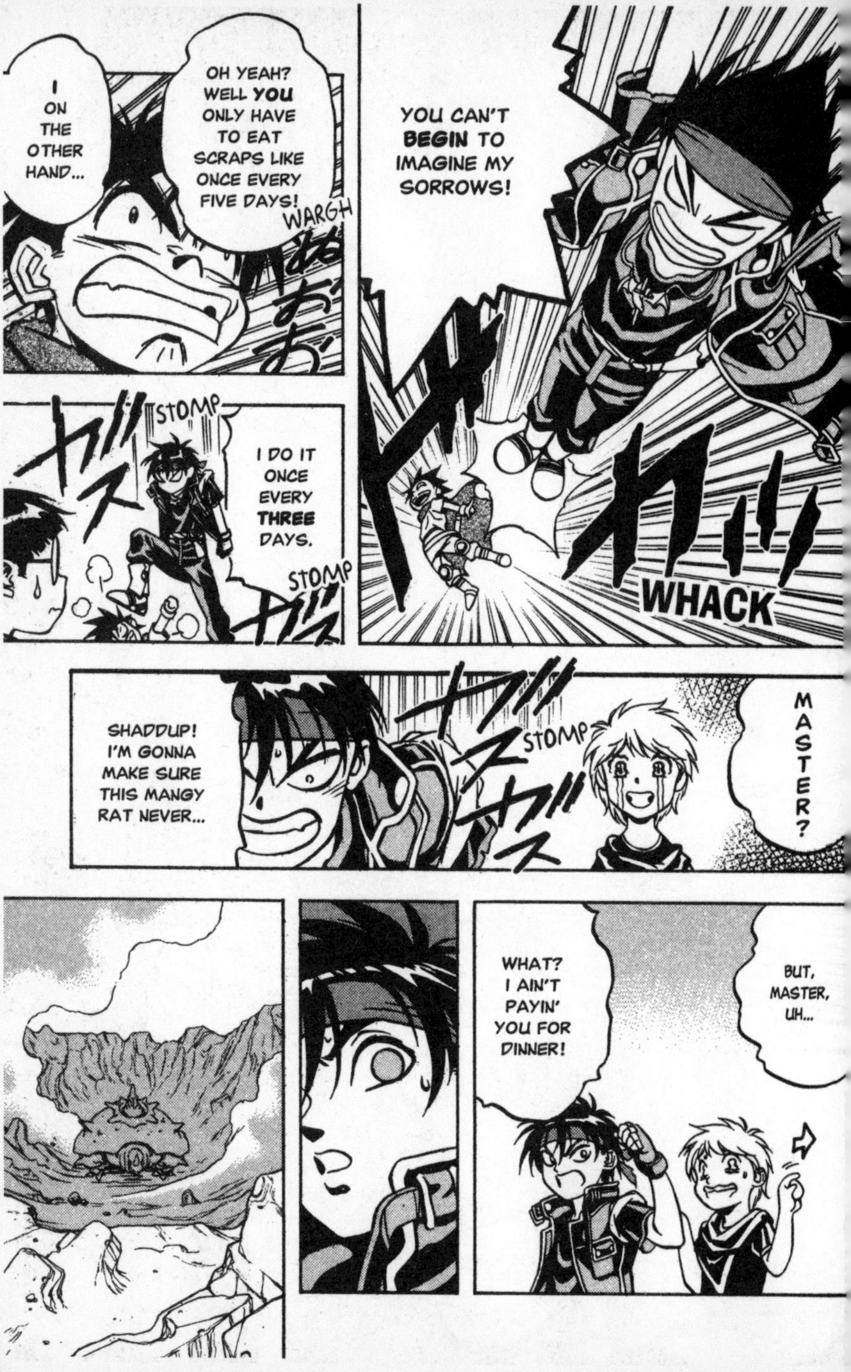
YOU CAN'T BEGIN TO IMAGINE MY SORROWS!
WHACK
OH YEAH? WELL YOU ONLY HAVE TO EAT SCRAPS LIKE ONCE EVERY FIVE DAYS!
I ON THE OTHER HAND...
WARGH
STOMP
I DO IT ONCE EVERY THREE DAYS.
STOMP
MASTER?
STOMP
SHADDUP! I'M GONNA MAKE SURE THIS MANGY RAT NEVER...
BUT, MASTER, UH...
WHAT? I AIN'T PAYIN' YOU FOR DINNER!

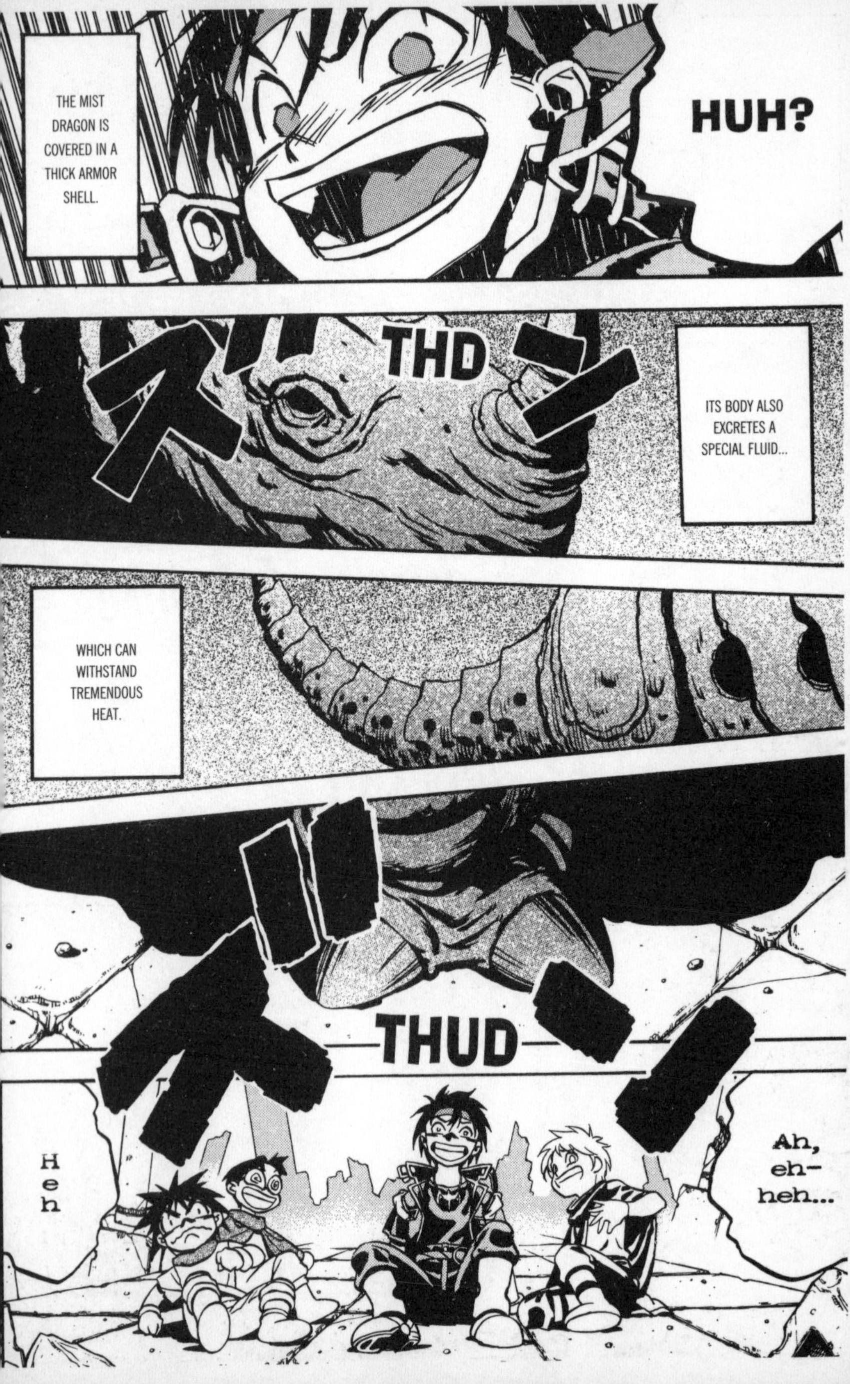
THE MIST DRAGON IS COVERED IN A THICK ARMOR SHELL.
HUH?
THD
ITS BODY ALSO EXCRETES A SPECIAL FLUID...
WHICH CAN WITHSTAND TREMENDOUS HEAT.
THUD
Ah, eh-heh...
Heh

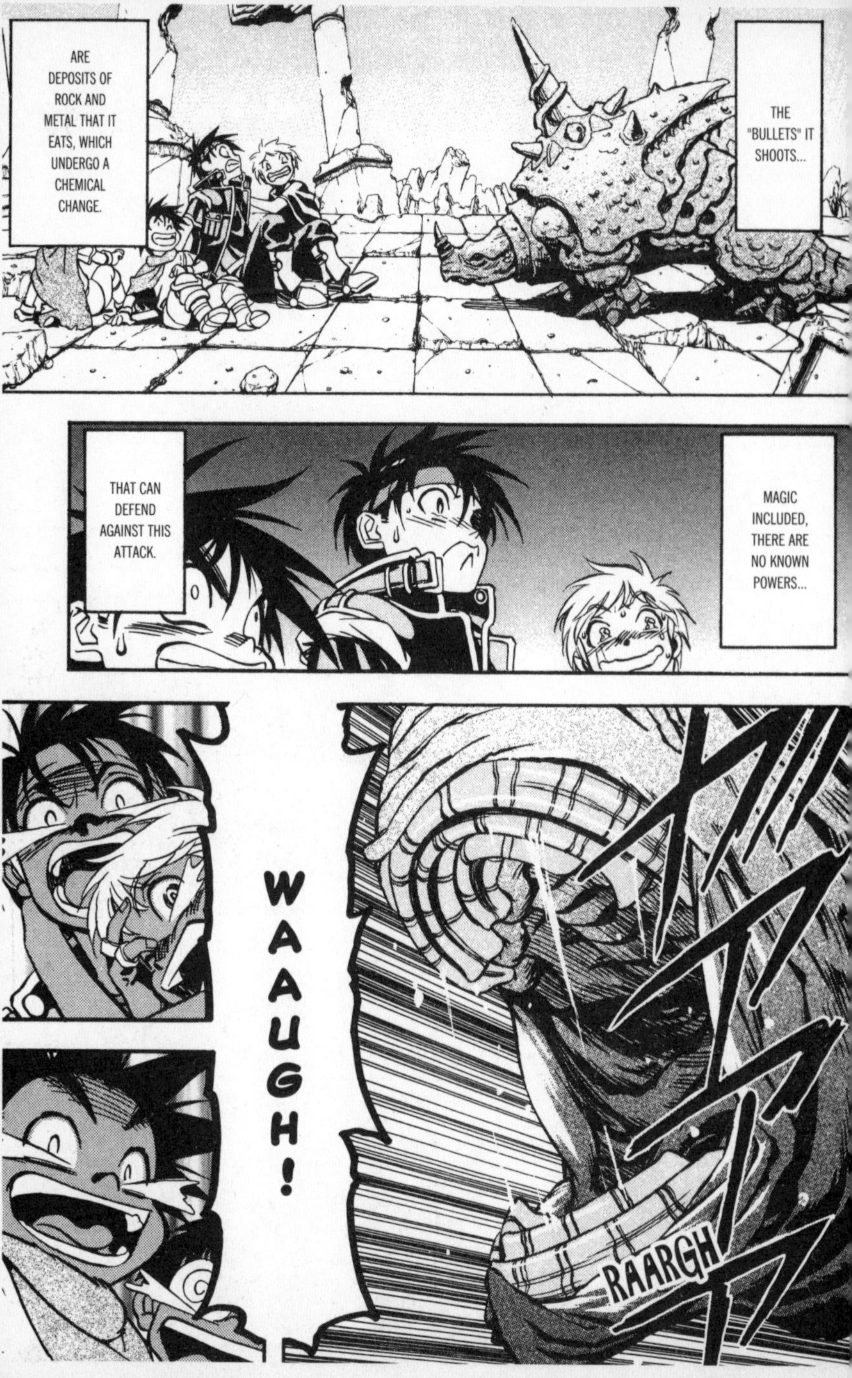
THE "BULLETS" IT SHOOTS...
ARE DEPOSITS OF ROCK AND METAL THAT IT EATS, WHICH UNDERGO A CHEMICAL CHANGE.
MAGIC INCLUDED, THERE ARE NO KNOWN POWERS...
THAT CAN DEFEND AGAINST THIS ATTACK.
RAARGH
WAAUGH!

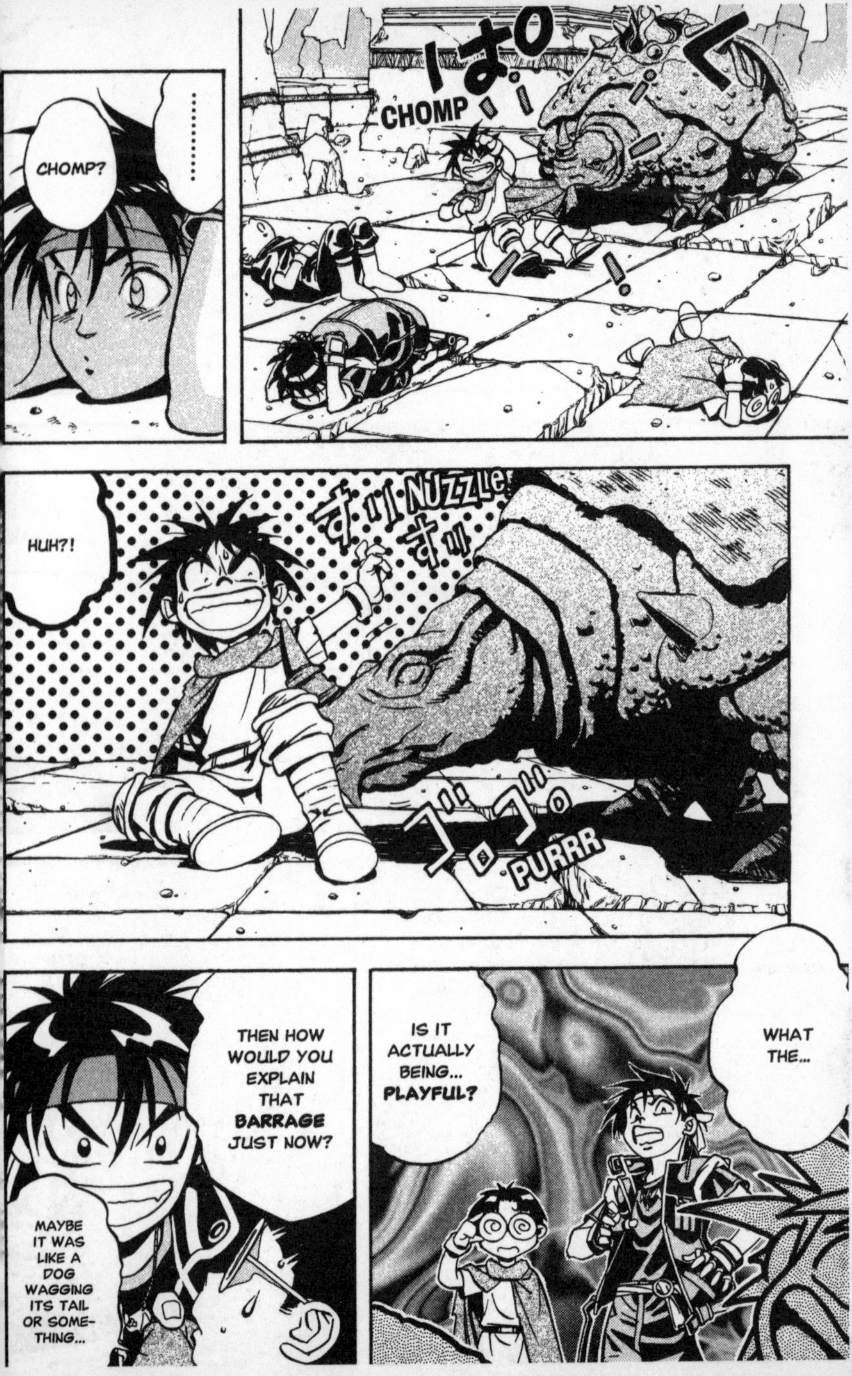
CHOMP
CHOMP?
......
NUZZLE
HUH?!
PURRR
WHAT THE...
IS IT ACTUALLY BEING... **PLAYFUL?**
THEN HOW WOULD YOU EXPLAIN THAT **BARRAGE** JUST NOW?
MAYBE IT WAS LIKE A DOG WAGGING ITS TAIL OR SOME-THING...

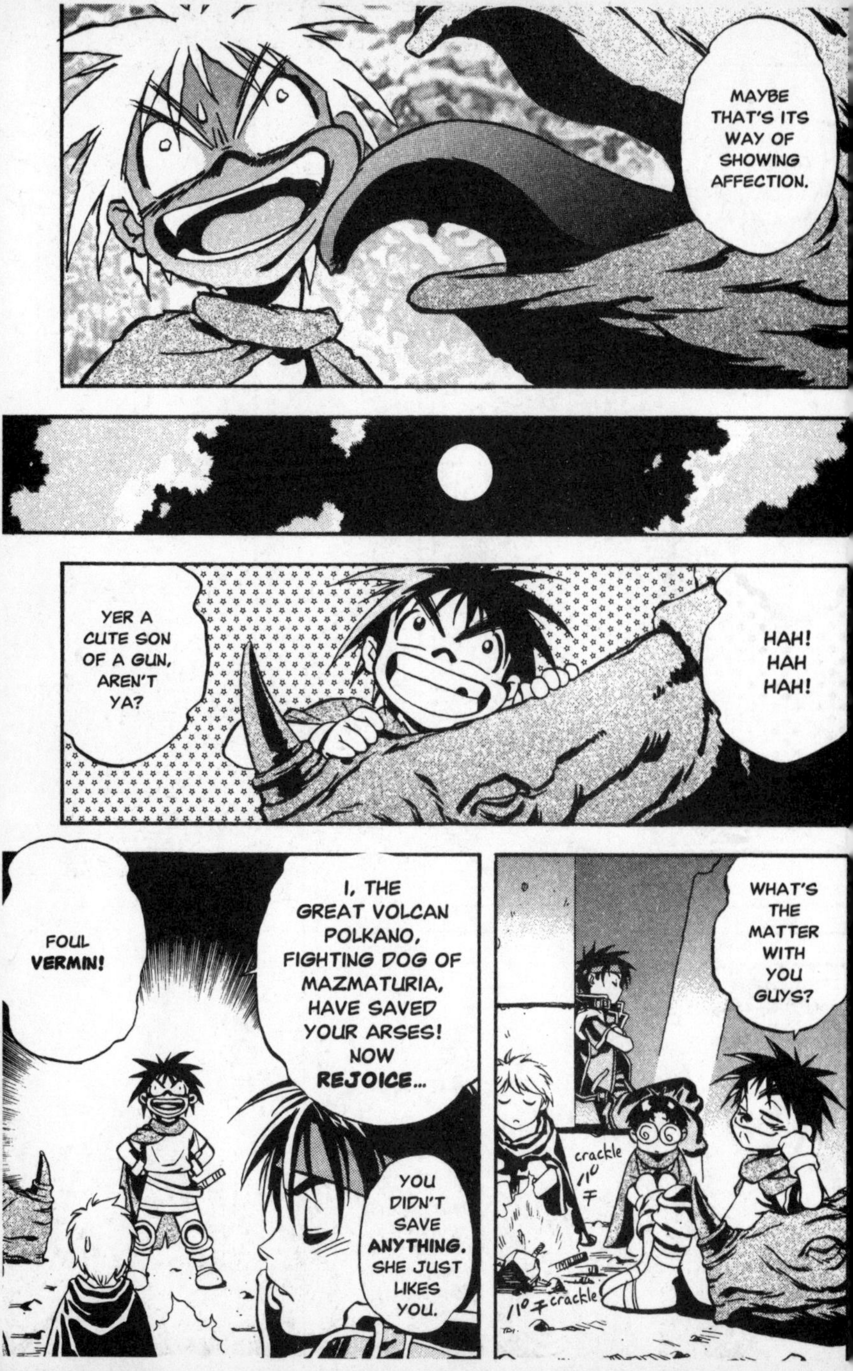
MAYBE THAT'S ITS WAY OF SHOWING AFFECTION.
YER A CUTE SON OF A GUN, AREN'T YA?
HAH! HAH HAH!
FOUL VERMIN!
I, THE GREAT VOLCAN POLKANO, FIGHTING DOG OF MAZMATURIA, HAVE SAVED YOUR ARSES! NOW REJOICE...
YOU DIDN'T SAVE ANYTHING. SHE JUST LIKES YOU.
WHAT'S THE MATTER WITH YOU GUYS?
crackle
crackle

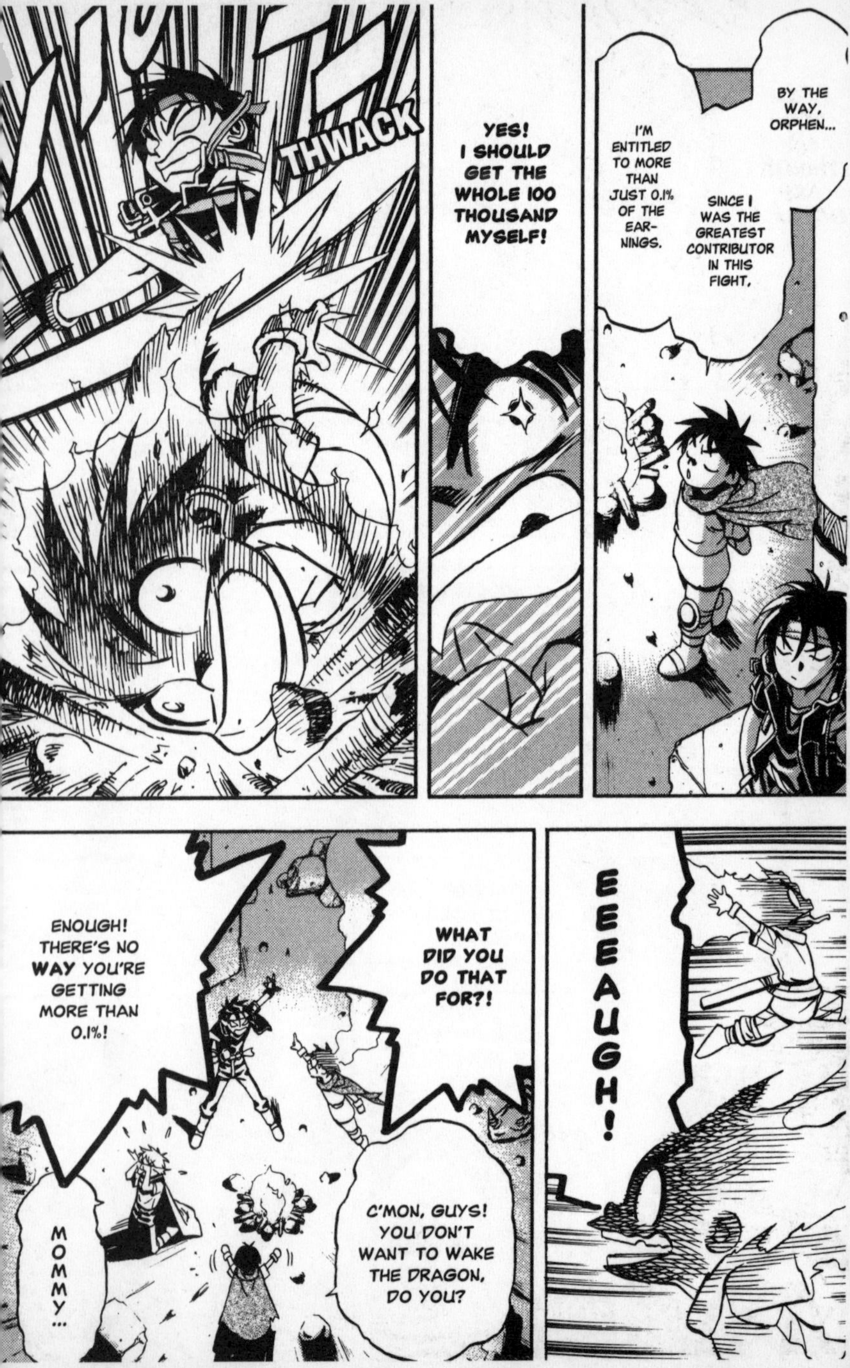
BY THE WAY, ORPHEN...
SINCE I WAS THE GREATEST CONTRIBUTOR IN THIS FIGHT,
I'M ENTITLED TO MORE THAN JUST 0.1% OF THE EARNINGS.
YES! I SHOULD GET THE WHOLE 100 THOUSAND MYSELF!
THWACK
EEEAUGH!
WHAT DID YOU DO THAT FOR?!
ENOUGH! THERE'S NO WAY YOU'RE GETTING MORE THAN 0.1%!
C'MON, GUYS! YOU DON'T WANT TO WAKE THE DRAGON, DO YOU?
MOMMY...

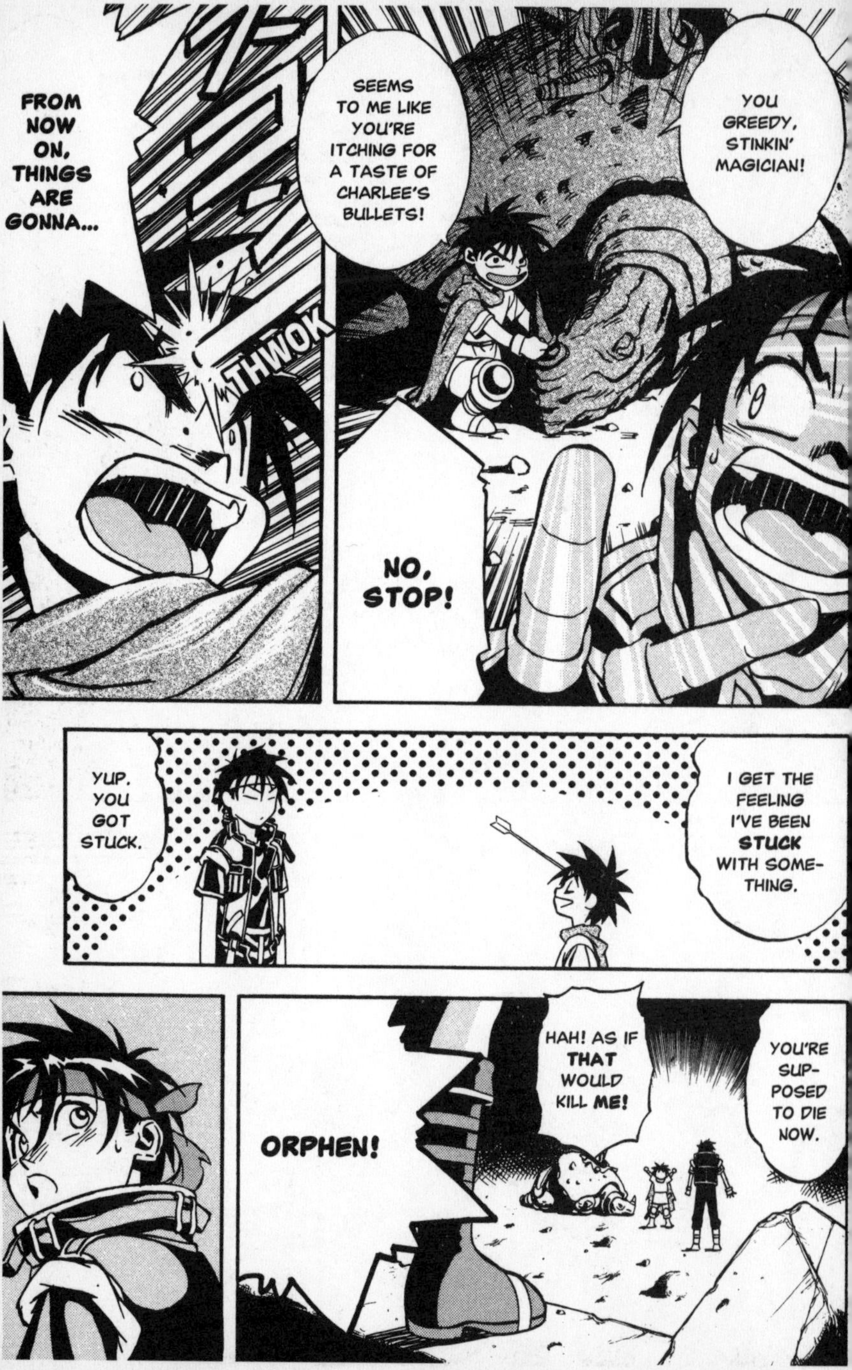

FROM NOW ON, THINGS ARE GONNA...
THWOK
SEEMS TO ME LIKE YOU'RE ITCHING FOR A TASTE OF CHARLEE'S BULLETS!
YOU GREEDY, STINKIN' MAGICIAN!
NO, STOP!
YUP. YOU GOT STUCK.
I GET THE FEELING I'VE BEEN STUCK WITH SOMETHING.
ORPHEN!
HAH! AS IF THAT WOULD KILL ME!
YOU'RE SUP-POSED TO DIE NOW.

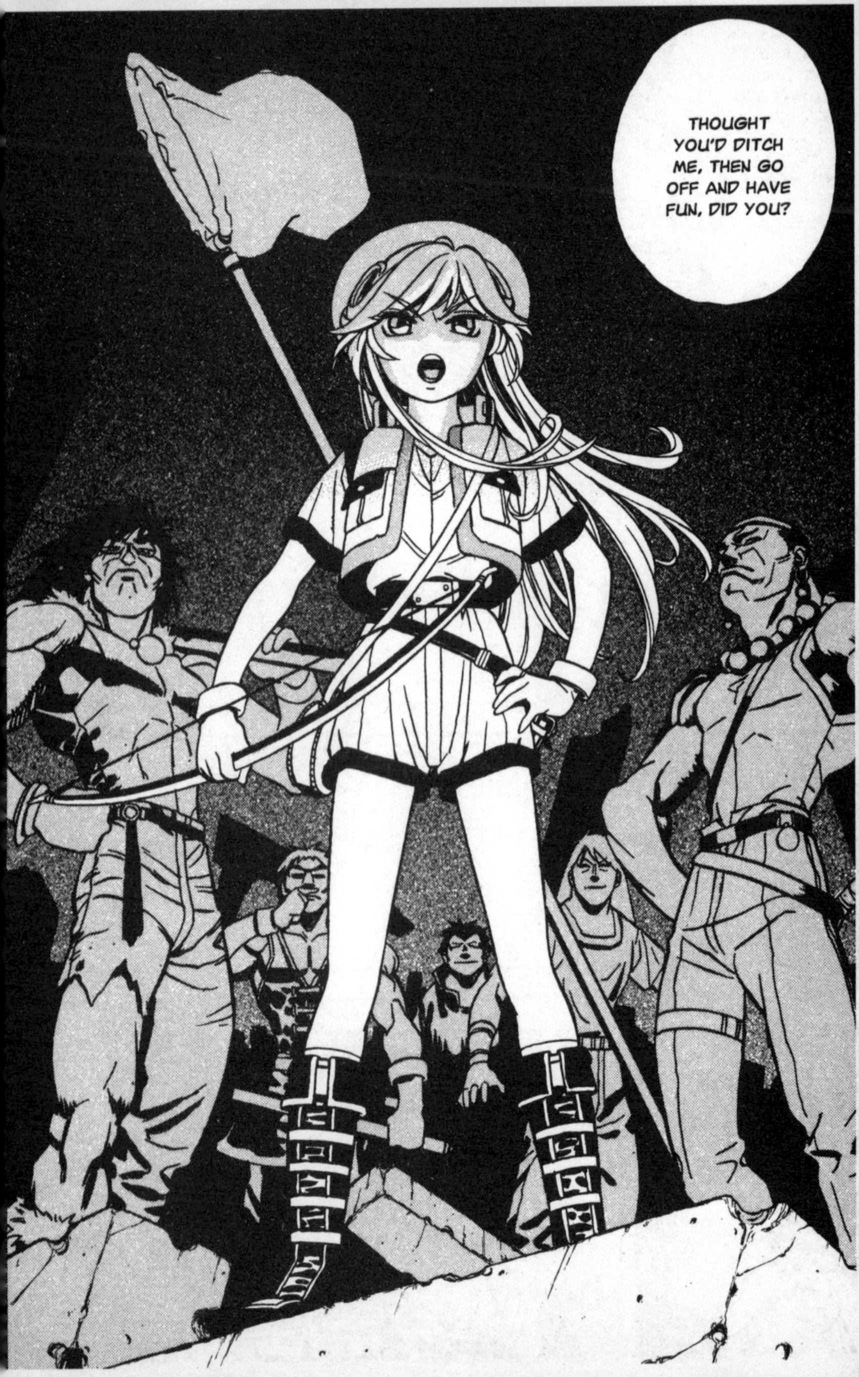
THOUGHT YOU'D DITCH ME, THEN GO OFF AND HAVE FUN, DID YOU?

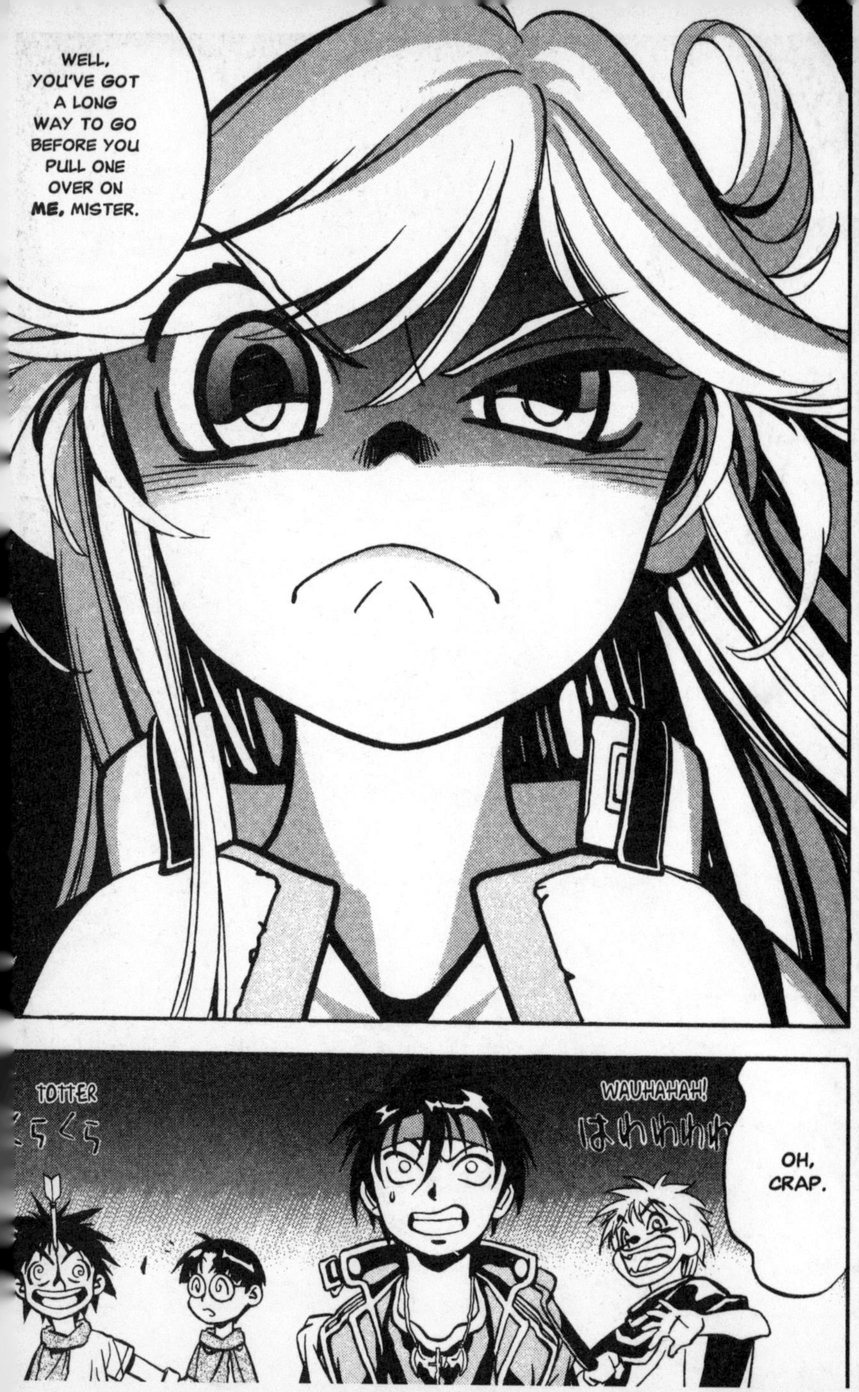
WELL, YOU'VE GOT A LONG WAY TO GO BEFORE YOU PULL ONE OVER ON ME, MISTER.
OH, CRAP.
WAUHAHAH!
はわわわわ
TOTTER

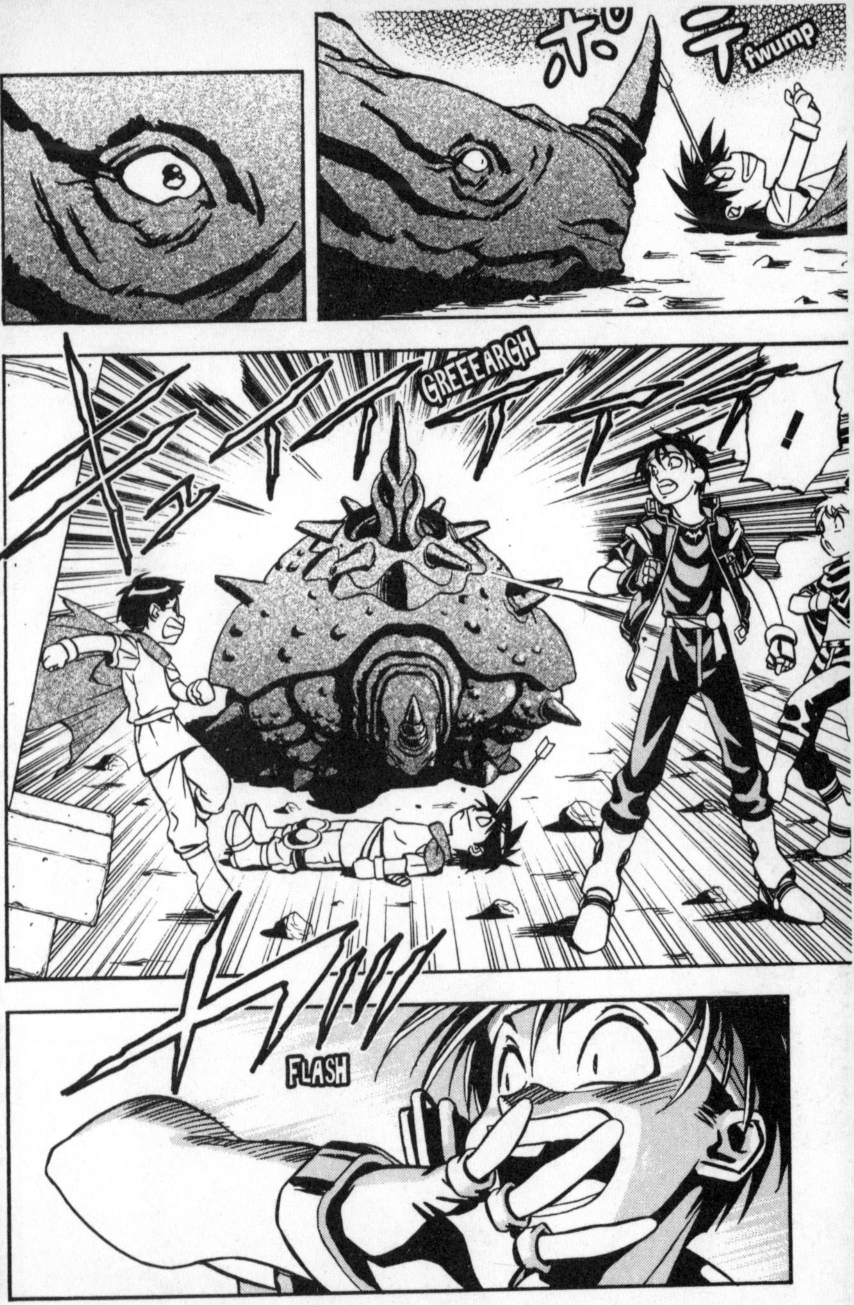
fwump
GREEEARGH
!
FLASH

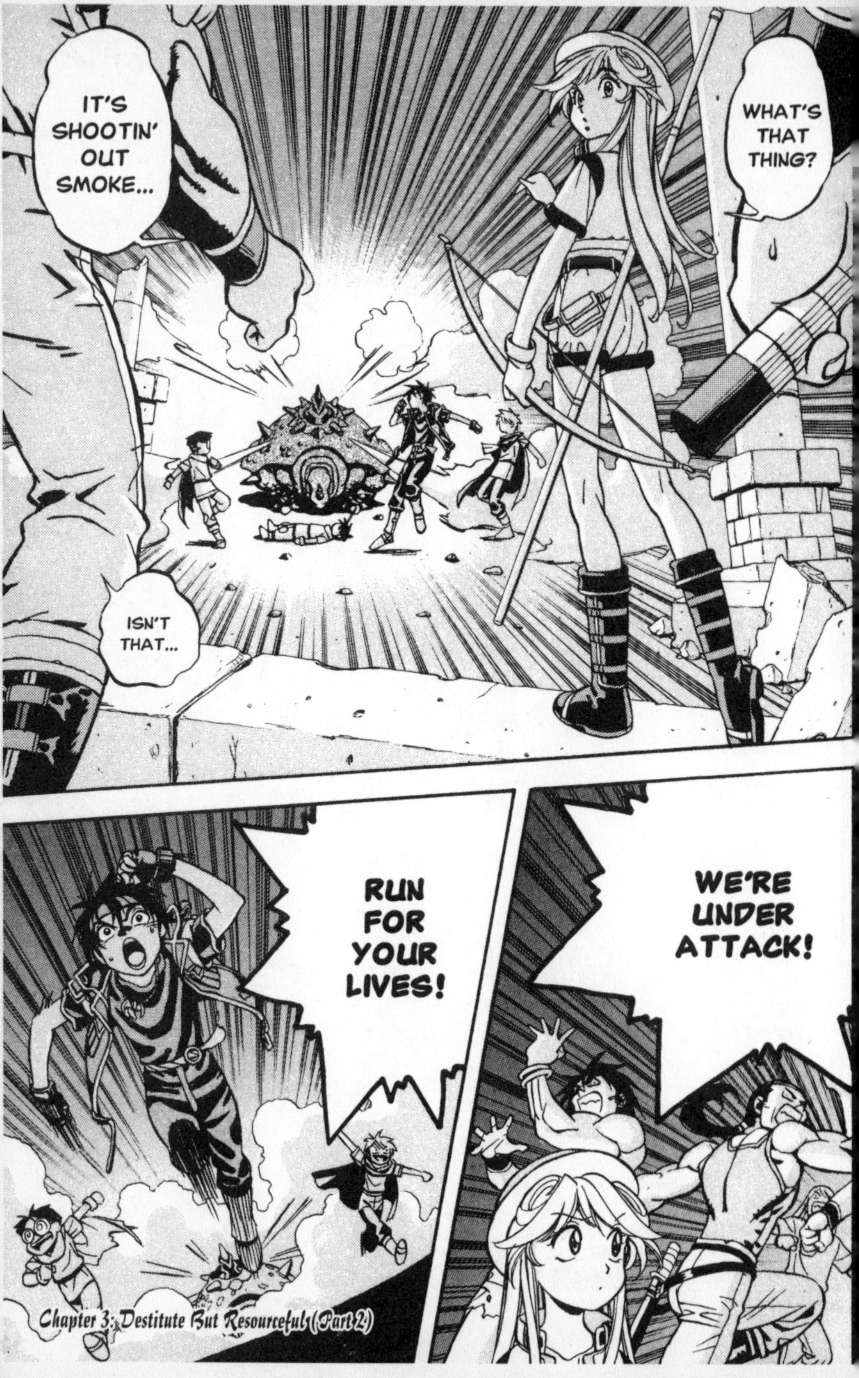
WHAT'S THAT THING?
IT'S SHOOTIN' OUT SMOKE...
ISN'T THAT...
WE'RE UNDER ATTACK!
RUN FOR YOUR LIVES!
Chapter 3: Destitute But Resourceful (Part 2)

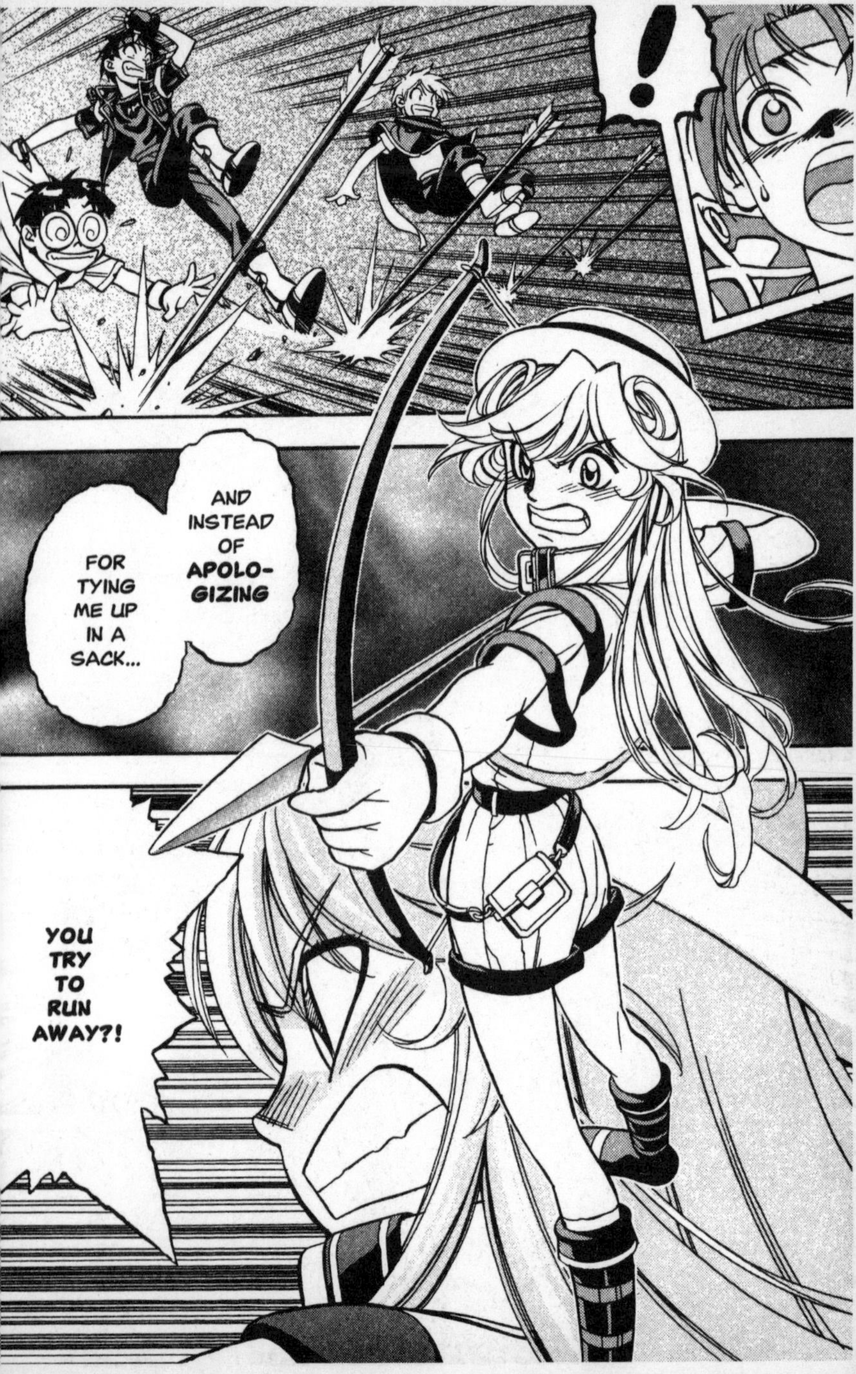
!
AND INSTEAD OF APOLOGIZING
FOR TYING ME UP IN A SACK...
YOU TRY TO RUN AWAY?!

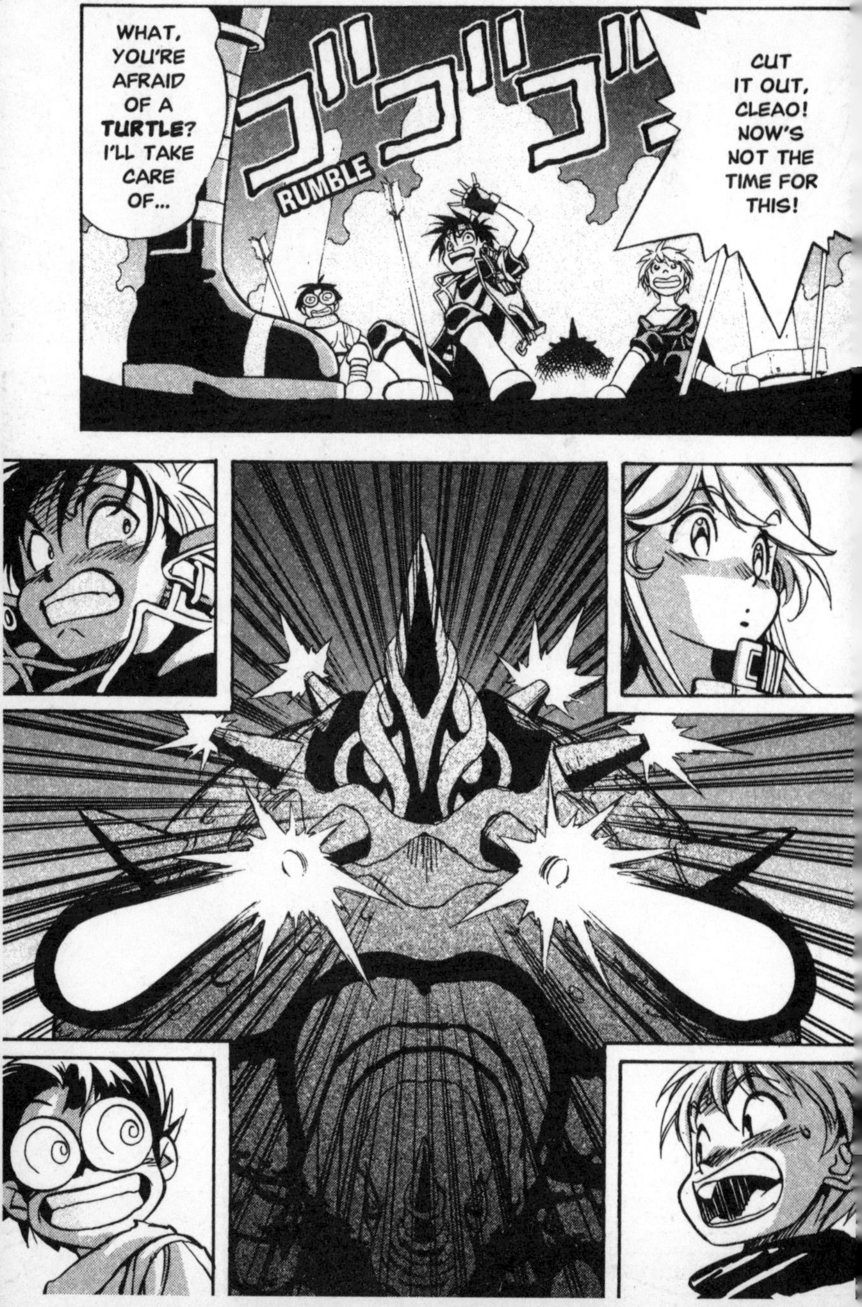
CUT IT OUT, CLEAO! NOW'S NOT THE TIME FOR THIS!
ゴゴゴ
RUMBLE
WHAT, YOU'RE AFRAID OF A TURTLE? I'LL TAKE CARE OF...

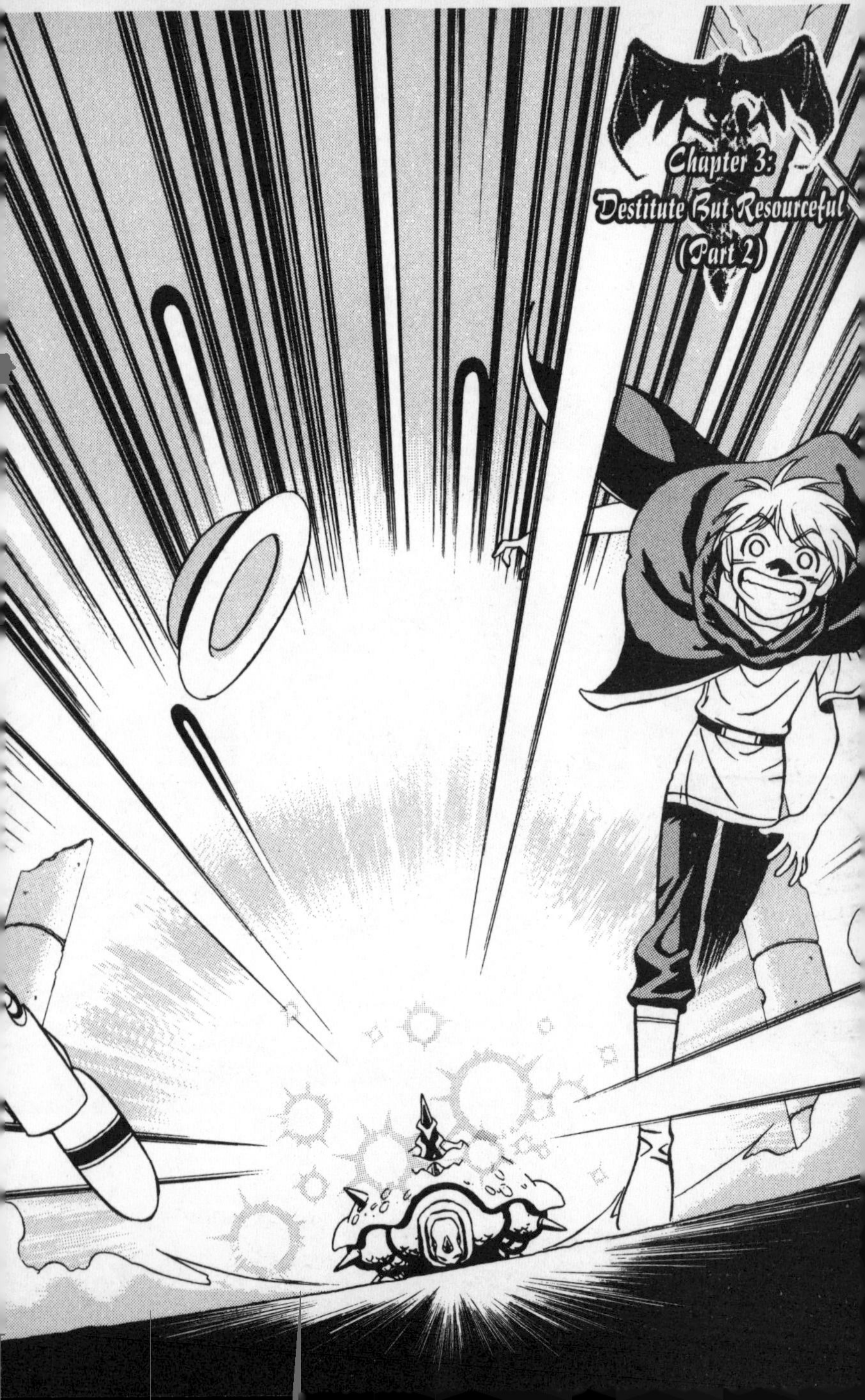
Chapter 3:
Destitute But Resourceful
(Part 2)

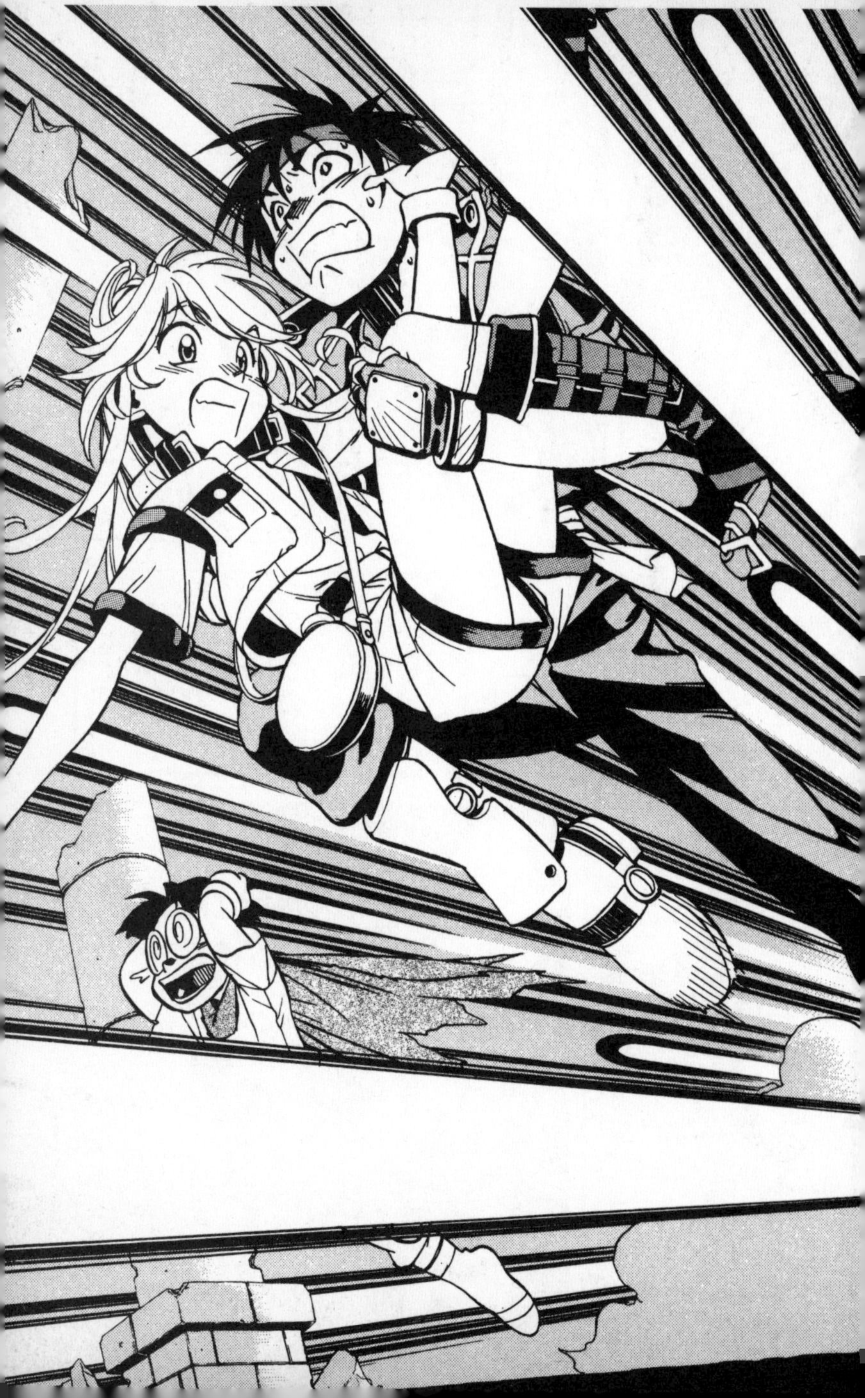

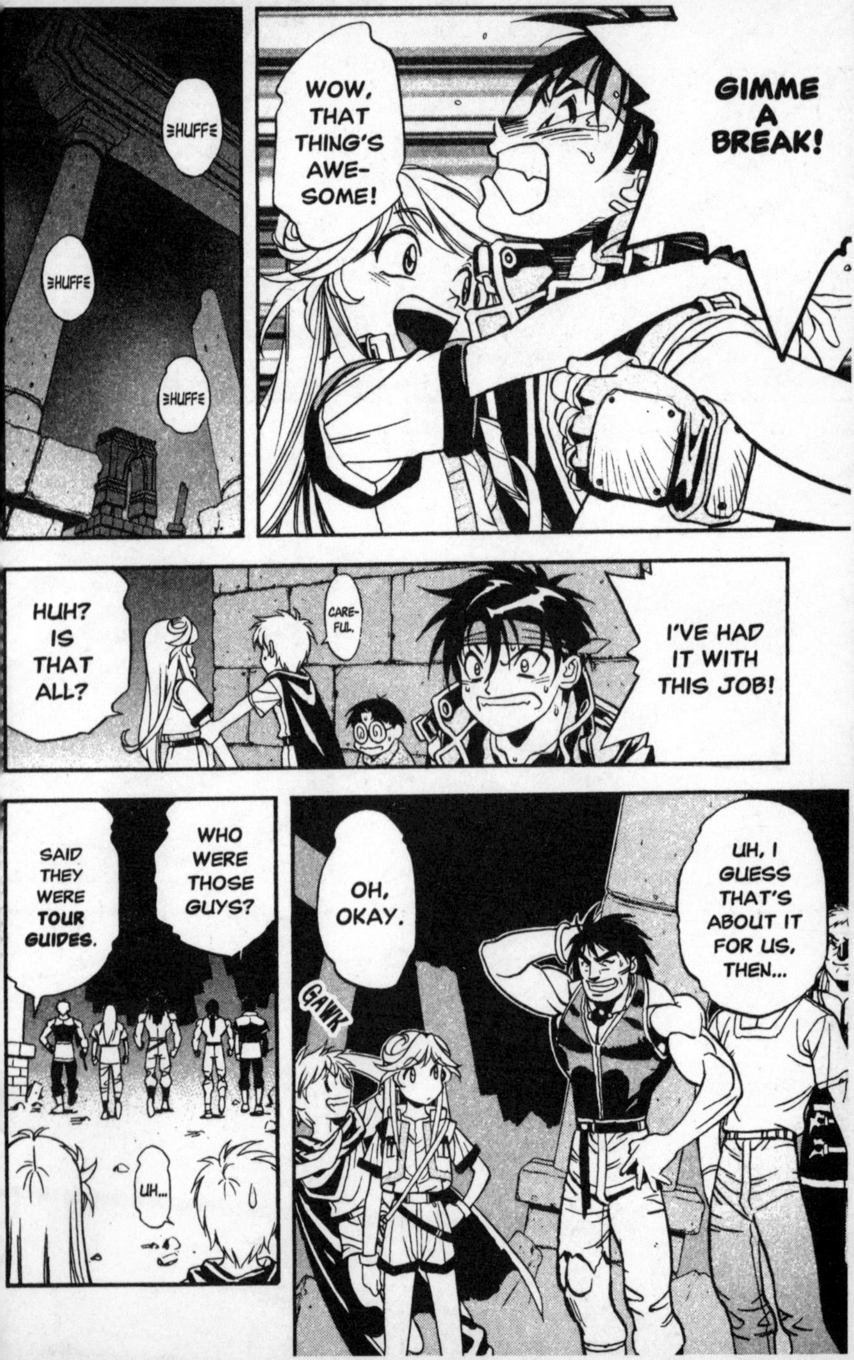
HUFF
HUFF
HUFF
WOW, THAT THING'S AWE-SOME!
GIMME A BREAK!
HUH? IS THAT ALL?
CARE-FUL.
I'VE HAD IT WITH THIS JOB!
WHO WERE THOSE GUYS?
SAID THEY WERE TOUR GUIDES.
UH...
UH, I GUESS THAT'S ABOUT IT FOR US, THEN...
OH, OKAY.
GAWK

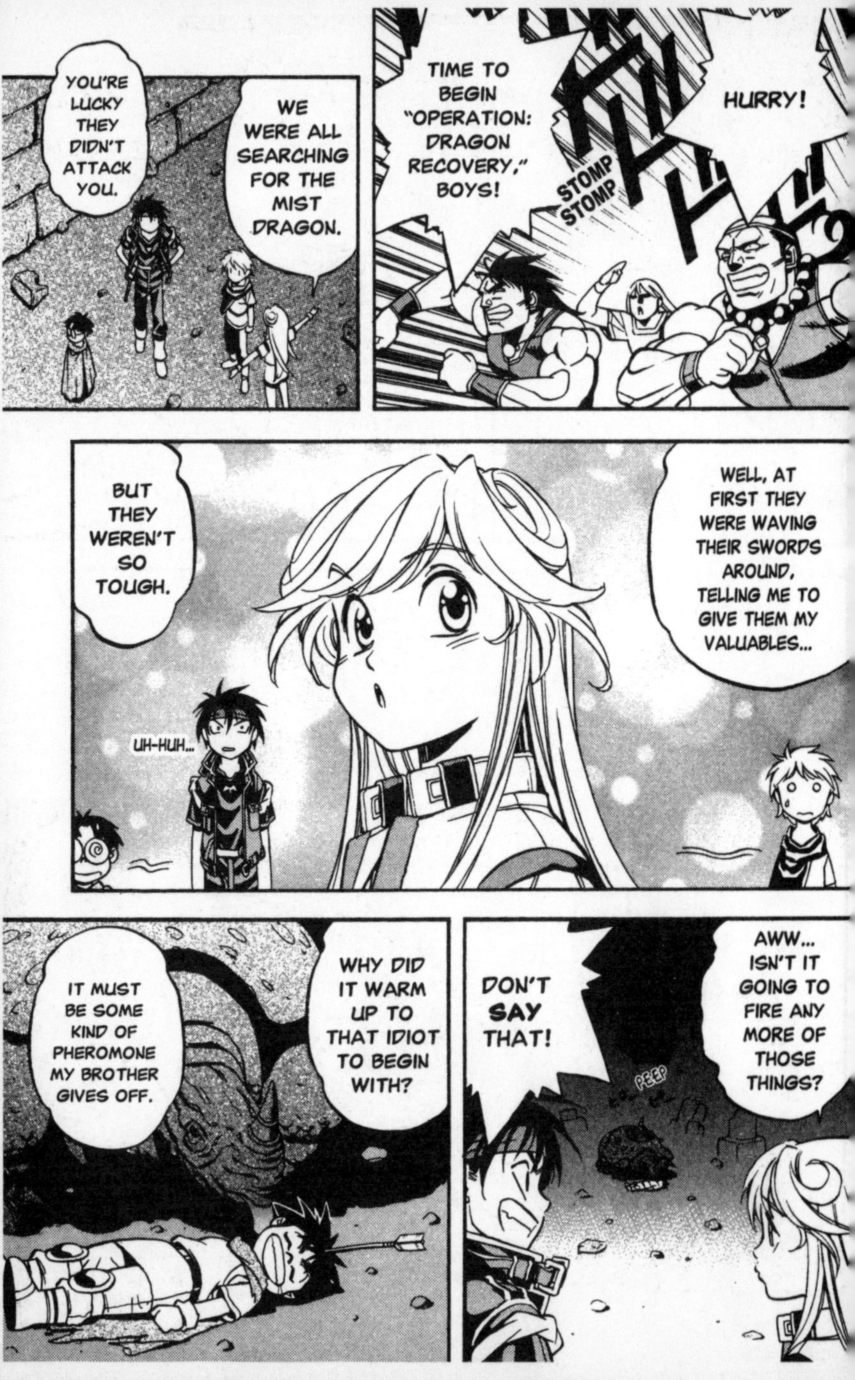
HURRY!
TIME TO BEGIN "OPERATION: DRAGON RECOVERY," BOYS!
STOMP STOMP
WE WERE ALL SEARCHING FOR THE MIST DRAGON.
YOU'RE LUCKY THEY DIDN'T ATTACK YOU.
WELL, AT FIRST THEY WERE WAVING THEIR SWORDS AROUND, TELLING ME TO GIVE THEM MY VALUABLES...
BUT THEY WEREN'T SO TOUGH.
UH-HUH...
AWW... ISN'T IT GOING TO FIRE ANY MORE OF THOSE THINGS?
DON'T SAY THAT!
PEEP
WHY DID IT WARM UP TO THAT IDIOT TO BEGIN WITH?
IT MUST BE SOME KIND OF PHEROMONE MY BROTHER GIVES OFF.

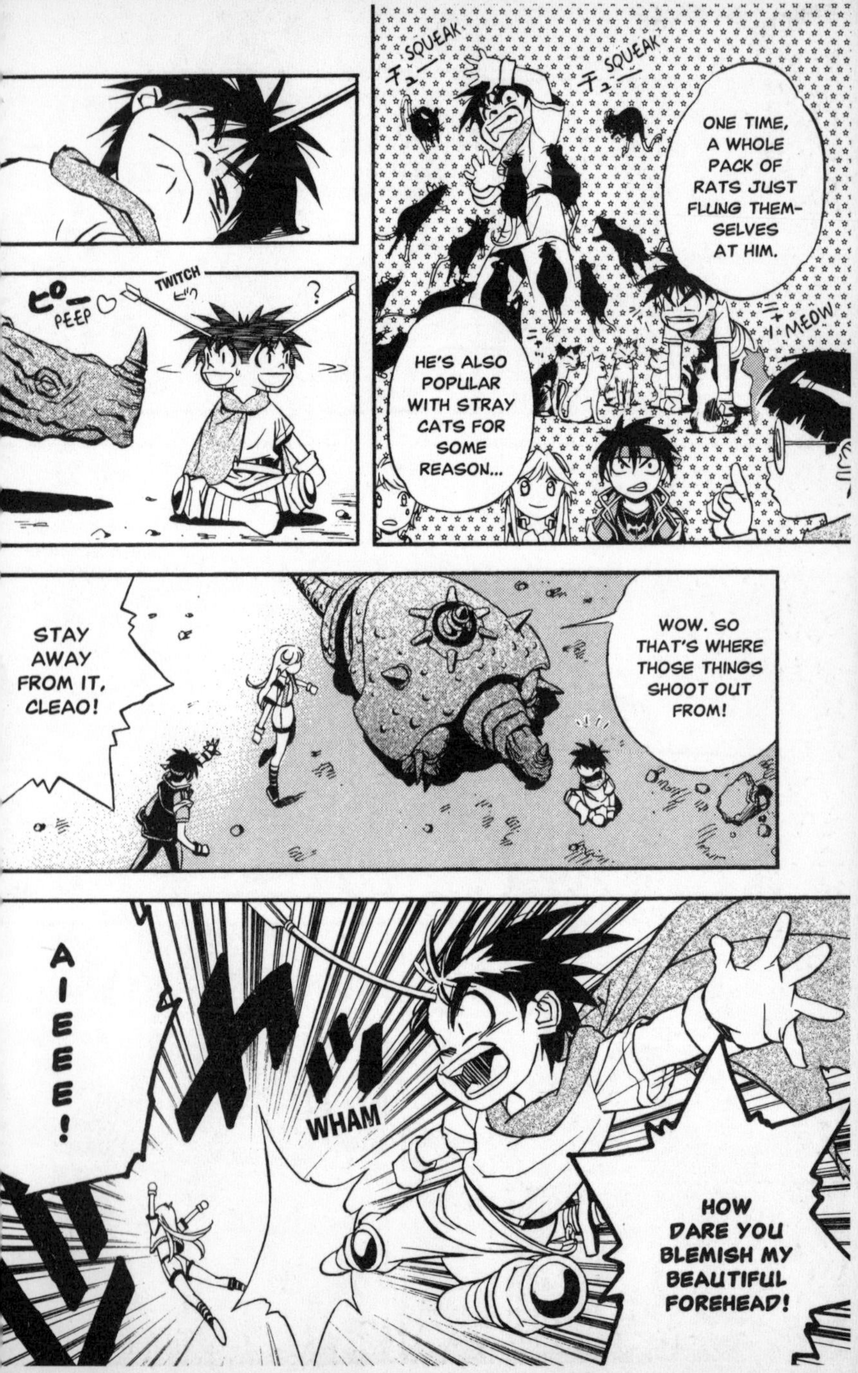

チュー SQUEAK
チュー SQUEAK
ONE TIME, A WHOLE PACK OF RATS JUST FLUNG THEM-SELVES AT HIM.
ニャー MEOW
HE'S ALSO POPULAR WITH STRAY CATS FOR SOME REASON...
ピロー PEEP
TWITCH ビク
?
WOW. SO THAT'S WHERE THOSE THINGS SHOOT OUT FROM!
STAY AWAY FROM IT, CLEAO!
AIEEEE!
WHAM
HOW DARE YOU BLEMISH MY BEAUTIFUL FOREHEAD!

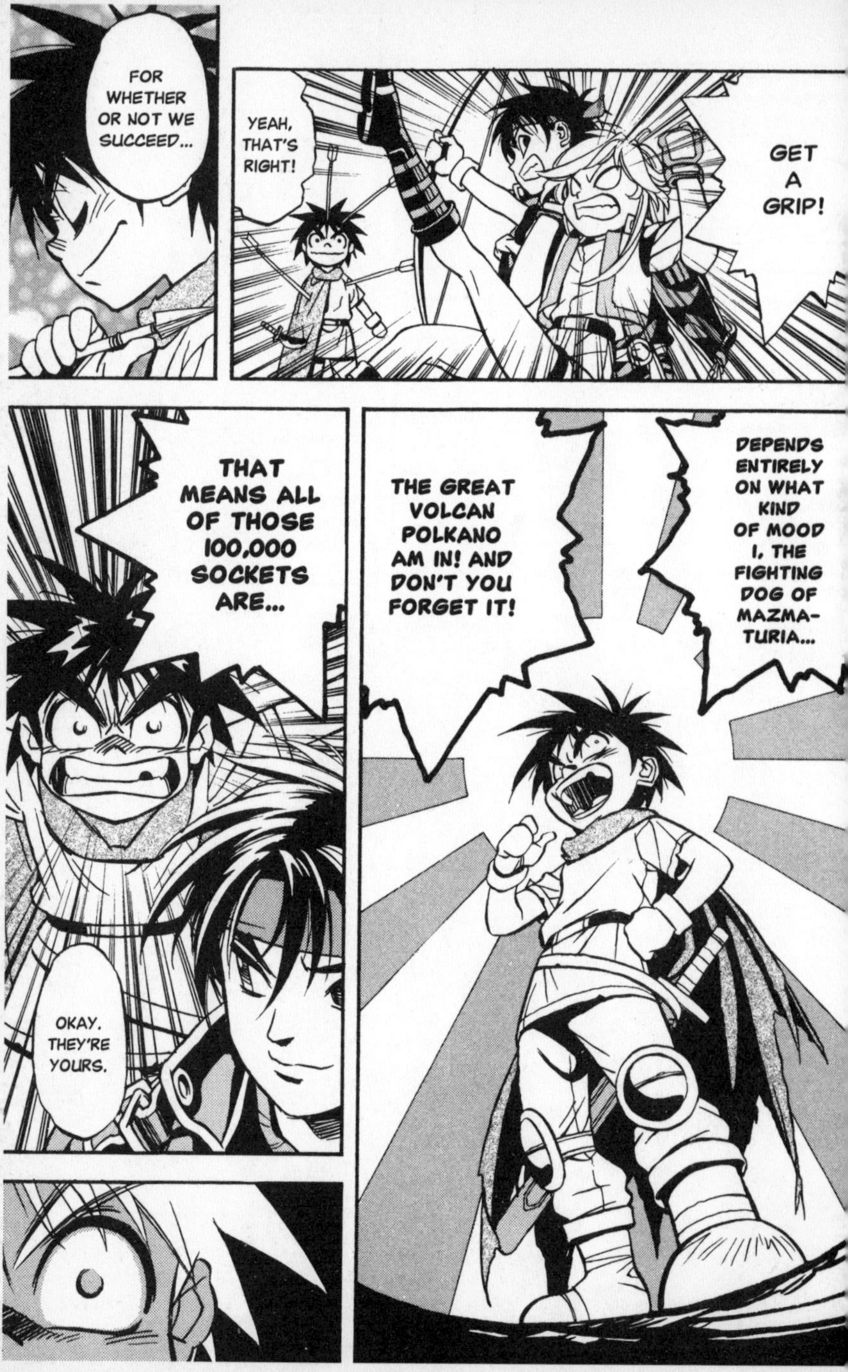
GET A GRIP!
YEAH, THAT'S RIGHT!
FOR WHETHER OR NOT WE SUCCEED...
DEPENDS ENTIRELY ON WHAT KIND OF MOOD I, THE FIGHTING DOG OF MAZMA-TURIA...
THE GREAT VOLCAN POLKANO AM IN! AND DON'T YOU FORGET IT!
THAT MEANS ALL OF THOSE 100,000 SOCKETS ARE...
OKAY. THEY'RE YOURS.

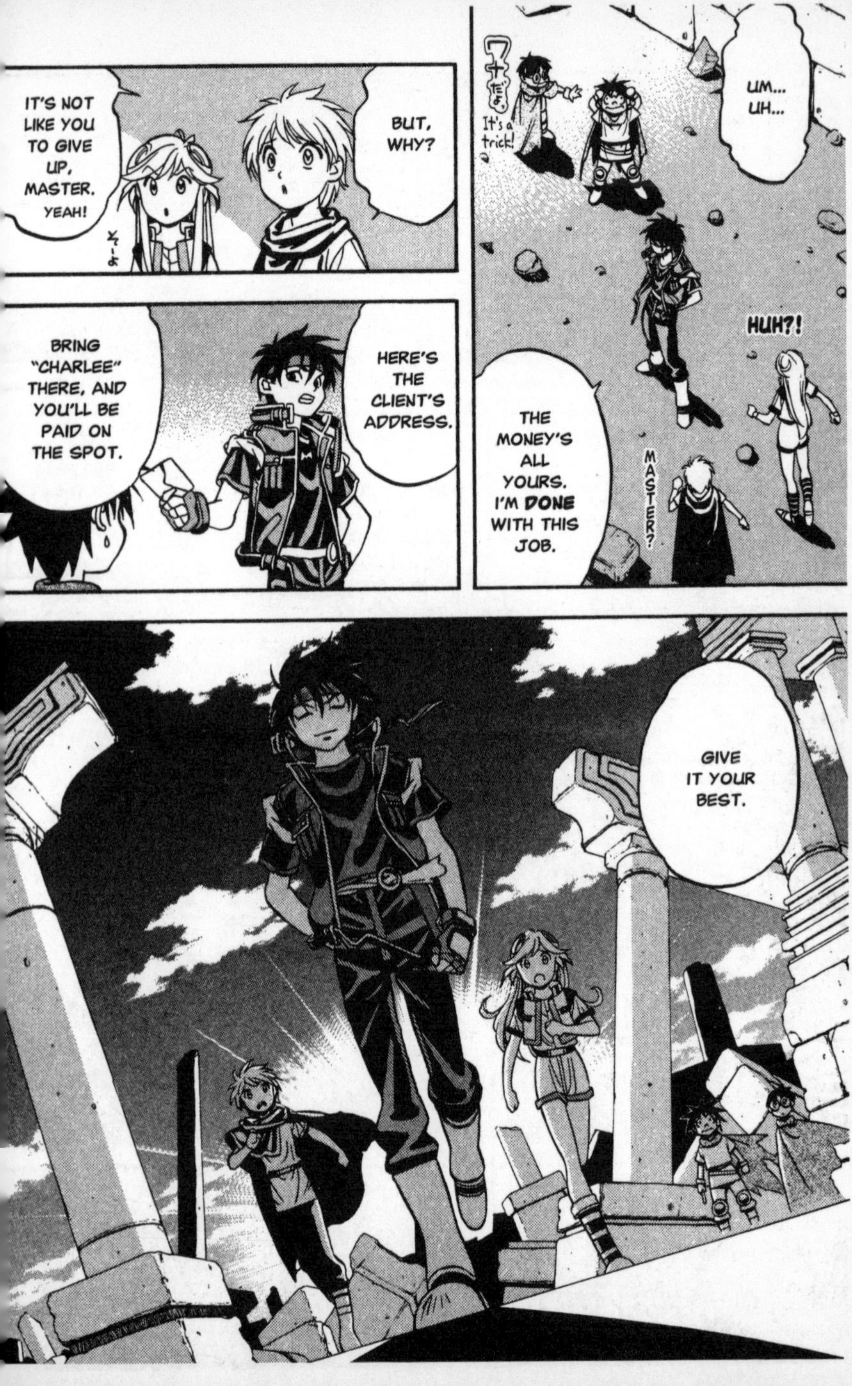

UM... UH...
ワナだよ。
It's a trick!
HUH?!
MASTER?
THE MONEY'S ALL YOURS. I'M **DONE** WITH THIS JOB.
BUT, WHY?
IT'S NOT LIKE YOU TO GIVE UP, MASTER.
YEAH!
HERE'S THE CLIENT'S ADDRESS.
BRING "CHARLEE" THERE, AND YOU'LL BE PAID ON THE SPOT.
GIVE IT YOUR BEST.

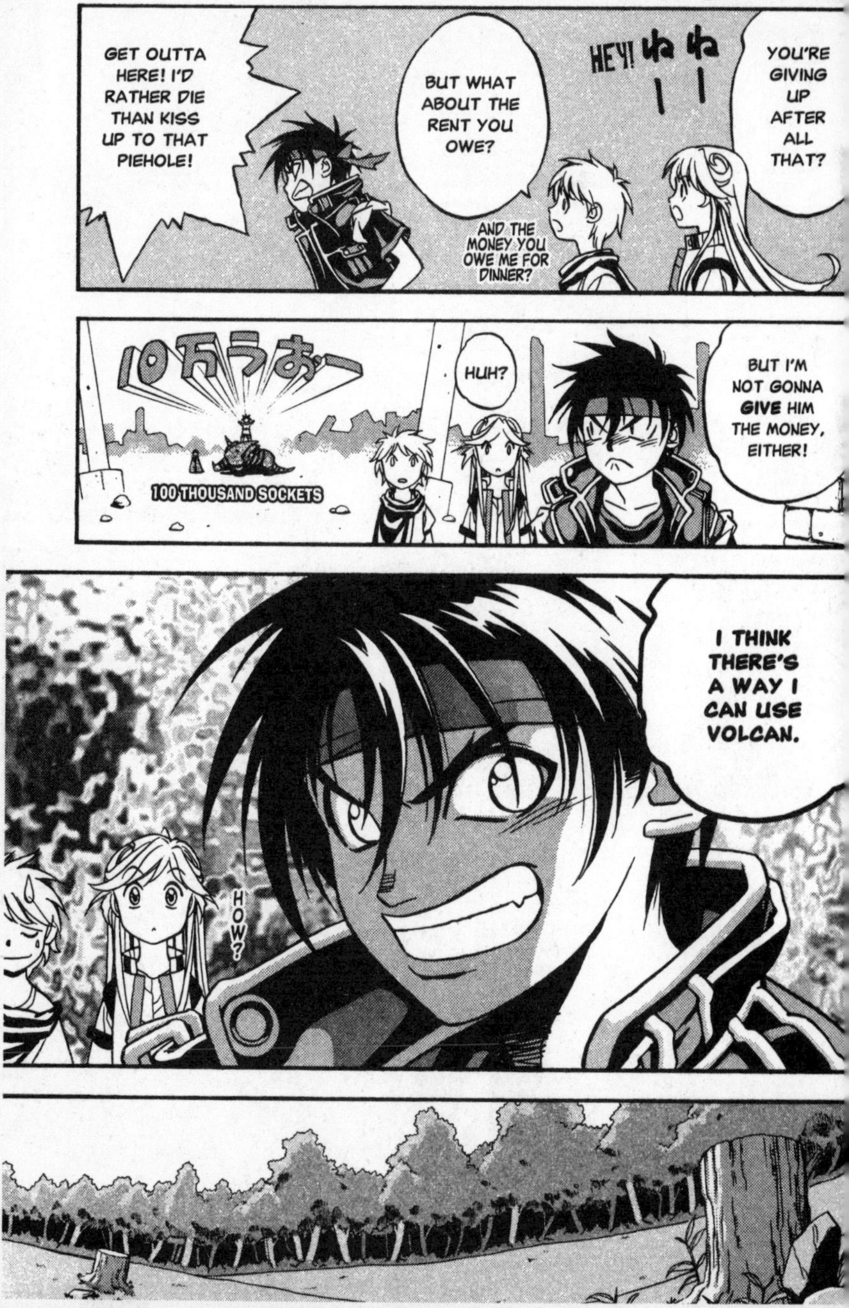
YOU'RE GIVING UP AFTER ALL THAT?
HEY!
BUT WHAT ABOUT THE RENT YOU OWE?
AND THE MONEY YOU OWE ME FOR DINNER?
GET OUTTA HERE! I'D RATHER DIE THAN KISS UP TO THAT PIEHOLE!
BUT I'M NOT GONNA GIVE HIM THE MONEY, EITHER!
HUH?
10万うぉー
100 THOUSAND SOCKETS
I THINK THERE'S A WAY I CAN USE VOLCAN.
HOW?

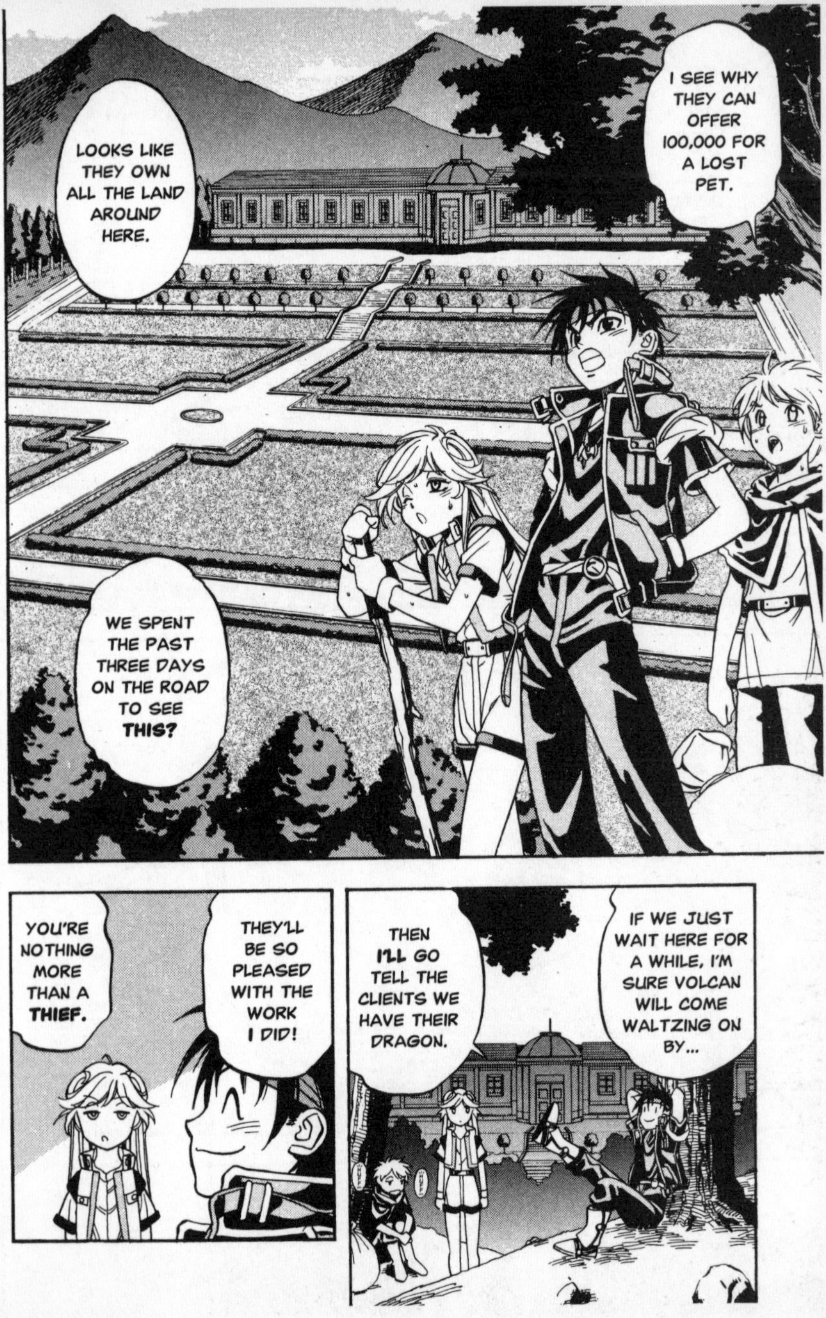
I SEE WHY THEY CAN OFFER 100,000 FOR A LOST PET.
LOOKS LIKE THEY OWN ALL THE LAND AROUND HERE.
WE SPENT THE PAST THREE DAYS ON THE ROAD TO SEE **THIS?**
IF WE JUST WAIT HERE FOR A WHILE, I'M SURE VOLCAN WILL COME WALTZING ON BY...
THEN **I'LL** GO TELL THE CLIENTS WE HAVE THEIR DRAGON.
THEY'LL BE SO PLEASED WITH THE WORK I DID!
YOU'RE NOTHING MORE THAN A **THIEF.**

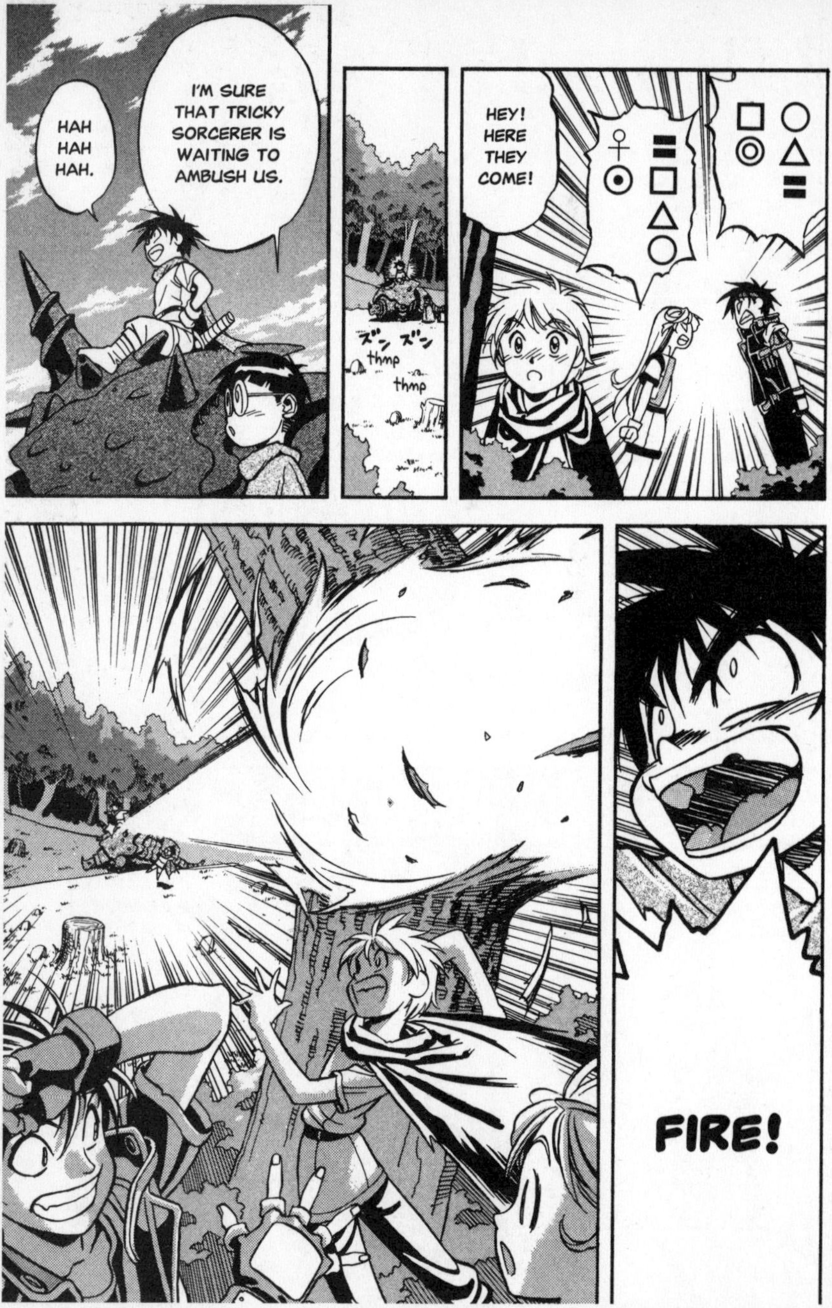

I'M SURE THAT TRICKY SORCERER IS WAITING TO AMBUSH US.
HAH HAH HAH.
ズン ズン
thmp thmp
HEY! HERE THEY COME!
○△〓
□◎
♀〓□△○
◉
FIRE!

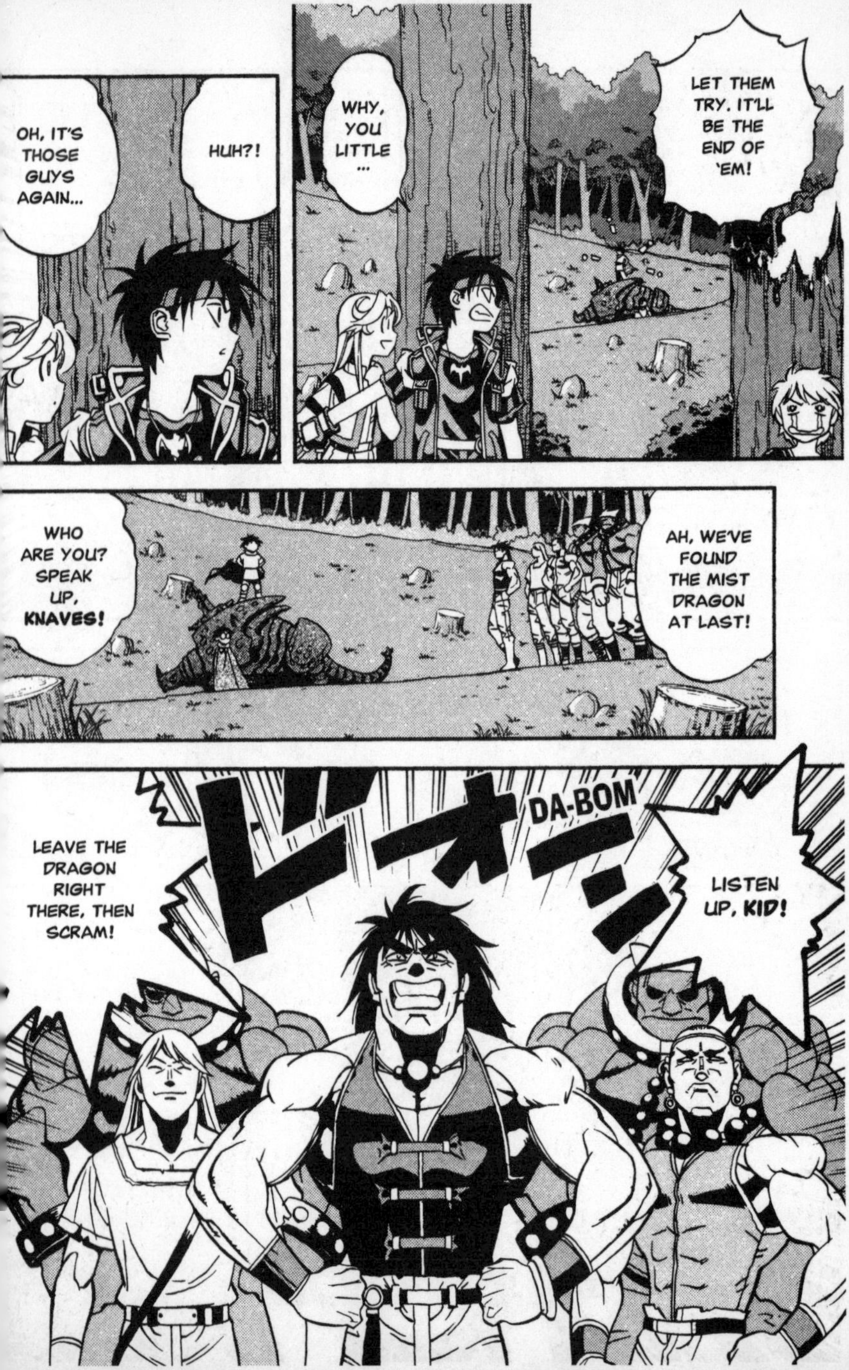
LET THEM TRY. IT'LL BE THE END OF 'EM!
WHY, YOU LITTLE ...
HUH?!
OH, IT'S THOSE GUYS AGAIN...
AH, WE'VE FOUND THE MIST DRAGON AT LAST!
WHO ARE YOU? SPEAK UP, KNAVES!
DA-BOM
LISTEN UP, KID!
LEAVE THE DRAGON RIGHT THERE, THEN SCRAM!

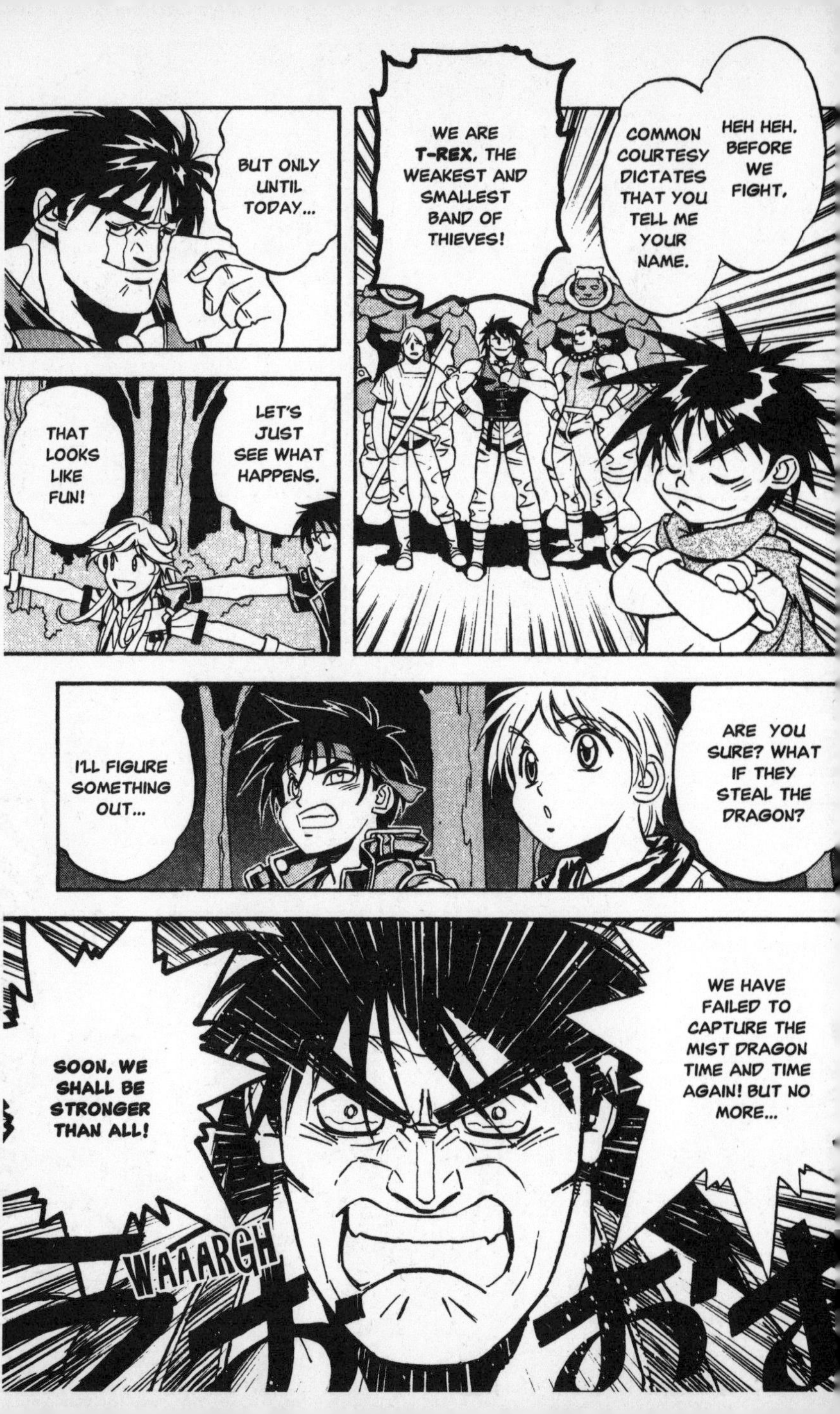
HEH HEH. BEFORE WE FIGHT,
COMMON COURTESY DICTATES THAT YOU TELL ME YOUR NAME.
WE ARE T-REX, THE WEAKEST AND SMALLEST BAND OF THIEVES!
BUT ONLY UNTIL TODAY...
LET'S JUST SEE WHAT HAPPENS.
THAT LOOKS LIKE FUN!
ARE YOU SURE? WHAT IF THEY STEAL THE DRAGON?
I'LL FIGURE SOMETHING OUT...
WE HAVE FAILED TO CAPTURE THE MIST DRAGON TIME AND TIME AGAIN! BUT NO MORE...
SOON, WE SHALL BE STRONGER THAN ALL!
WAAARGH

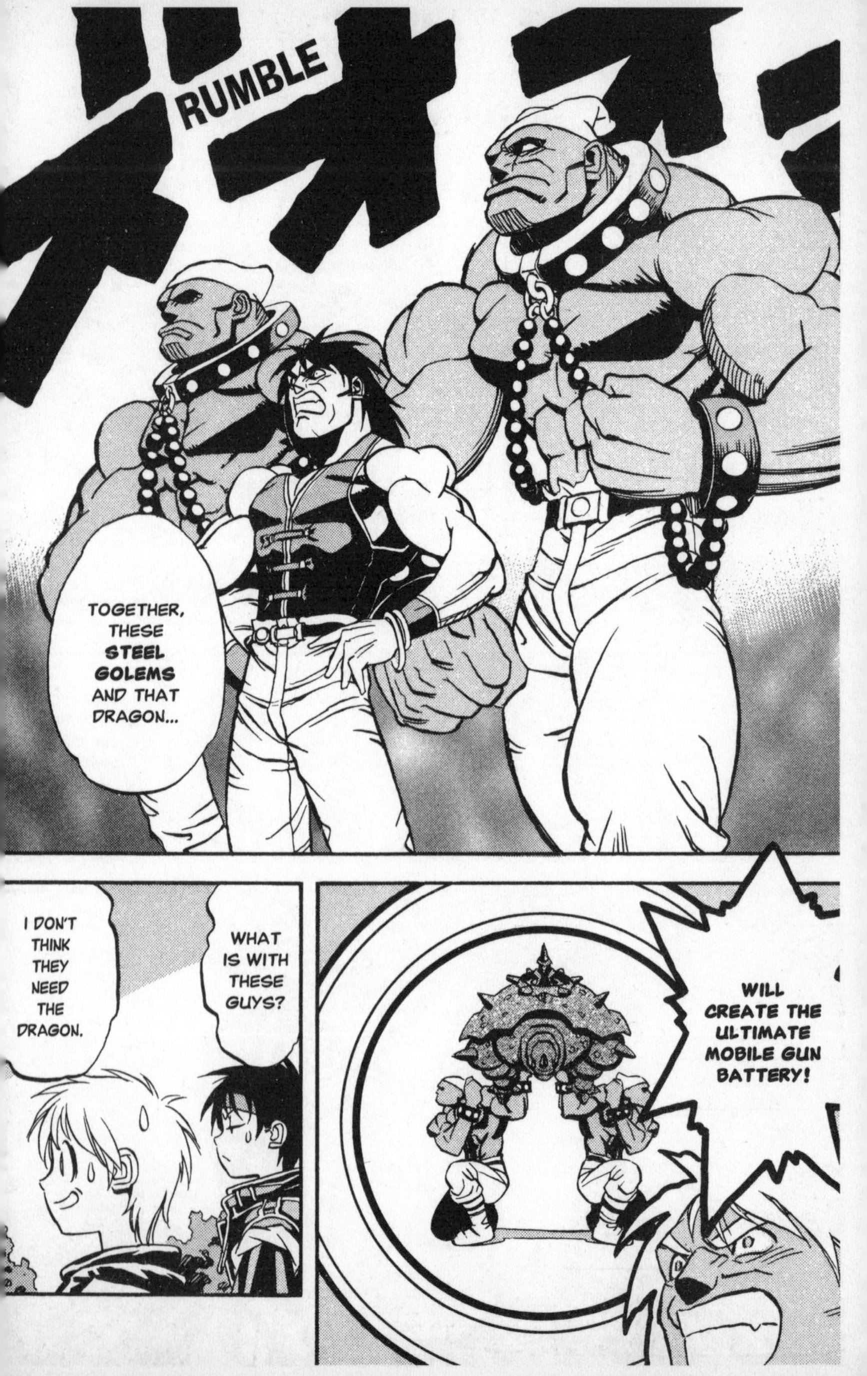
RUMBLE
TOGETHER, THESE STEEL GOLEMS AND THAT DRAGON...
WILL CREATE THE ULTIMATE MOBILE GUN BATTERY!
WHAT IS WITH THESE GUYS?
I DON'T THINK THEY NEED THE DRAGON.

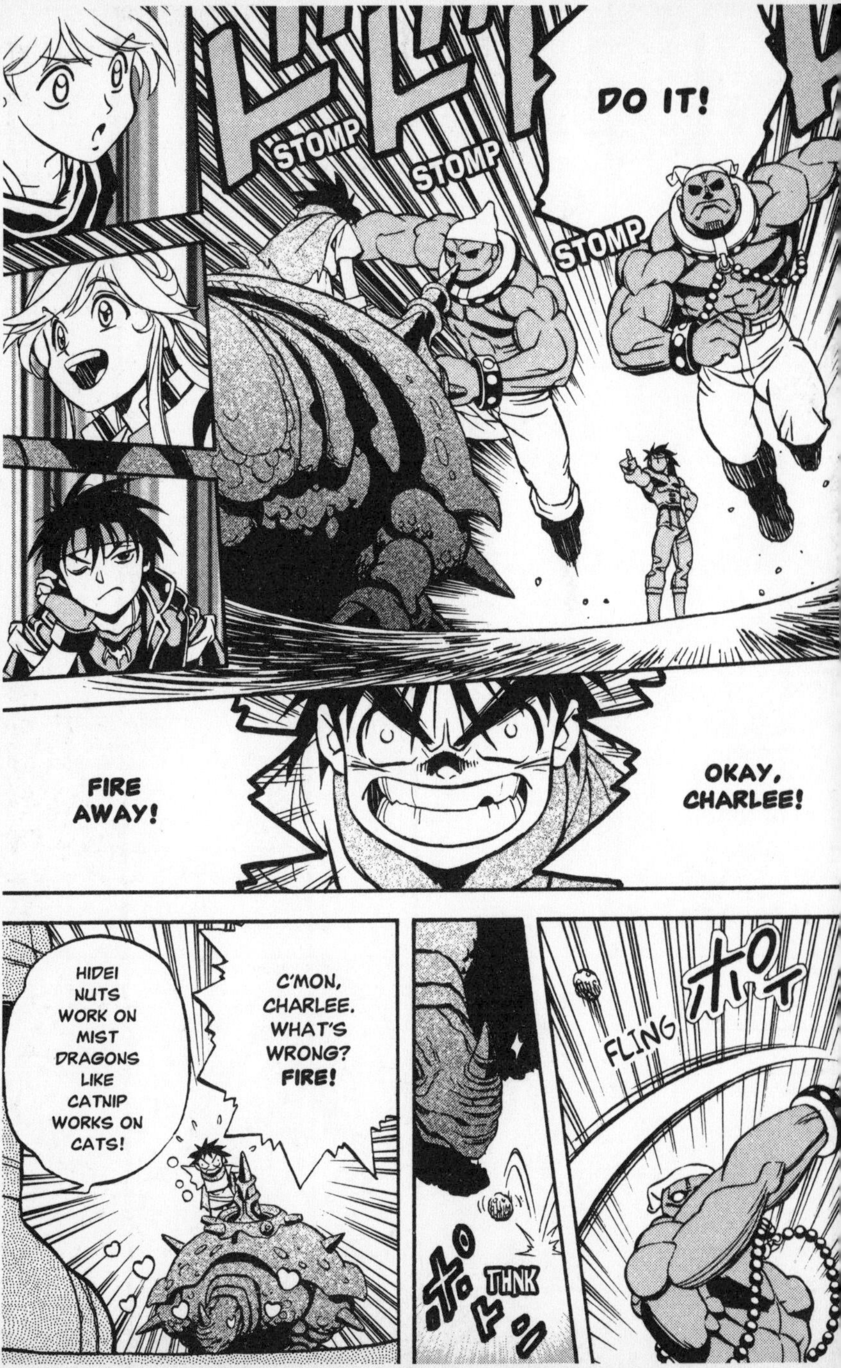
STOMP
STOMP
DO IT!
STOMP
OKAY, CHARLEE!
FIRE AWAY!
FLING
THNK
C'MON, CHARLEE. WHAT'S WRONG? FIRE!
HIDEI NUTS WORK ON MIST DRAGONS LIKE CATNIP WORKS ON CATS!

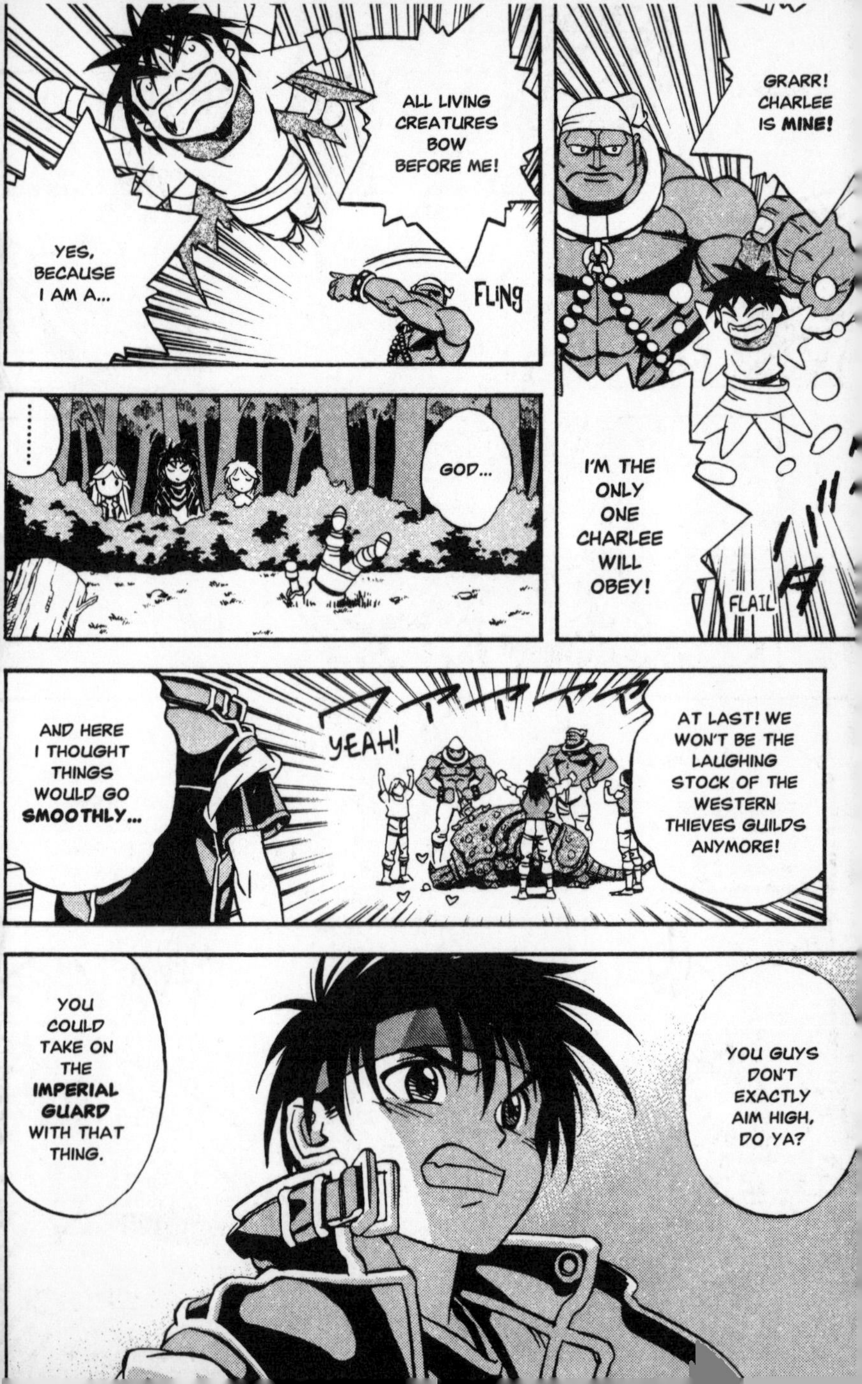
ALL LIVING CREATURES BOW BEFORE ME!
YES, BECAUSE I AM A...
FLING
GOD...
......
GRARR! CHARLEE IS MINE!
I'M THE ONLY ONE CHARLEE WILL OBEY!
FLAIL
AT LAST! WE WON'T BE THE LAUGHING STOCK OF THE WESTERN THIEVES GUILDS ANYMORE!
YEAH!
AND HERE I THOUGHT THINGS WOULD GO SMOOTHLY...
YOU GUYS DON'T EXACTLY AIM HIGH, DO YA?
YOU COULD TAKE ON THE IMPERIAL GUARD WITH THAT THING.

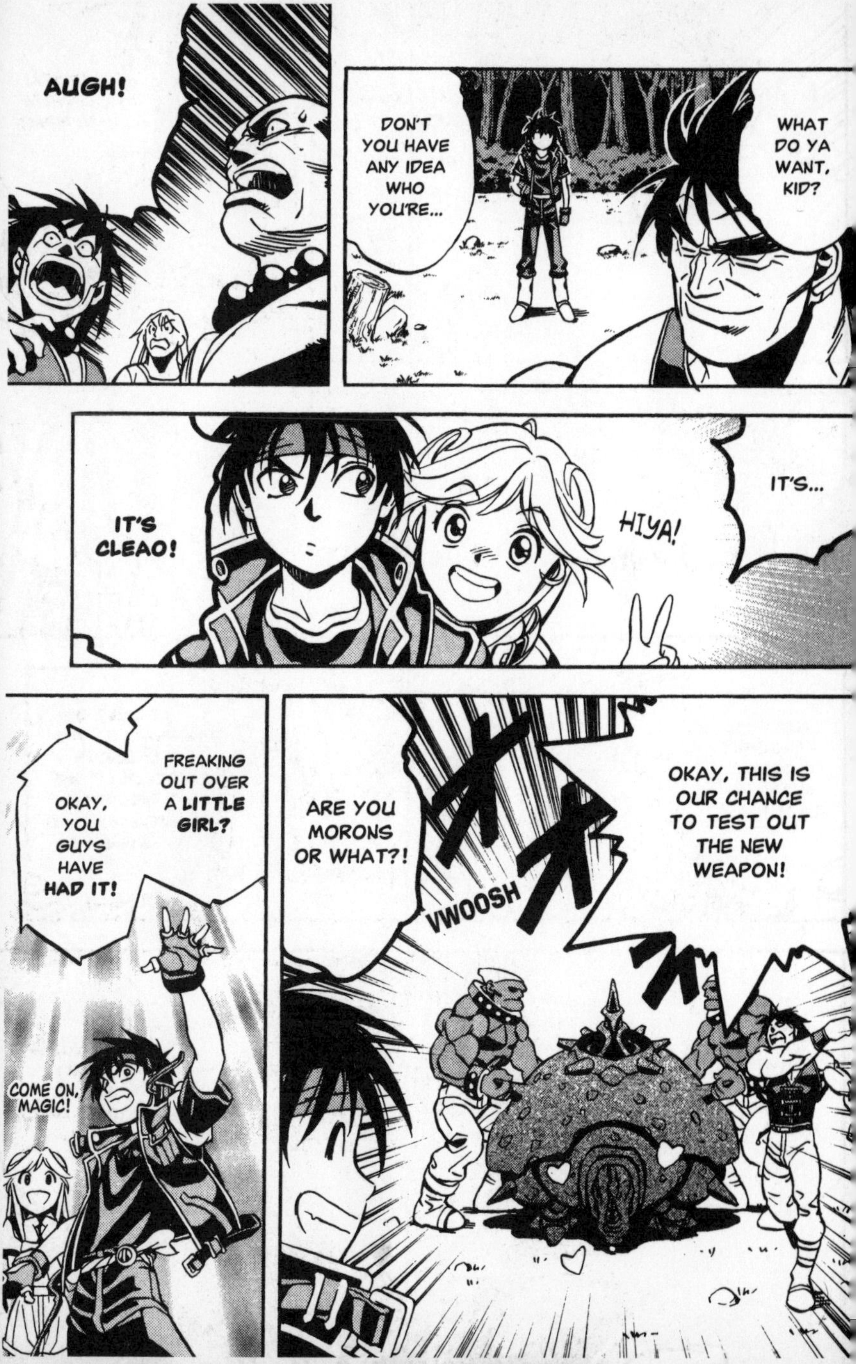
WHAT DO YA WANT, KID?
DON'T YOU HAVE ANY IDEA WHO YOU'RE...
AUGH!
IT'S...
HIYA!
IT'S CLEAO!
OKAY, THIS IS OUR CHANCE TO TEST OUT THE NEW WEAPON!
VWOOSH
ARE YOU MORONS OR WHAT?!
FREAKING OUT OVER A LITTLE GIRL?
OKAY, YOU GUYS HAVE HAD IT!
COME ON, MAGIC!

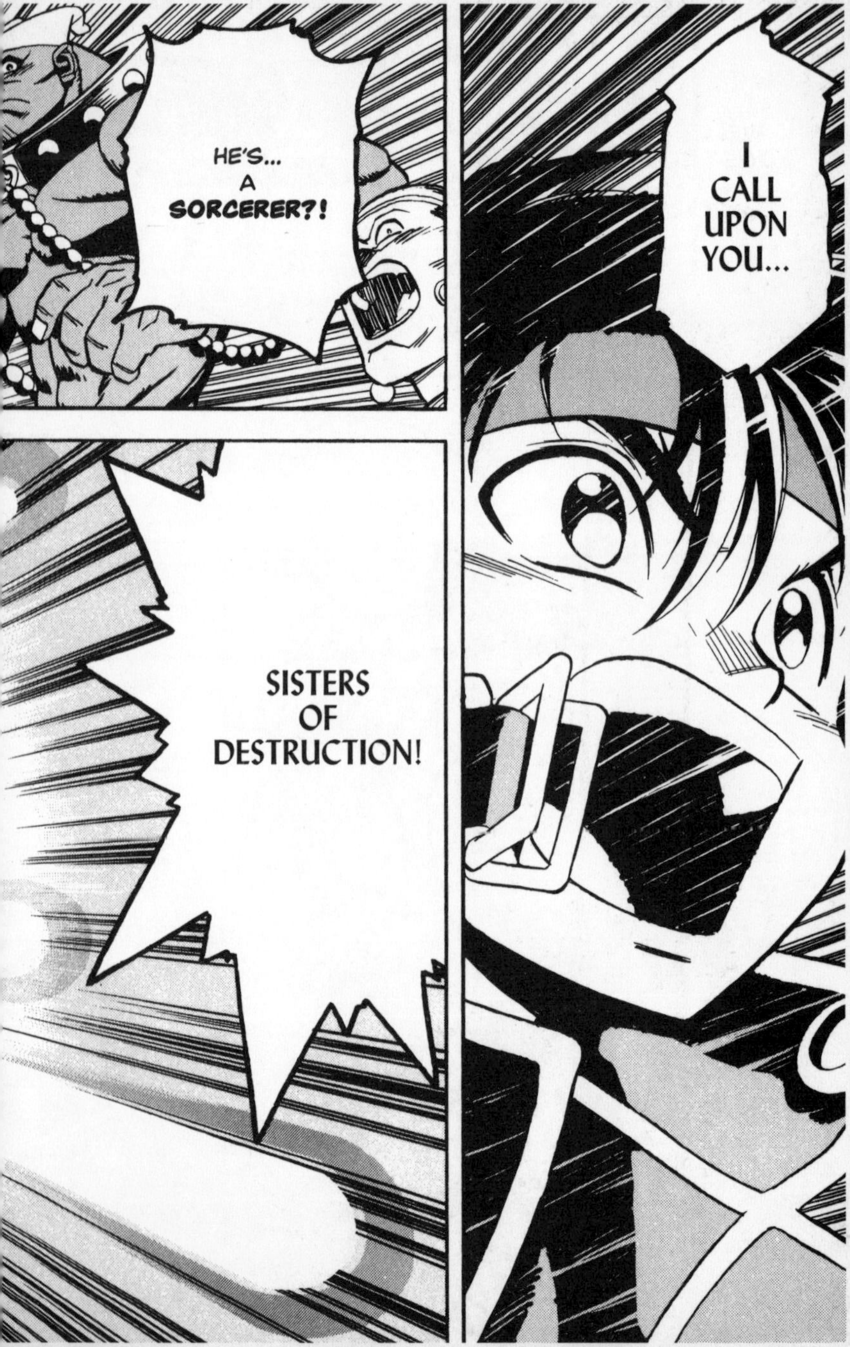
I CALL UPON YOU...
HE'S... A SORCERER?!
SISTERS OF DESTRUCTION!

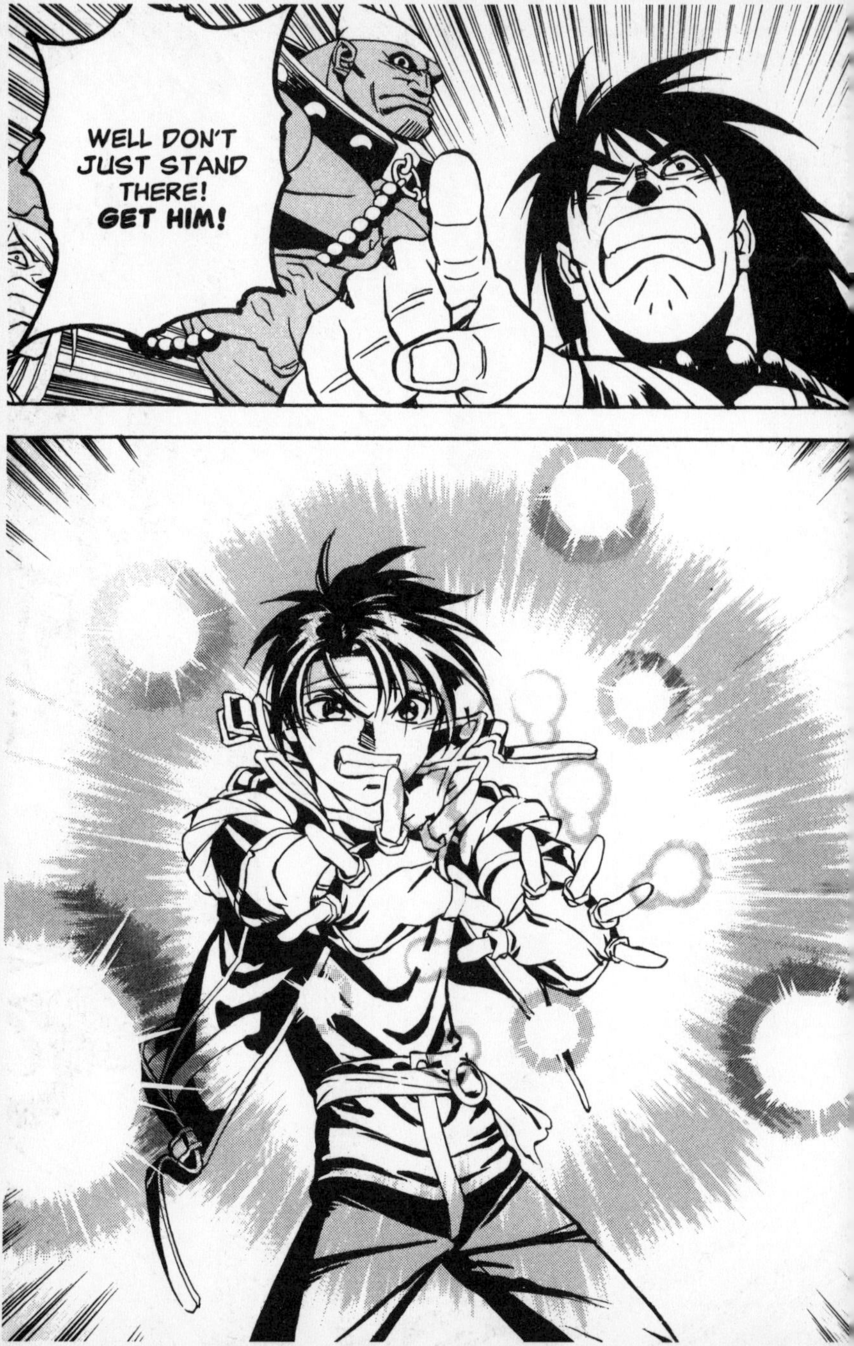
WELL DON'T JUST STAND THERE! GET HIM!

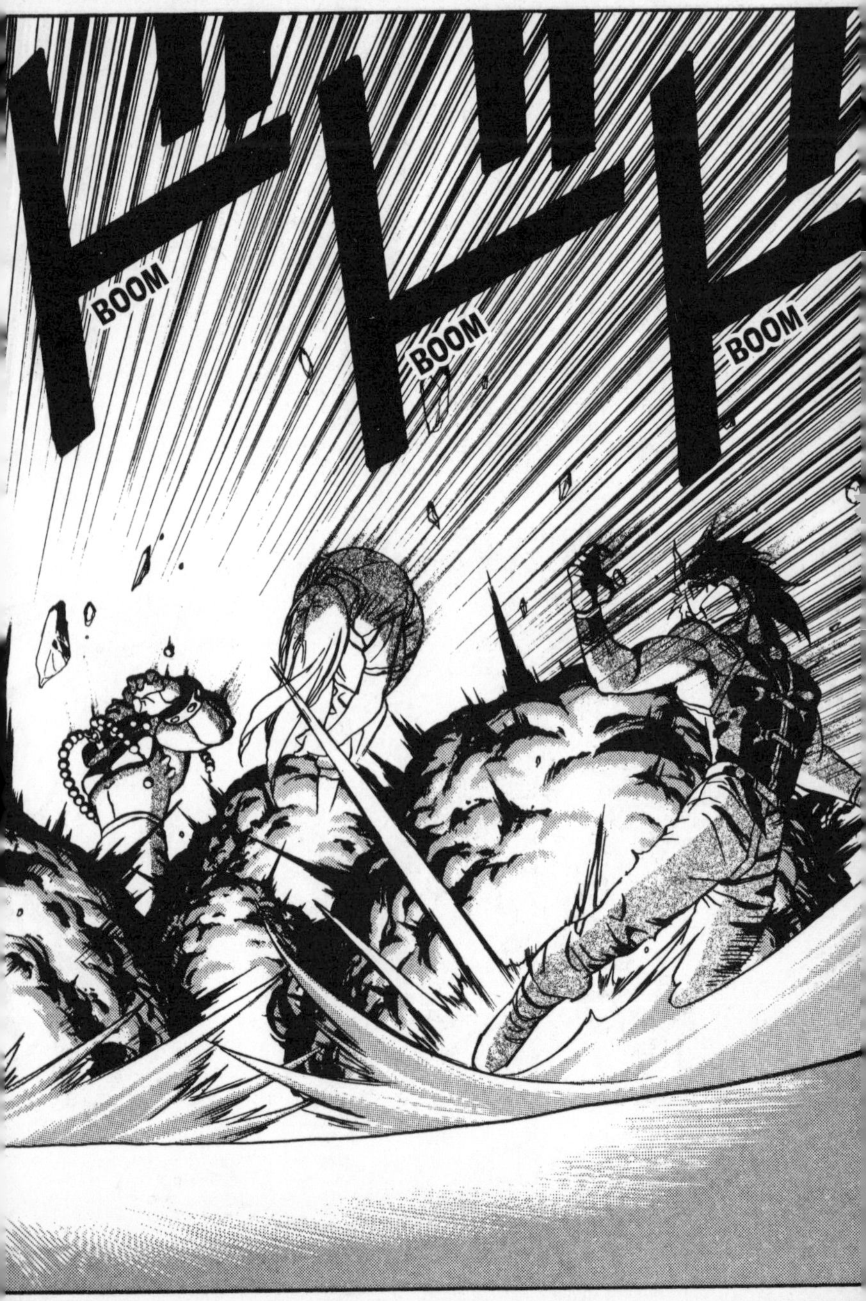
BOOM
BOOM
BOOM

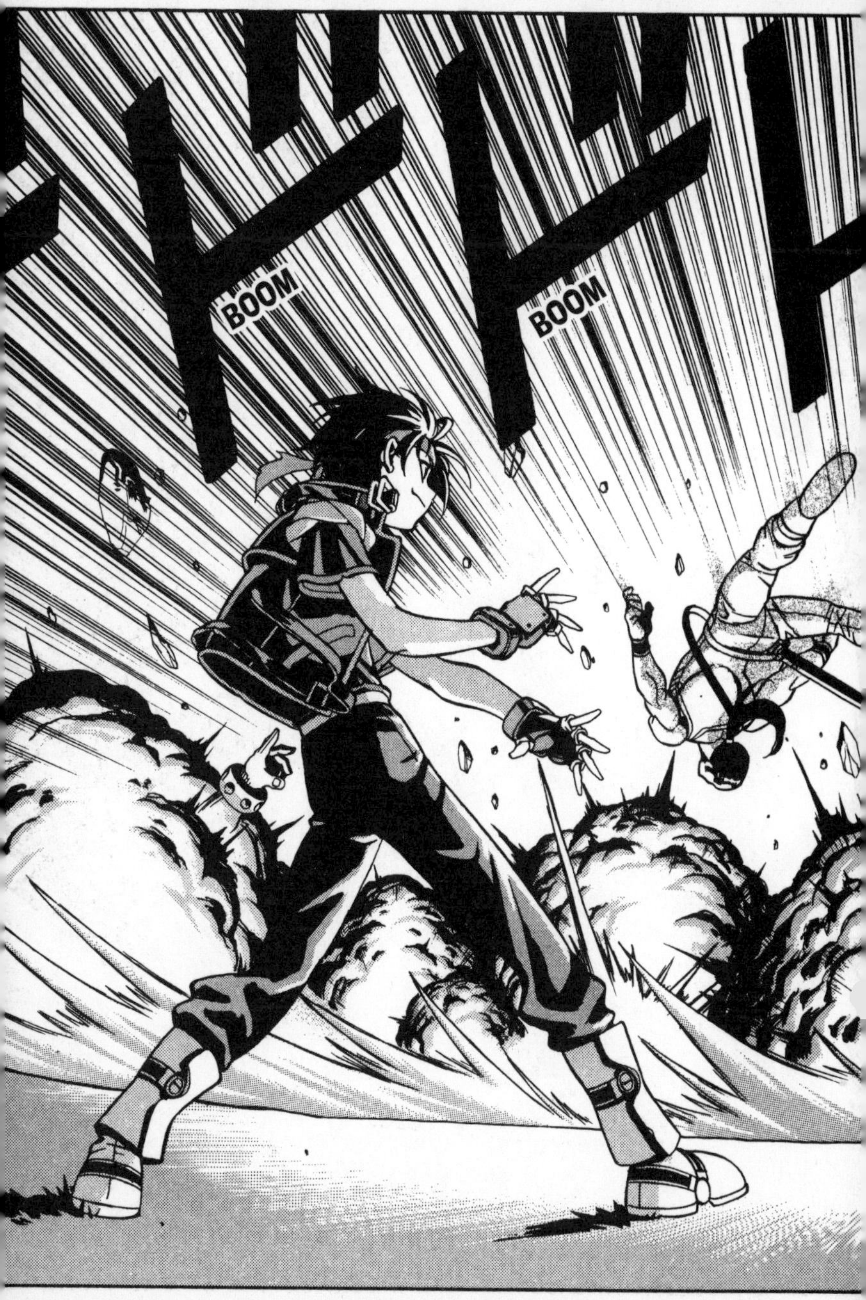
BOOM
BOOM

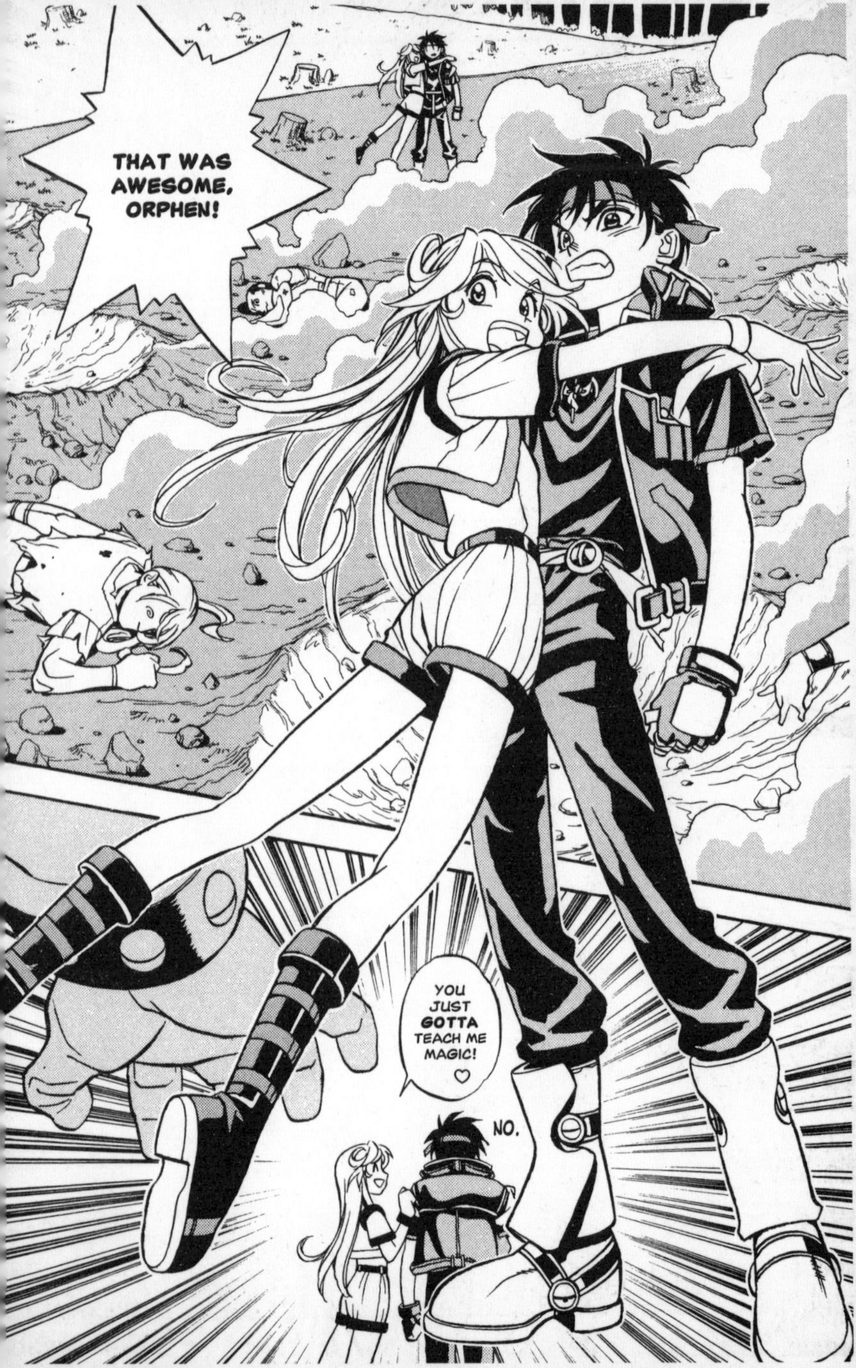
THAT WAS AWESOME, ORPHEN!
YOU JUST GOTTA TEACH ME MAGIC! ♡
NO.

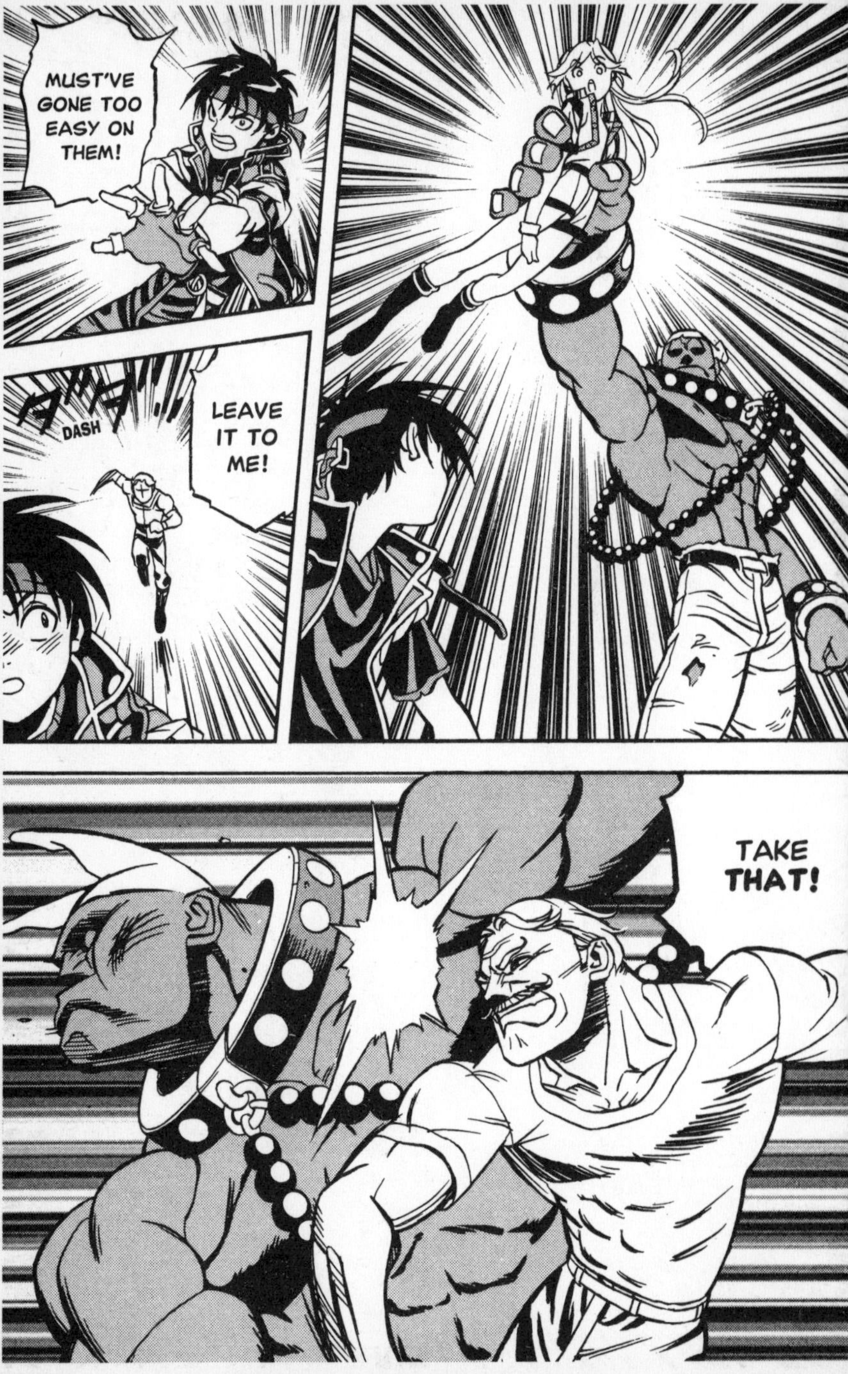
MUST'VE GONE TOO EASY ON THEM!
DASH
LEAVE IT TO ME!
TAKE THAT!

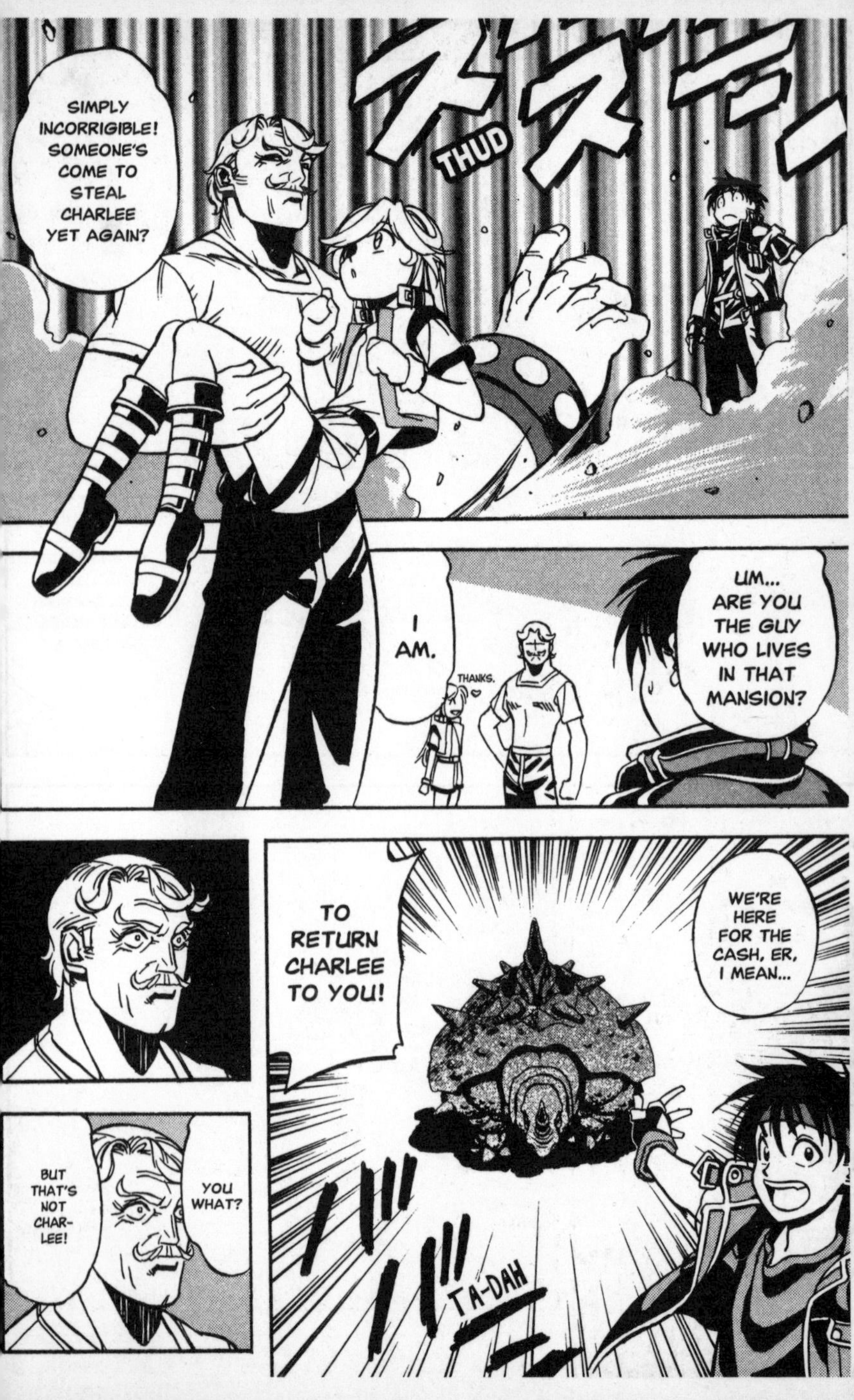
THUD
SIMPLY INCORRIGIBLE! SOMEONE'S COME TO STEAL CHARLEE YET AGAIN?
UM... ARE YOU THE GUY WHO LIVES IN THAT MANSION?
THANKS.
I AM.
WE'RE HERE FOR THE CASH, ER, I MEAN...
TO RETURN CHARLEE TO YOU!
TA-DAH
YOU WHAT?
BUT THAT'S NOT CHAR-LEE!

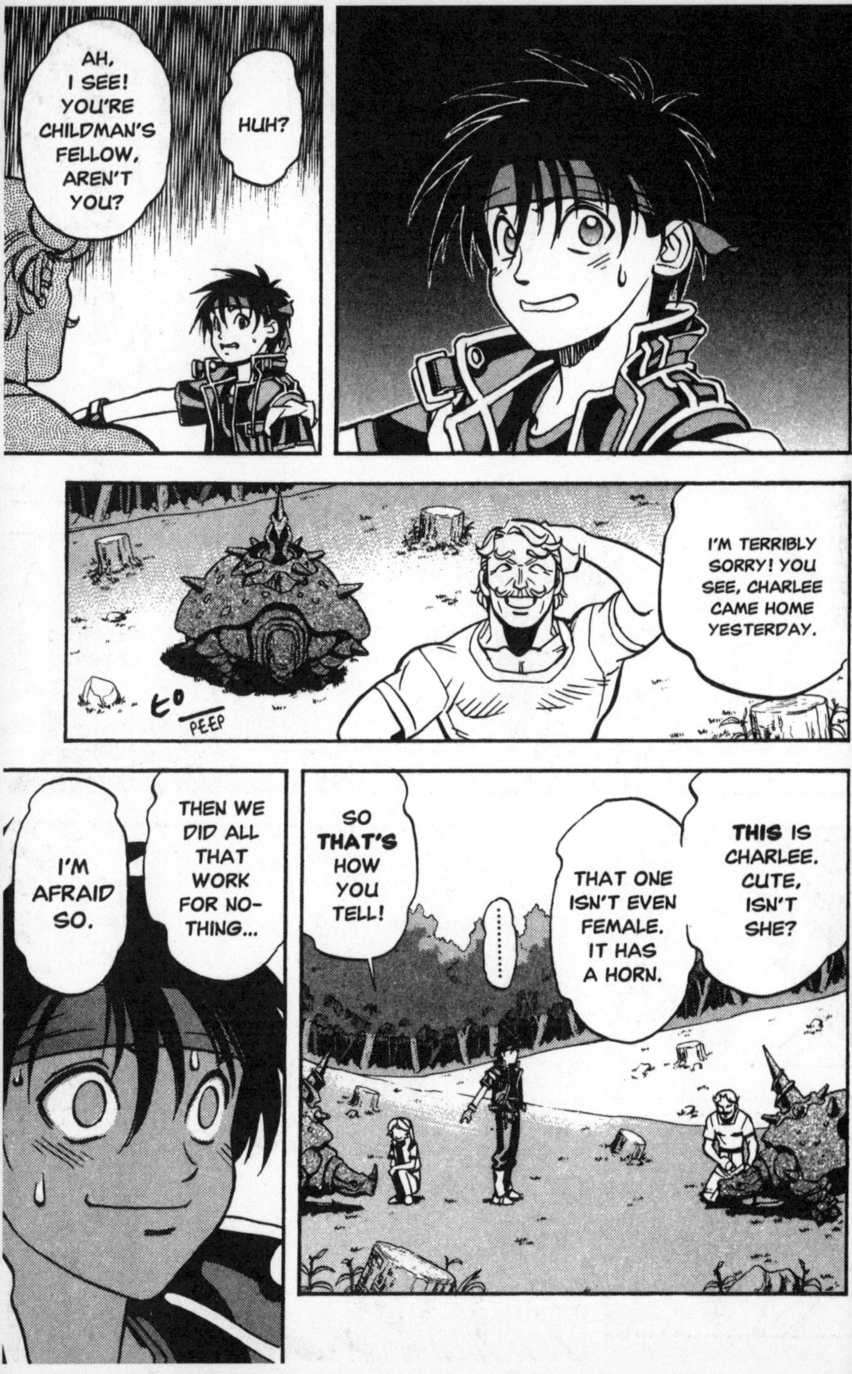
HUH?
AH, I SEE! YOU'RE CHILDMAN'S FELLOW, AREN'T YOU?
I'M TERRIBLY SORRY! YOU SEE, CHARLEE CAME HOME YESTERDAY.
ピ
PEEP
THIS IS CHARLEE. CUTE, ISN'T SHE?
THAT ONE ISN'T EVEN FEMALE. IT HAS A HORN.
....
SO THAT'S HOW YOU TELL!
THEN WE DID ALL THAT WORK FOR NO-THING...
I'M AFRAID SO.

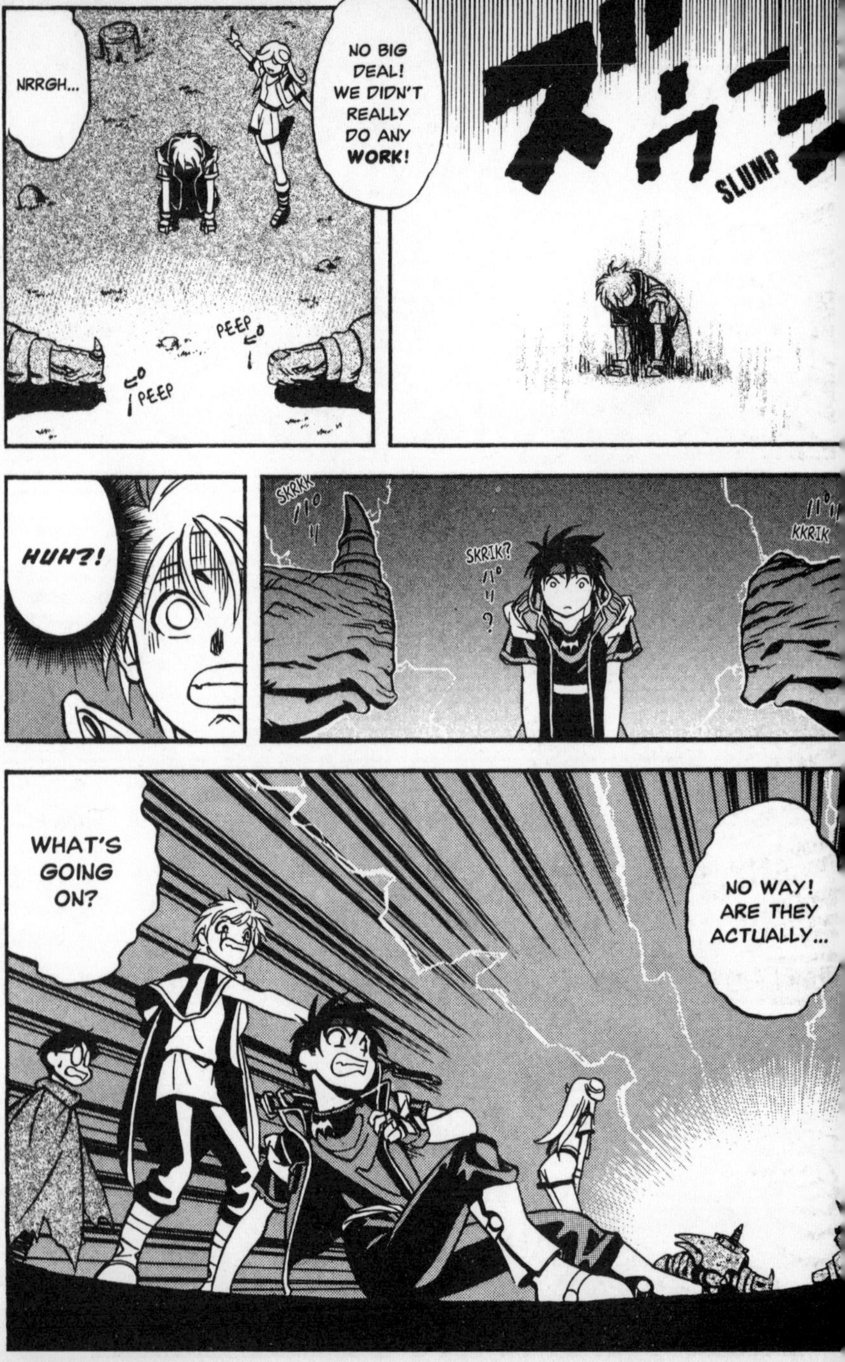
SLUMP
NO BIG DEAL! WE DIDN'T REALLY DO ANY **WORK**!
NRRGH...
PEEP
PEEP
KKRIK
SKRIK?
SKRKK
HUH?!
NO WAY! ARE THEY ACTUALLY...
WHAT'S GOING ON?

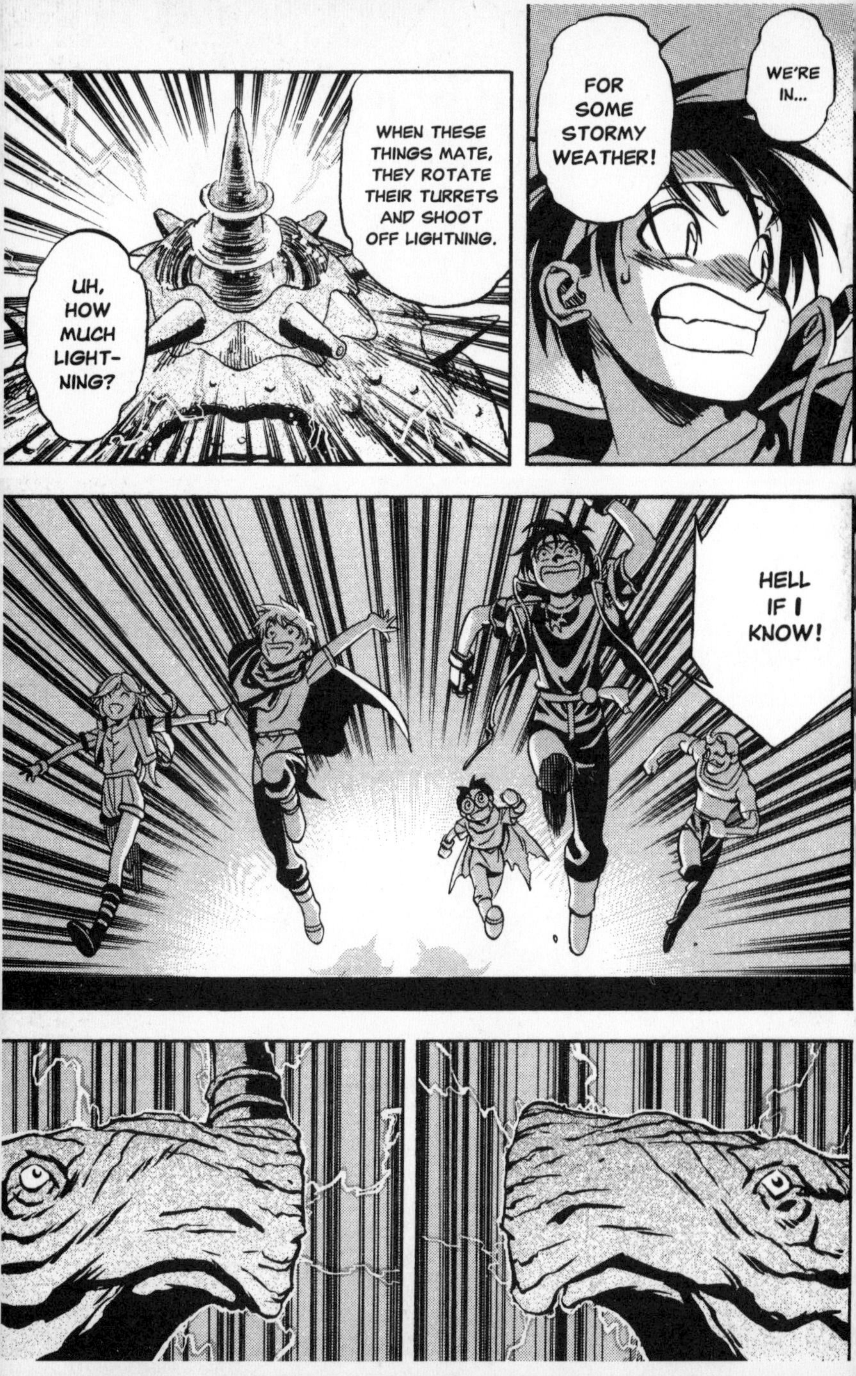
WE'RE IN...
FOR SOME STORMY WEATHER!
WHEN THESE THINGS MATE, THEY ROTATE THEIR TURRETS AND SHOOT OFF LIGHTNING.
UH, HOW MUCH LIGHT-NING?
HELL IF I KNOW!

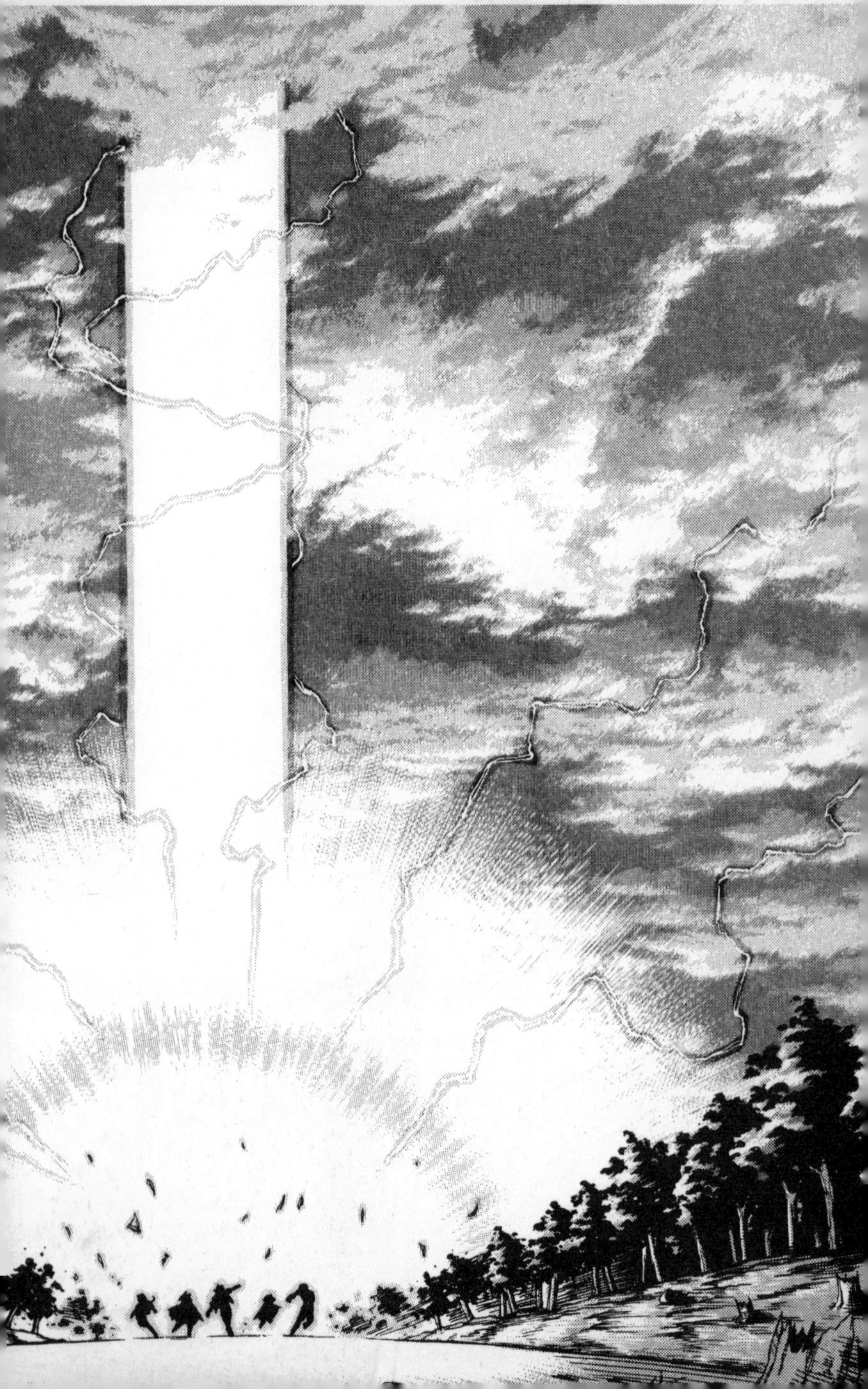

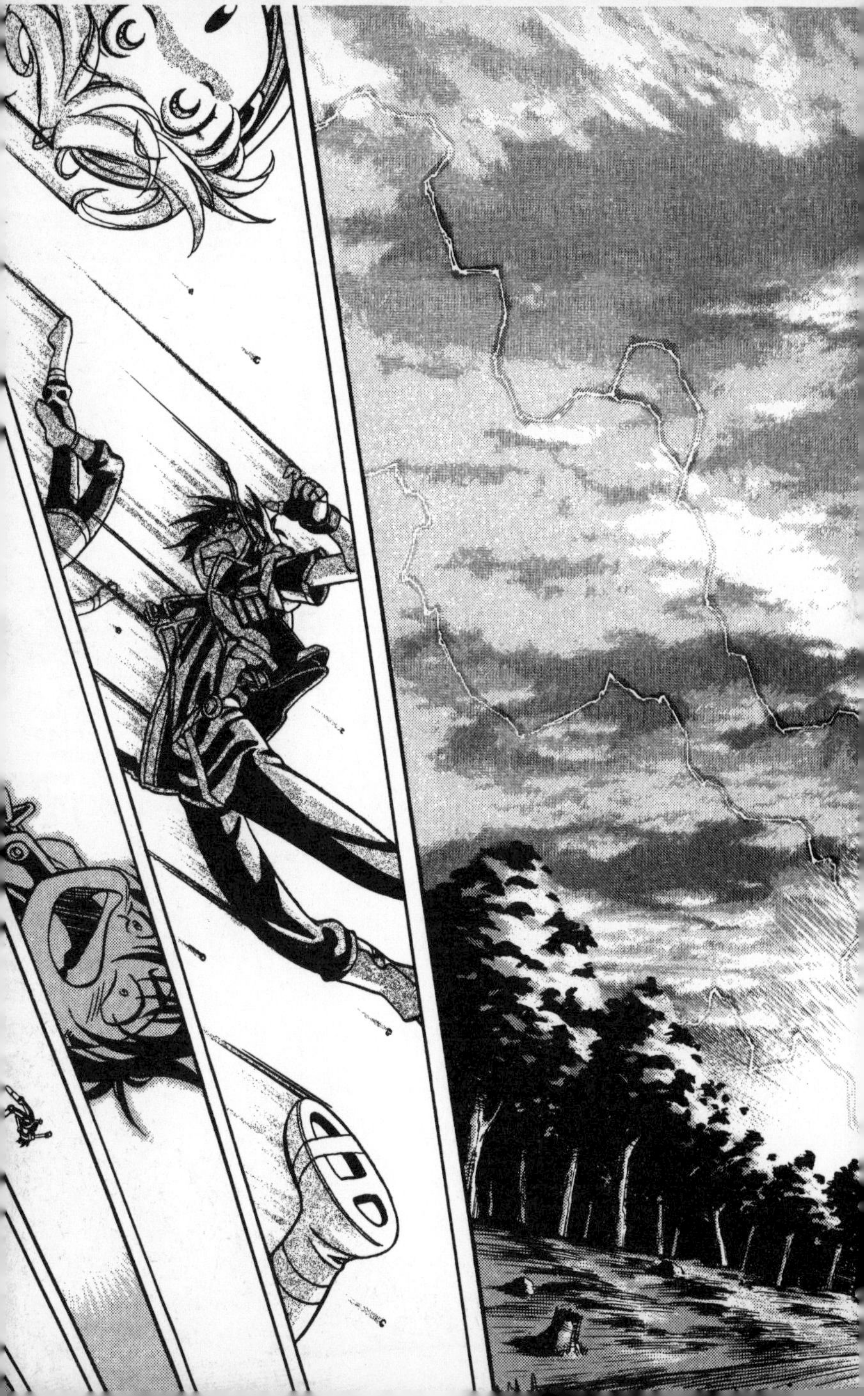

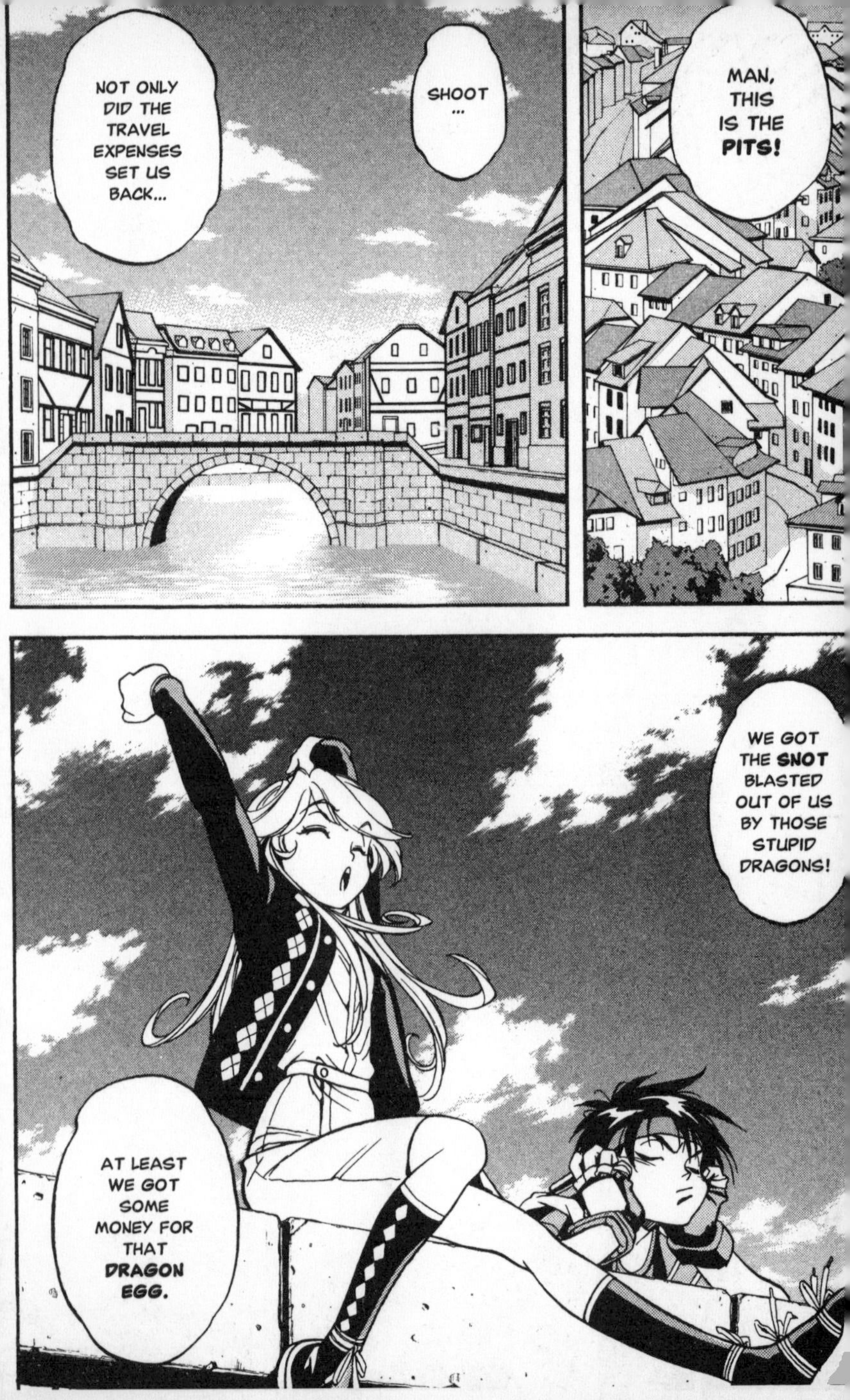
MAN, THIS IS THE **PITS!**
SHOOT ...
NOT ONLY DID THE TRAVEL EXPENSES SET US BACK...
WE GOT THE **SNOT** BLASTED OUT OF US BY THOSE STUPID DRAGONS!
AT LEAST WE GOT SOME MONEY FOR THAT **DRAGON EGG.**

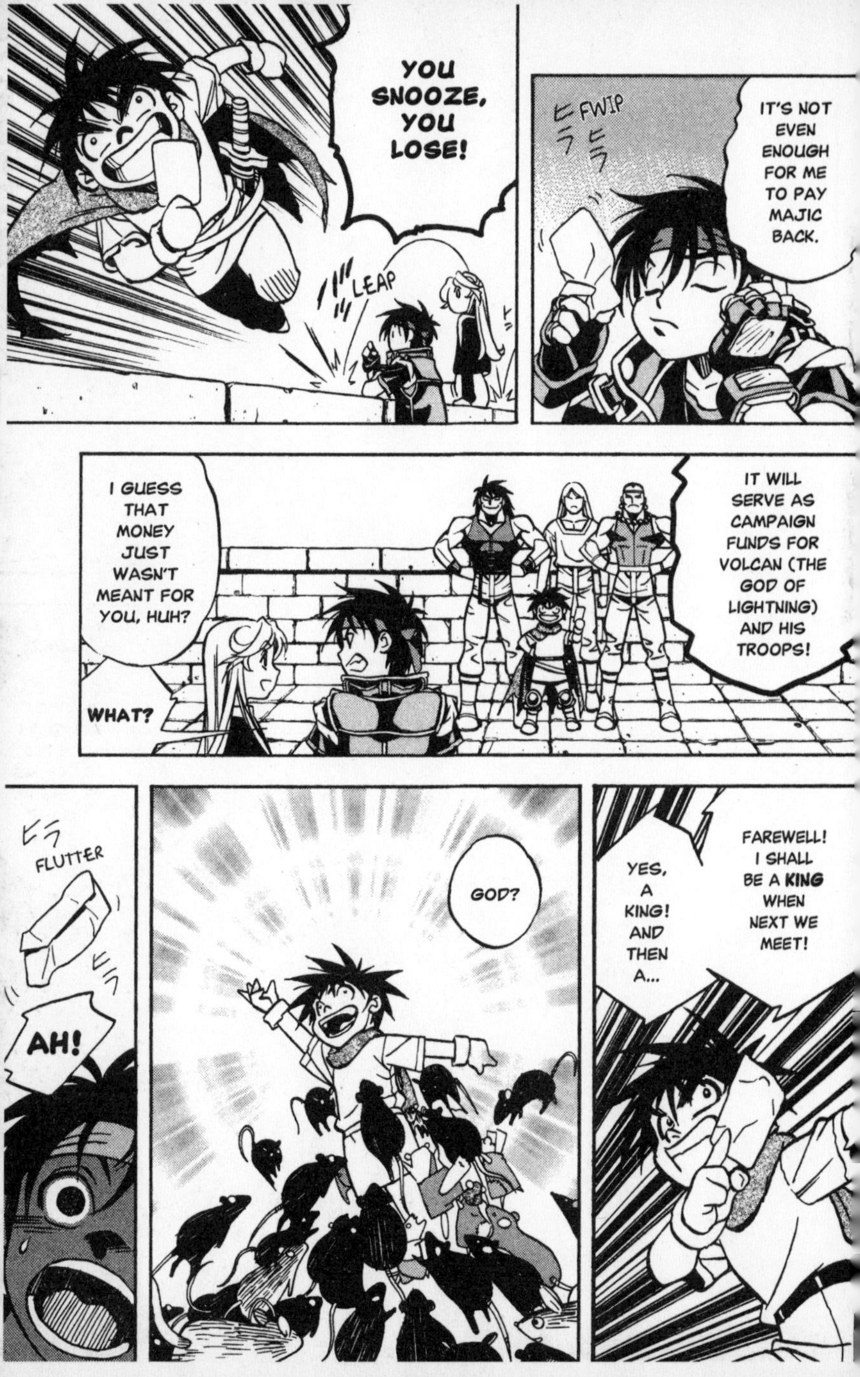

ヒラ FWIP ヒラ
IT'S NOT EVEN ENOUGH FOR ME TO PAY MAJIC BACK.
YOU SNOOZE, YOU LOSE!
LEAP
IT WILL SERVE AS CAMPAIGN FUNDS FOR VOLCAN (THE GOD OF LIGHTNING) AND HIS TROOPS!
I GUESS THAT MONEY JUST WASN'T MEANT FOR YOU, HUH?
WHAT?
FAREWELL! I SHALL BE A **KING** WHEN NEXT WE MEET!
YES, A KING! AND THEN A...
GOD?
ヒラ FLUTTER ヒラ
AH!

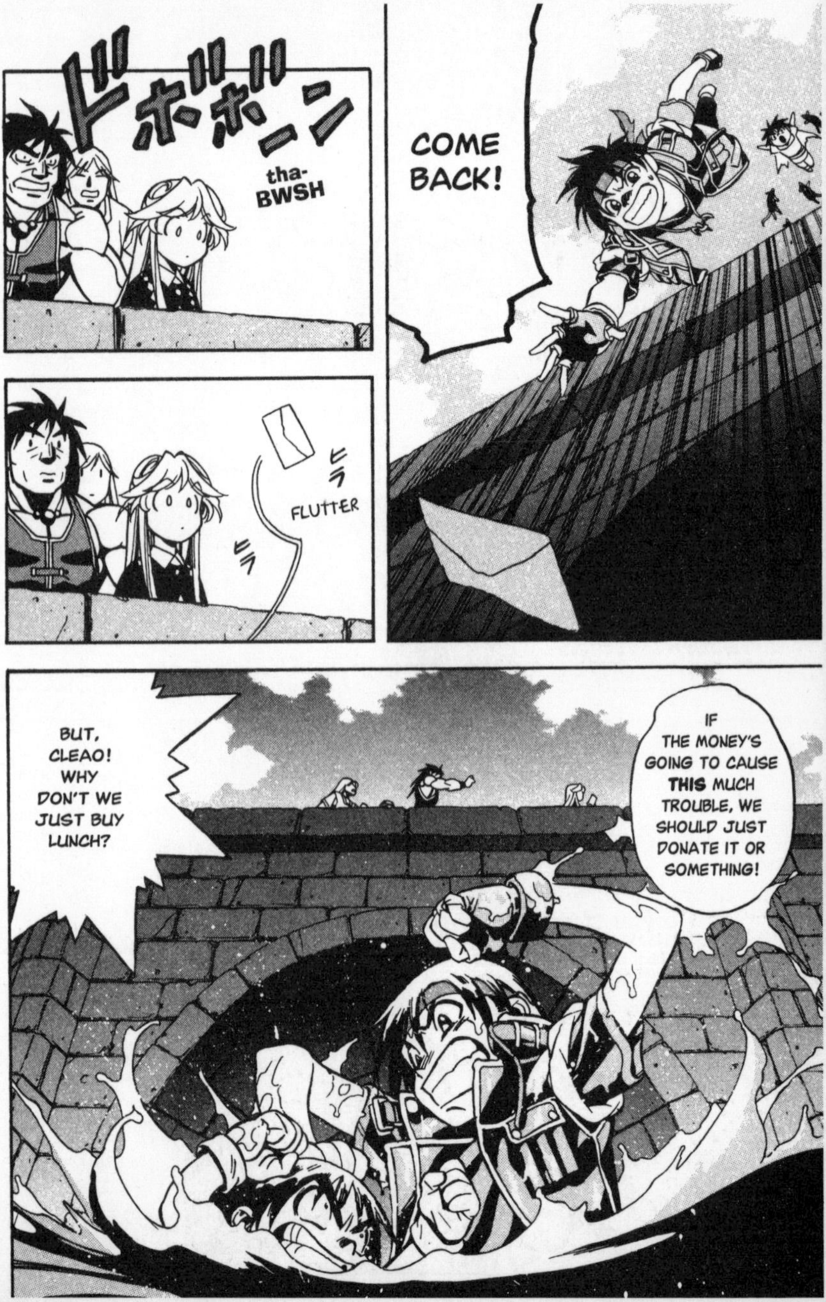
COME BACK!
ドボボーン
tha-BWSH
ヒラ
FLUTTER
ヒラ
IF THE MONEY'S GOING TO CAUSE **THIS** MUCH TROUBLE, WE SHOULD JUST DONATE IT OR SOMETHING!
BUT, CLEAO! WHY DON'T WE JUST BUY LUNCH?

ORPHEN

The Demon Witch

NUZZLE
HUH?!
PURRR

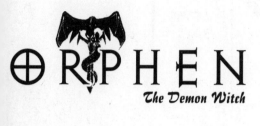

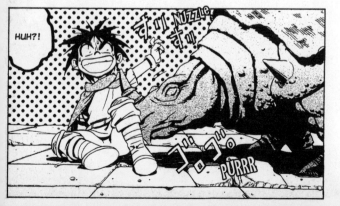

ORPHEN

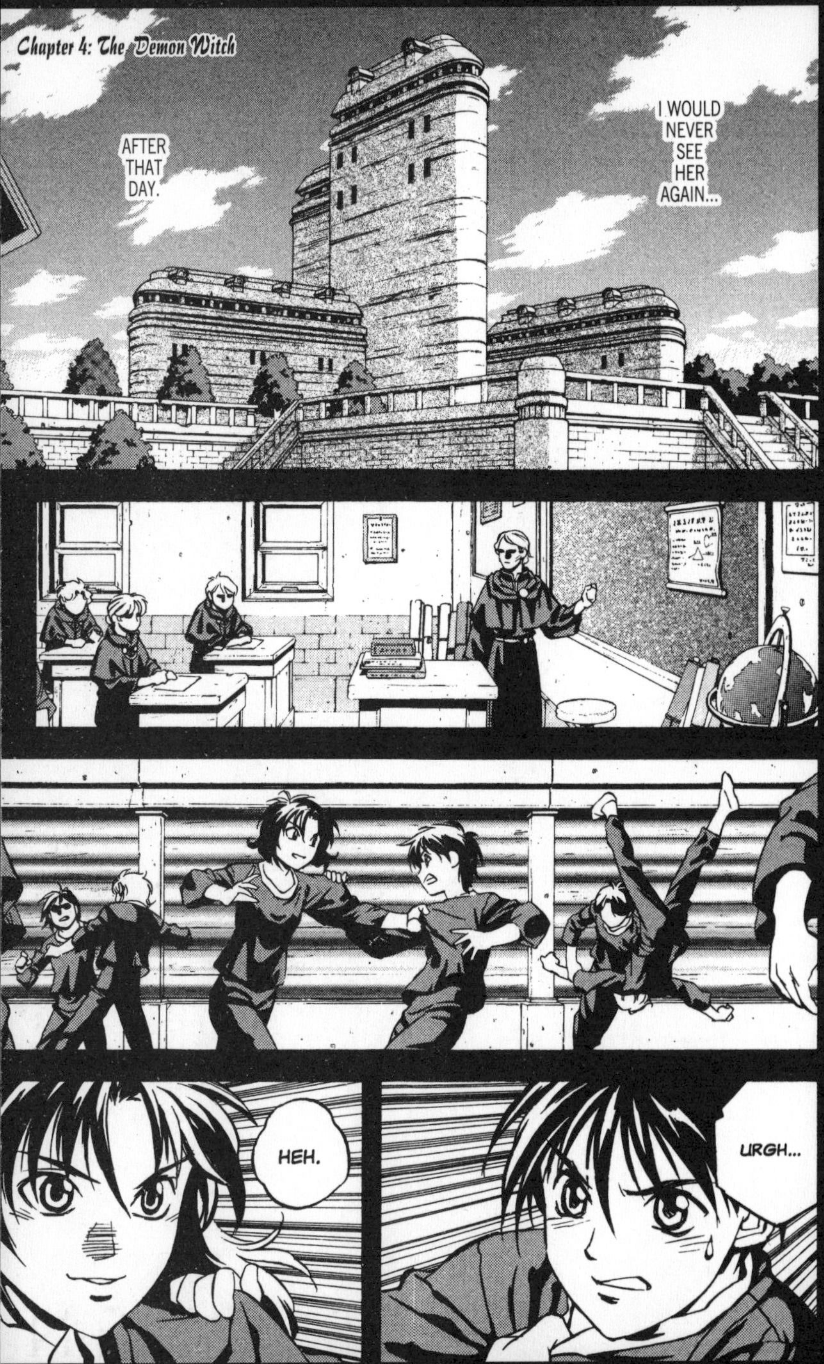
Chapter 4: The Demon Witch
AFTER THAT DAY,
I WOULD NEVER SEE HER AGAIN...
HEH.
URGH...

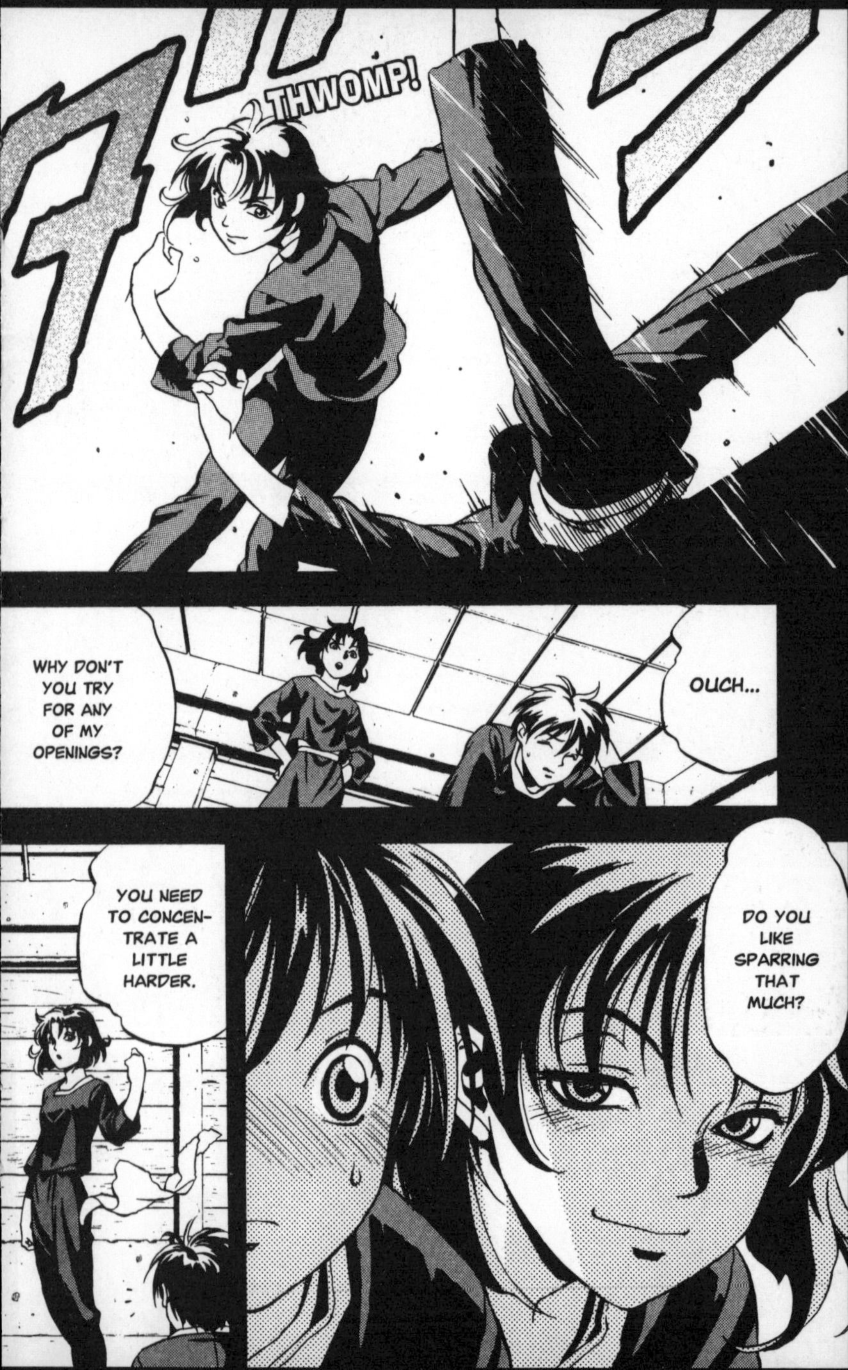
THWOMP!
OUCH...
WHY DON'T YOU TRY FOR ANY OF MY OPENINGS?
DO YOU LIKE SPARRING THAT MUCH?
YOU NEED TO CONCEN-TRATE A LITTLE HARDER.

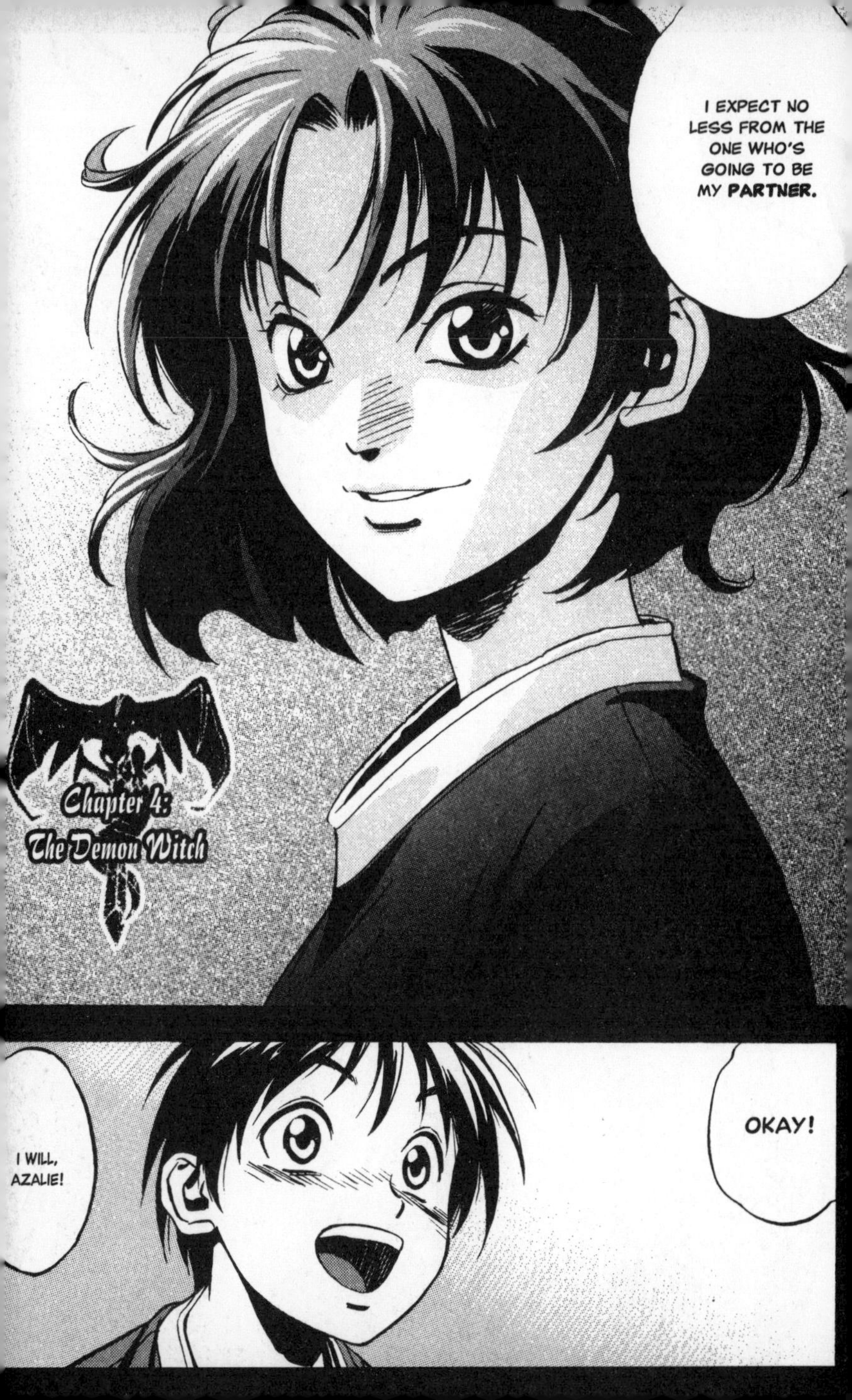
I EXPECT NO LESS FROM THE ONE WHO'S GOING TO BE MY **PARTNER.**
Chapter 4: The Demon Witch
OKAY!
I WILL, AZALIE!

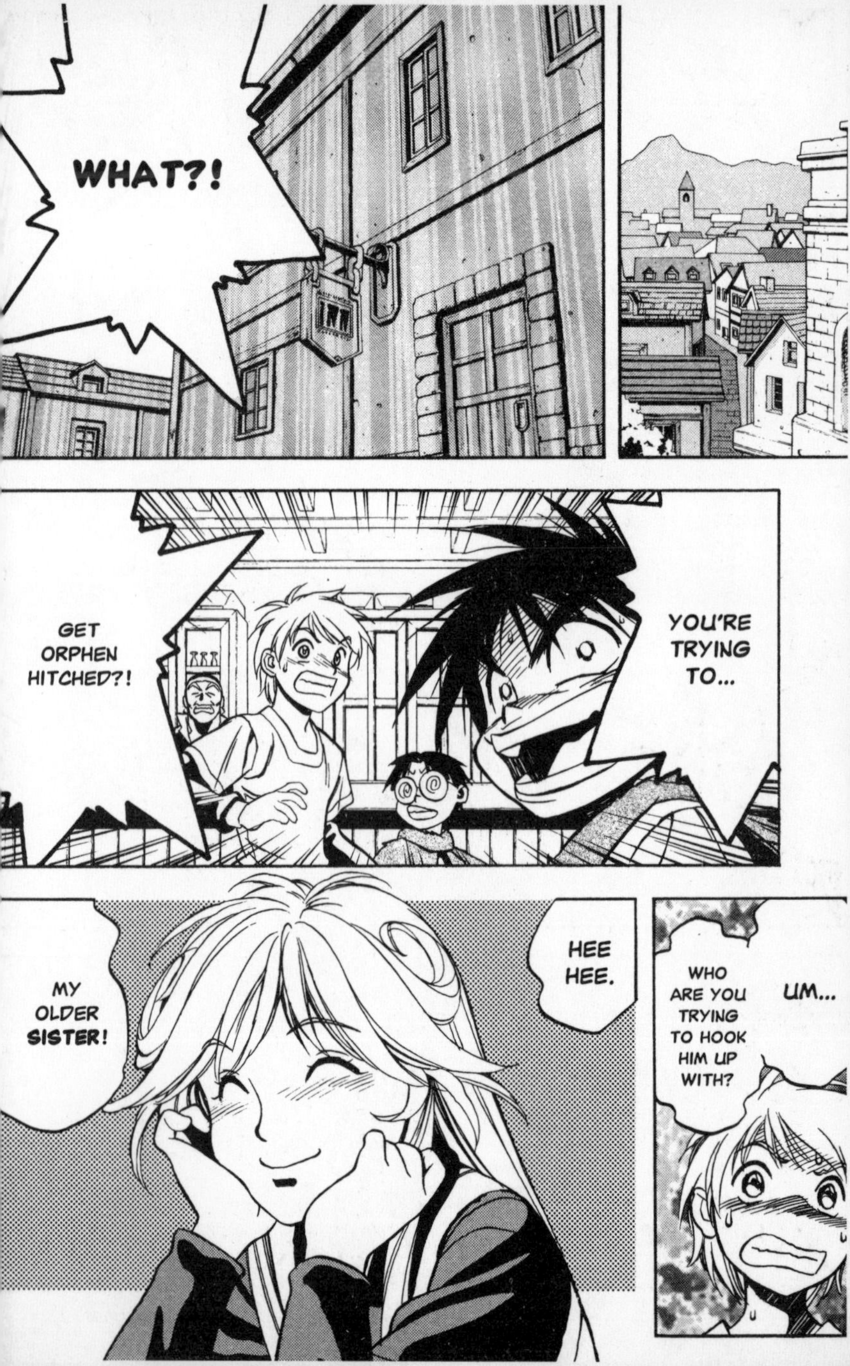
WHAT?!
YOU'RE TRYING TO...
GET ORPHEN HITCHED?!
UM...
WHO ARE YOU TRYING TO HOOK HIM UP WITH?
HEE HEE.
MY OLDER SISTER!

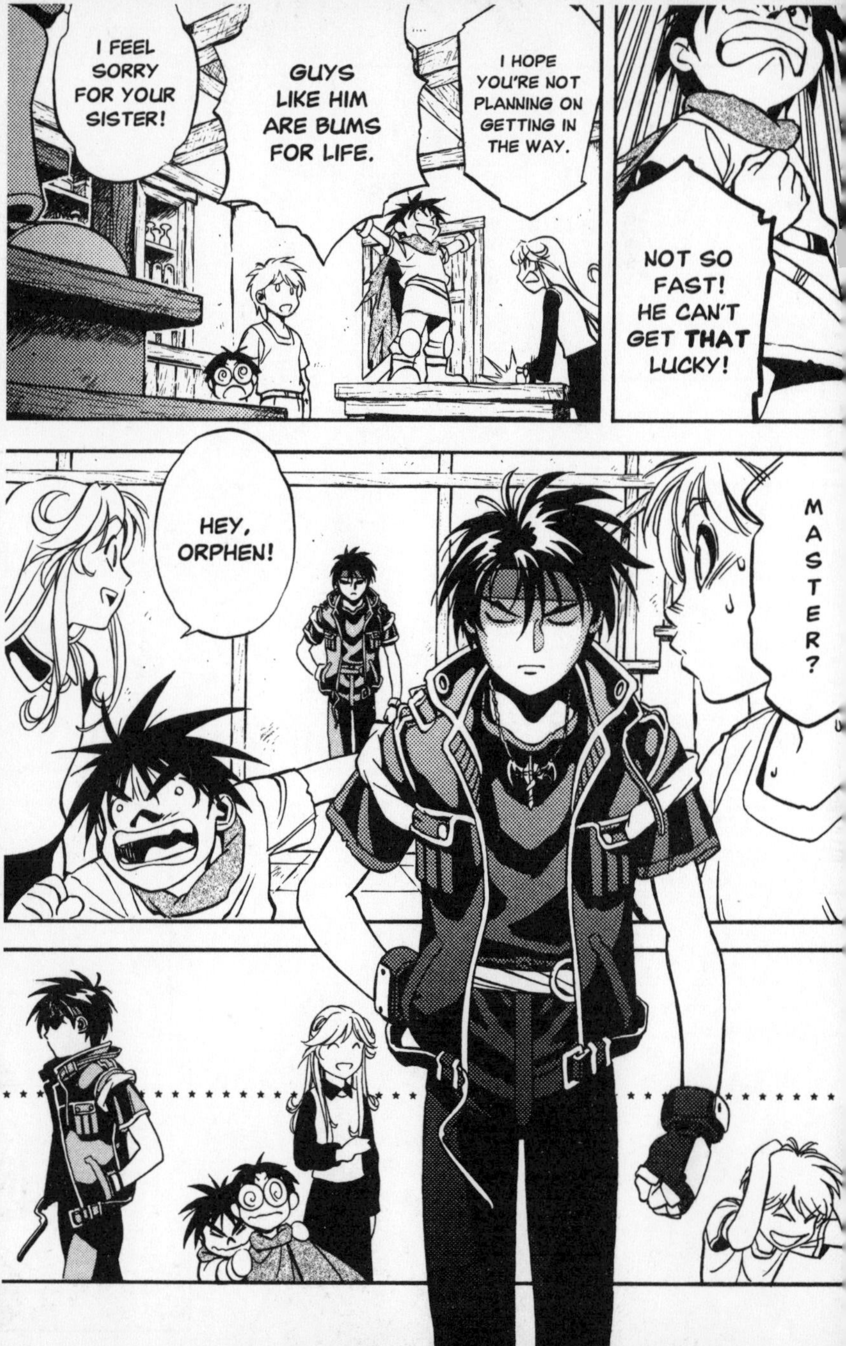
I FEEL SORRY FOR YOUR SISTER!
GUYS LIKE HIM ARE BUMS FOR LIFE.
I HOPE YOU'RE NOT PLANNING ON GETTING IN THE WAY.
NOT SO FAST! HE CAN'T GET THAT LUCKY!
HEY, ORPHEN!
MASTER?

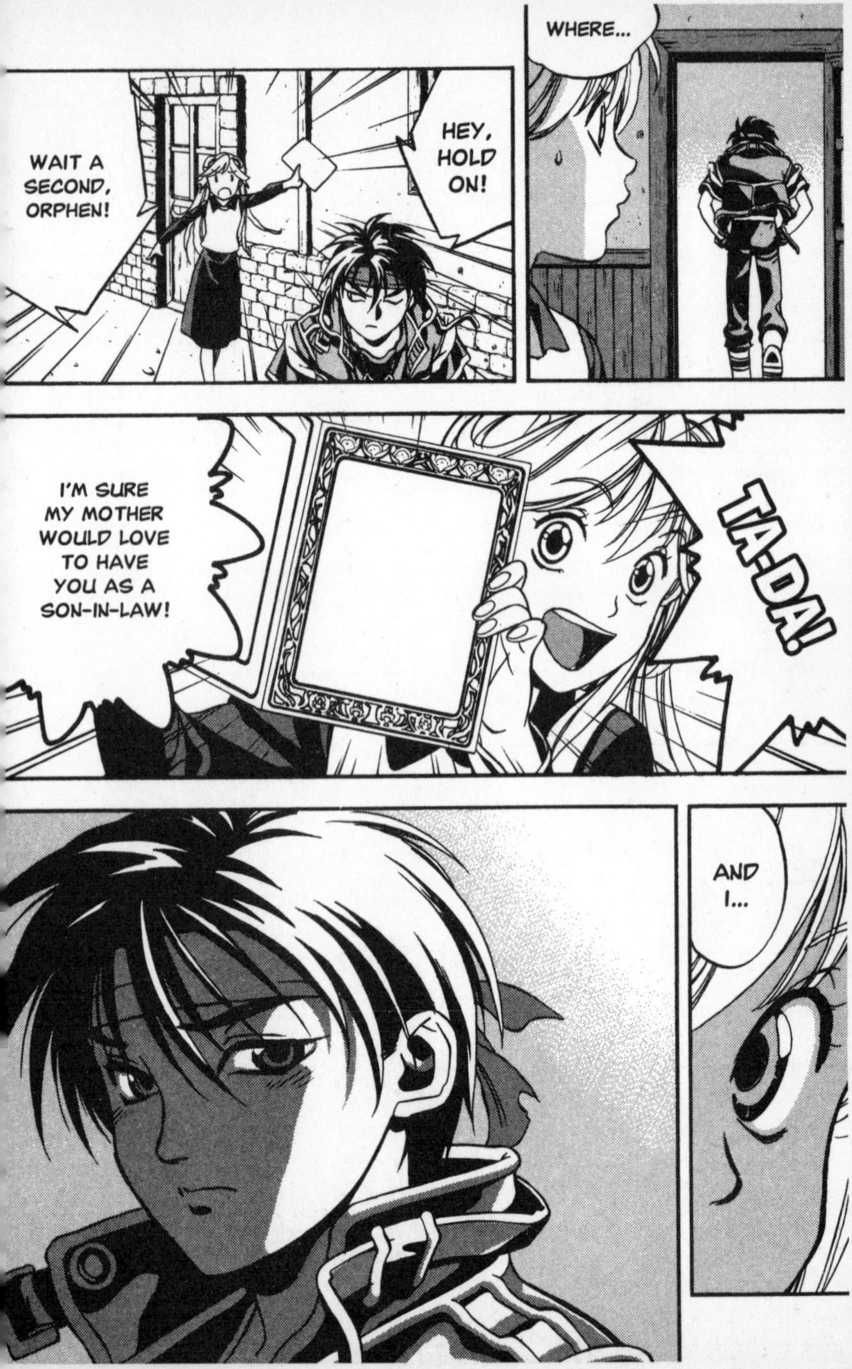
WAIT A SECOND, ORPHEN!
HEY, HOLD ON!
WHERE...
I'M SURE MY MOTHER WOULD LOVE TO HAVE YOU AS A SON-IN-LAW!
TA-DA!
AND I...

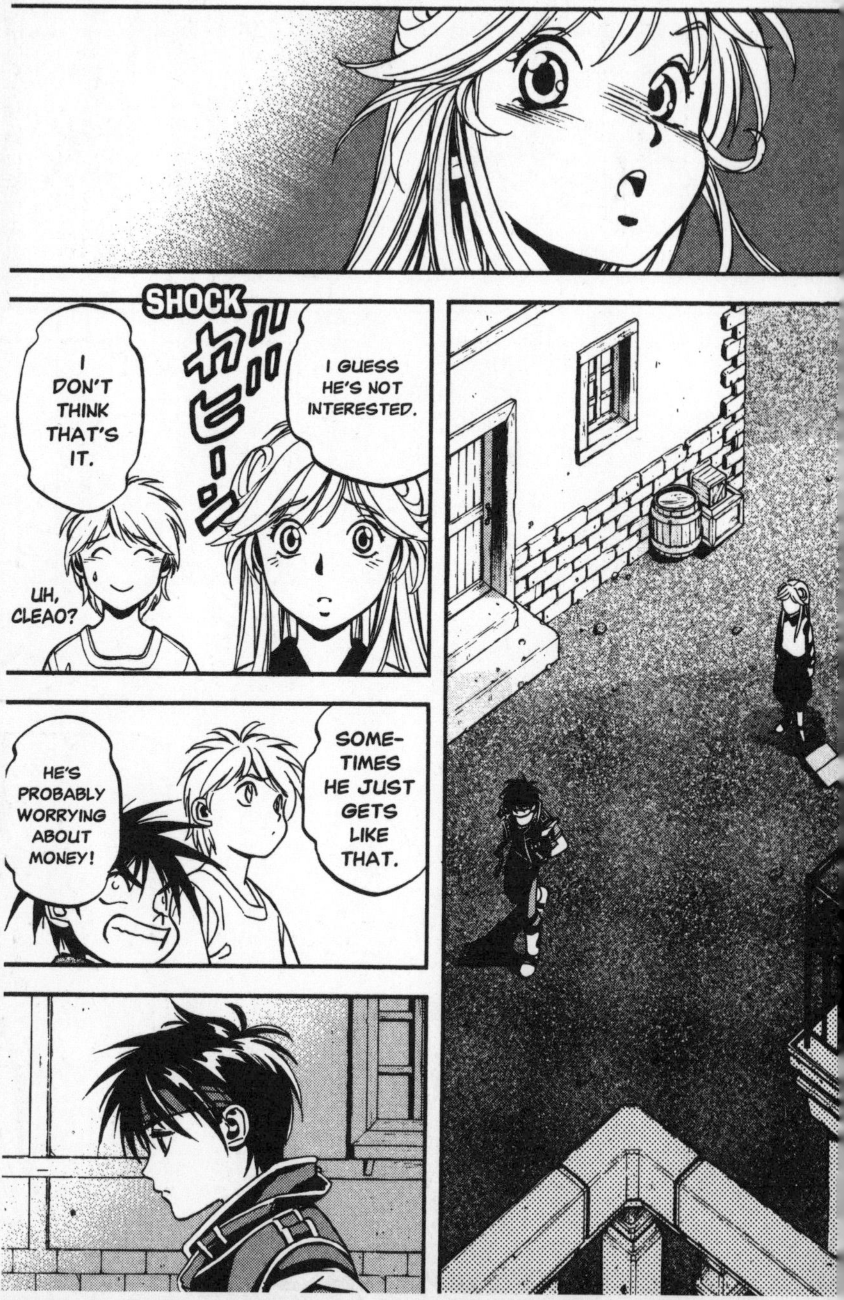
I GUESS HE'S NOT INTERESTED.
SHOCK
I DON'T THINK THAT'S IT.
UH, CLEAO?
SOME-TIMES HE JUST GETS LIKE THAT.
HE'S PROBABLY WORRYING ABOUT MONEY!

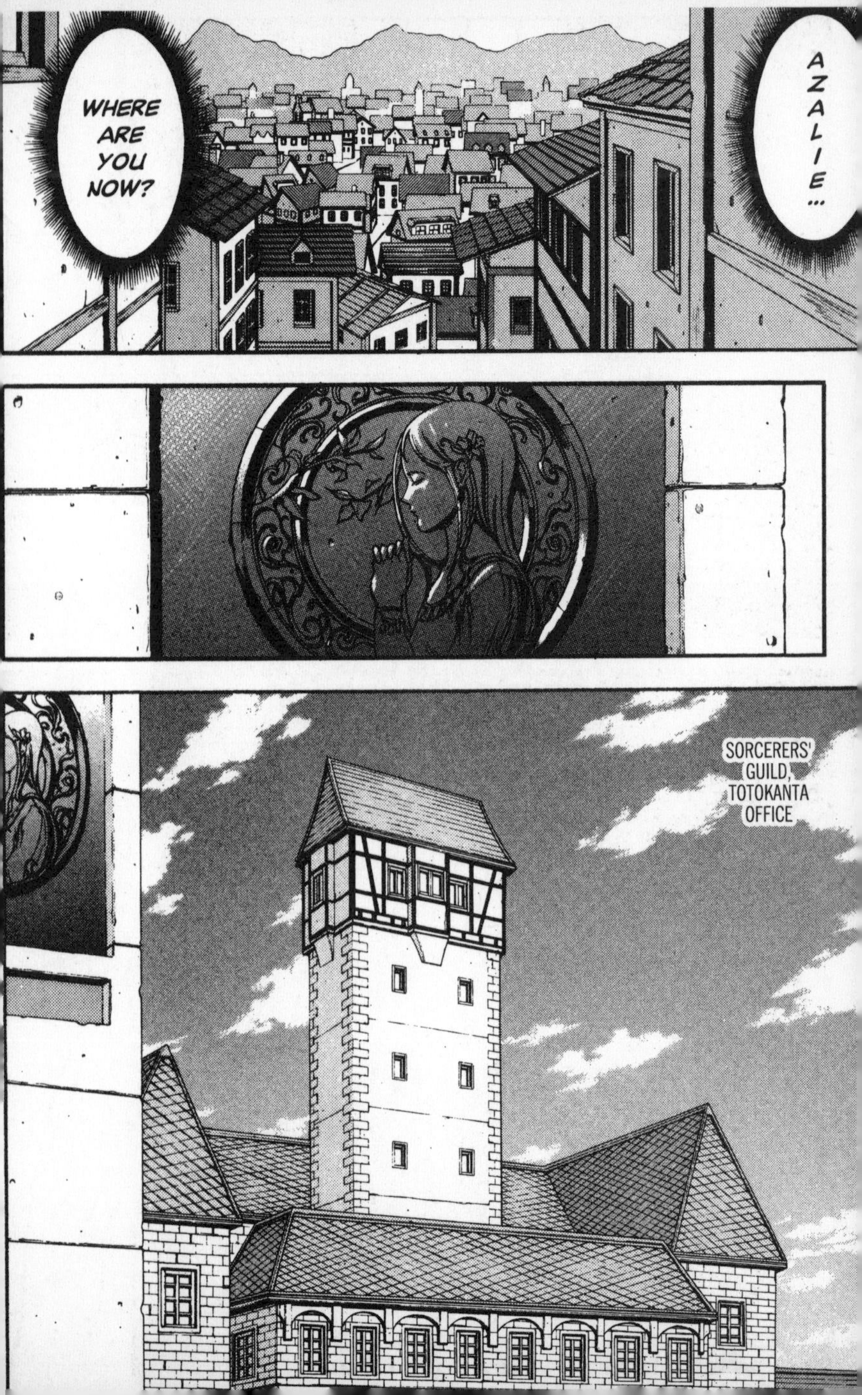
AZALIE...
WHERE ARE YOU NOW?
SORCERERS' GUILD, TOTOKANTA OFFICE

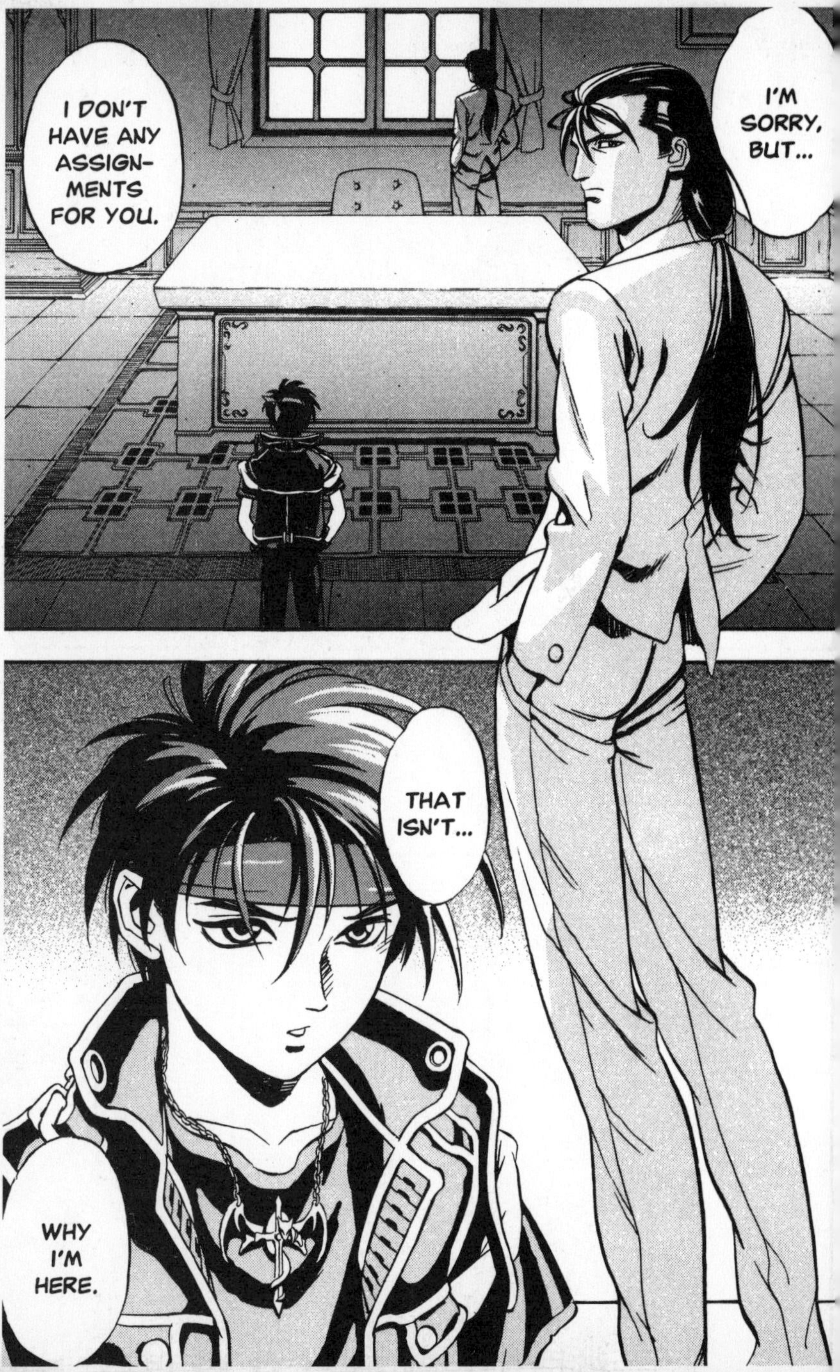
I'M SORRY, BUT...
I DON'T HAVE ANY ASSIGN- MENTS FOR YOU.
THAT ISN'T...
WHY I'M HERE.

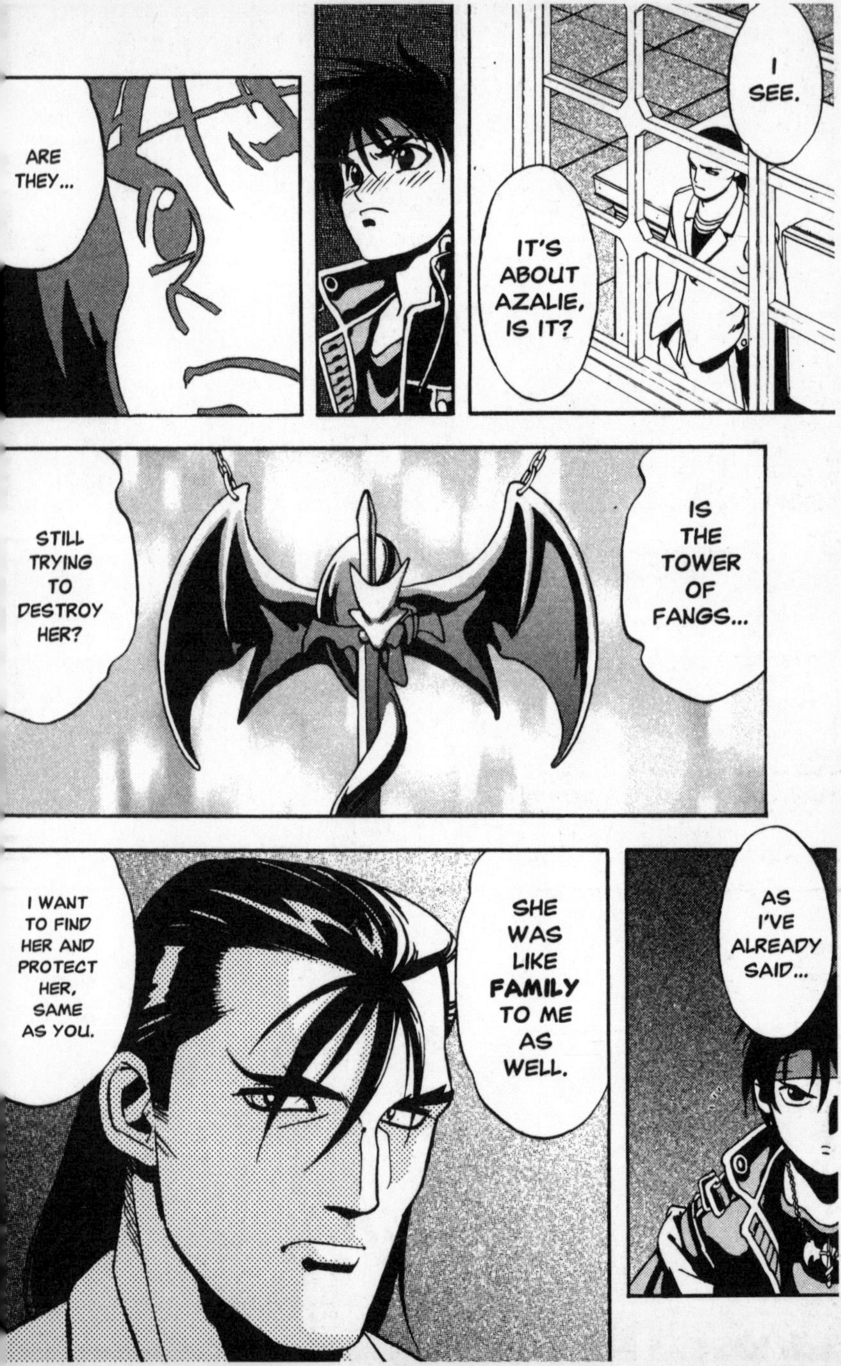
I SEE.
IT'S ABOUT AZALIE, IS IT?
ARE THEY...
IS THE TOWER OF FANGS...
STILL TRYING TO DESTROY HER?
AS I'VE ALREADY SAID...
SHE WAS LIKE **FAMILY** TO ME AS WELL.
I WANT TO FIND HER AND PROTECT HER, SAME AS YOU.

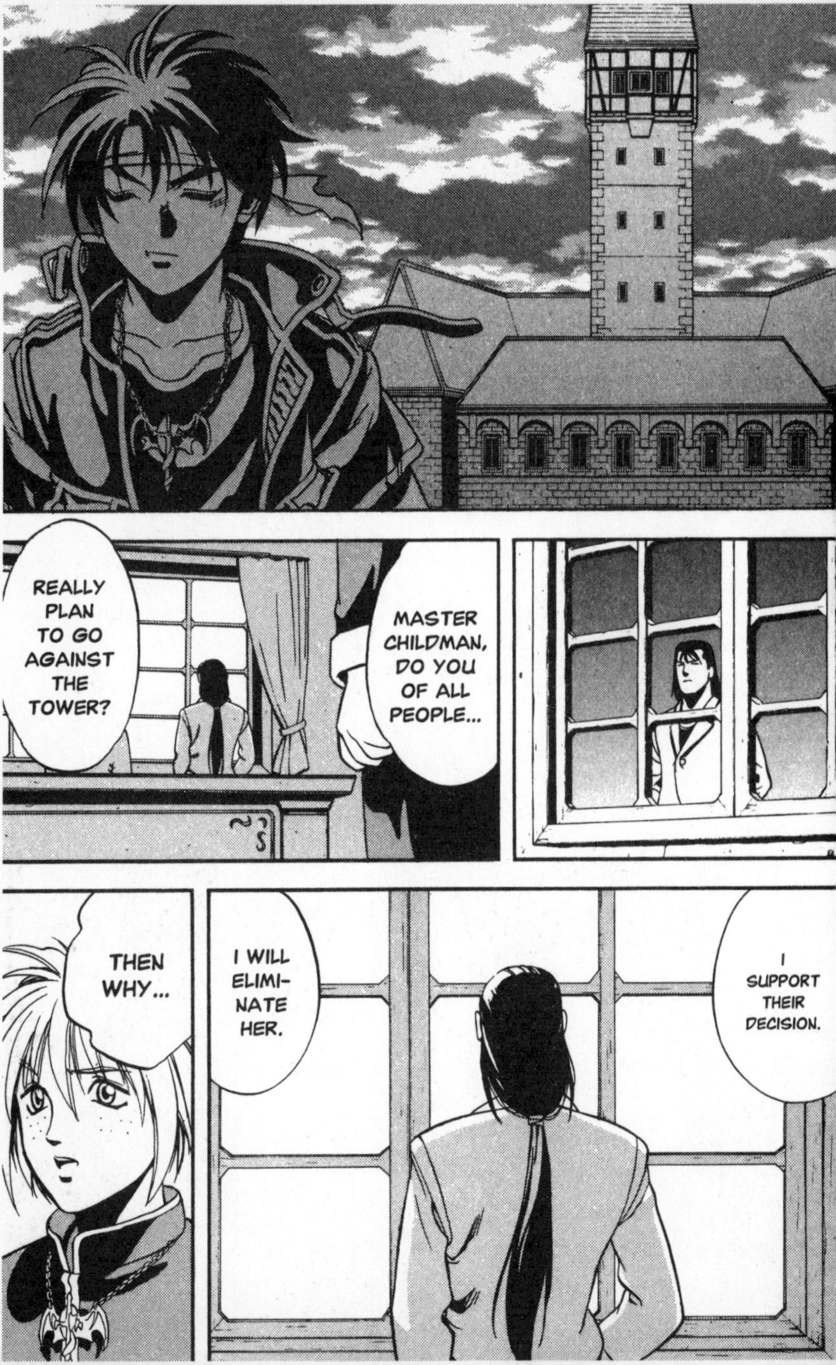
MASTER CHILDMAN, DO YOU OF ALL PEOPLE...
REALLY PLAN TO GO AGAINST THE TOWER?
I SUPPORT THEIR DECISION.
I WILL ELIMI-NATE HER.
THEN WHY...

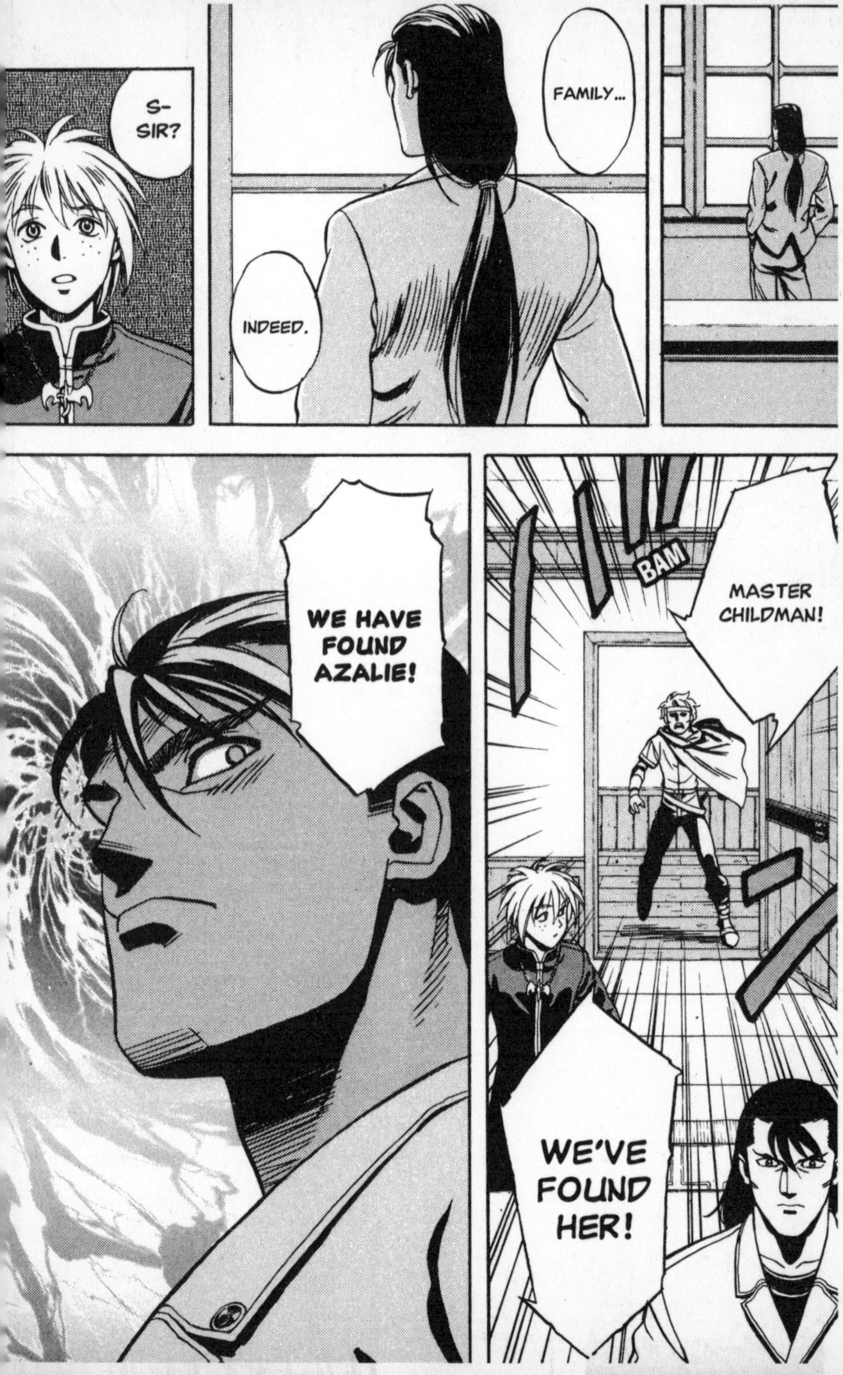
S-SIR?
FAMILY...
INDEED.
WE HAVE FOUND AZALIE!
BAM
MASTER CHILDMAN!
WE'VE FOUND HER!

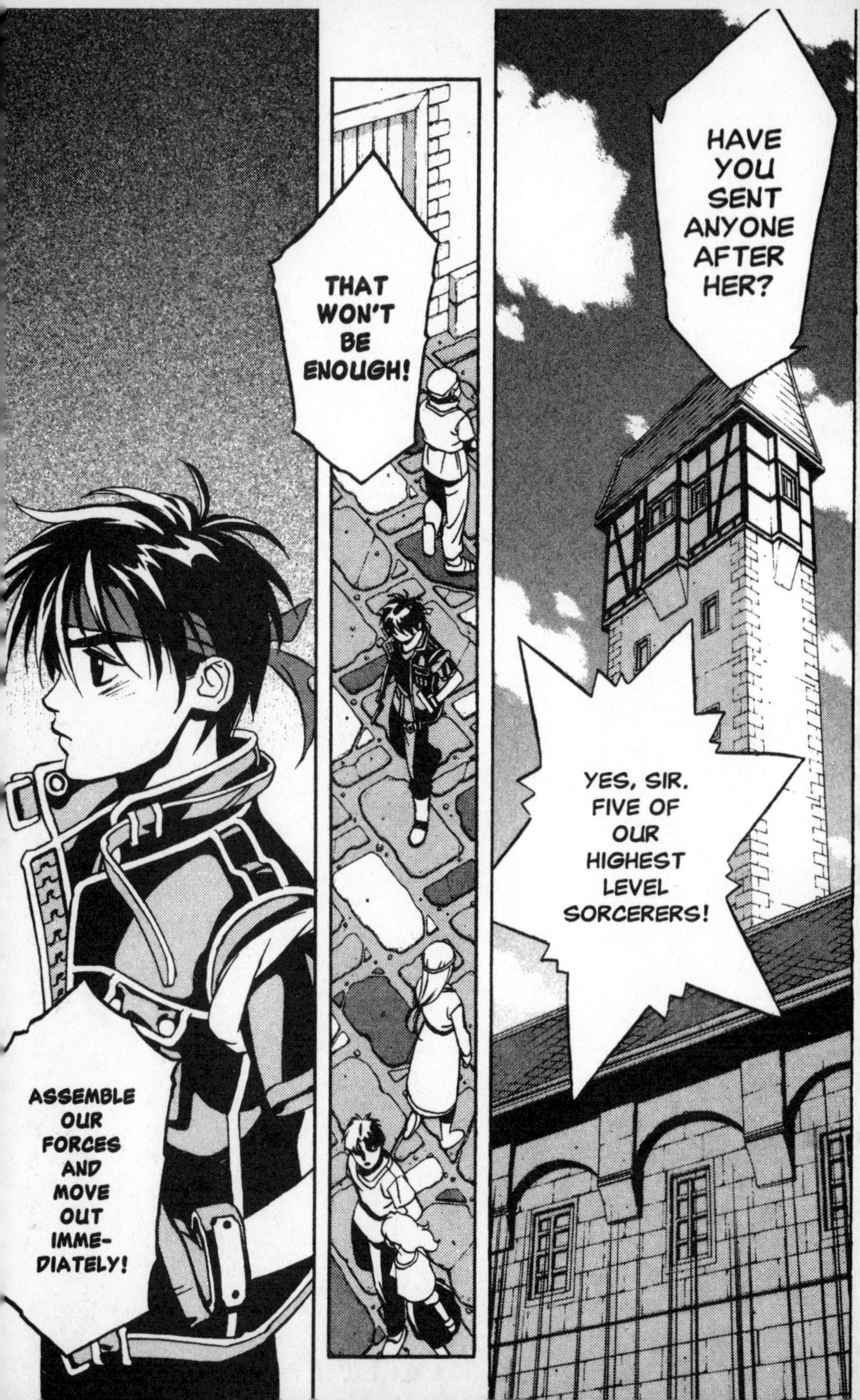
HAVE YOU SENT ANYONE AFTER HER?
YES, SIR. FIVE OF OUR HIGHEST LEVEL SORCERERS!
THAT WON'T BE ENOUGH!
ASSEMBLE OUR FORCES AND MOVE OUT IMME-DIATELY!

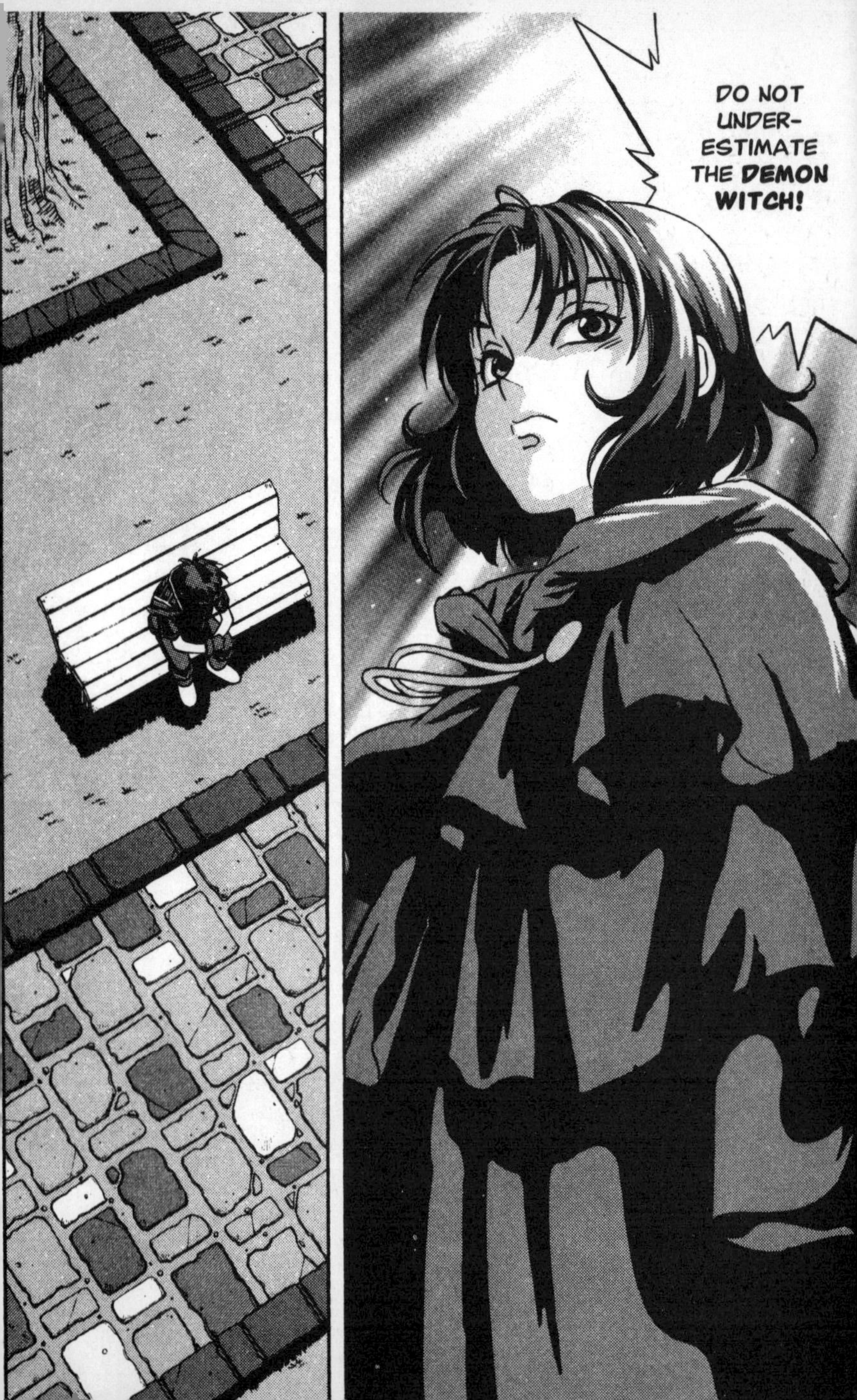
DO NOT UNDER-ESTIMATE THE DEMON WITCH!

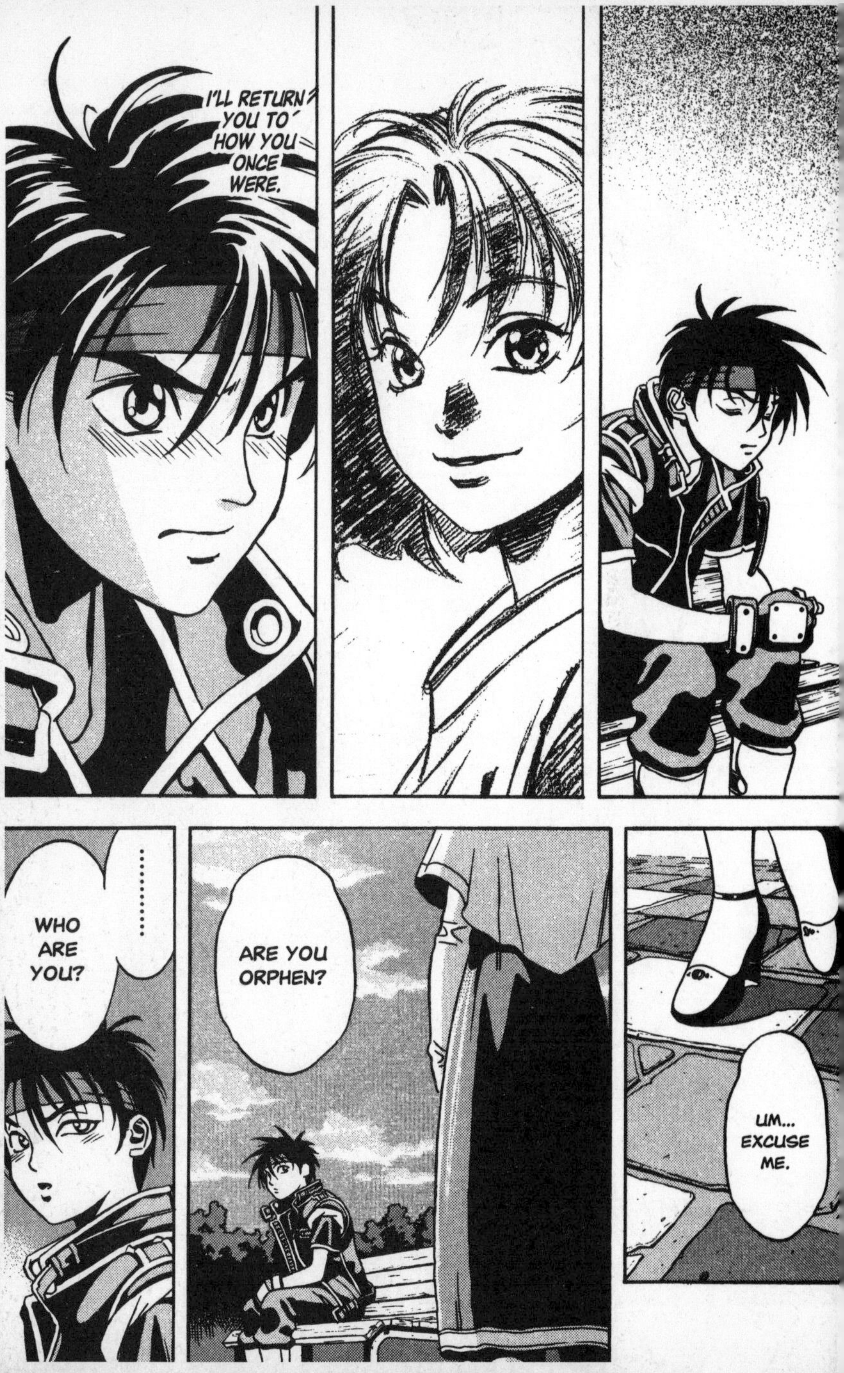
I'LL RETURN YOU TO HOW YOU ONCE WERE.
UM... EXCUSE ME.
ARE YOU ORPHEN?
....
WHO ARE YOU?

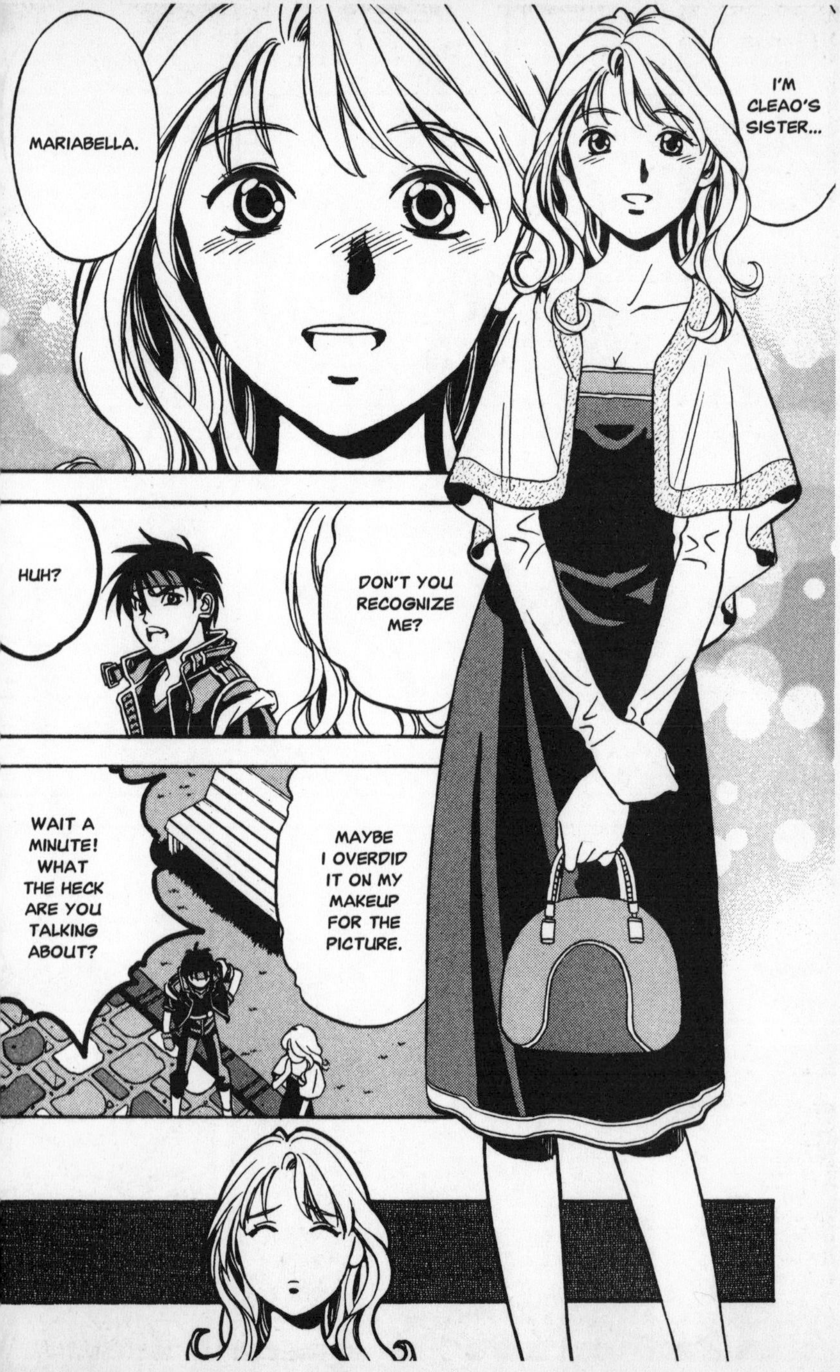
I'M CLEAO'S SISTER...
MARIABELLA.
DON'T YOU RECOGNIZE ME?
HUH?
MAYBE I OVERDID IT ON MY MAKEUP FOR THE PICTURE.
WAIT A MINUTE! WHAT THE HECK ARE YOU TALKING ABOUT?

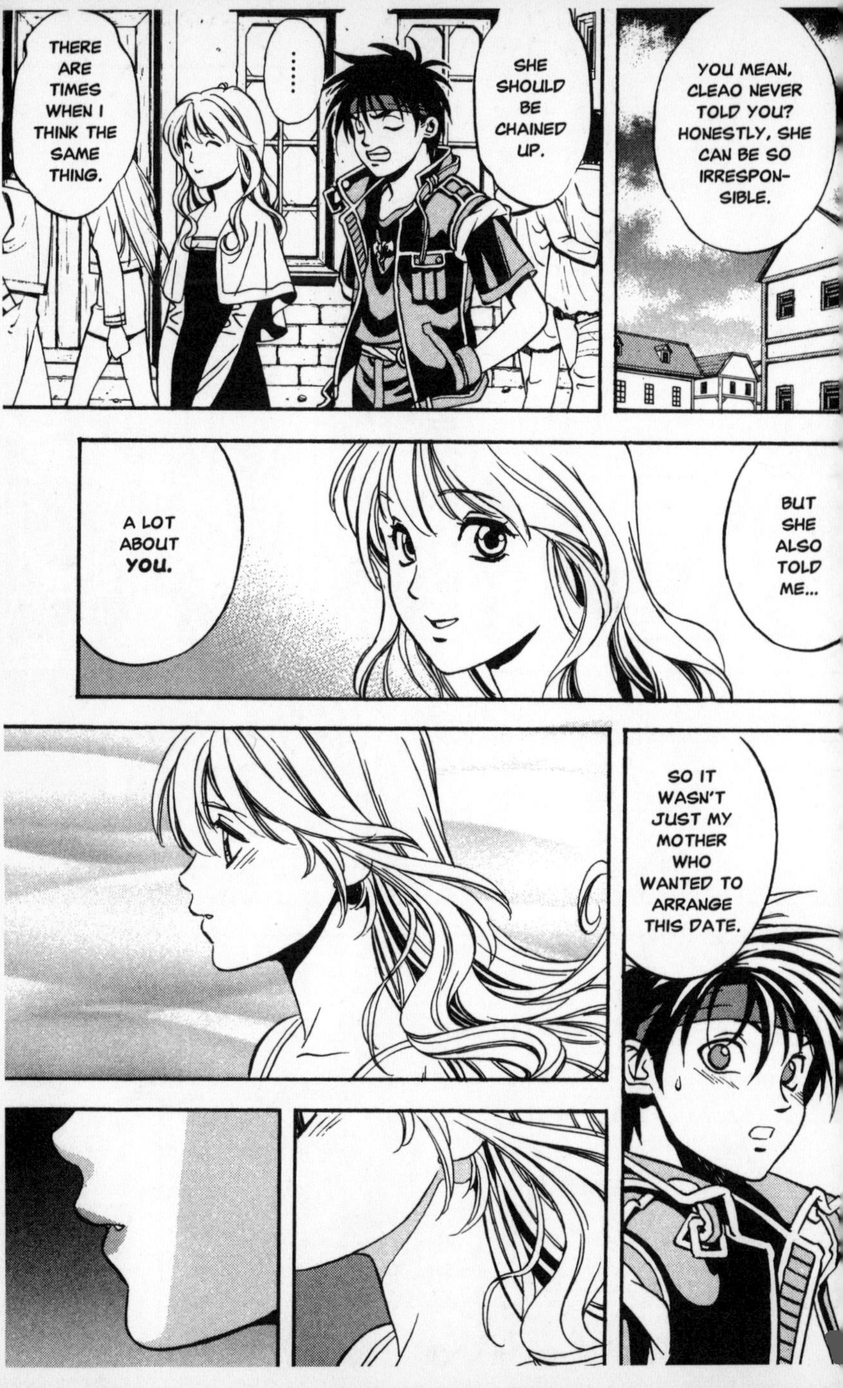
YOU MEAN, CLEAO NEVER TOLD YOU? HONESTLY, SHE CAN BE SO IRRESPON-SIBLE.
SHE SHOULD BE CHAINED UP.
......
THERE ARE TIMES WHEN I THINK THE SAME THING.
BUT SHE ALSO TOLD ME...
A LOT ABOUT **YOU.**
SO IT WASN'T JUST MY MOTHER WHO WANTED TO ARRANGE THIS DATE.

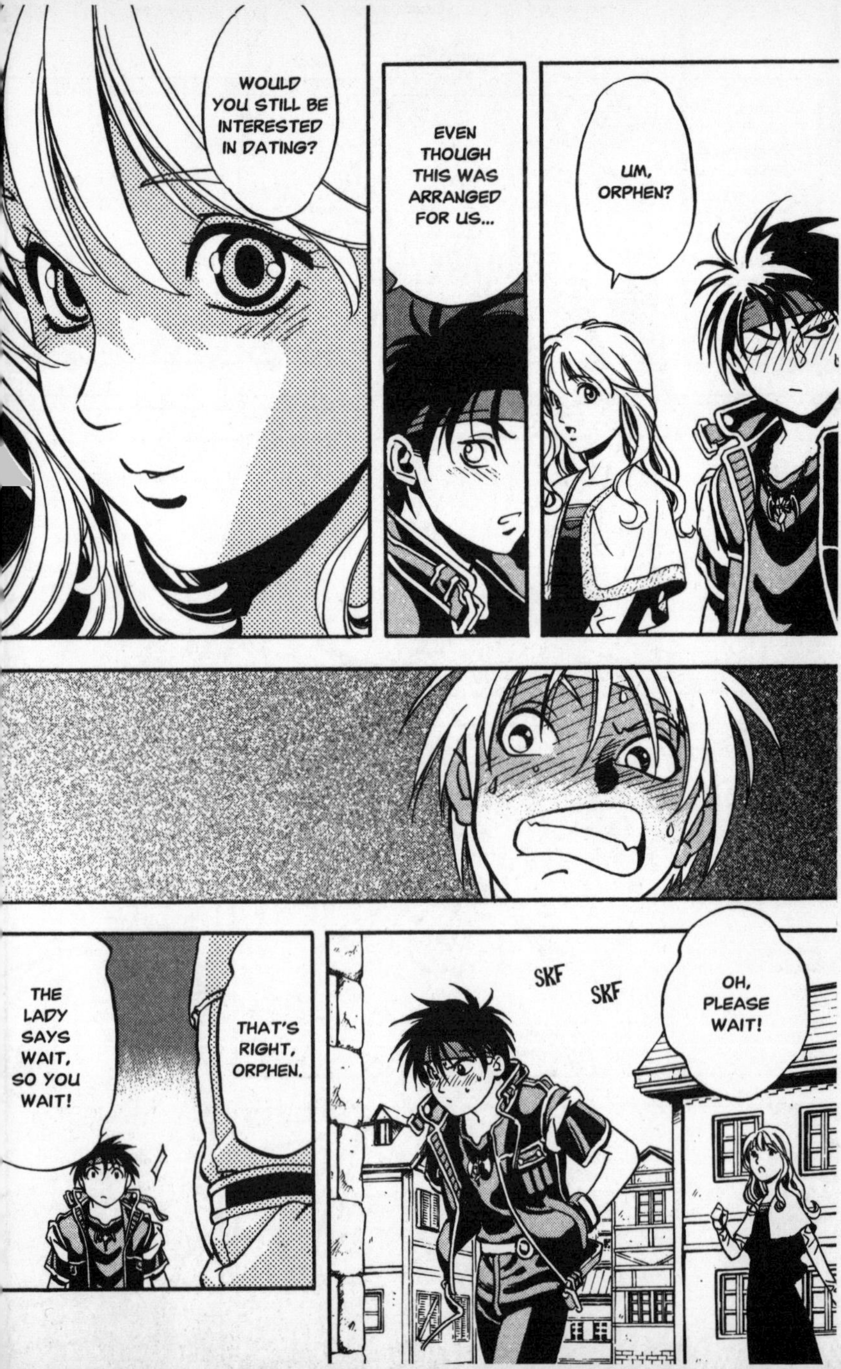
UM, ORPHEN?
EVEN THOUGH THIS WAS ARRANGED FOR US...
WOULD YOU STILL BE INTERESTED IN DATING?
OH, PLEASE WAIT!
SKF
SKF
THAT'S RIGHT, ORPHEN.
THE LADY SAYS WAIT, SO YOU WAIT!

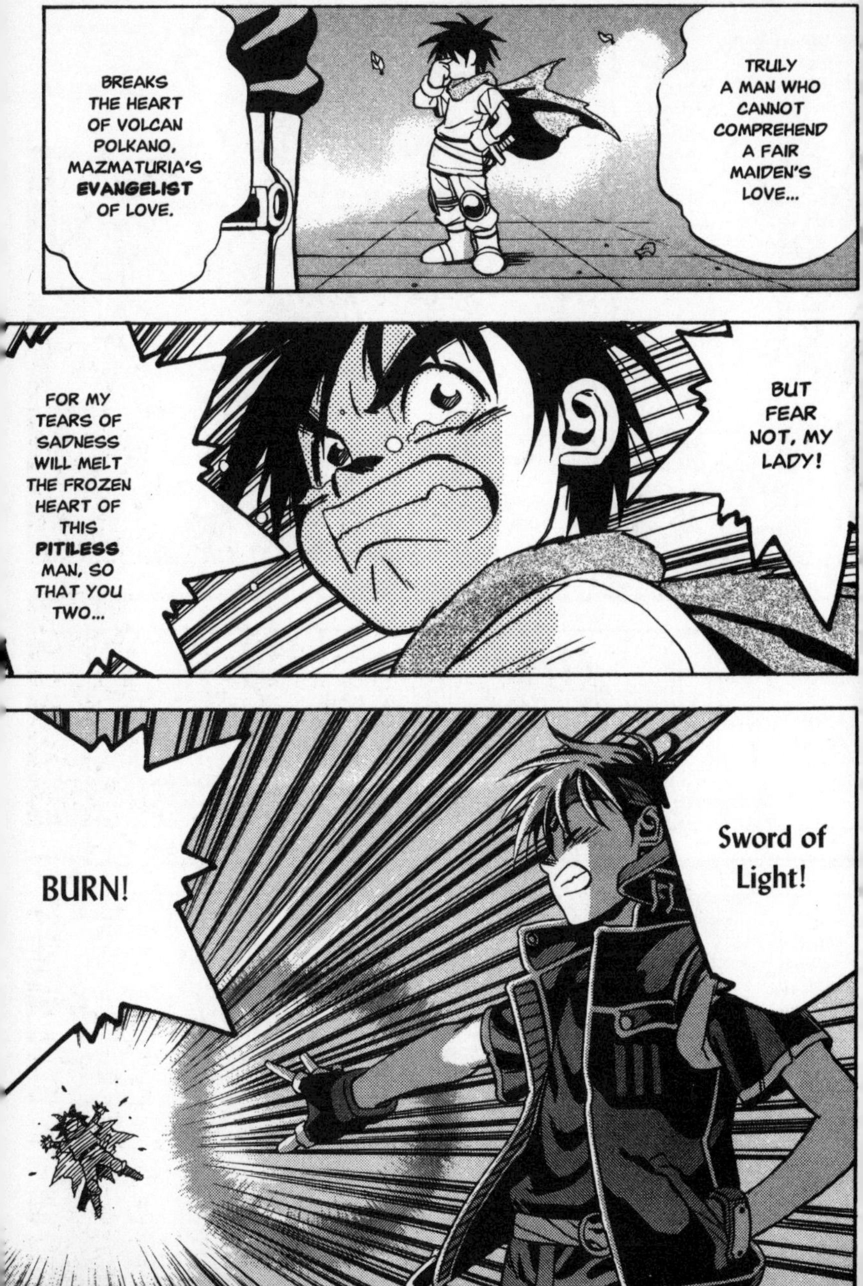
TRULY A MAN WHO CANNOT COMPREHEND A FAIR MAIDEN'S LOVE...
BREAKS THE HEART OF VOLCAN POLKANO, MAZMATURIA'S EVANGELIST OF LOVE.
BUT FEAR NOT, MY LADY!
FOR MY TEARS OF SADNESS WILL MELT THE FROZEN HEART OF THIS PITILESS MAN, SO THAT YOU TWO...
Sword of Light!
BURN!

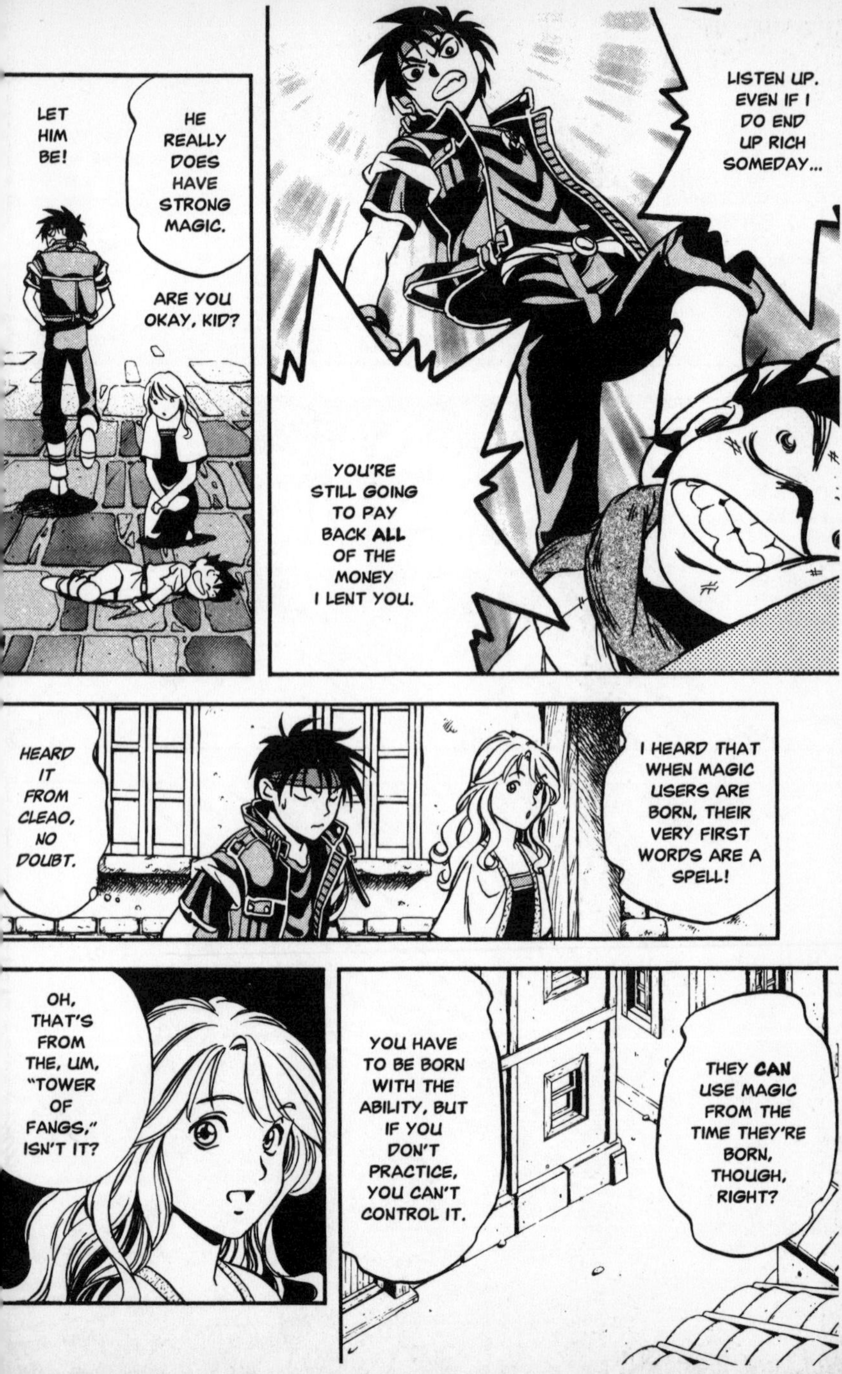
LISTEN UP. EVEN IF I DO END UP RICH SOMEDAY...
YOU'RE STILL GOING TO PAY BACK **ALL** OF THE MONEY I LENT YOU.
HE REALLY DOES HAVE STRONG MAGIC.
LET HIM BE!
ARE YOU OKAY, KID?
I HEARD THAT WHEN MAGIC USERS ARE BORN, THEIR VERY FIRST WORDS ARE A SPELL!
HEARD IT FROM CLEAO, NO DOUBT.
THEY **CAN** USE MAGIC FROM THE TIME THEY'RE BORN, THOUGH, RIGHT?
YOU HAVE TO BE BORN WITH THE ABILITY, BUT IF YOU DON'T PRACTICE, YOU CAN'T CONTROL IT.
OH, THAT'S FROM THE, UM, "TOWER OF FANGS," ISN'T IT?

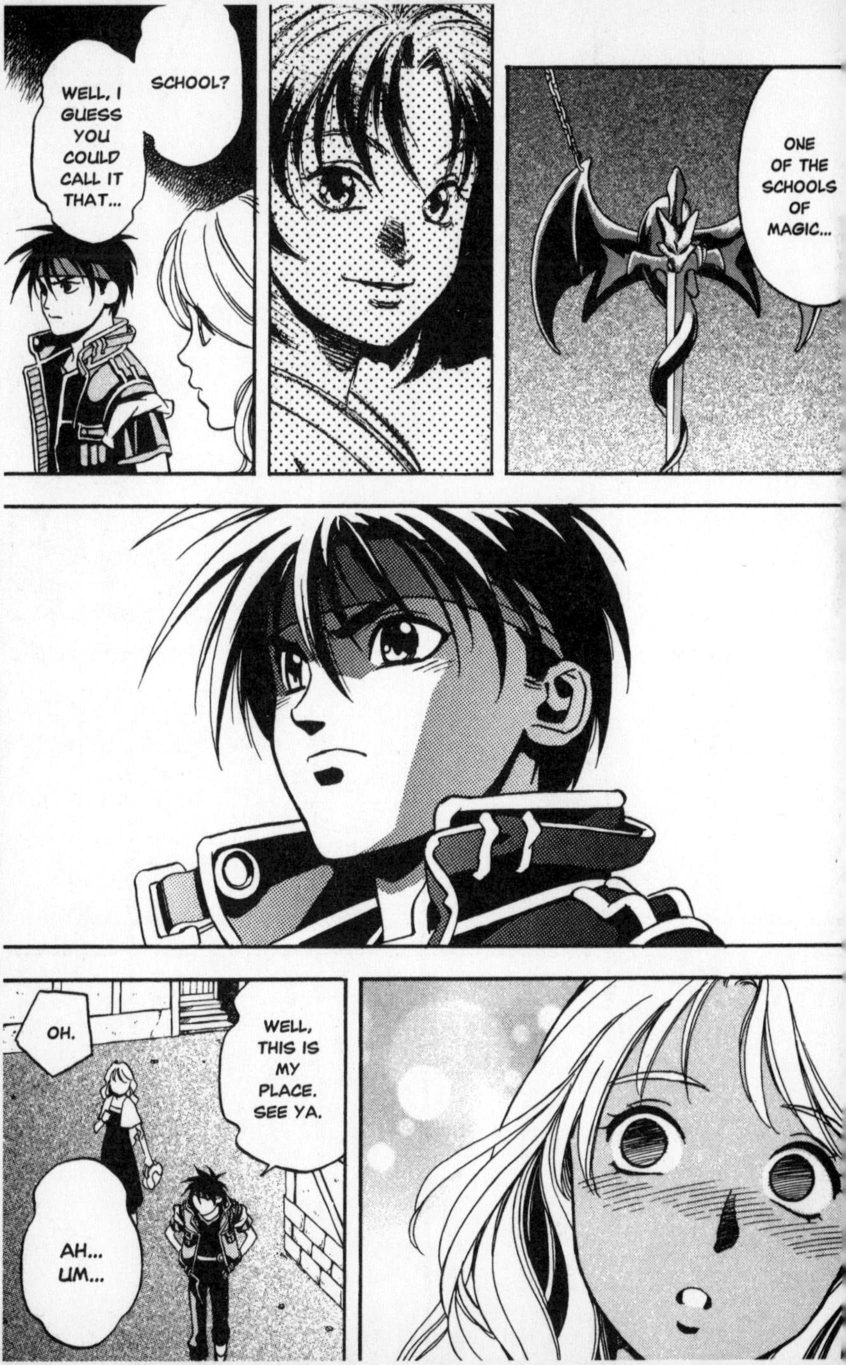
ONE OF THE SCHOOLS OF MAGIC...
SCHOOL?
WELL, I GUESS YOU COULD CALL IT THAT...
WELL, THIS IS MY PLACE. SEE YA.
OH.
AH... UM...

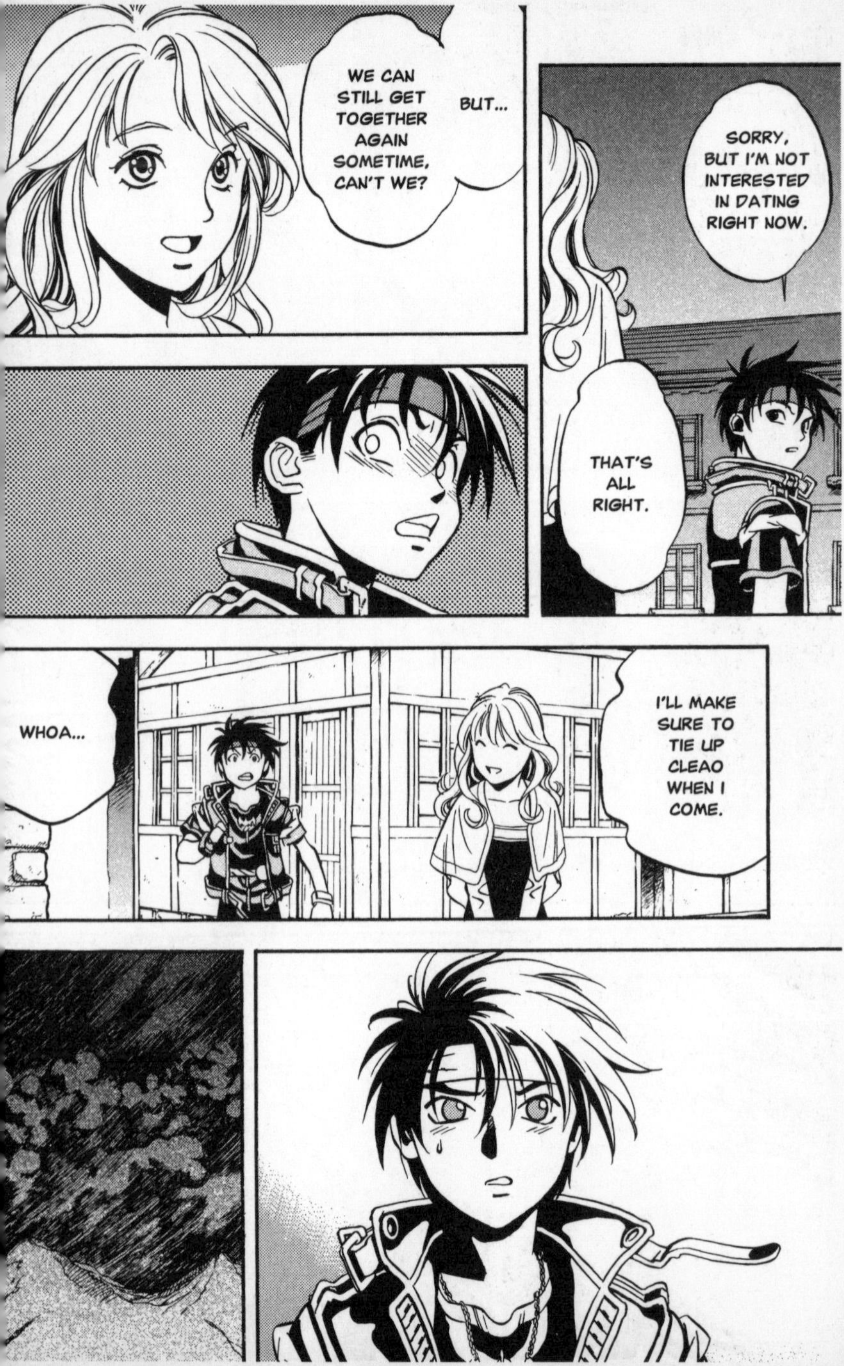
SORRY, BUT I'M NOT INTERESTED IN DATING RIGHT NOW.
THAT'S ALL RIGHT.
WE CAN STILL GET TOGETHER AGAIN SOMETIME, CAN'T WE?
BUT...
I'LL MAKE SURE TO TIE UP CLEAO WHEN I COME.
WHOA...

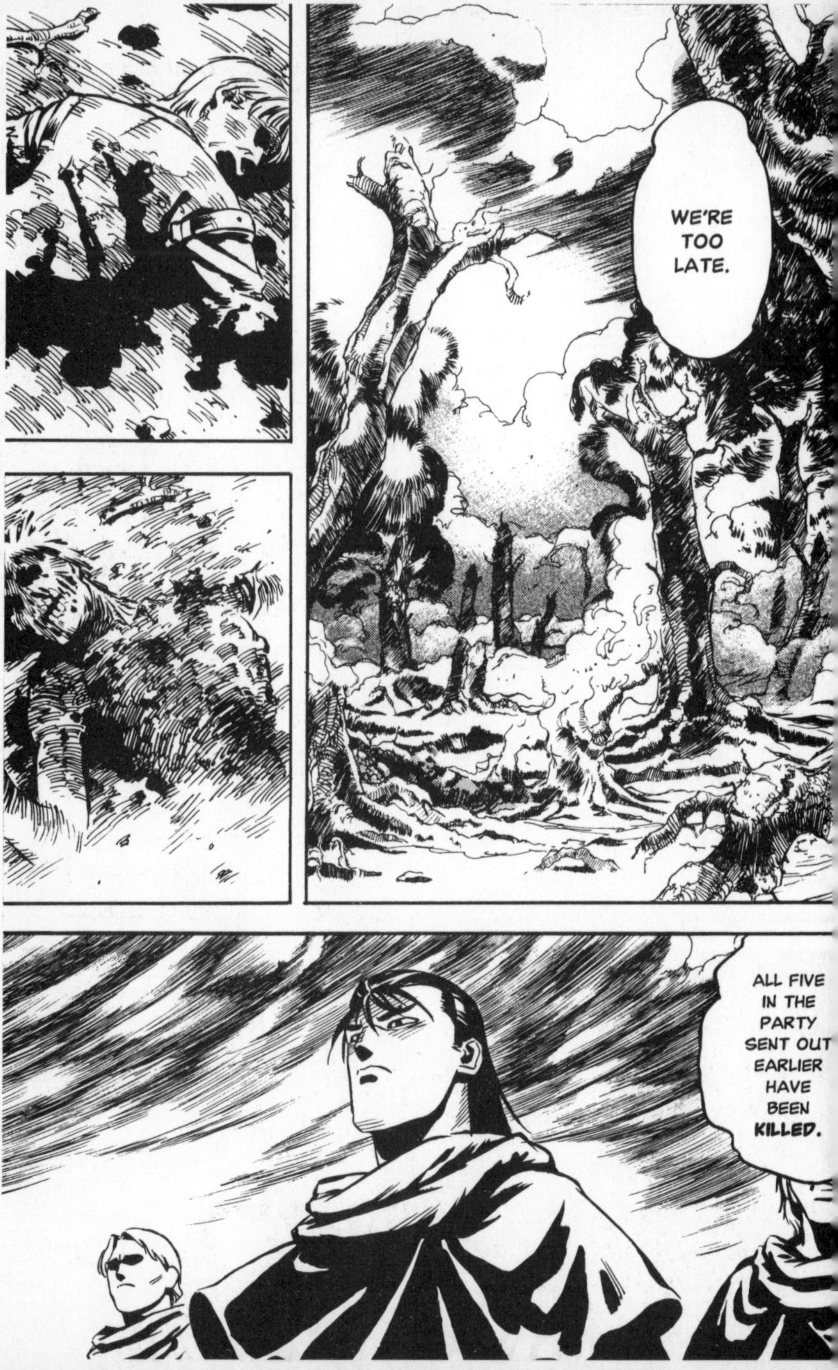
WE'RE TOO LATE.
ALL FIVE IN THE PARTY SENT OUT EARLIER HAVE BEEN **KILLED.**

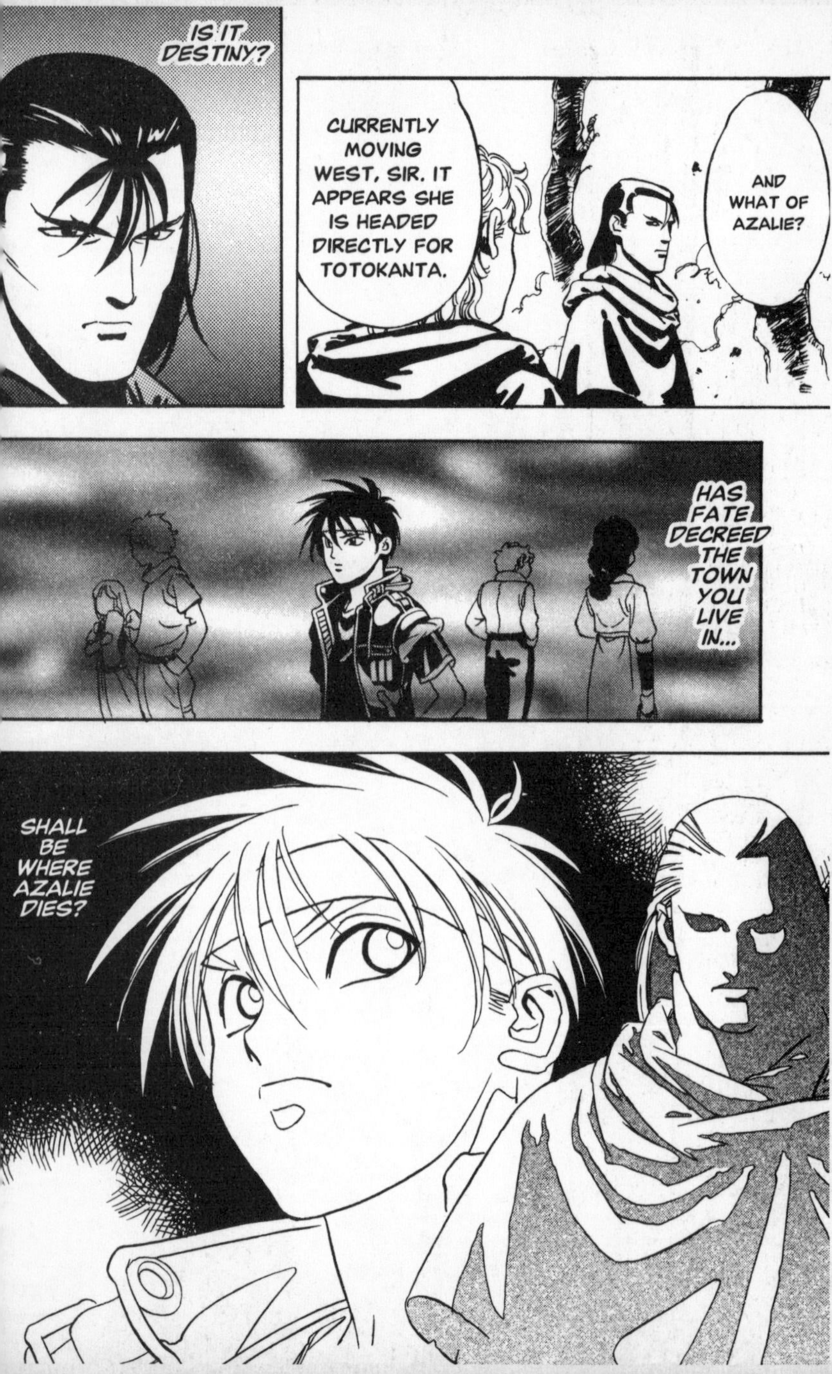
IS IT DESTINY?
AND WHAT OF AZALIE?
CURRENTLY MOVING WEST, SIR. IT APPEARS SHE IS HEADED DIRECTLY FOR TOTOKANTA.
HAS FATE DECREED THE TOWN YOU LIVE IN...
SHALL BE WHERE AZALIE DIES?

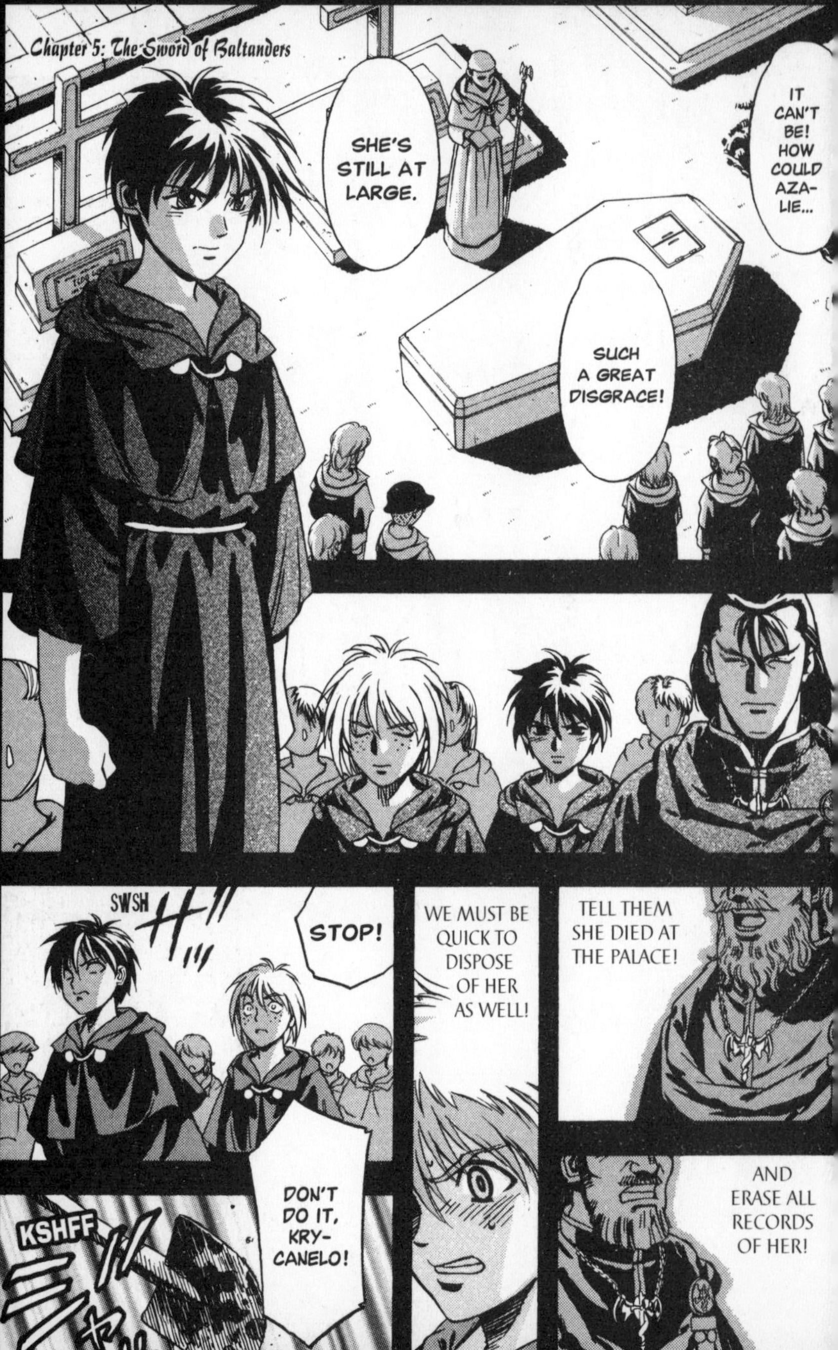
Chapter 5: The Sword of Baltanders
IT CAN'T BE! HOW COULD AZA-LIE...
SUCH A GREAT DISGRACE!
SHE'S STILL AT LARGE.
TELL THEM SHE DIED AT THE PALACE!
WE MUST BE QUICK TO DISPOSE OF HER AS WELL!
STOP!
SWSH
AND ERASE ALL RECORDS OF HER!
DON'T DO IT, KRY-CANELO!
KSHFF

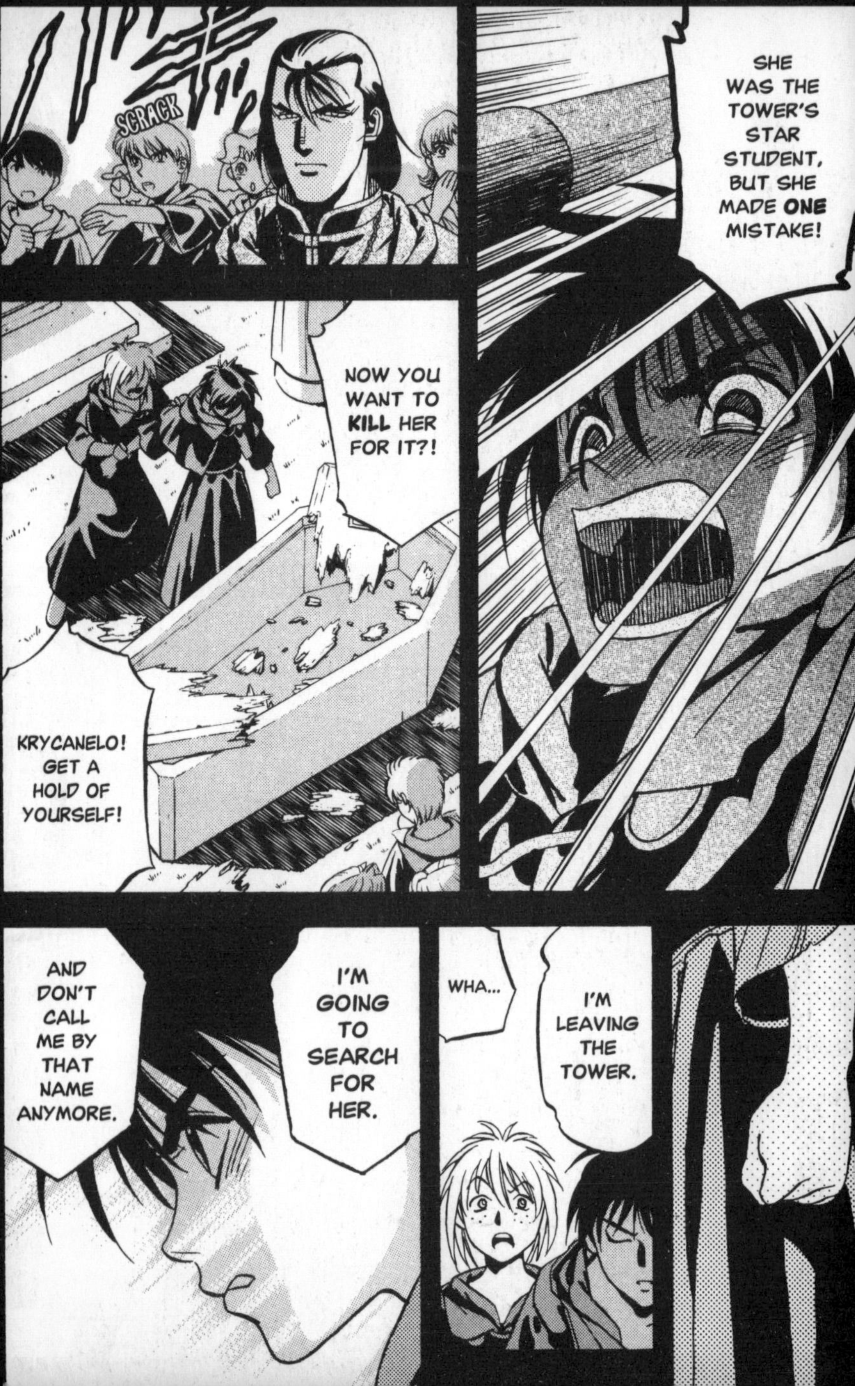
SCRACK
SHE WAS THE TOWER'S STAR STUDENT, BUT SHE MADE ONE MISTAKE!
NOW YOU WANT TO KILL HER FOR IT?!
KRYCANELO! GET A HOLD OF YOURSELF!
AND DON'T CALL ME BY THAT NAME ANYMORE.
I'M GOING TO SEARCH FOR HER.
WHA...
I'M LEAVING THE TOWER.

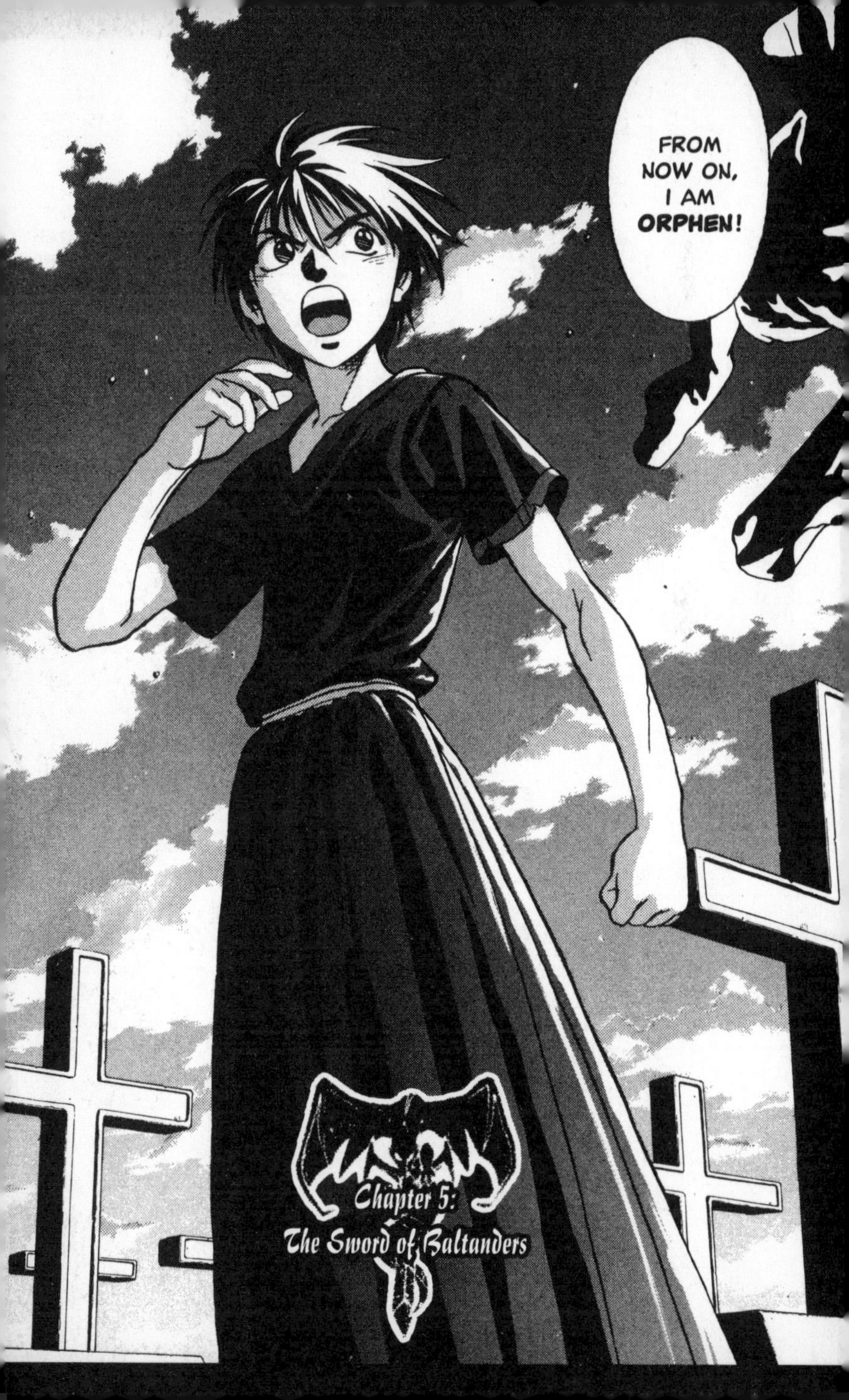
FROM NOW ON, I AM ORPHEN!
Chapter 5:
The Sword of Baltanders

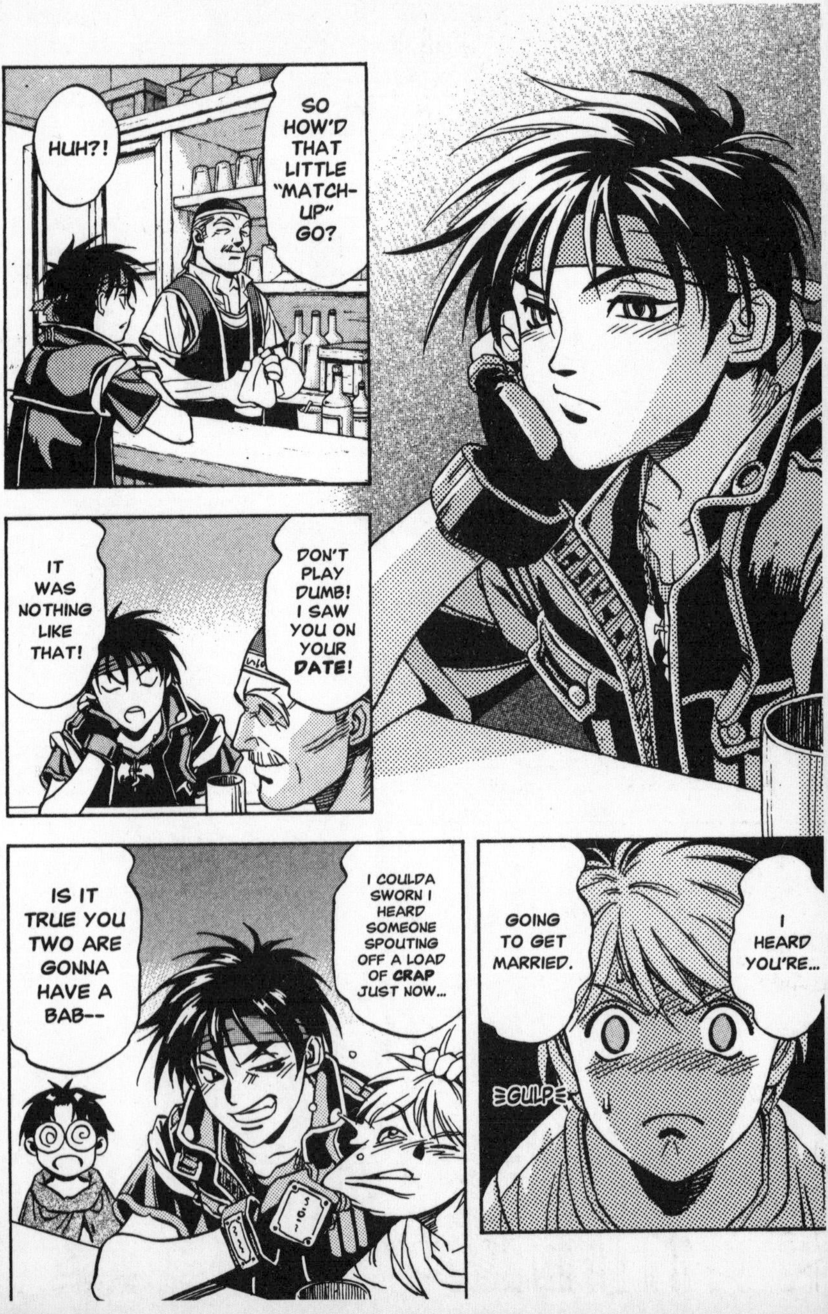
SO HOW'D THAT LITTLE "MATCH-UP" GO?
HUH?!
DON'T PLAY DUMB! I SAW YOU ON YOUR DATE!
IT WAS NOTHING LIKE THAT!
I HEARD YOU'RE...
GOING TO GET MARRIED.
GULP
IS IT TRUE YOU TWO ARE GONNA HAVE A BAB--
I COULDA SWORN I HEARD SOMEONE SPOUTING OFF A LOAD OF CRAP JUST NOW...

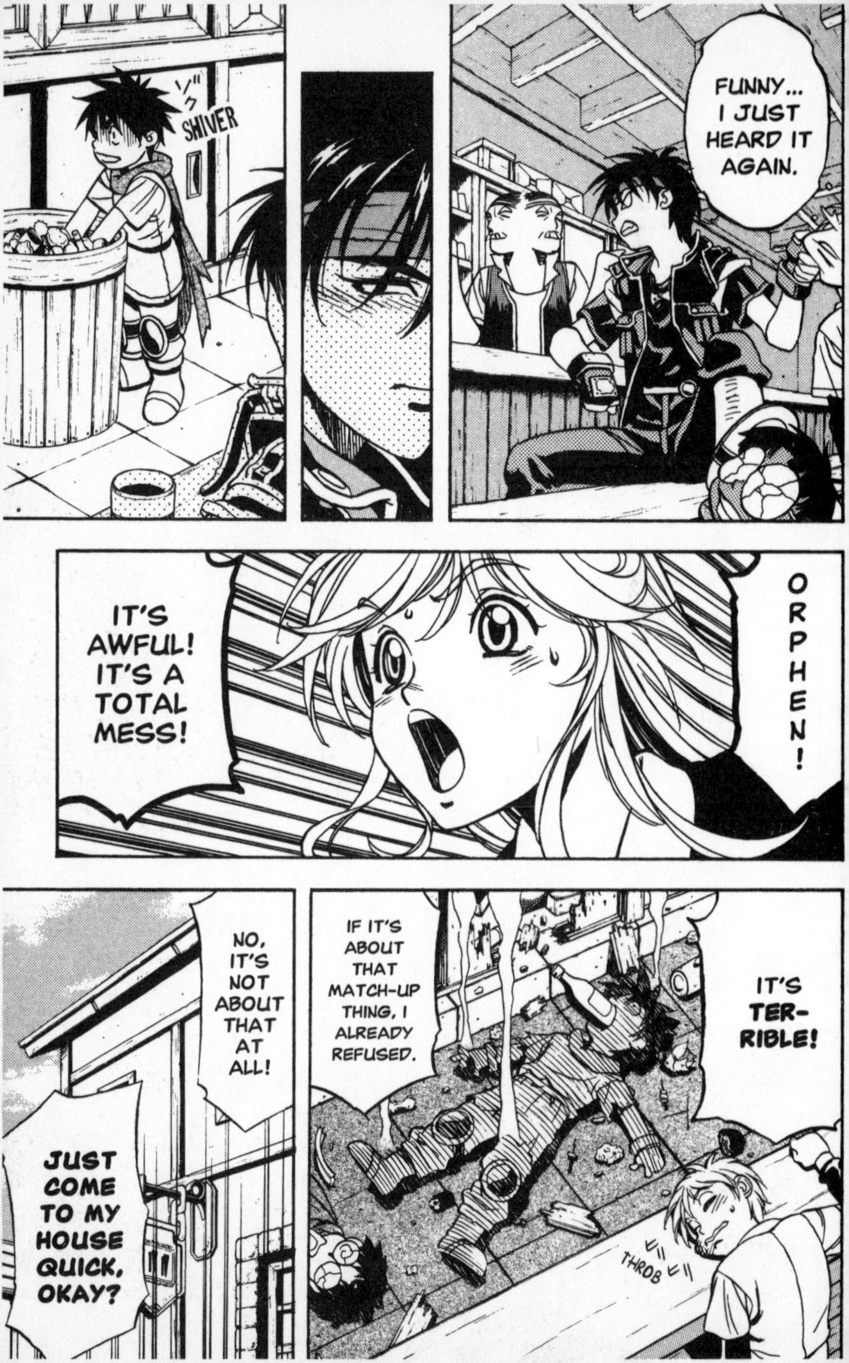
FUNNY... I JUST HEARD IT AGAIN.
ゾク
SHIVER
ORPHEN!
IT'S AWFUL! IT'S A TOTAL MESS!
IT'S TER-RIBLE!
IF IT'S ABOUT THAT MATCH-UP THING, I ALREADY REFUSED.
THROB
NO, IT'S NOT ABOUT THAT AT ALL!
JUST COME TO MY HOUSE QUICK, OKAY?

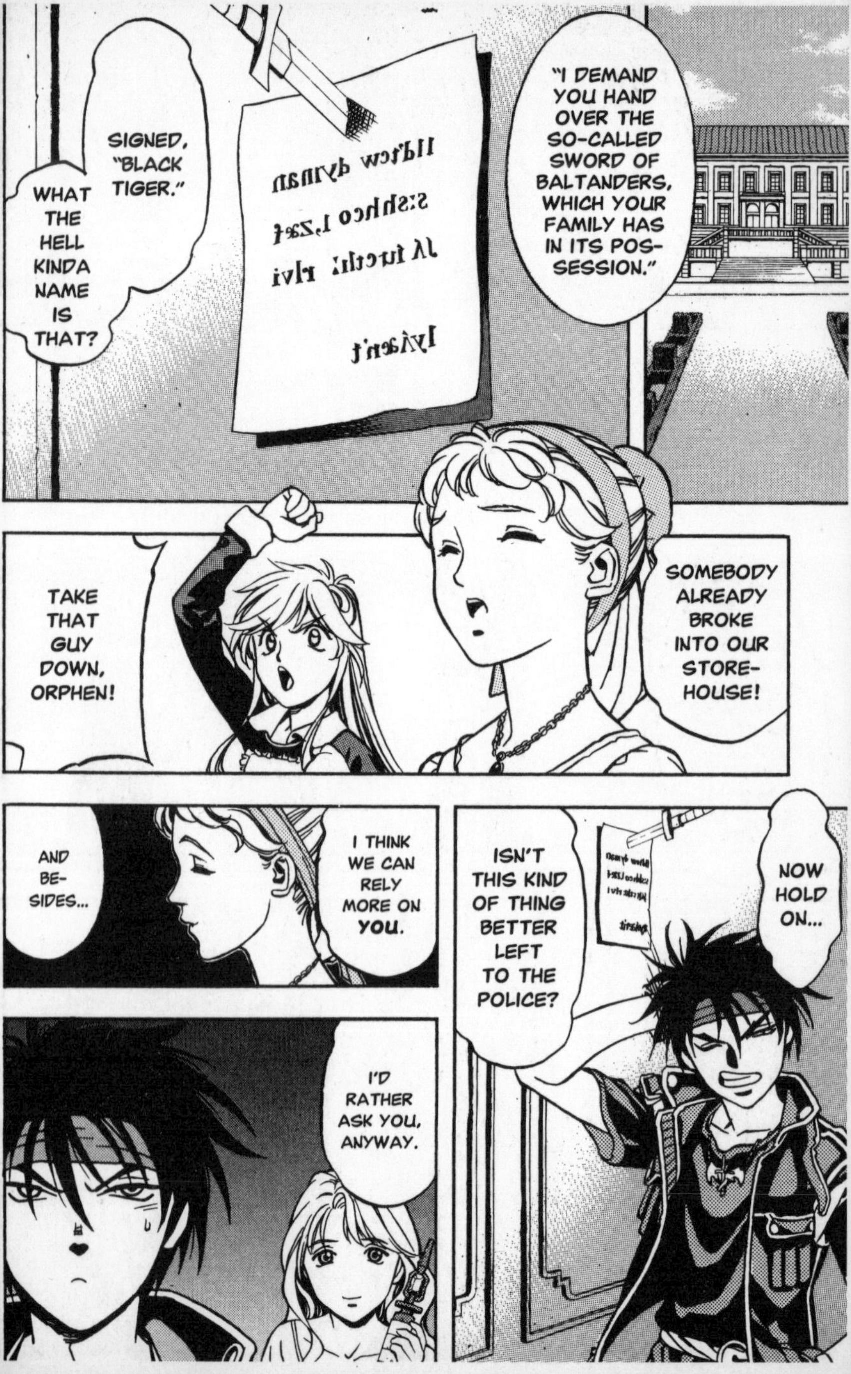
"I DEMAND YOU HAND OVER THE SO-CALLED SWORD OF BALTANDERS, WHICH YOUR FAMILY HAS IN ITS POSSESSION."
SIGNED, "BLACK TIGER."
WHAT THE HELL KINDA NAME IS THAT?
SOMEBODY ALREADY BROKE INTO OUR STOREHOUSE!
TAKE THAT GUY DOWN, ORPHEN!
NOW HOLD ON...
ISN'T THIS KIND OF THING BETTER LEFT TO THE POLICE?
I THINK WE CAN RELY MORE ON **YOU**.
AND BESIDES...
I'D RATHER ASK YOU, ANYWAY.

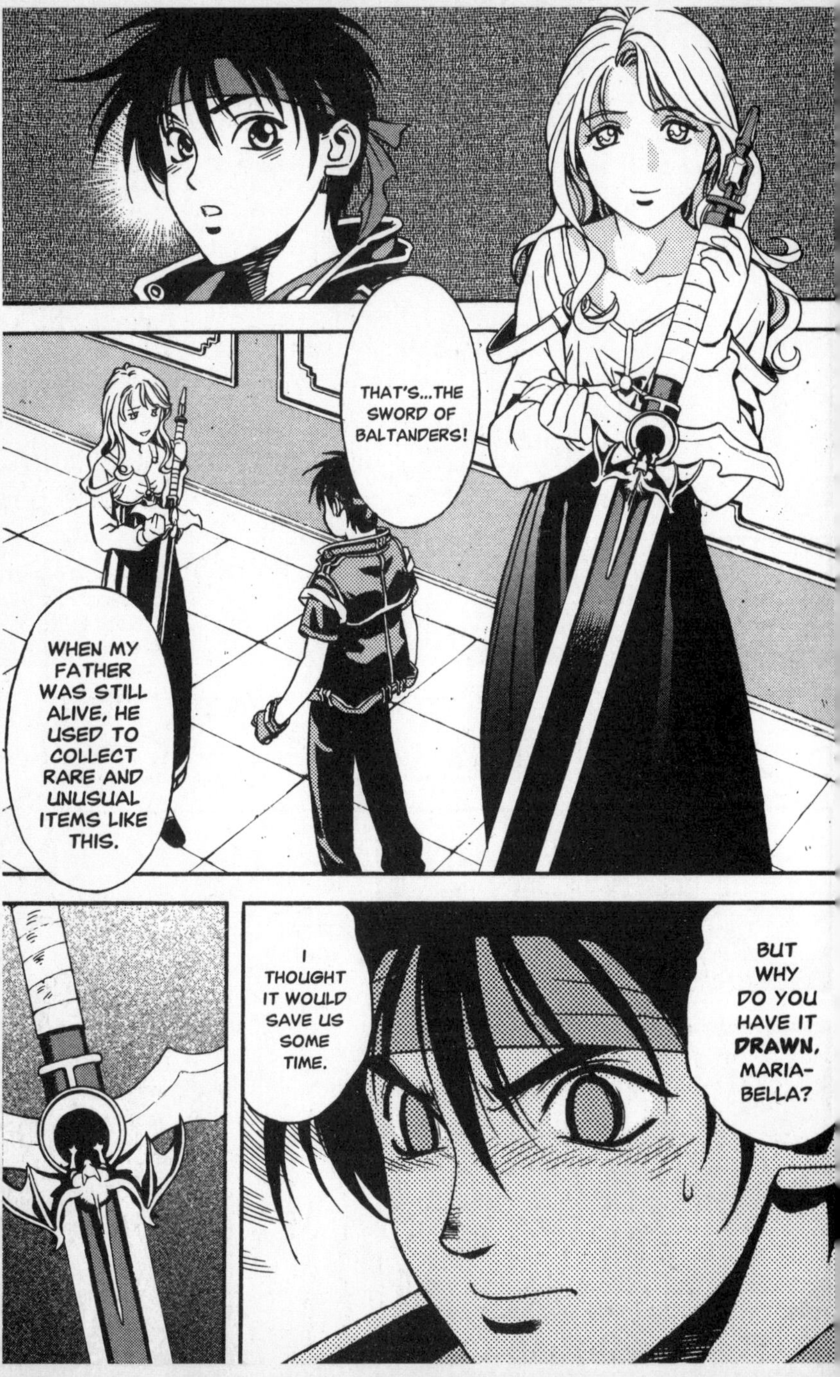
THAT'S...THE SWORD OF BALTANDERS!
WHEN MY FATHER WAS STILL ALIVE, HE USED TO COLLECT RARE AND UNUSUAL ITEMS LIKE THIS.
BUT WHY DO YOU HAVE IT DRAWN, MARIA-BELLA?
I THOUGHT IT WOULD SAVE US SOME TIME.

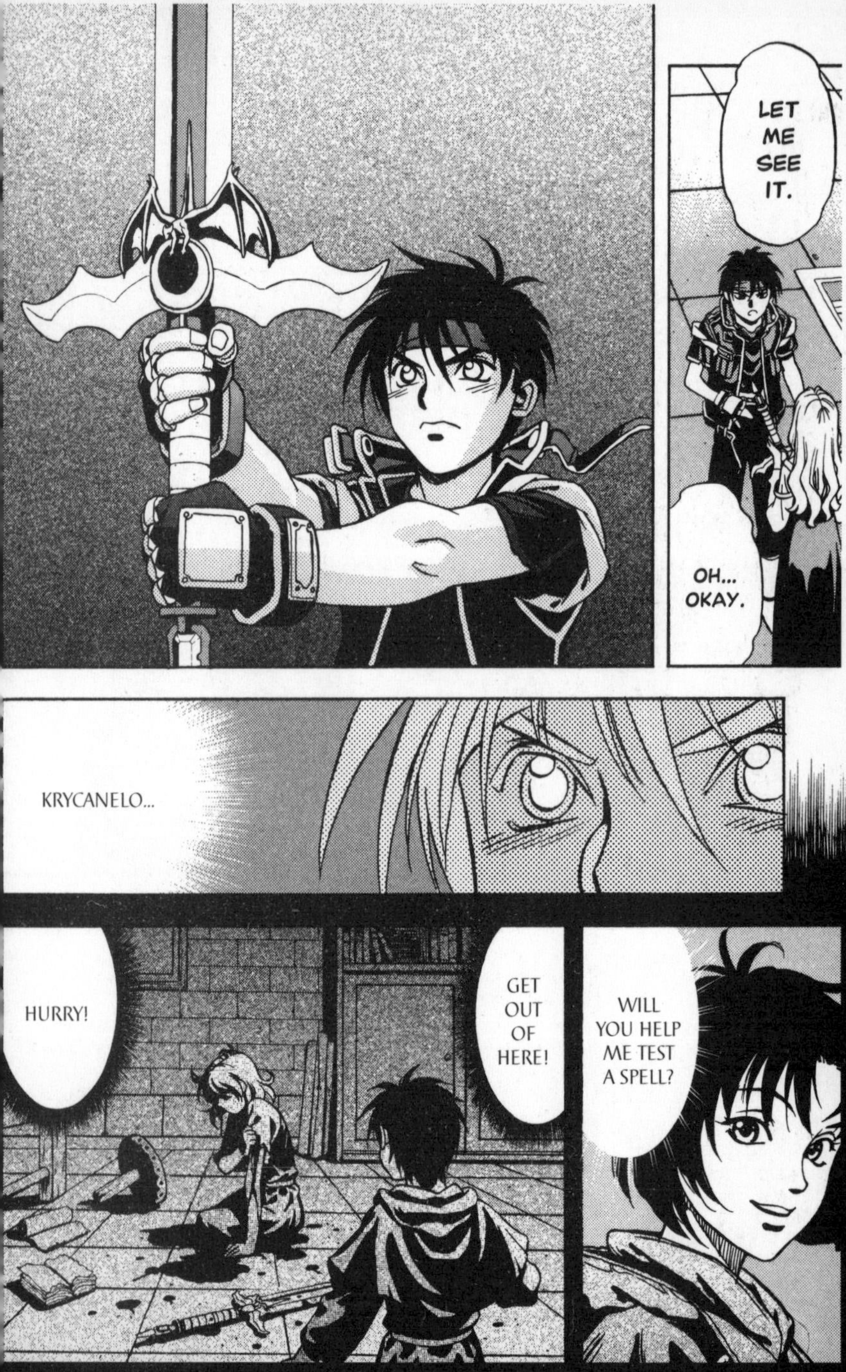
LET ME SEE IT.
OH... OKAY.
KRYCANELO...
WILL YOU HELP ME TEST A SPELL?
GET OUT OF HERE!
HURRY!

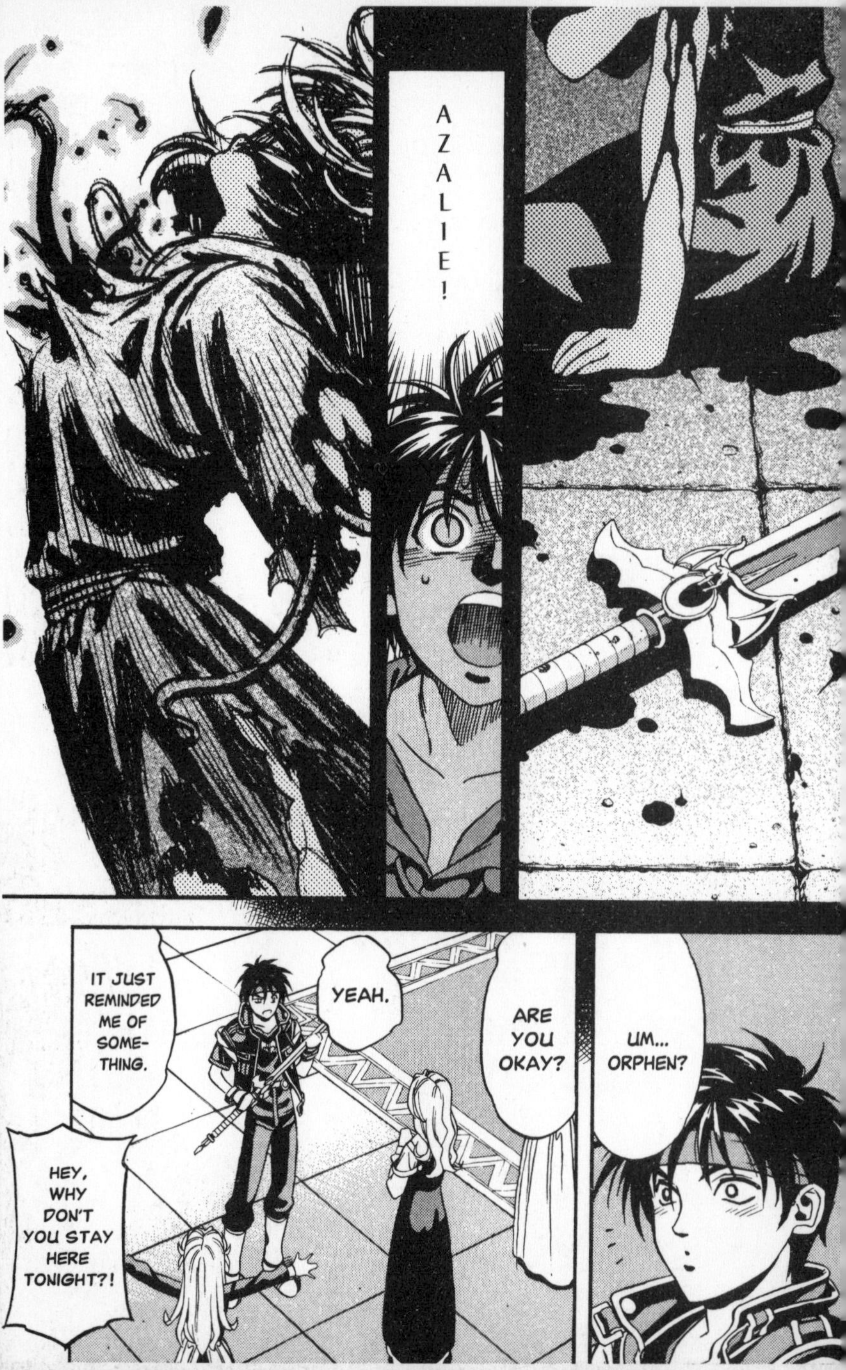
AZALIE!
UM... ORPHEN?
ARE YOU OKAY?
YEAH.
IT JUST REMINDED ME OF SOME-THING.
HEY, WHY DON'T YOU STAY HERE TONIGHT?!

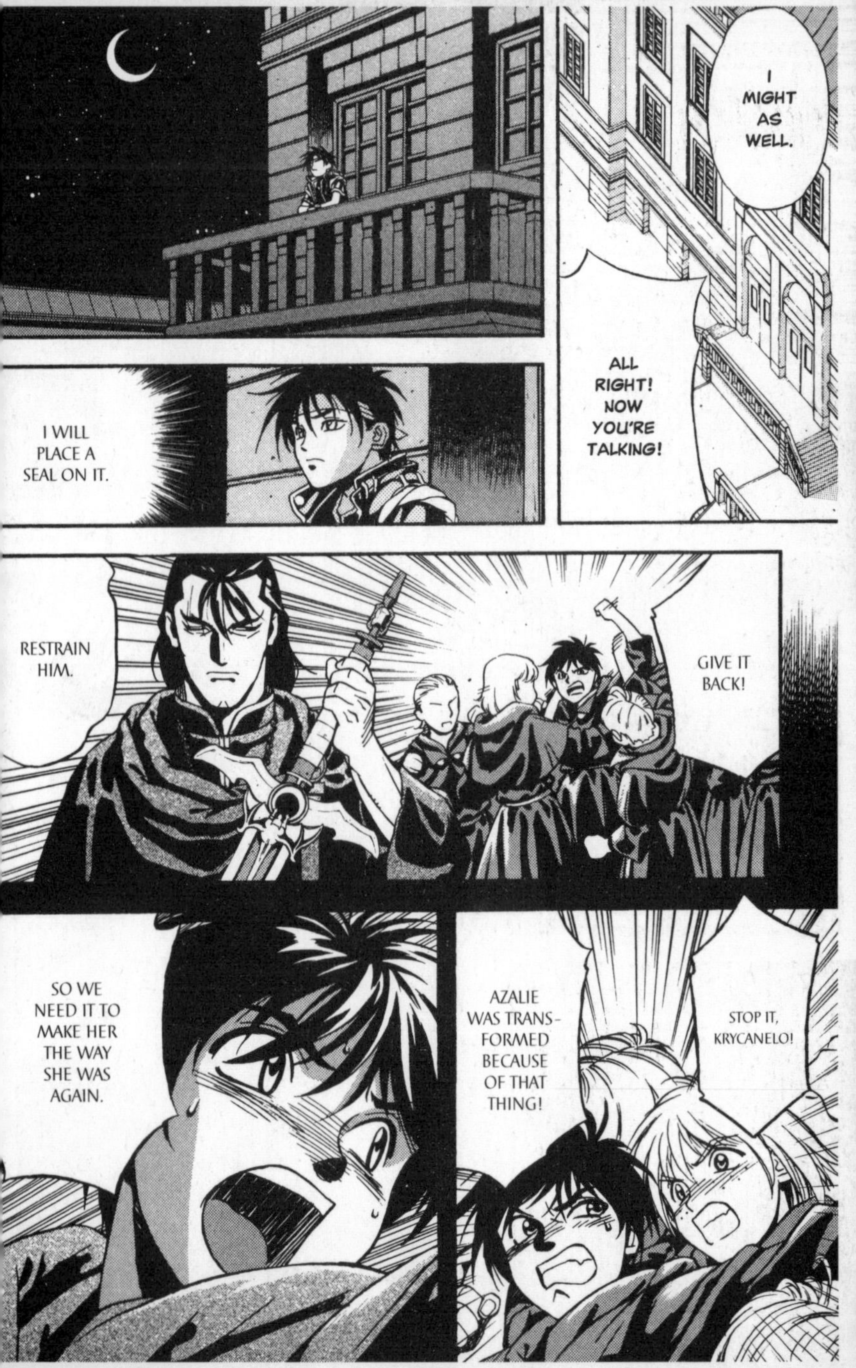
I MIGHT AS WELL.
ALL RIGHT! NOW YOU'RE TALKING!
I WILL PLACE A SEAL ON IT.
GIVE IT BACK!
RESTRAIN HIM.
STOP IT, KRYCANELO!
AZALIE WAS TRANS-FORMED BECAUSE OF THAT THING!
SO WE NEED IT TO MAKE HER THE WAY SHE WAS AGAIN.

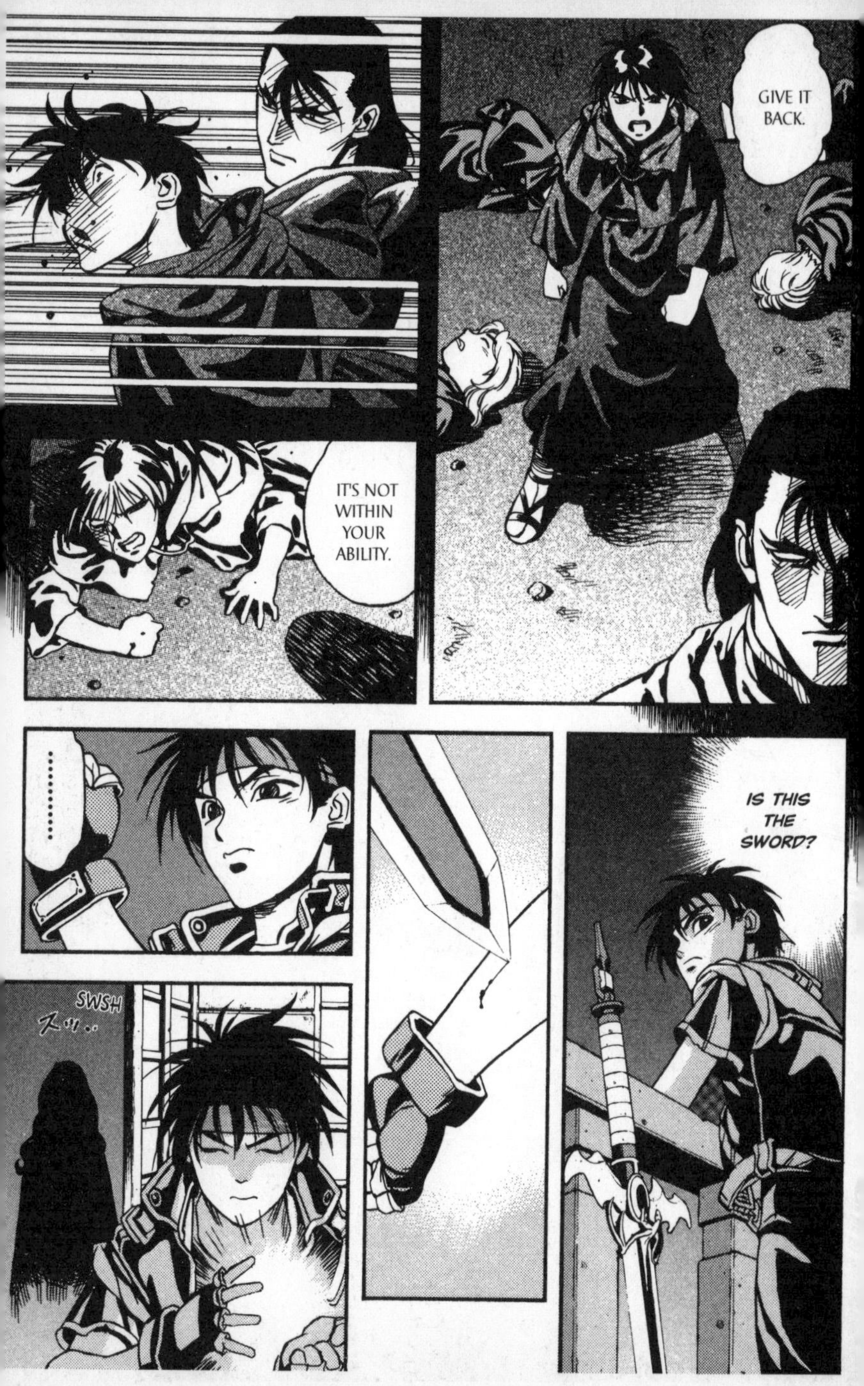
GIVE IT BACK.
IT'S NOT WITHIN YOUR ABILITY.
IS THIS THE SWORD?
....
SWSH

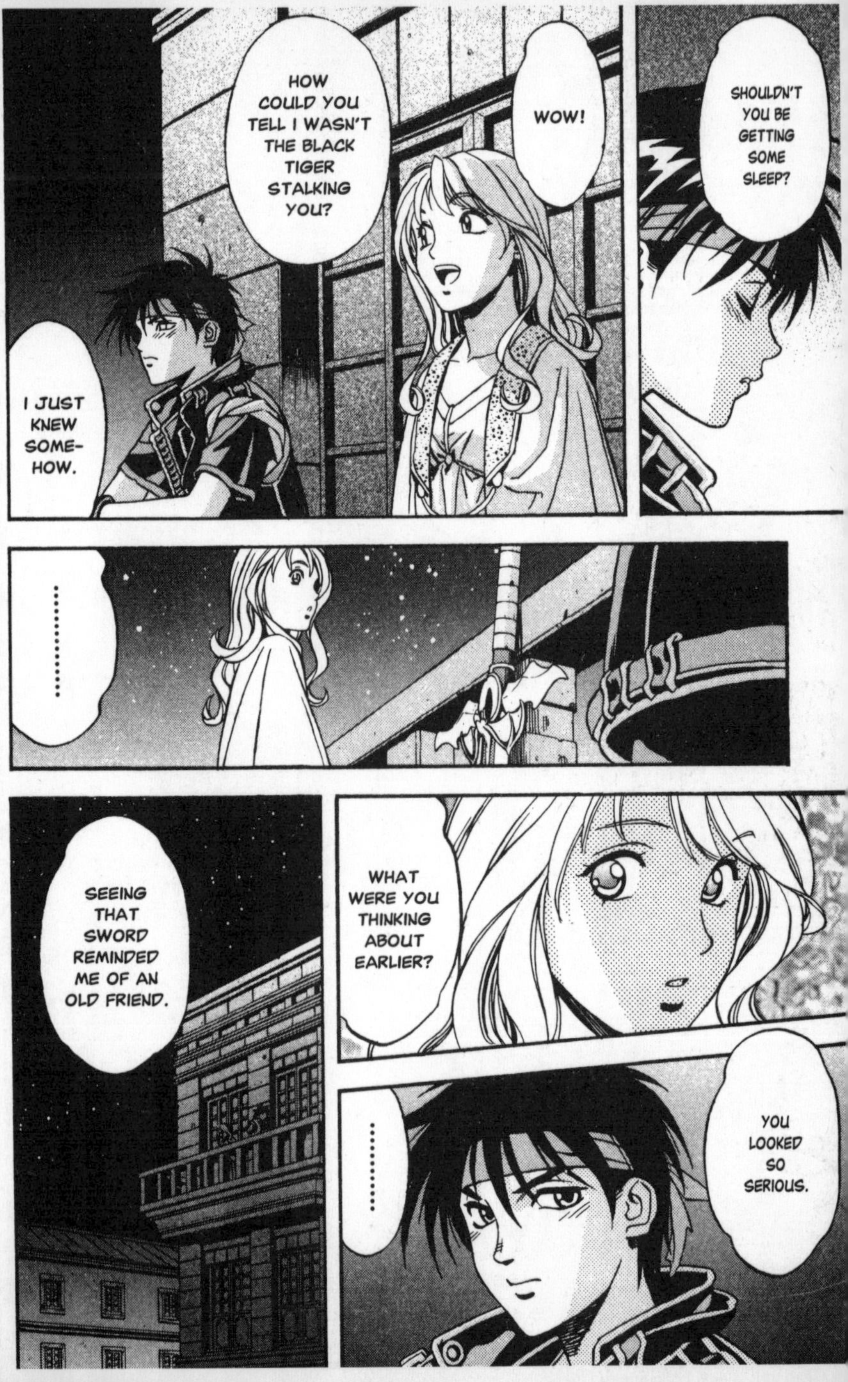

SHOULDN'T YOU BE GETTING SOME SLEEP?
WOW!
HOW COULD YOU TELL I WASN'T THE BLACK TIGER STALKING YOU?
I JUST KNEW SOME-HOW.
......
WHAT WERE YOU THINKING ABOUT EARLIER?
YOU LOOKED SO SERIOUS.
......
SEEING THAT SWORD REMINDED ME OF AN OLD FRIEND.

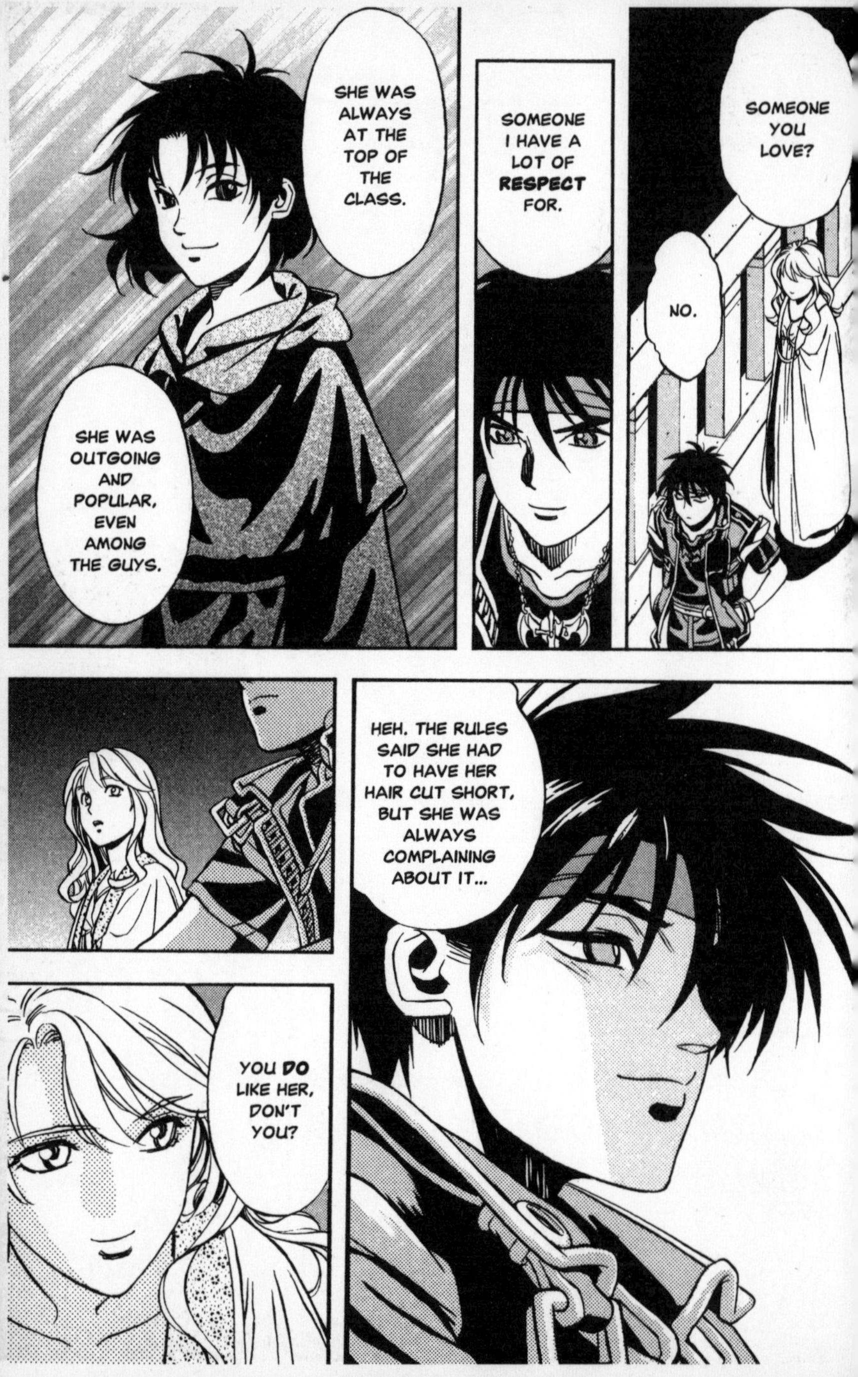
SHE WAS ALWAYS AT THE TOP OF THE CLASS.
SHE WAS OUTGOING AND POPULAR, EVEN AMONG THE GUYS.
SOMEONE I HAVE A LOT OF **RESPECT** FOR.
SOMEONE YOU LOVE?
NO.
HEH. THE RULES SAID SHE HAD TO HAVE HER HAIR CUT SHORT, BUT SHE WAS ALWAYS COMPLAINING ABOUT IT...
YOU **DO** LIKE HER, DON'T YOU?

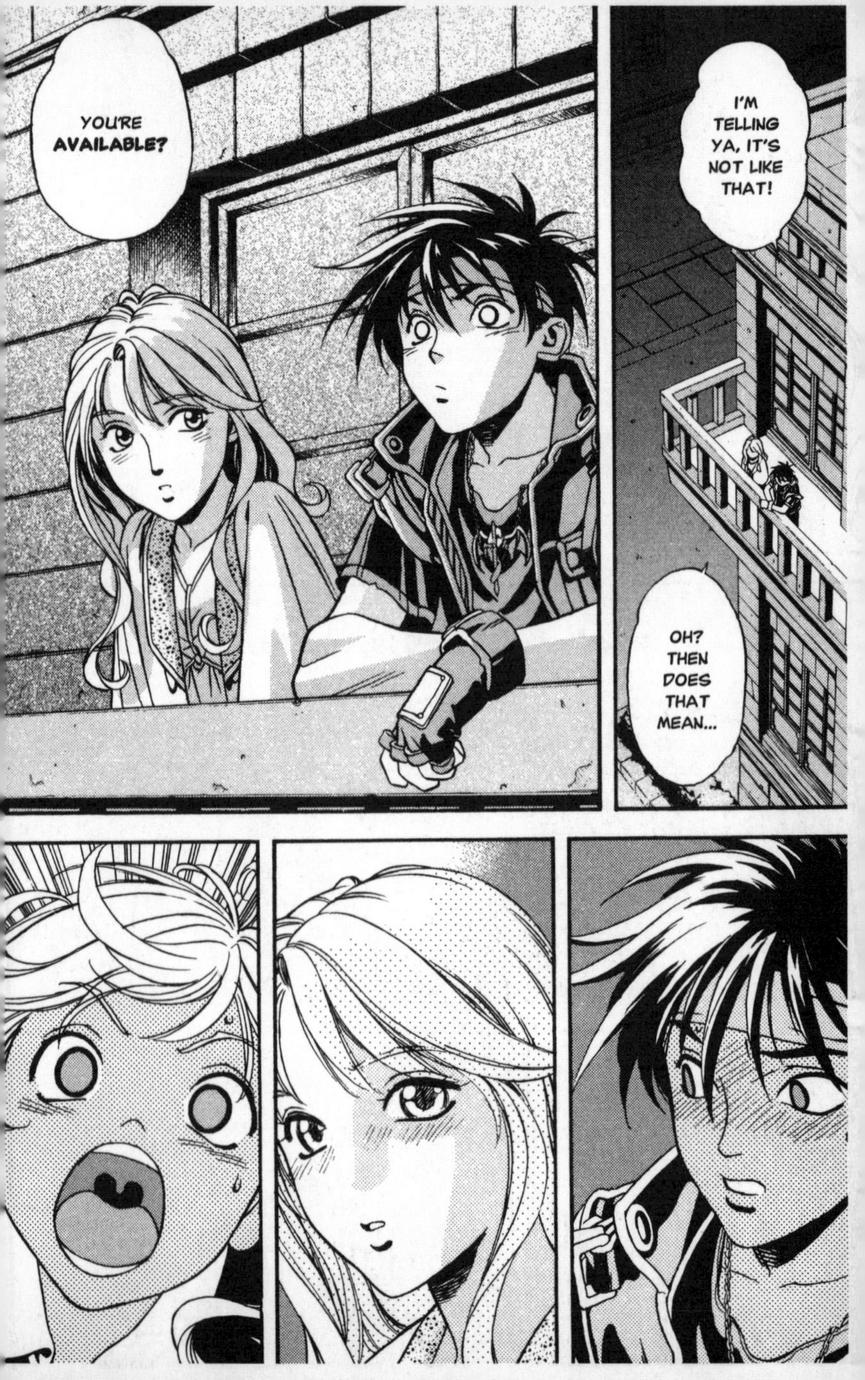
I'M TELLING YA, IT'S NOT LIKE THAT!
OH? THEN DOES THAT MEAN...
YOU'RE AVAILABLE?

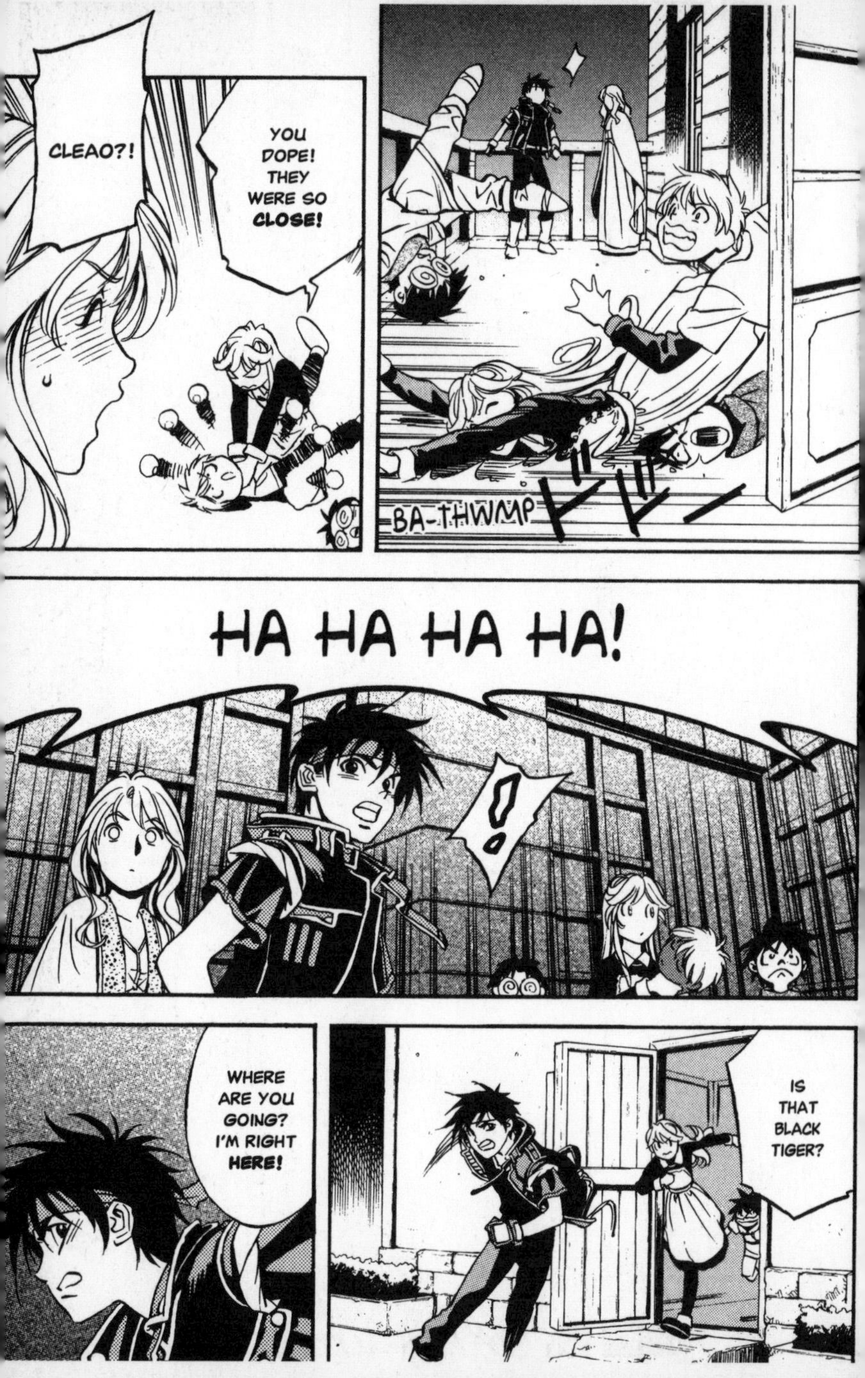
BA-THWMP
YOU DOPE! THEY WERE SO CLOSE!
CLEAO?!
HA HA HA HA!
IS THAT BLACK TIGER?
WHERE ARE YOU GOING? I'M RIGHT HERE!

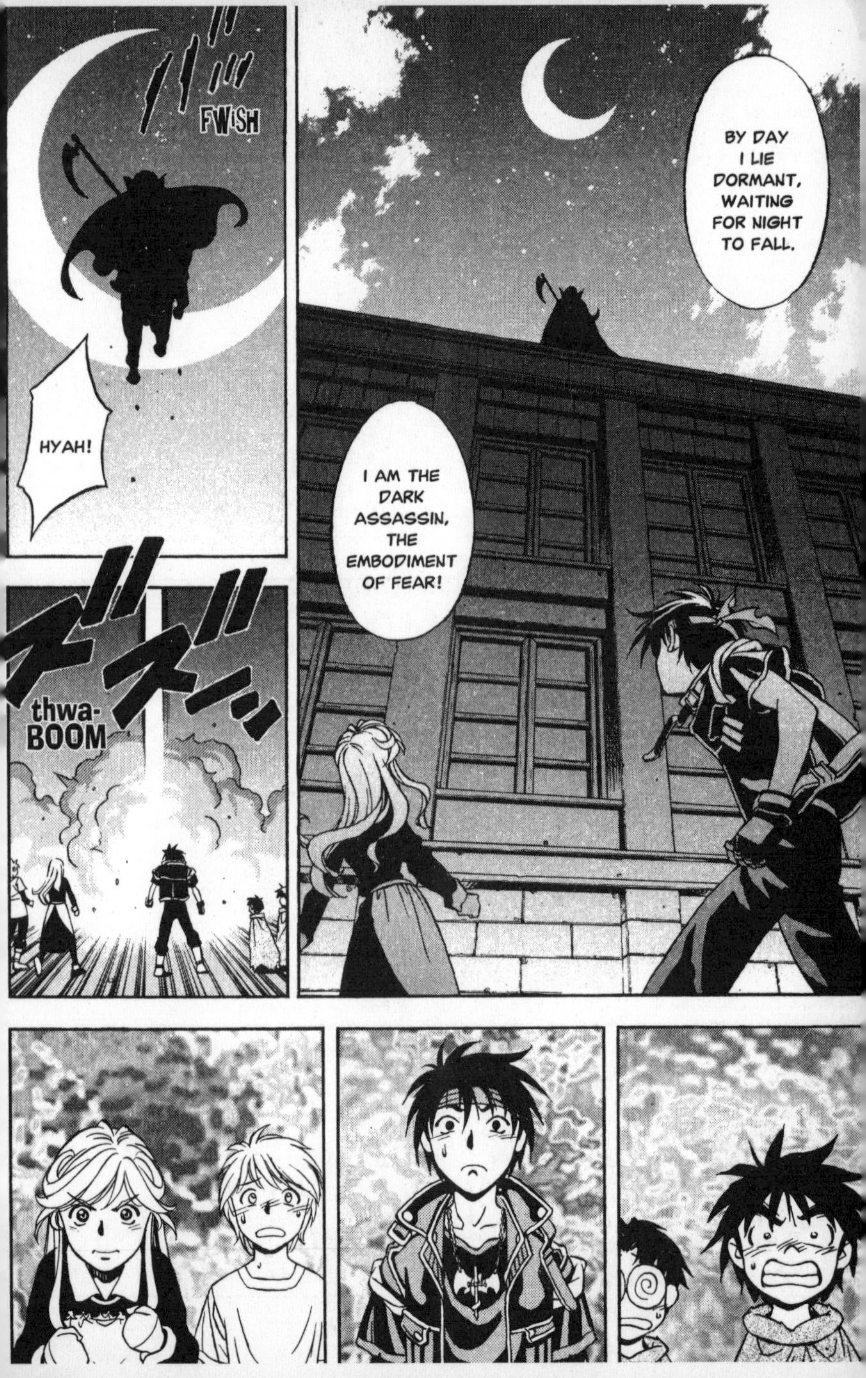
BY DAY I LIE DORMANT, WAITING FOR NIGHT TO FALL.
I AM THE DARK ASSASSIN, THE EMBODIMENT OF FEAR!
FWISH
HYAH!
thwa-BOOM

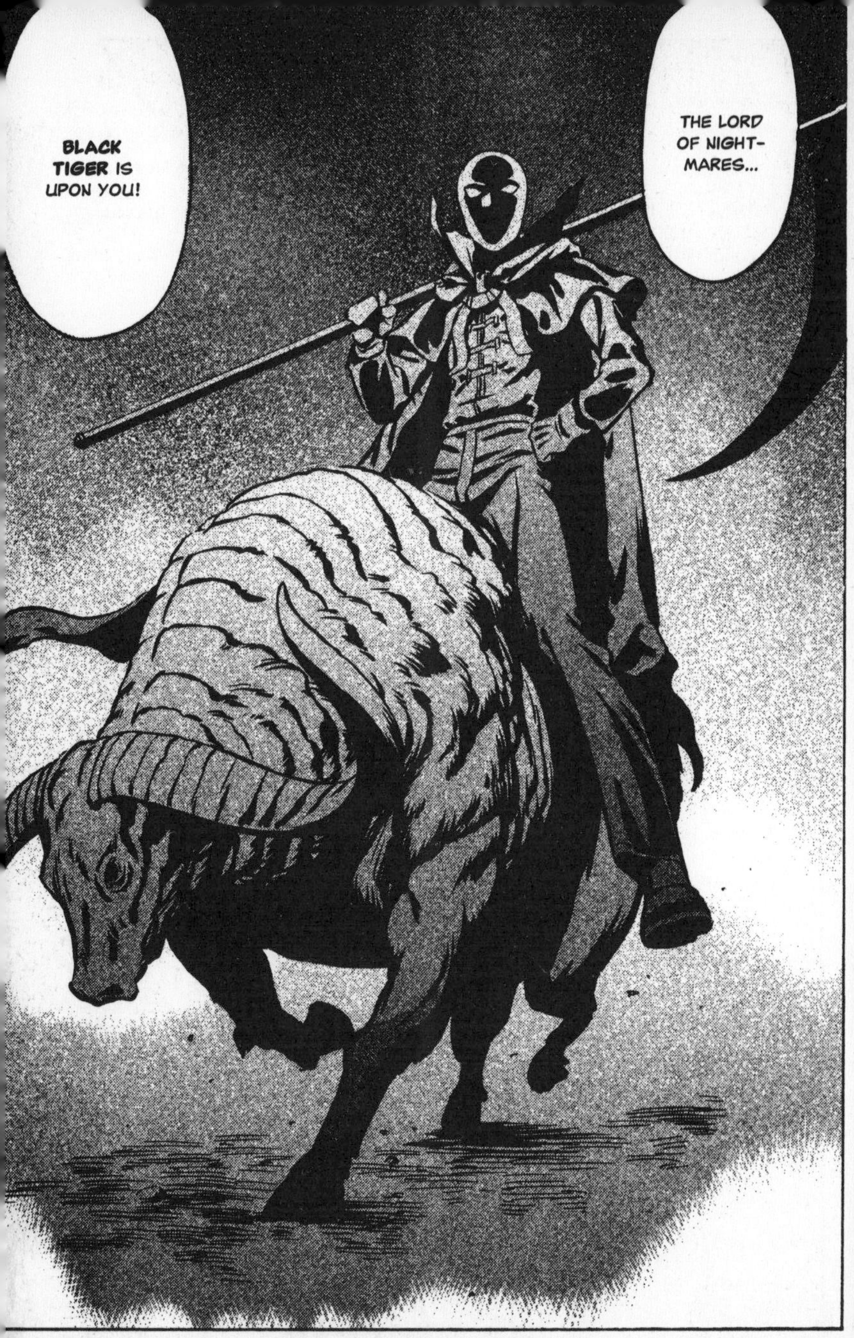
THE LORD OF NIGHT-MARES...
BLACK TIGER IS UPON YOU!

To be continued in Volume 2...

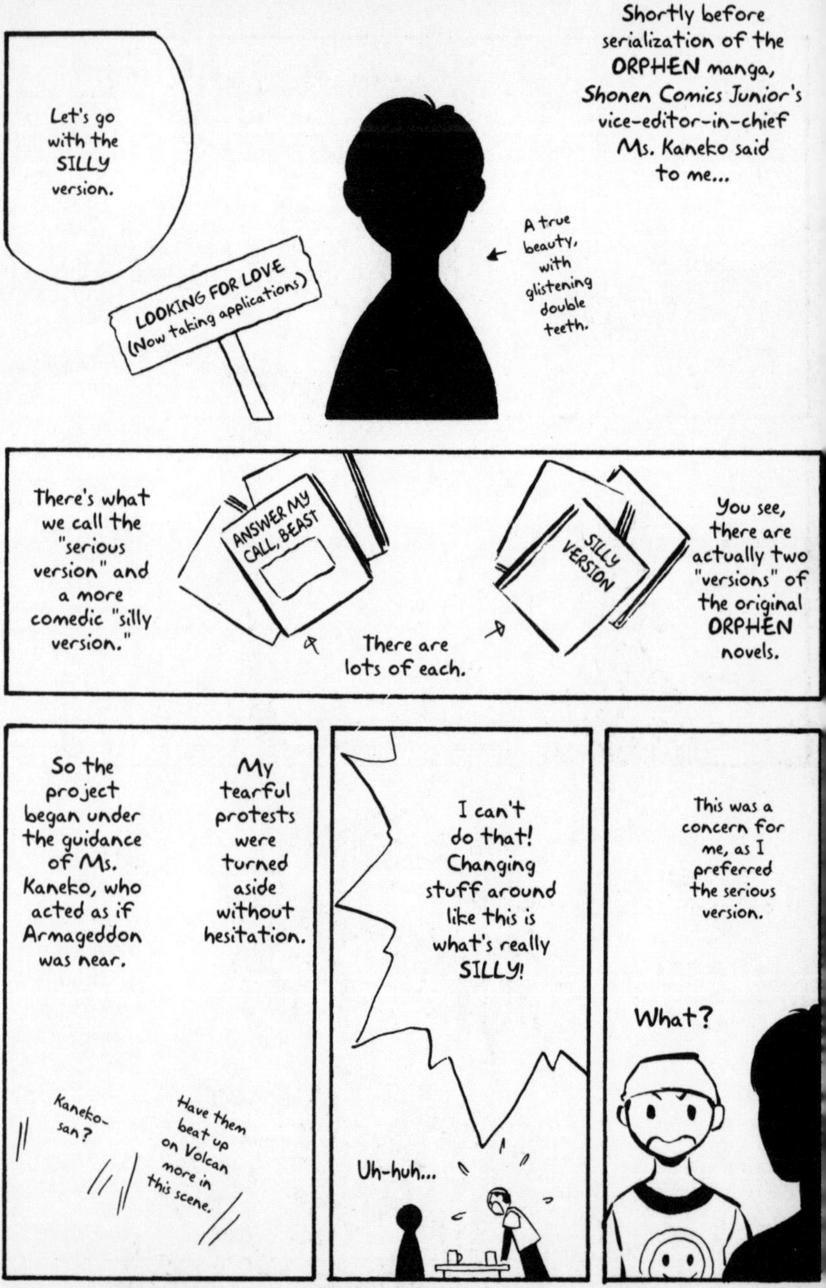
Shortly before serialization of the ORPHEN manga, Shonen Comics Junior's vice-editor-in-chief Ms. Kaneko said to me...
A true beauty, with glistening double teeth.
LOOKING FOR LOVE (Now taking applications)
Let's go with the SILLY version.
You see, there are actually two "versions" of the original ORPHEN novels.
SILLY VERSION
There are lots of each.
ANSWER MY CALL, BEAST
There's what we call the "serious version" and a more comedic "silly version."
This was a concern for me, as I preferred the serious version.
What?
I can't do that! Changing stuff around like this is what's really SILLY!
Uh-huh...
My tearful protests were turned aside without hesitation.
So the project began under the guidance of Ms. Kaneko, who acted as if Armageddon was near.
Have them beat up on Volcan more in this scene.
Kaneko-san?

STAFF/KIYOHIKO SASAKI, KOJI OOTA, ISAO MAKINO, DAISUKE UJIHARA, TAKUO HOSHIHATA, MOTOTAKA MATSUO

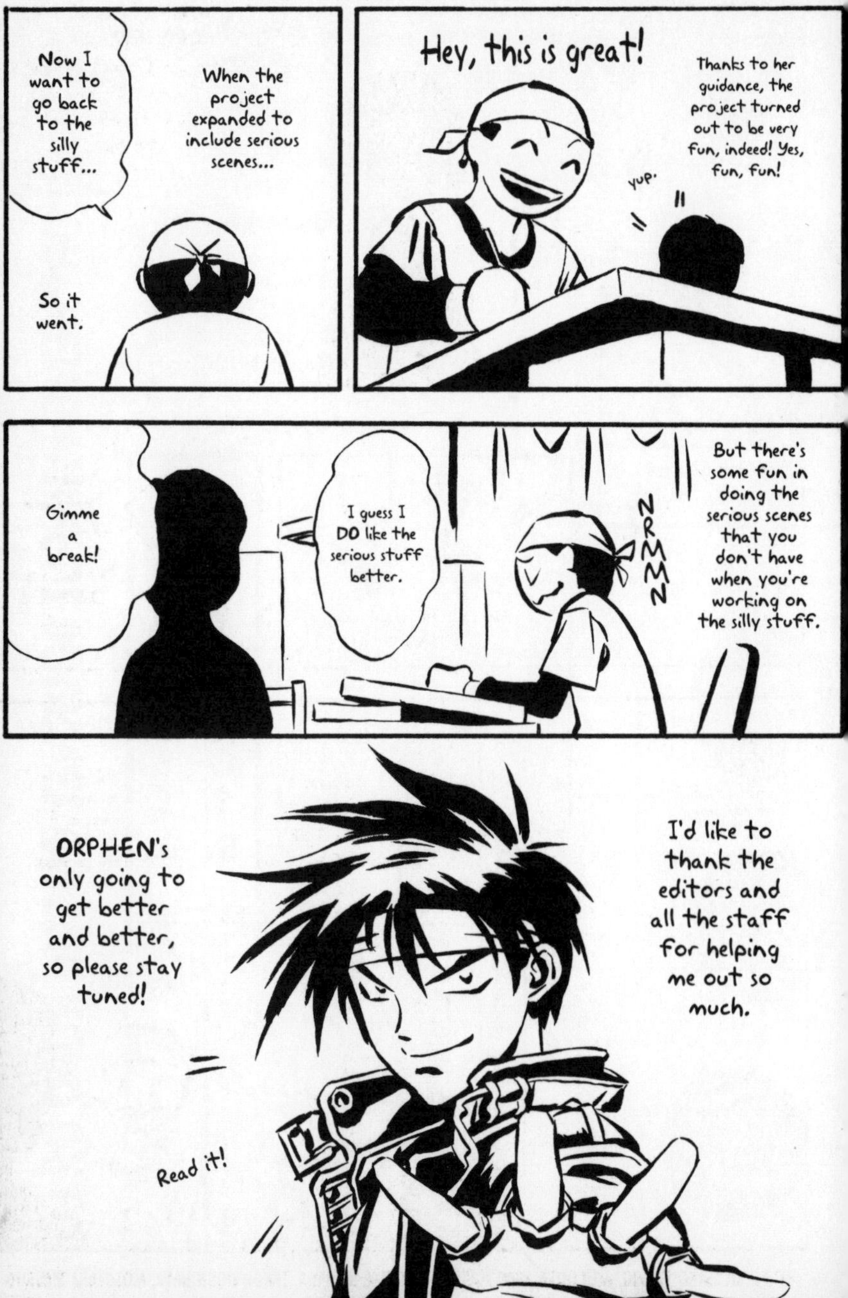

Now I want to go back to the silly stuff...
When the project expanded to include serious scenes...
So it went.
Hey, this is great!
Thanks to her guidance, the project turned out to be very fun, indeed! Yes, fun, fun!
yup.
Gimme a break!
I guess I DO like the serious stuff better.
NRMMN
But there's some fun in doing the serious scenes that you don't have when you're working on the silly stuff.
ORPHEN's only going to get better and better, so please stay tuned!
I'd like to thank the editors and all the staff for helping me out so much.
Read it!

BONUS

ORPHEN'S PAINFUL JOURNEY ON THE ROAD OF LOVE

LET'S WASTE OUR LIVES AWAY ON WOMEN! ♫

START

After money, what is the next most important thing in life?

A. Romance B. Love C. Weirdness

YES or A. / NO or B.

A.

Sometimes you think, "I don't believe in love."

C.

You are a born entertainer; use your talent to make this world a little brighter. Don't waste your time on LOVE!

B.

With a little love, you could overcome any obstacle!

Yeah, a hot body's more important than a pretty face.

For a first date, you'd take her to...
A. The amusement park.
B. A quiet beach.

You are head over heels for an earnest girl.

This would make a good present:
A. An expensive bouquet.
B. An expensive accessory.

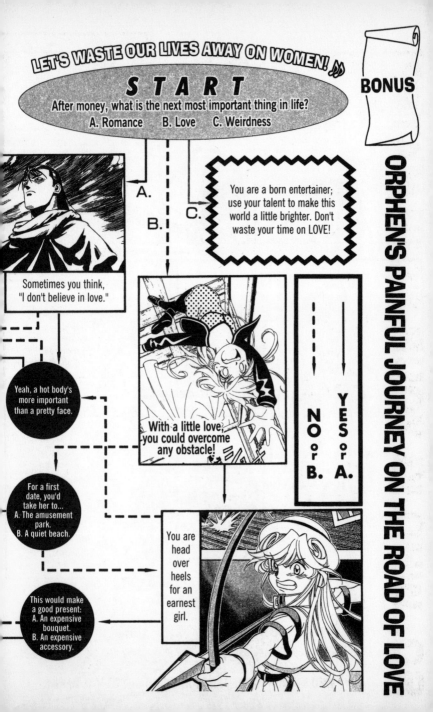

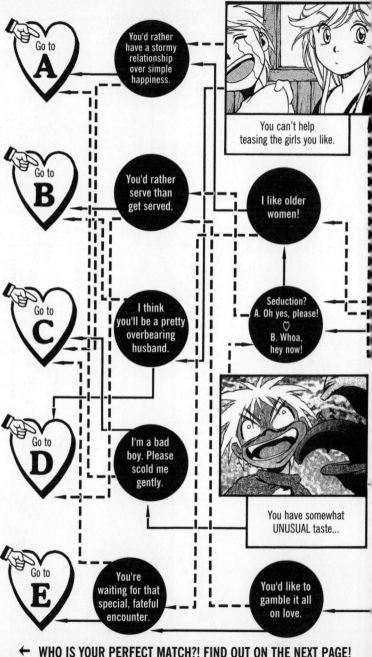

Go to **A**

You'd rather have a stormy relationship over simple happiness.

You can't help teasing the girls you like.

Go to **B**

You'd rather serve than get served.

I like older women!

Go to **C**

I think you'll be a pretty overbearing husband.

Seduction?
A. Oh yes, please!
♡
B. Whoa, hey now!

Go to **D**

I'm a bad boy. Please scold me gently.

You have somewhat UNUSUAL taste...

Go to **E**

You're waiting for that special, fateful encounter.

You'd like to gamble it all on love.

← WHO IS YOUR PERFECT MATCH?! FIND OUT ON THE NEXT PAGE!

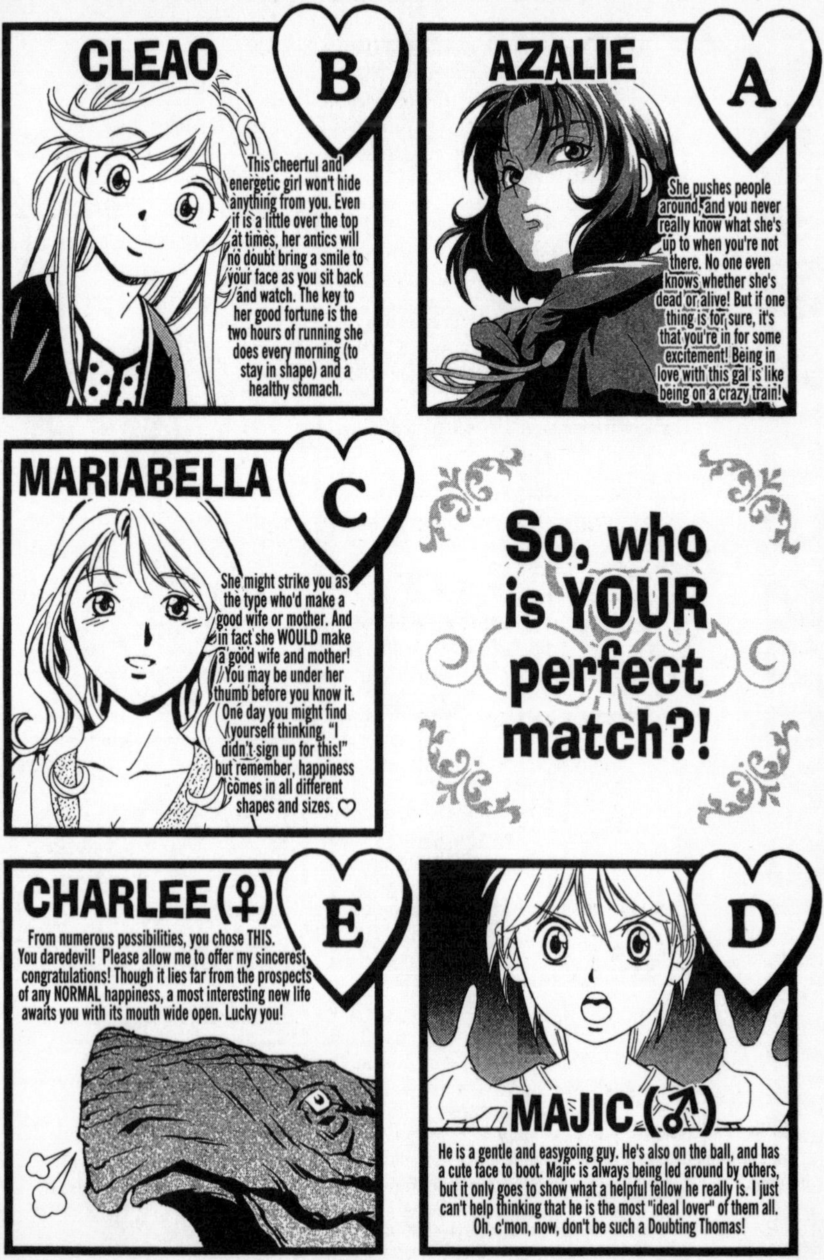

CLEAO
B
This cheerful and energetic girl won't hide anything from you. Even if is a little over the top at times, her antics will no doubt bring a smile to your face as you sit back and watch. The key to her good fortune is the two hours of running she does every morning (to stay in shape) and a healthy stomach.
AZALIE
A
She pushes people around, and you never really know what she's up to when you're not there. No one even knows whether she's dead or alive! But if one thing is for sure, it's that you're in for some excitement! Being in love with this gal is like being on a crazy train!
MARIABELLA
C
She might strike you as the type who'd make a good wife or mother. And in fact she WOULD make a good wife and mother! You may be under her thumb before you know it. One day you might find yourself thinking, "I didn't sign up for this!" but remember, happiness comes in all different shapes and sizes. ♡
So, who is YOUR perfect match?!
CHARLEE (♀)
E
From numerous possibilities, you chose THIS. You daredevil! Please allow me to offer my sincerest congratulations! Though it lies far from the prospects of any NORMAL happiness, a most interesting new life awaits you with its mouth wide open. Lucky you!
D
MAJIC (♂)
He is a gentle and easygoing guy. He's also on the ball, and has a cute face to boot. Majic is always being led around by others, but it only goes to show what a helpful fellow he really is. I just can't help thinking that he is the most "ideal lover" of them all. Oh, c'mon, now, don't be such a Doubting Thomas!

Orphen Volume One

© 1998 Yoshinobu Akita/Hajime Sawada
© 1998 Yuuya Kusaka
Originally published in Japan in 1998 by
KADOKAWA SHOTEN PUBLISHING CO., LTD., Tokyo
English translation rights arranged with
KADOKAWA SHOTEN PUBLISHING CO., LTD., Tokyo.

Translator BRENDAN FRAYNE
Lead Translator/Translation Supervisor JAVIER LOPEZ
ADV Manga Translation Staff KAY BERTRAND & AMY FORSYTH

Print Production/Art Studio Manager LISA PUCKETT
Pre-press Manager KLYS REEDYK
Sr. Designer/Creative Manager JORGE ALVARADO
Graphic Designer/Group Leader GEORGE REYNOLDS
Graphic Designers HEATHER GARY & NATALIA MORALES
Graphic Intern MARK MEZA

International Coordinators TORU IWAKAMI,
ATSUSHI KANBAYASHI & KYOKO DRUMHELLER

Publishing Editor SUSAN ITIN
Assistant Editor MARGARET SCHAROLD
Editorial Assistant SHERIDAN JACOBS
Editorial Intern MIKE ESSMYER
Research/Traffic Coordinator MARSHA ARNOLD

Executive VP, CFO, COO KEVIN CORCORAN

President, C.E.O & Publisher JOHN LEDFORD

Email: editor@adv-manga.com
www.adv-manga.com
www.advfilms.com

For sales and distribution inquiries please call 1.800.282.7202

ADV MANGA™ is a division of A.D. Vision, Inc.
10114 W. Sam Houston Parkway, Suite 200, Houston, Texas 77099

English text © 2005 published by A.D. Vision, Inc. under exclusive license.
ADV MANGA is a trademark of A.D. Vision, Inc.

ISBN: 1-4139-0266-9
First printing, March 2005
10 9 8 7 6 5 4 3 2 1
Printed in Canada

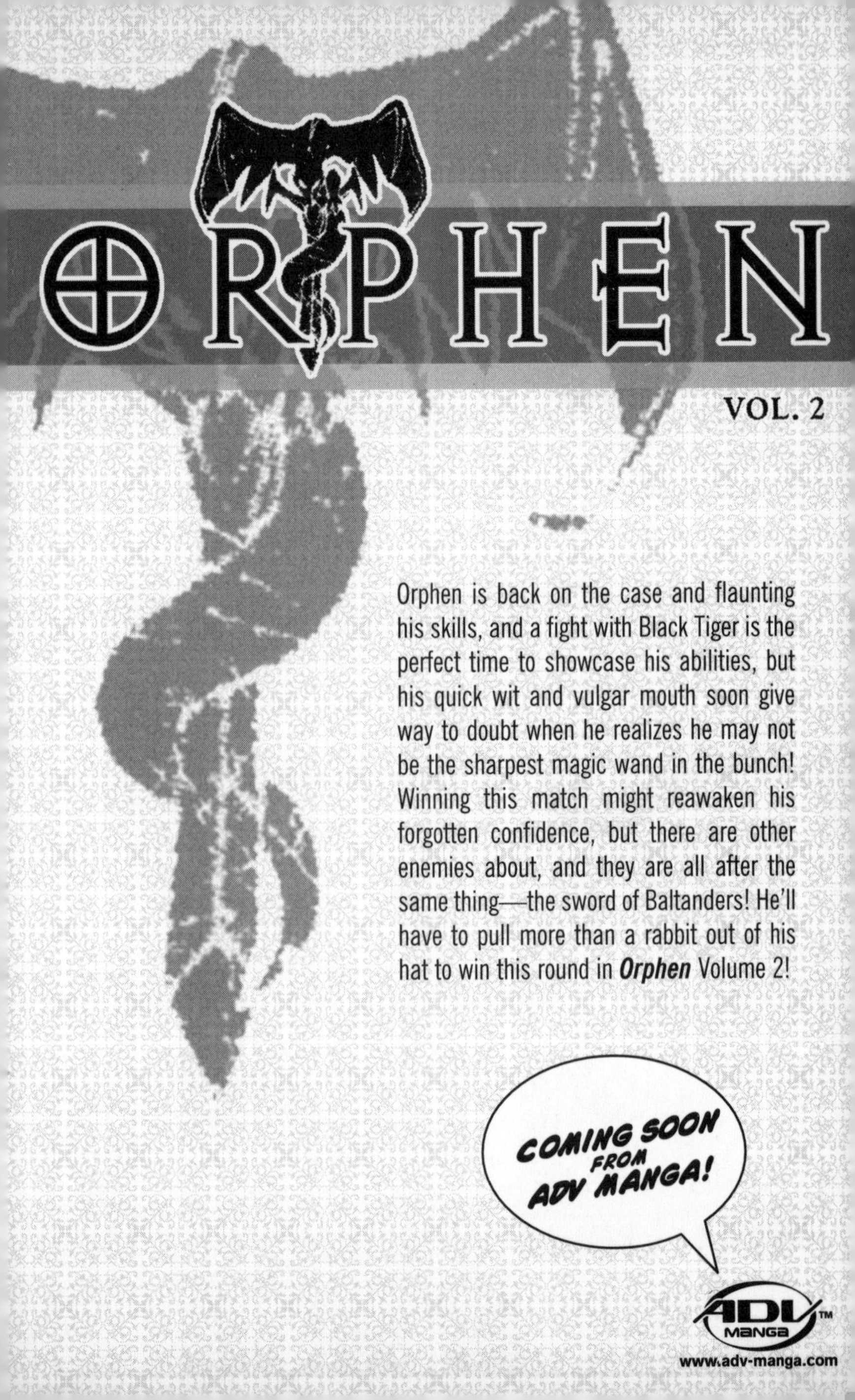
ORPHEN
VOL. 2
Orphen is back on the case and flaunting his skills, and a fight with Black Tiger is the perfect time to showcase his abilities, but his quick wit and vulgar mouth soon give way to doubt when he realizes he may not be the sharpest magic wand in the bunch! Winning this match might reawaken his forgotten confidence, but there are other enemies about, and they are all after the same thing—the sword of Baltanders! He'll have to pull more than a rabbit out of his hat to win this round in ***Orphen*** Volume 2!
COMING SOON FROM ADV MANGA!
ADV Manga™
www.adv-manga.com

DO YOU HAVE WHAT IT TAKES TO MAKE IT IN CROMARTIE HIGH?

Do you have a tough nickname?

❑ Yes ❑ No

How many fights have you been in?

❑ None ❑ More than 100

❑ 5-10 ❑ None – no one ever had the stones to challenge me

What's in your bookbag?

❑ My homework ❑ Porn ❑ A metal plate

How tough do you look? Check all that apply.

❑ Pompadour ❑ Handlebar mustache ❑ Shaved eyebrows

❑ Carpet of chest hair ❑ Lazy swagger ❑ Menacing glare

Say you checked out eleven adult videos. Three of those were new releases, so you had to return them the next day. How many videos do you have left?

❑ 3 ❑ 8 ❑ 11 – I would never give them back.

How did you rate?

10 points or less	**Errand Boy**
10 – 15	**Wannabe Punk**
30 – 40	**One Badass Dude**
More than 100	**Champ by Default**

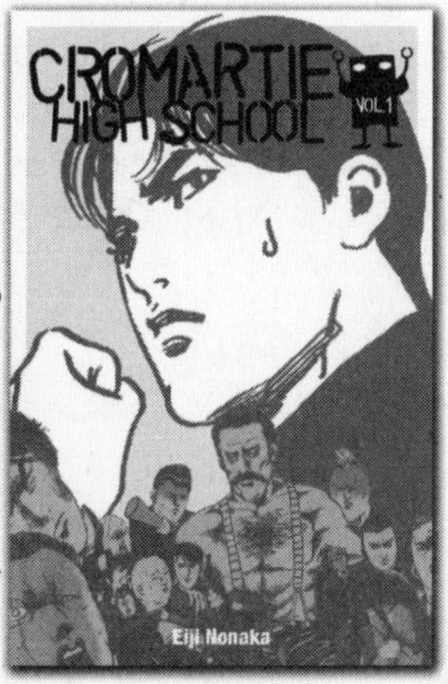
CROMARTIE HIGH SCHOOL
VOL.1
Eiji Nonaka

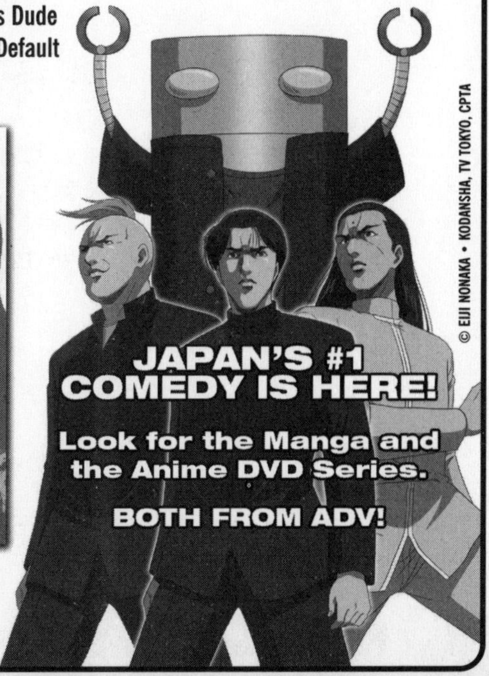
JAPAN'S #1 COMEDY IS HERE!
Look for the Manga and the Anime DVD Series.
BOTH FROM ADV!

ADV Manga™

www.adv-manga.com

What do you do when you see a pig, a dog, and a...Puchu?

you head for cover!

Puchu
(from Excel Saga)

Saizo
(from Peacemaker Kurogane)

Menchi
(from Excel Saga)

"CAP YOUR SKULL!"

Suggested Retail Price: $14.99

To find your favorite retailer or shop online visit:www.advfilms.com

 **MANGA SURVEY**

PLEASE MAIL THE COMPLETED FORM TO: EDITOR – ADV MANGA
C/o A.D. Vision, Inc. 10114 W. Sam Houston Pkwy., Suite 200 Houston, TX 77099

Name:_____

Address:_____

City, State, Zip:_____

E-Mail:_____

Male ☐   Female ☐   Age:_____

☐ **CHECK HERE IF YOU WOULD LIKE TO RECEIVE OTHER INFORMATION OR FUTURE OFFERS FROM ADV.**

All information provided will be used for internal purposes only. We promise not to sell or otherwise divulge your information.

1. Annual Household Income (*Check only one*)
☐ Under $25,000
☐ $25,000 to $50,000
☐ $50,000 to $75,000
☐ Over $75,000

2. How do you hear about new Manga releases? (*Check all that apply*)
☐ Browsing in Store   ☐ Magazine Ad
☐ Internet Reviews   ☐ Online Advertising
☐ Anime News Websites   ☐ Conventions
☐ Direct Email Campaigns   ☐ TV Advertising
☐ Online forums (message boards and chat rooms)
☐ Carrier pigeon
☐ Other:_____

3. Which magazines do you read? (*Check all that apply*)
☐ Wizard   ☐ YRB
☐ SPIN   ☐ EGM
☐ Animerica   ☐ Newtype USA
☐ Rolling Stone   ☐ SciFi
☐ Maxim   ☐ Starlog
☐ DC Comics   ☐ Wired
☐ URB   ☐ Vice
☐ Polygon   ☐ BPM
☐ Original Play Station Magazine ☐ I hate reading
☐ Entertainment Weekly   ☐ Other:_____

4. Have you visited the ADV Manga website?
- ☐ Yes
- ☐ No

5. Have you made any manga purchases online from the ADV website?
- ☐ Yes
- ☐ No

6. If you have visited the ADV Manga website, how would you rate your online experience?
- ☐ Excellent
- ☐ Good
- ☐ Average
- ☐ Poor

7. What genre of manga do you prefer?
(*Check all that apply*)
- ☐ adventure
- ☐ romance
- ☐ detective
- ☐ action
- ☐ horror
- ☐ sci-fi/fantasy
- ☐ sports
- ☐ comedy

8. How many manga titles have you purchased in the last 6 months?
- ☐ none
- ☐ 1-4
- ☐ 5-10
- ☐ 11+

9. Where do you make your manga purchases? (*Check all that apply*)
- ☐ comic store
- ☐ bookstore
- ☐ newsstand
- ☐ online
- ☐ other:_____
- ☐ department store
- ☐ grocery store
- ☐ video store
- ☐ video game store

10. Which bookstores do you usually make your manga purchases at?
(*Check all that apply*)
- ☐ Barnes & Noble
- ☐ Walden Books
- ☐ Suncoast
- ☐ Best Buy
- ☐ Amazon.com
- ☐ Borders
- ☐ Books-A-Million
- ☐ Toys "Я" Us
- ☐ Other bookstore:
  _____

11. What's your favorite anime/manga website? (*Check all that apply*)
- ☐ adv-manga.com
- ☐ advfilms.com
- ☐ rightstuf.com
- ☐ animenewsservice.com
- ☐ animenewsnetwork.com
- ☐ Other:_____
- ☐ animeondvd.com
- ☐ anipike.com
- ☐ animeonline.net
- ☐ planetanime.com
- ☐ animenation.com

All information provided will be used for internal purposes only. We promise not to sell or otherwise divulge your information.